SWORD ART ONLINE

abec Artworks

Wanderers

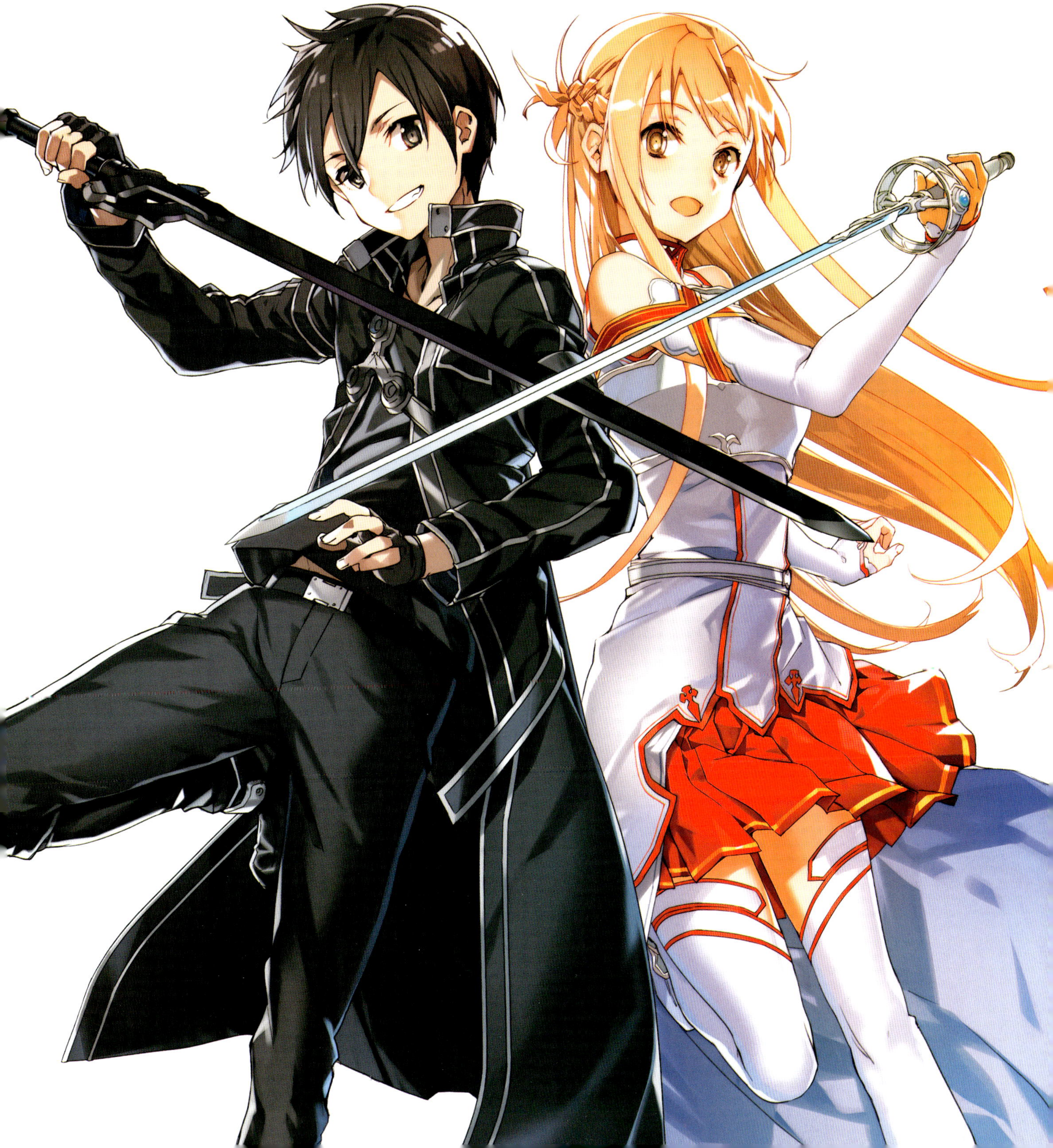

SWORD ART ONLINE

Alicization Running

The volume that depicts Kirito and Eugeo's life at North Centoria Imperial Swordcraft Academy. In a way, uniforms are kind of like the face of a series, even more than the characters, so I think that the uniforms at this academy are actually a major piece of iconography for the Alicization saga.

Dengeki Bunko
Sword Art Online 10: Alicization Running
Cover: July 2012

For this cover, I was asked to draw Kirito and Sortiliena. They've both got elegance and strength. I really enjoyed working with those qualities here.

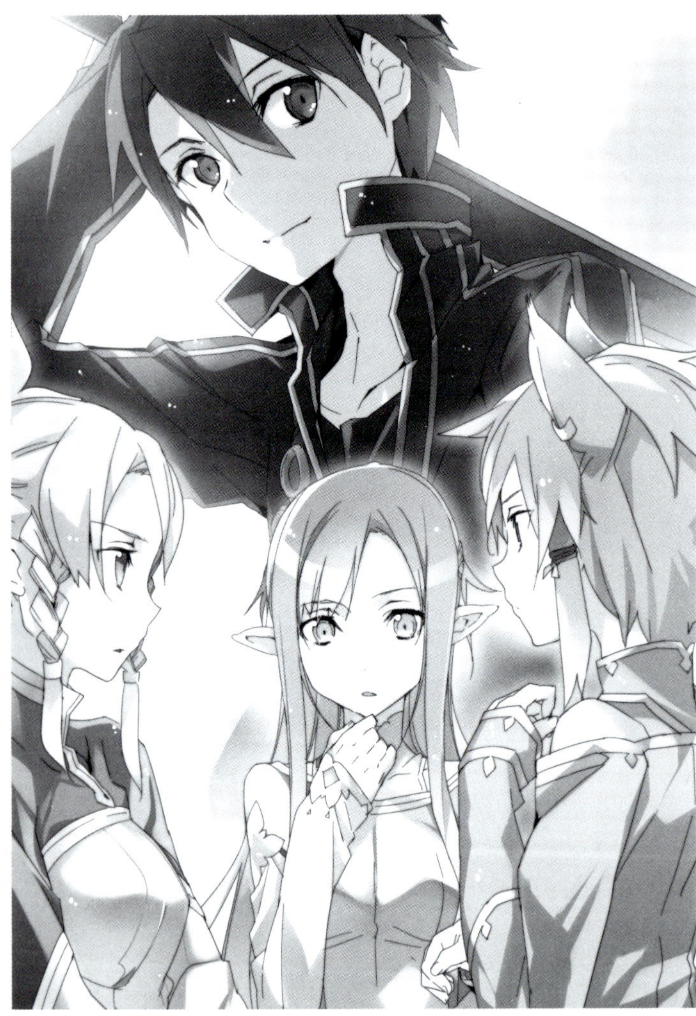

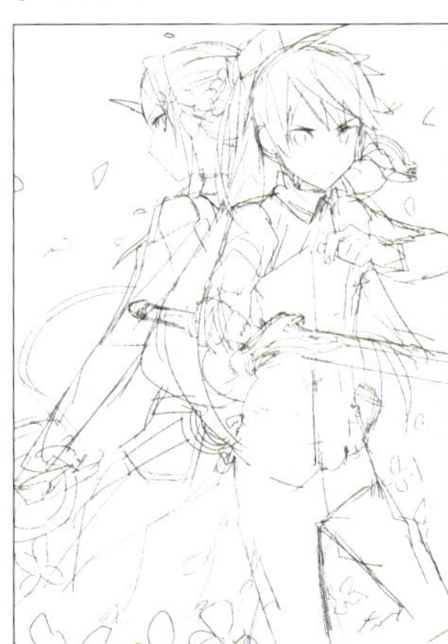

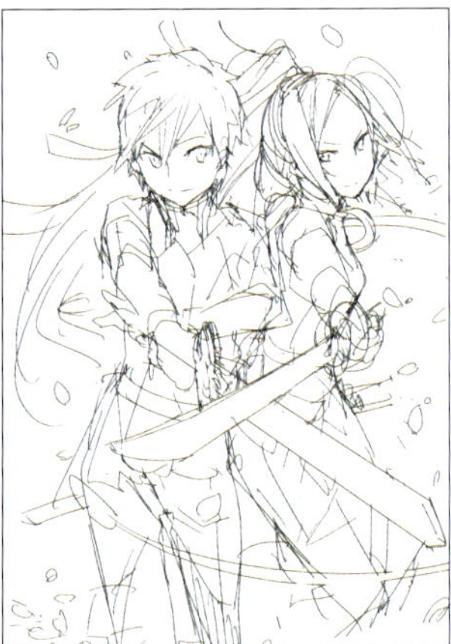

Alternate Cover Sketches

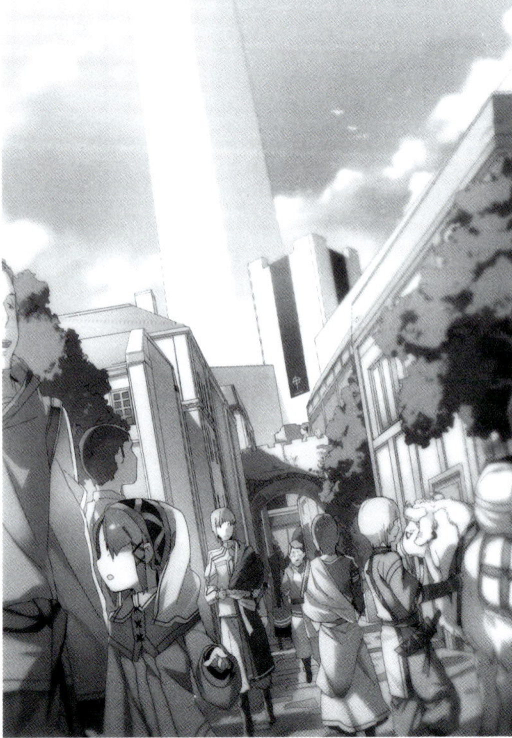

Dengeki Bunko
Sword Art Online 10: Alicization Running
Illustration: July 2012

I wanted to bring out the feeling of life in the Underworld here, so I drew some people wearing toga-like robes, but in later designs, I wasn't able to preserve that idea. I kind of regret that now.

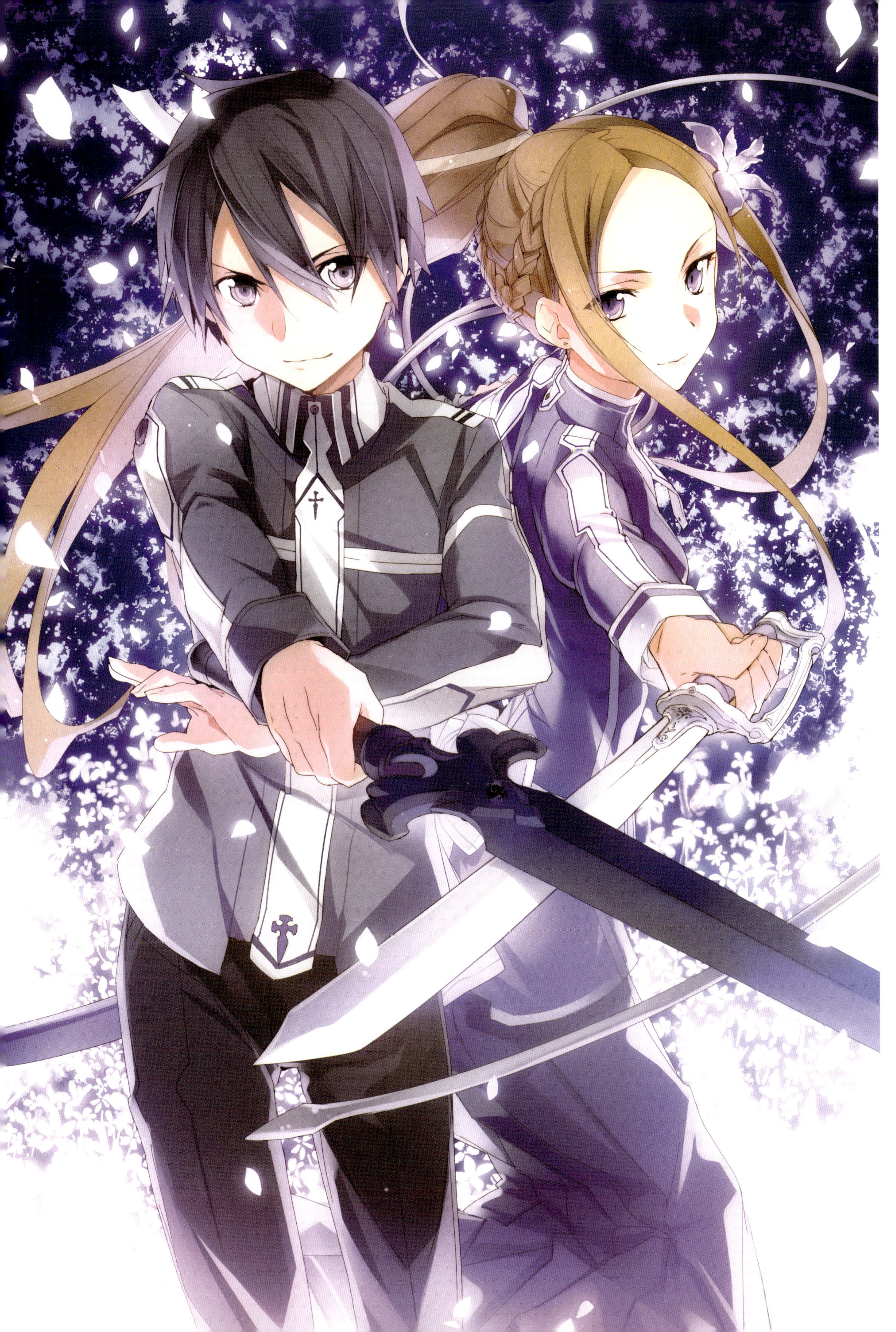

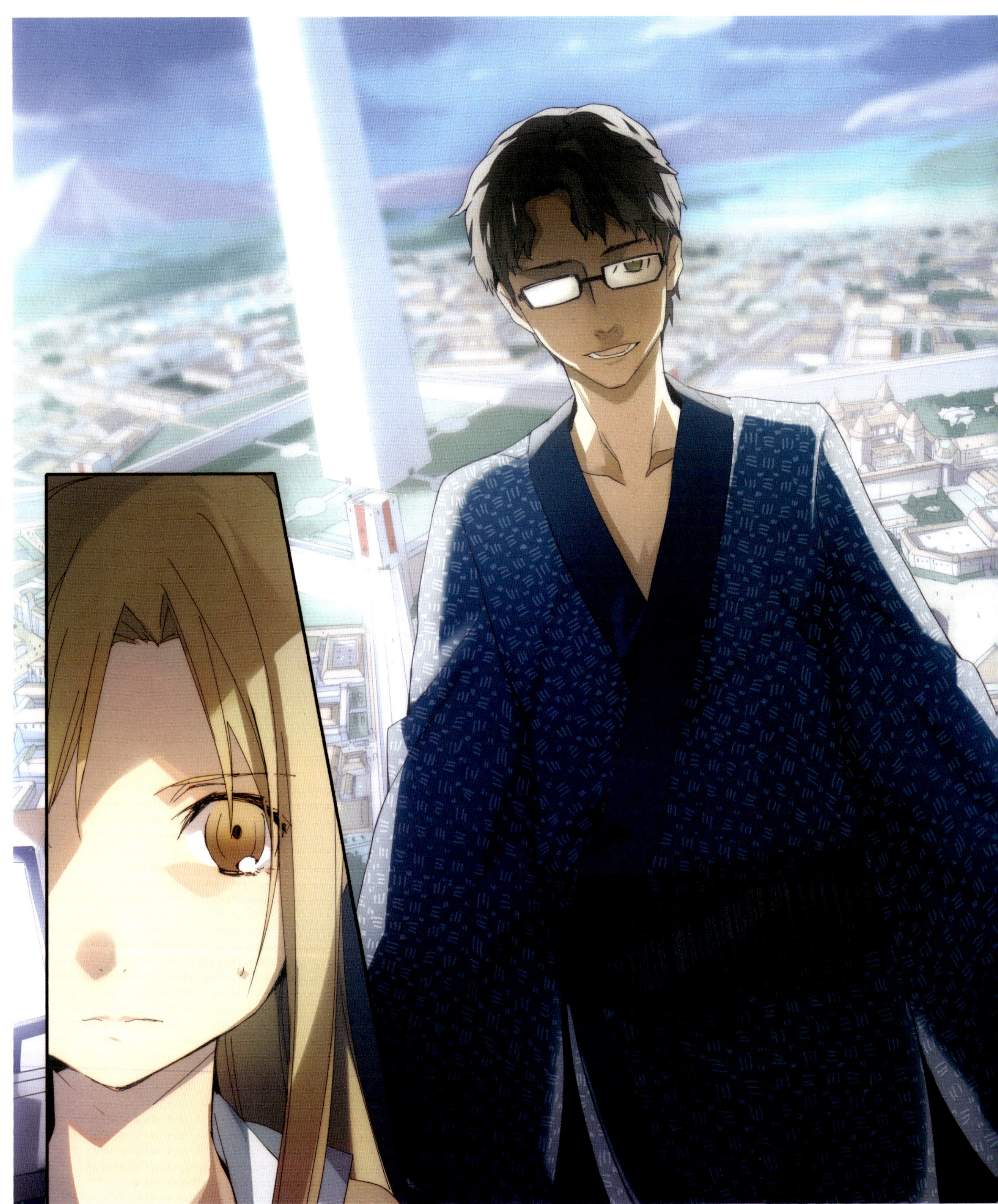

Dengeki Bunko, *Sword Art Online 10: Alicization Running*
Frontispiece: July 2012

All I remember is having to draw a long-distance view of Centoria and thinking, "Aaaah!!" But in the image itself, Kikuoka-san's wickedness stands out more. That mysterious light glinting off only the glasses is just a traditional technique at this point.

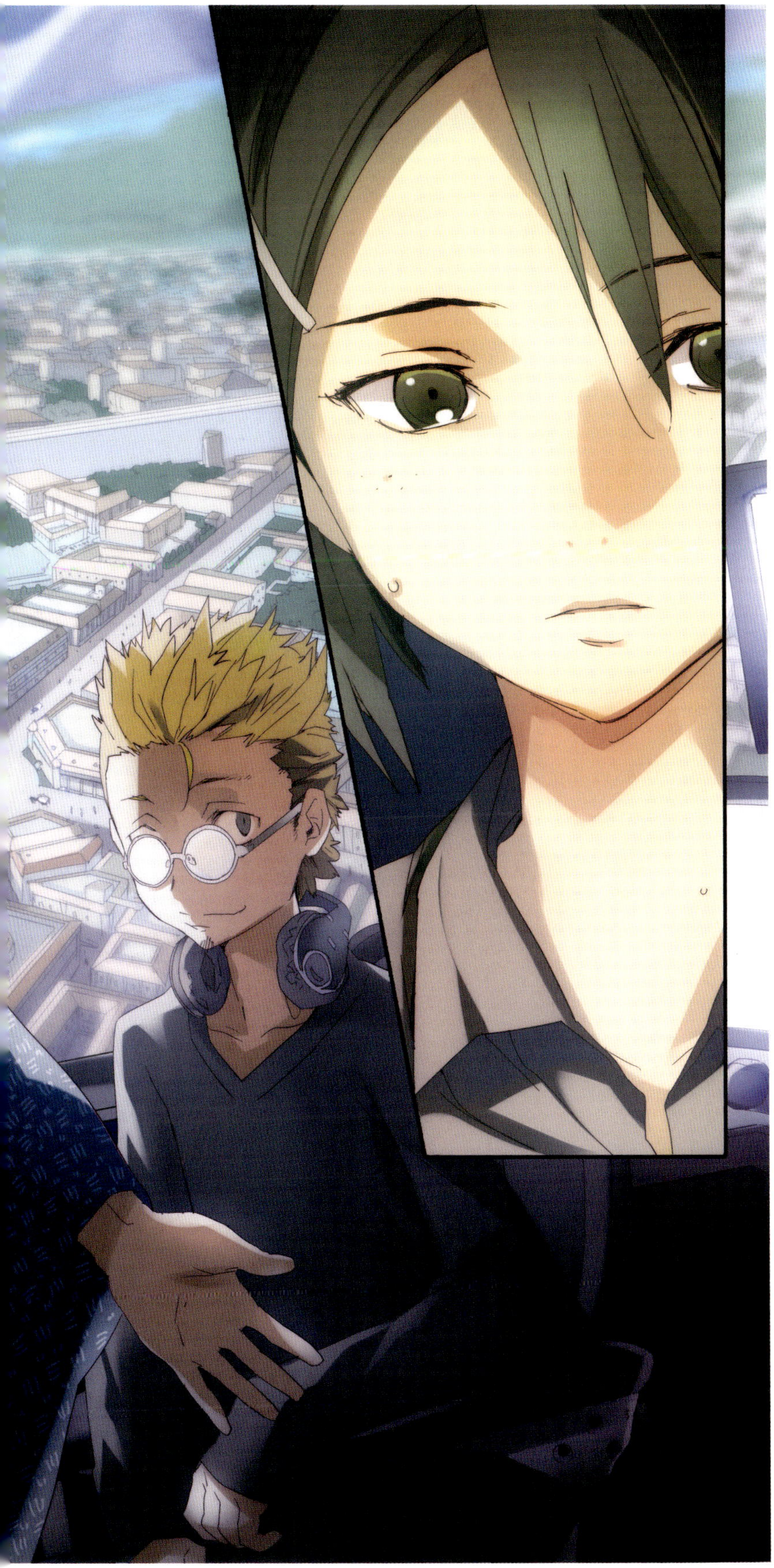

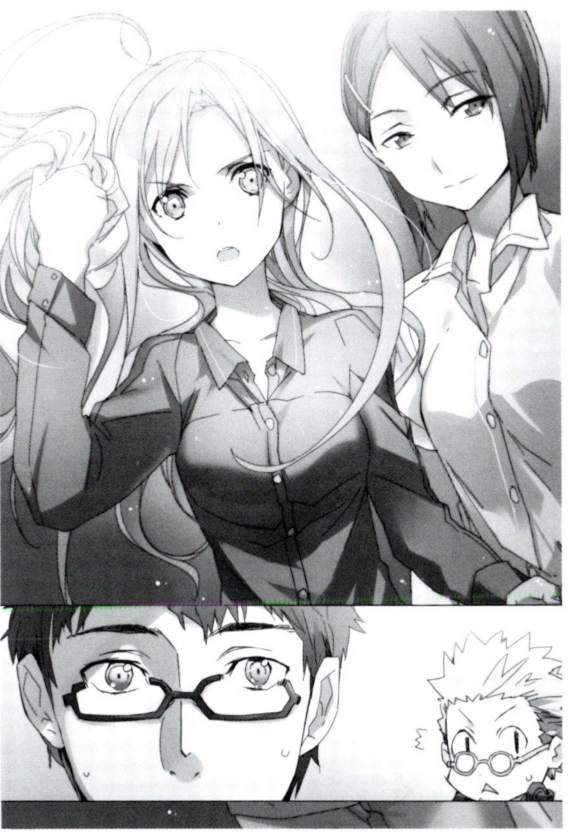

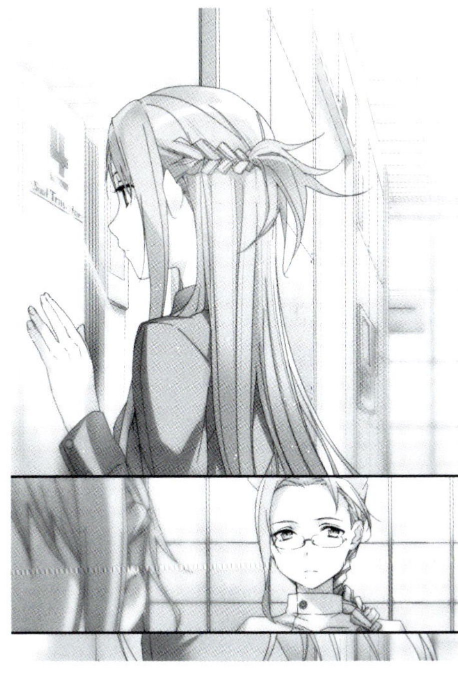

Dengeki Bunko
Sword Art Online 10: Alicization Running
Illustration: July 2012

Because the number of illustrations in a book is quite limited, it's not easy to show a before-and-after change in emotion through art alone. Anyway, I think Asuna's just a lovely person, with the way she can spring into action when the time calls for it.

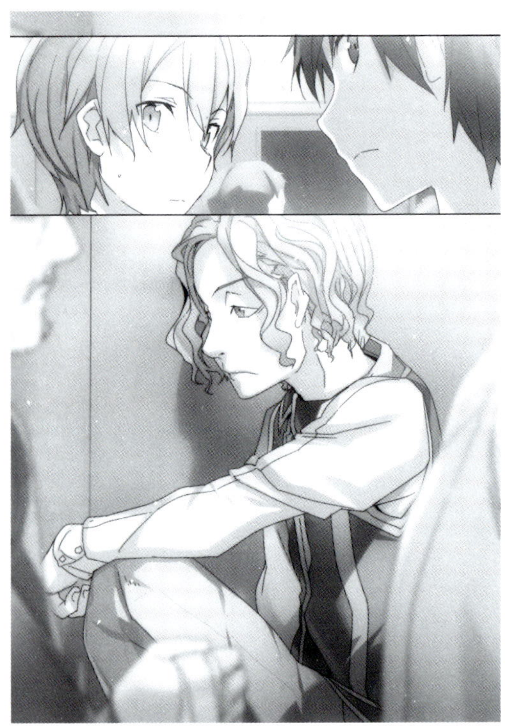

Dengeki Bunko
Sword Art Online 10: Alicization Running
Illustration: July 2012

Egome's just kind of a random side character, but somehow he got two illustrations.

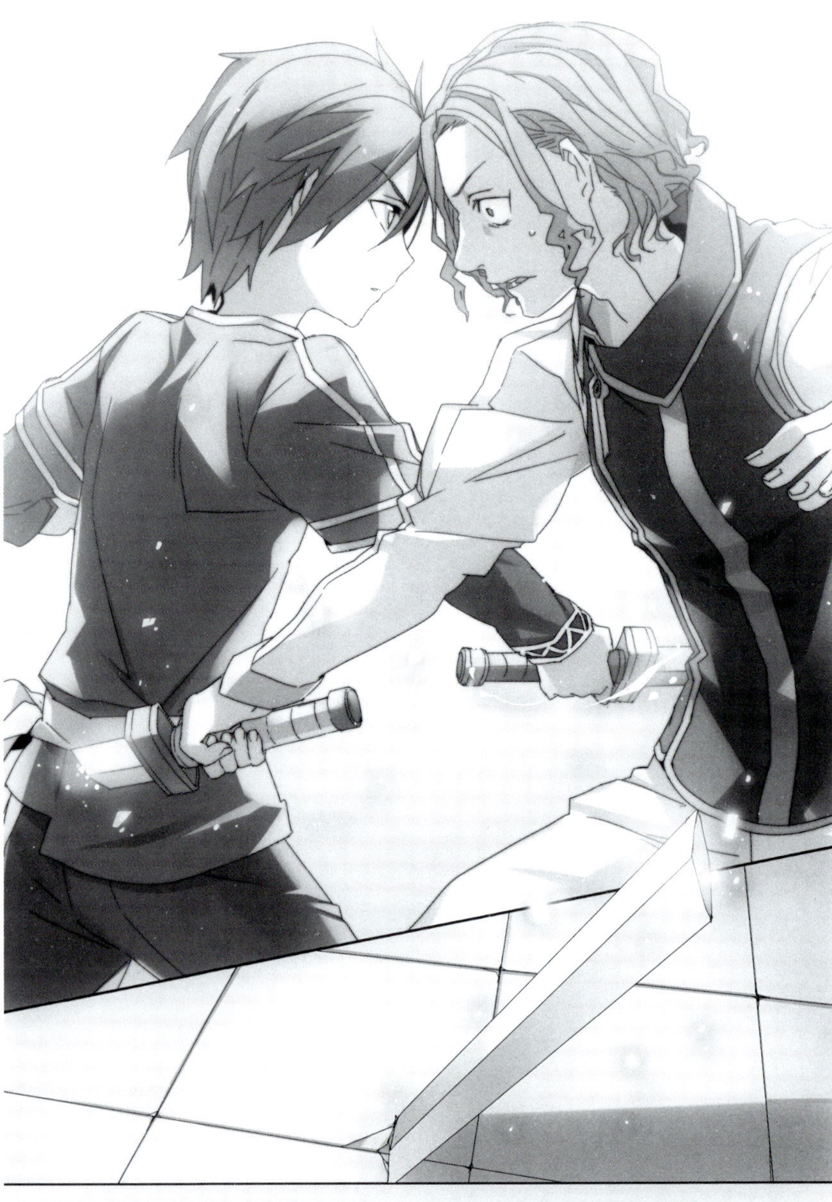

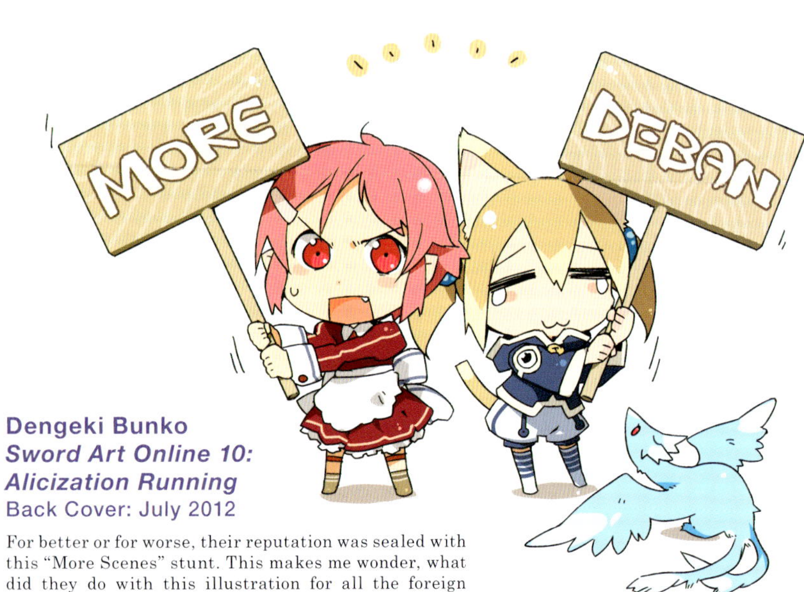

Dengeki Bunko
Sword Art Online 10: Alicization Running
Back Cover: July 2012

For better or for worse, their reputation was sealed with this "More Scenes" stunt. This makes me wonder, what did they do with this illustration for all the foreign language editions?

Dengeki Bunko
Sword Art Online 10: Alicization Running
Frontispiece: July 2012

Unlike the black-and-white illustration, Kirito seems to be the one getting pushed around here.

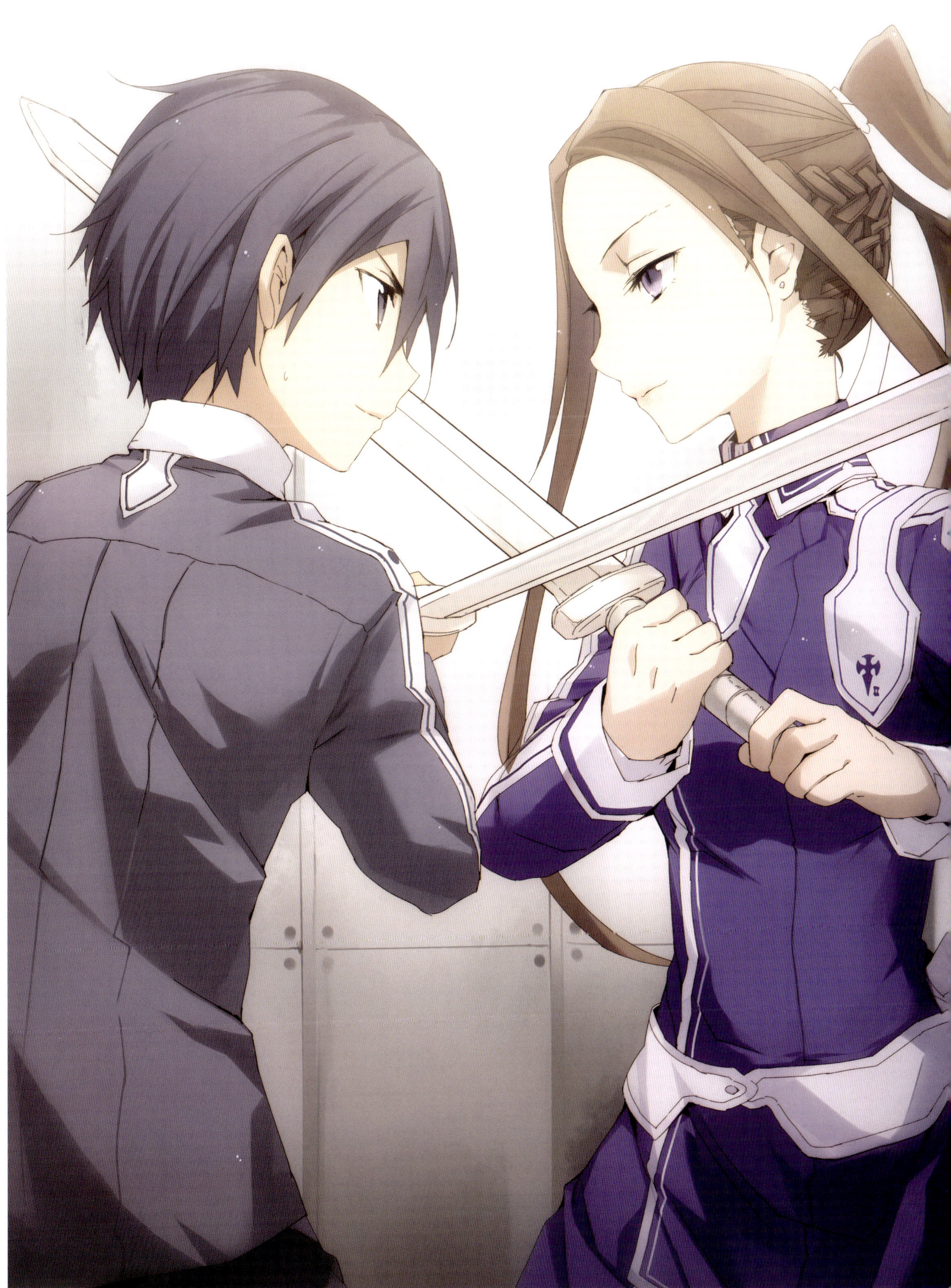

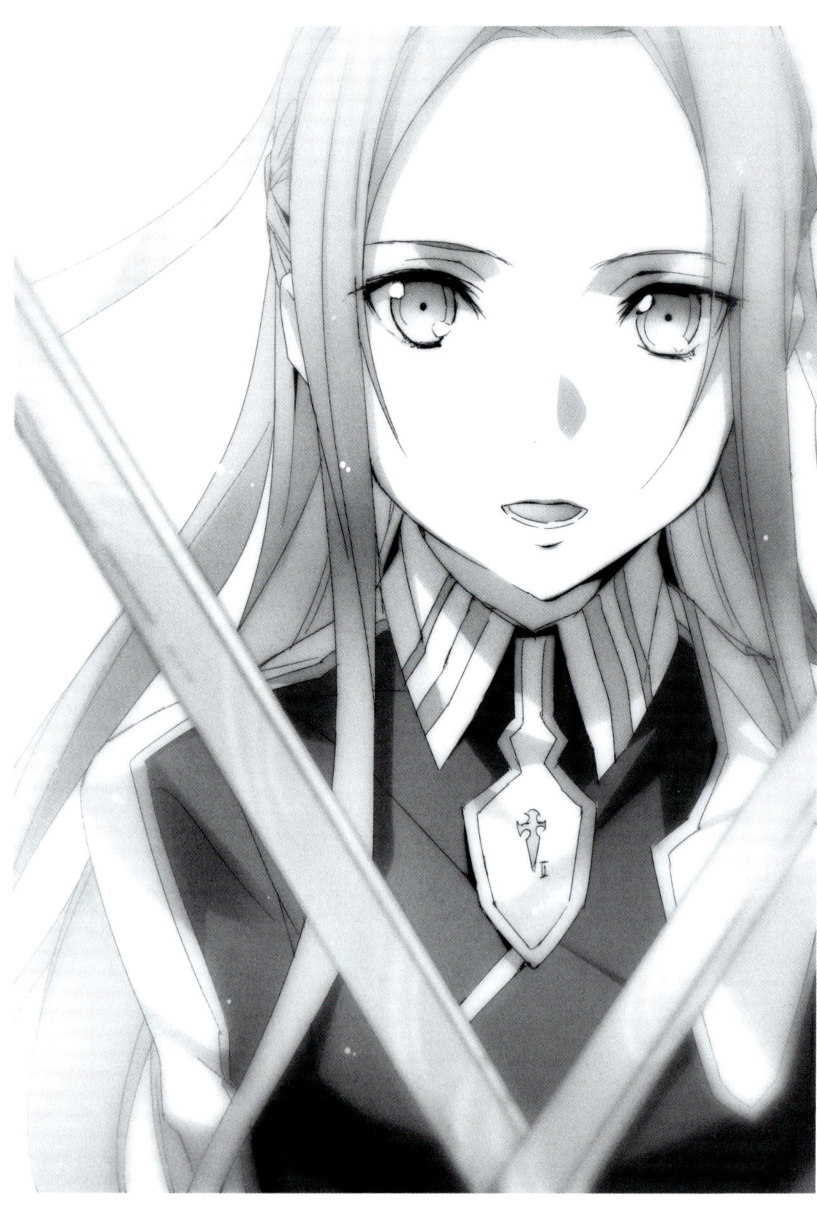

Dengeki Bunko
Sword Art Online 10: Alicization Running
Illustration: July 2012

I love characters in roles like Miss Azurica and Sortiliena, and since they have very limited appearances, it tends to result in me trying to get the most out of them, with samey results.

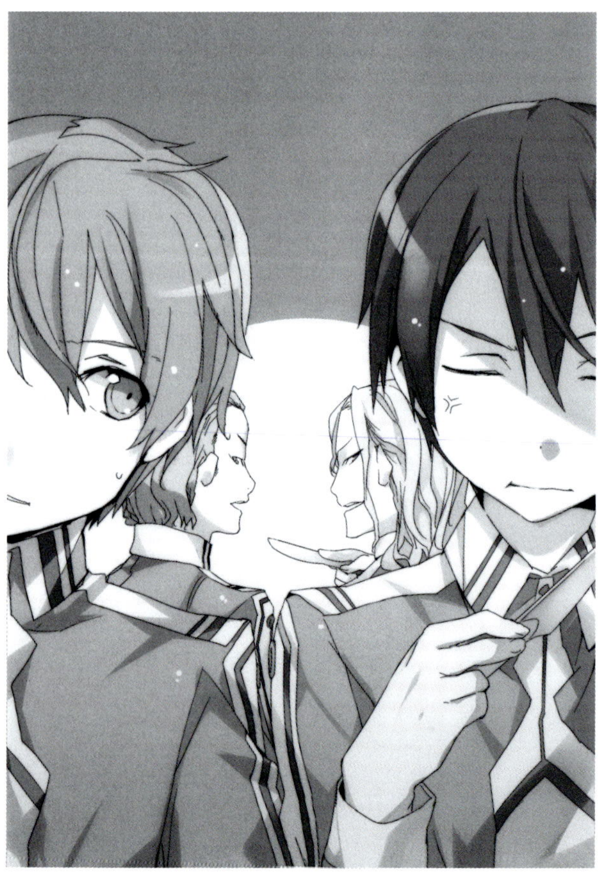

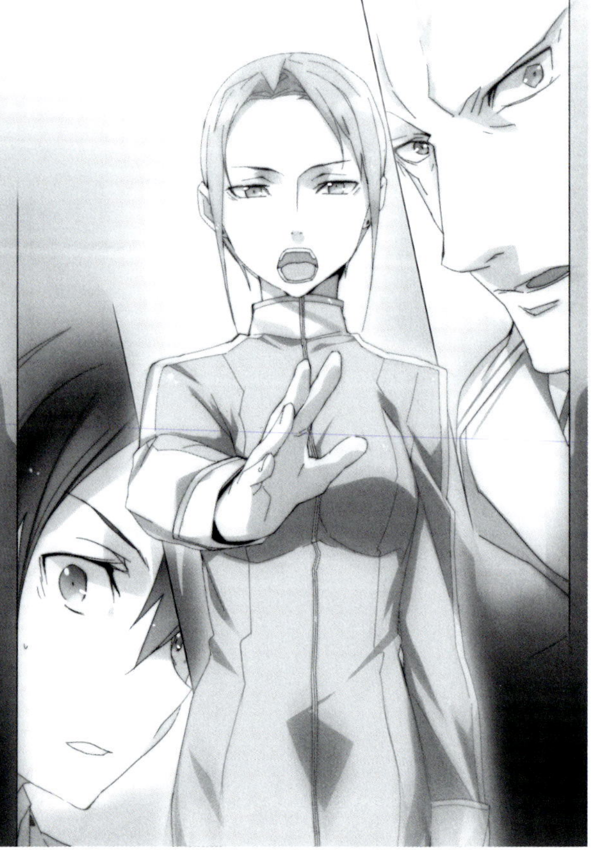

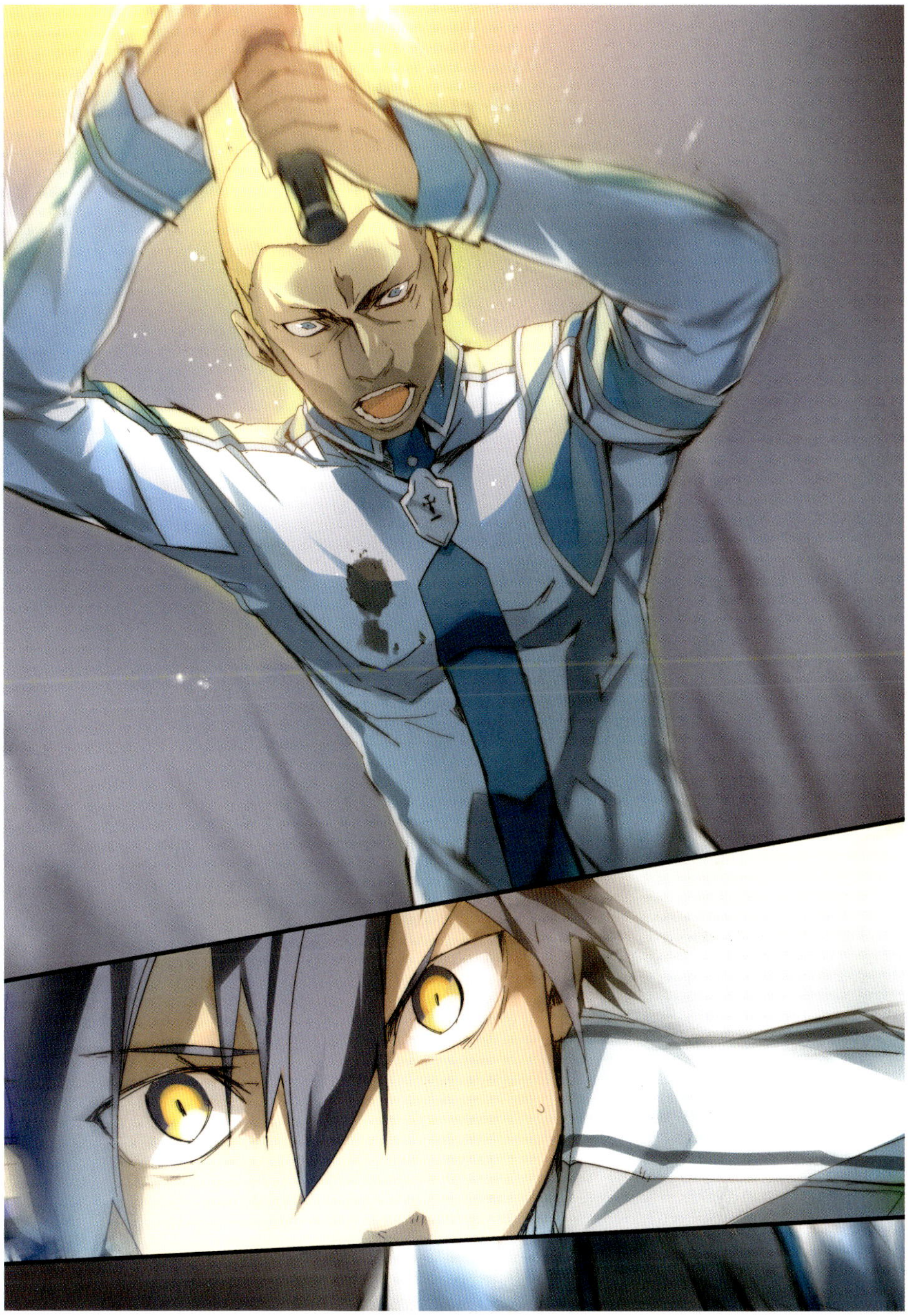

Dengeki Bunko
Sword Art Online 10: Alicization Running
Frontispiece: July 2012

The cover and frontispiece (i.e. color) illustrations are designed for text to go over them, so it always weirds me out to see them looking empty when that text is removed...Looking at the interior illustrations, I always wish I could put in some sound effects, like "Wham!" or "Boom!" The strange thing is that the presence or absence of sound effects completely changes the way those images come across. What am I trying to say, you ask? I'm just making excuses toward anyone who looked at this piece and thought it looked cheap and boring. Sorry.

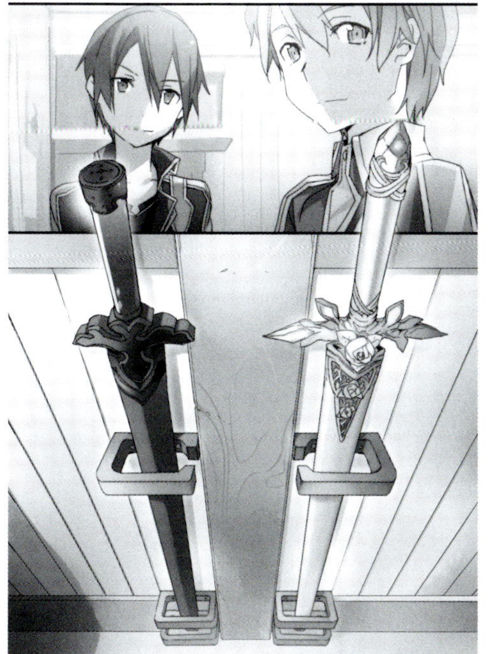

Dengeki Bunko
Sword Art Online 10: Alicization Running
Illustration: July 2012

Based on the system of item priority in the Underworld, that sword stand would have to have a really high priority, too. It's a fascinating world, the more you think about it.

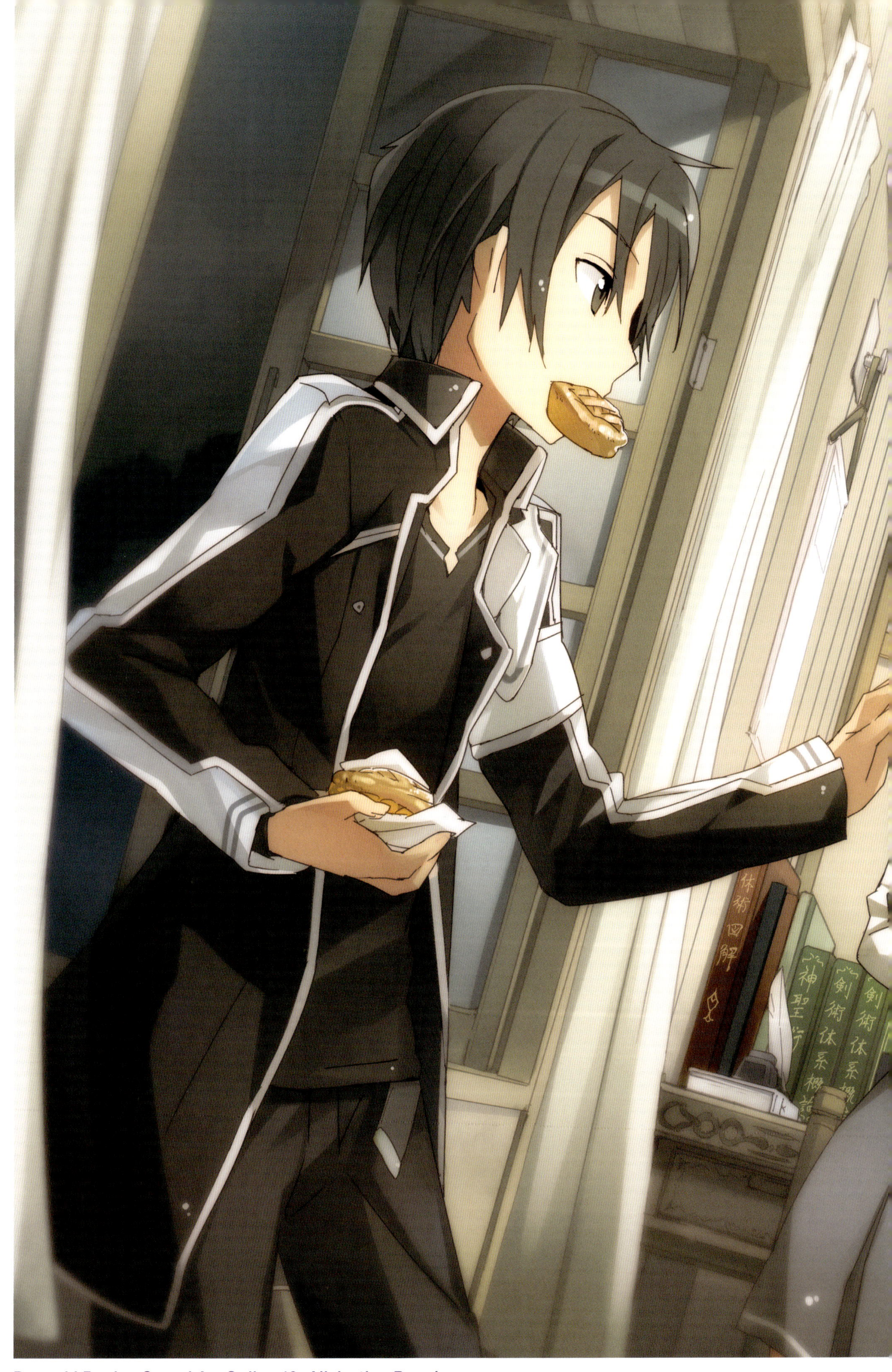

Dengeki Bunko, *Sword Art Online 10: Alicization Running*
Frontispiece: July 2012

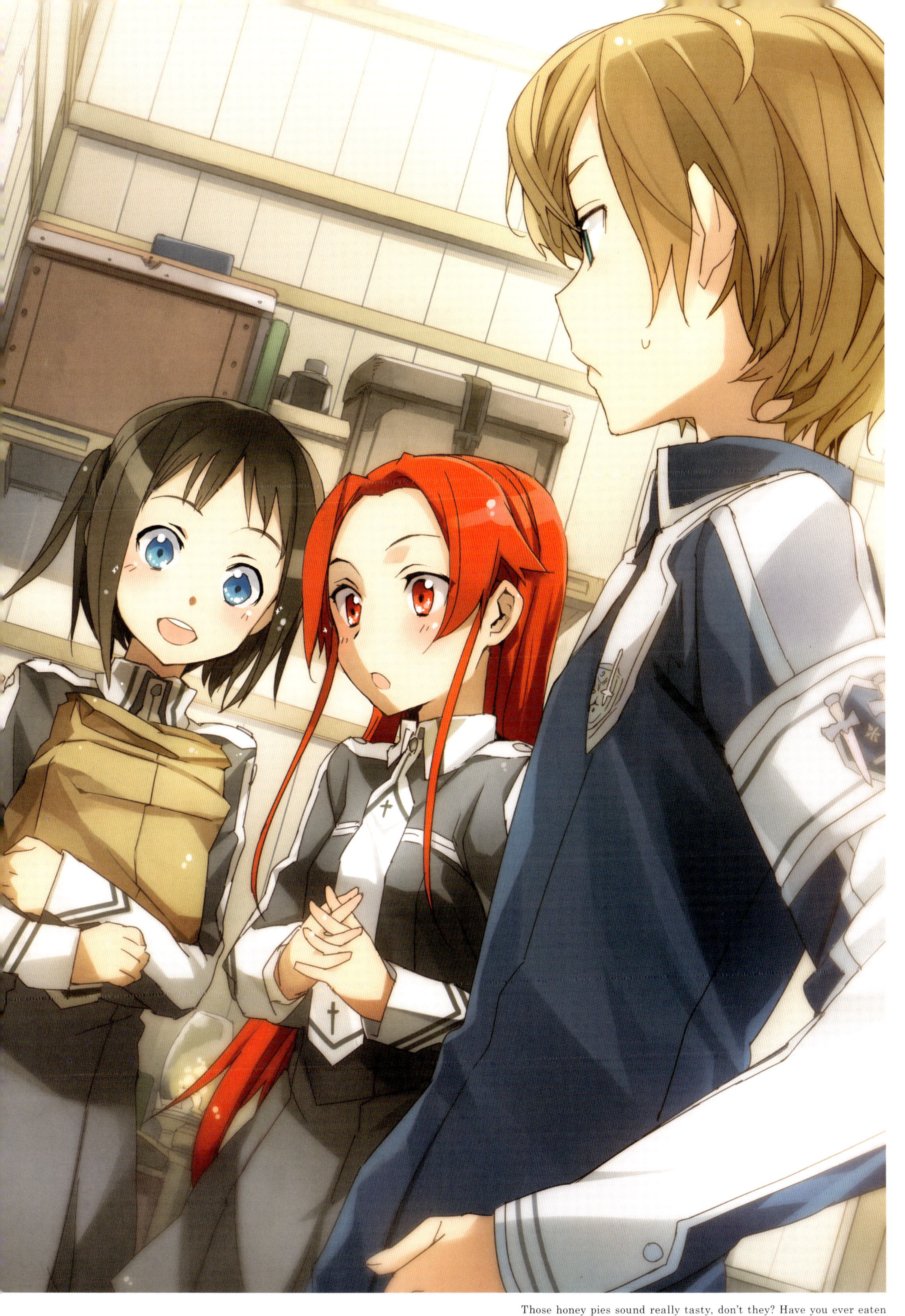

Those honey pies sound really tasty, don't they? Have you ever eaten one? Also, I remember that I specifically drew Kirito's shirt open here because I wanted to show what he was wearing under the uniform.

SWORD ART ONLINE

Alicization Turning

Now elite disciples, Kirito and Eugeo leave the academy behind and begin climbing Central Cathedral in this turning point for the saga.

Dengeki Bunko
Sword Art Online 11: Alicization Turning
Cover: December 2012

Kirito is very subtly chained up here. In the Japanese release, the book has a strip of promotional paper around the bottom, so it's almost entirely hidden. In the rough design, Tiese is holding her own sword, but in the end, I changed it so that she's holding the Blue Rose Sword. Eugeo's not on the cover itself, but he is central to the story, after all.

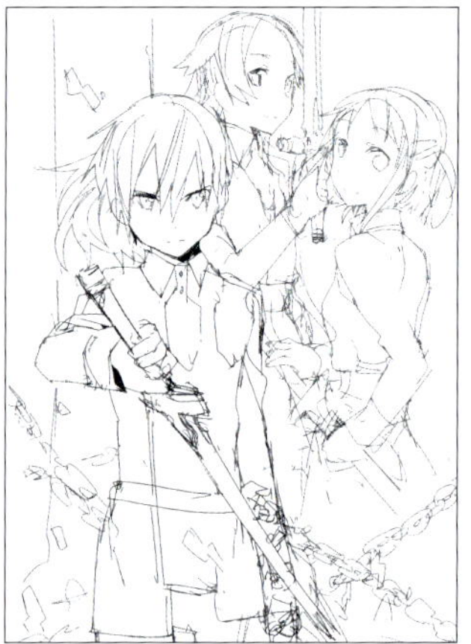

Alternate Cover Sketch

Dengeki Bunko
Sword Art Online 11: Alicization Turning
Illustration: December 2012

If you just look at the interior illustrations, it really is like Eugeo is the protagonist of this book. Something about that all-white uniform kind of looks like a joke, doesn't it? I mean, I get that he wanted his color to be unified, but it's just hard to take him seriously that way. Incidentally, Ichiemon's design came straight from Kawahara-sensei.

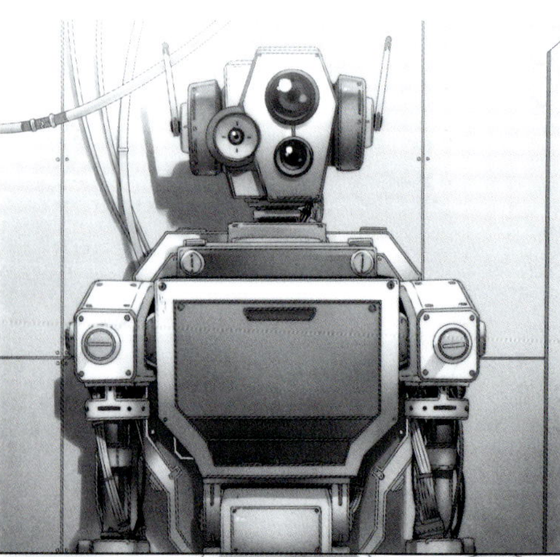

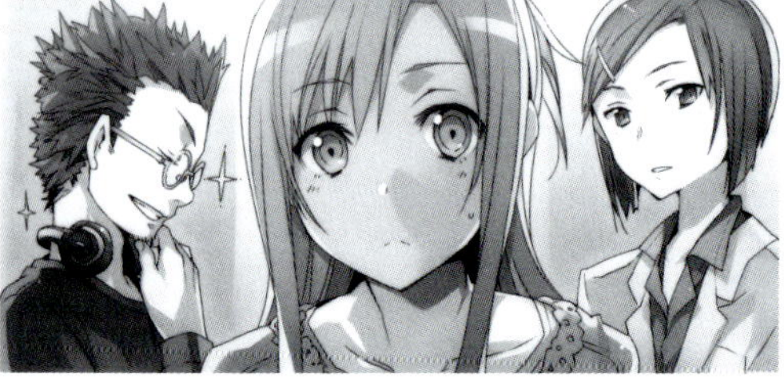

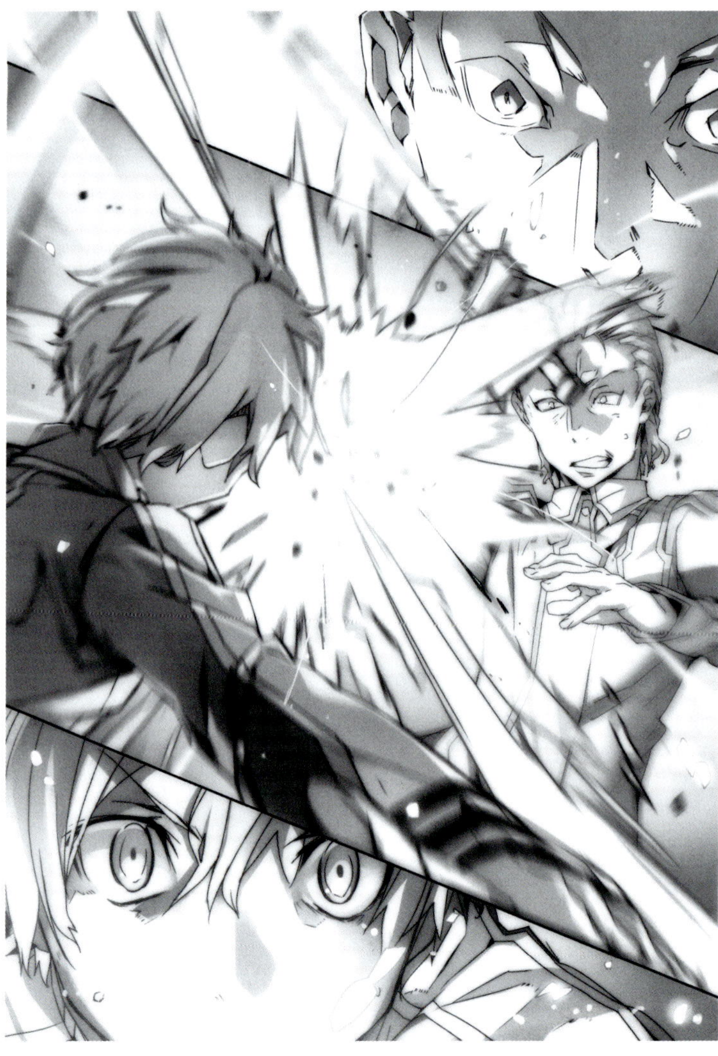

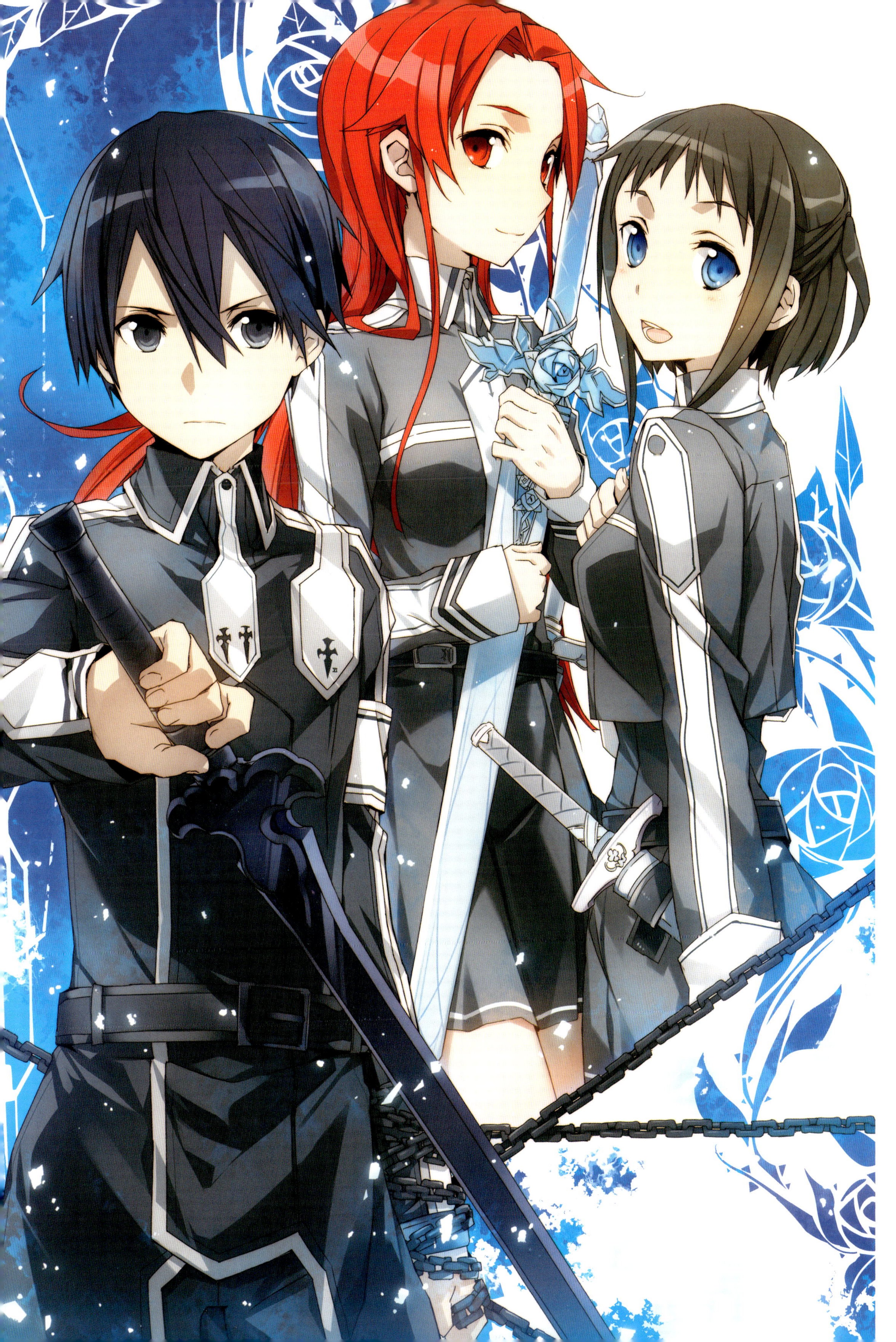

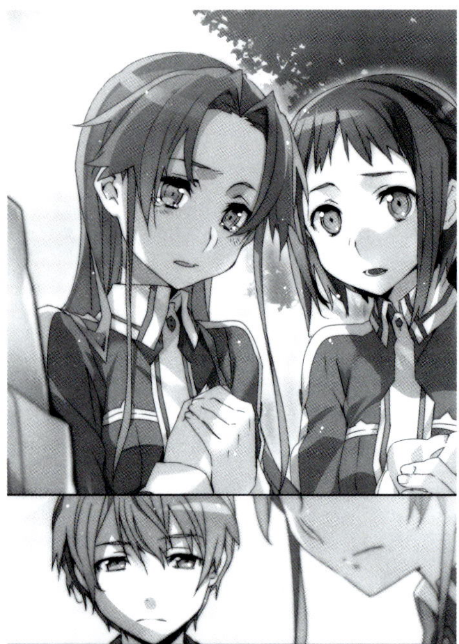

Dengeki Bunko
Sword Art Online 11: Alicization Turning
Illustration: December 2012

If Eugeo's the protagonist of this volume, then Tiese is the heroine. Unfortunately, because she always comes in a set with Ronie, that lowers her heroine quotient. A shame.

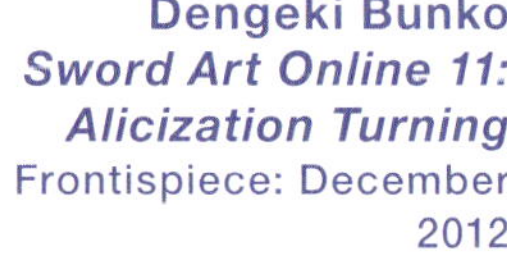

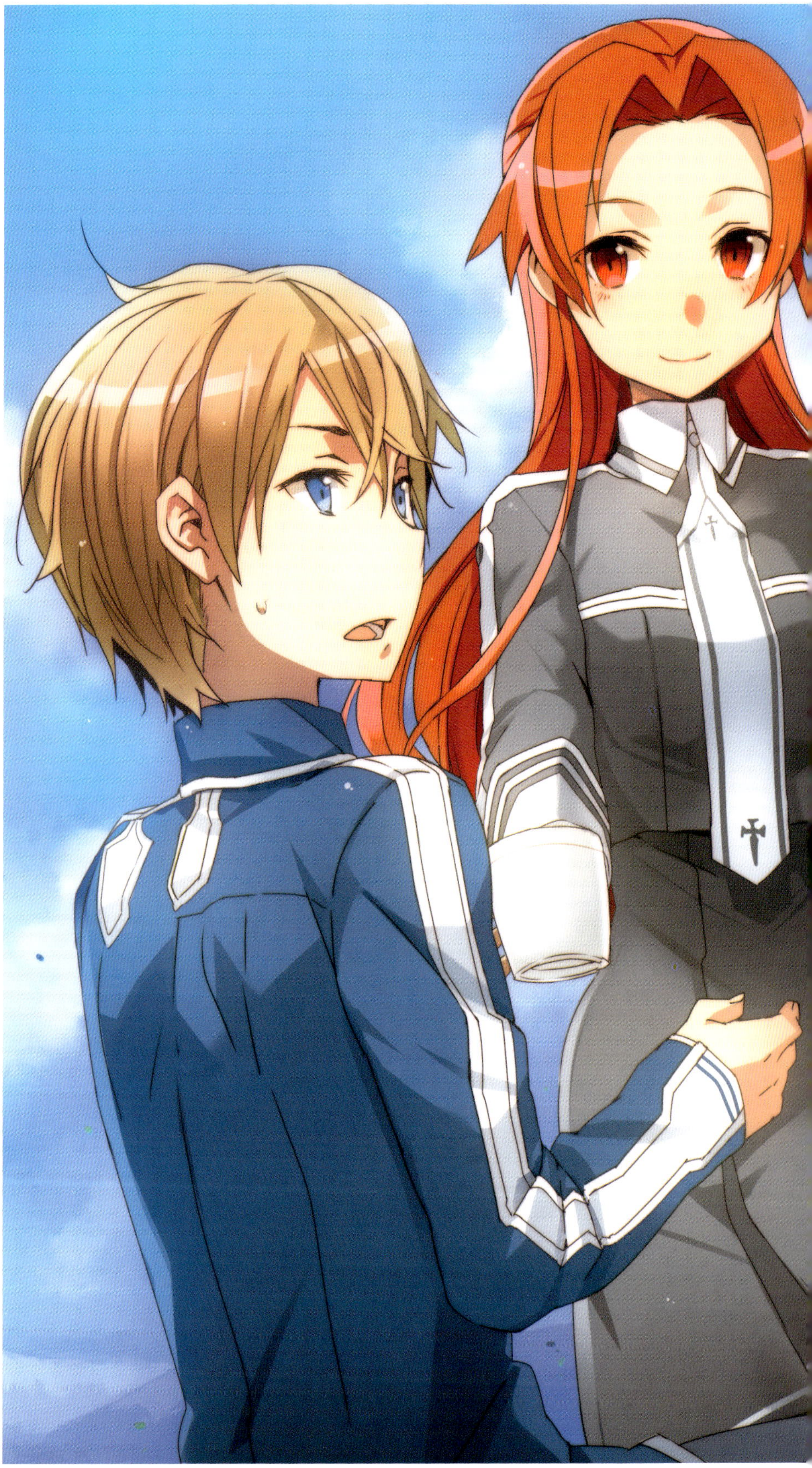

Dengeki Bunko
Sword Art Online 11: Alicization Turning
Frontispiece: December 2012

A relaxing picnic. I really wanted to do this piece for the huge contrast with the next one.

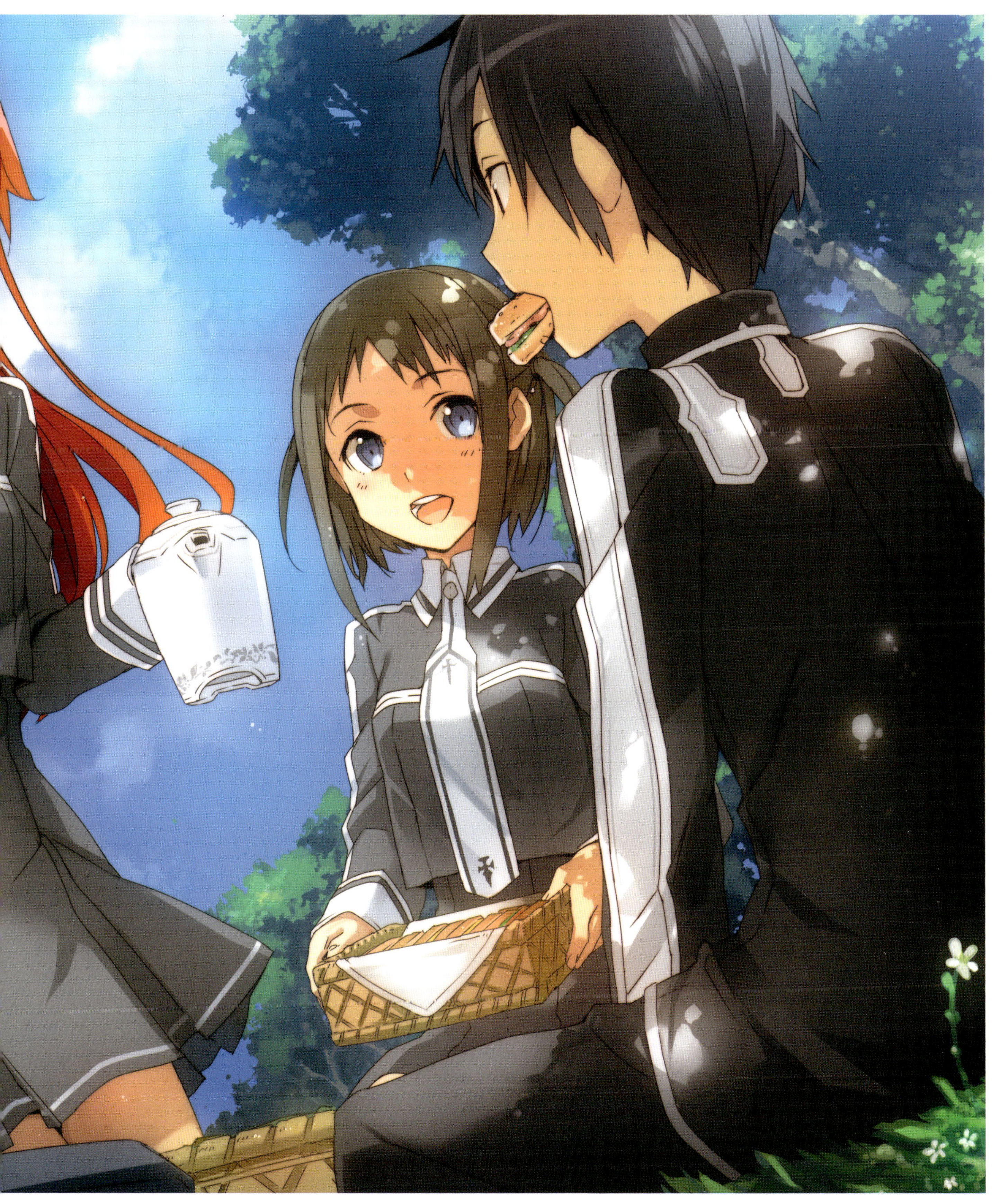

Dengeki Bunko
Sword Art Online 11: Alicization Turning
Frontispiece: December 2012

This is the contrast scene. I took extra care to make it as dramatic as possible so it didn't come across like some kind of aggressive fan service scene.

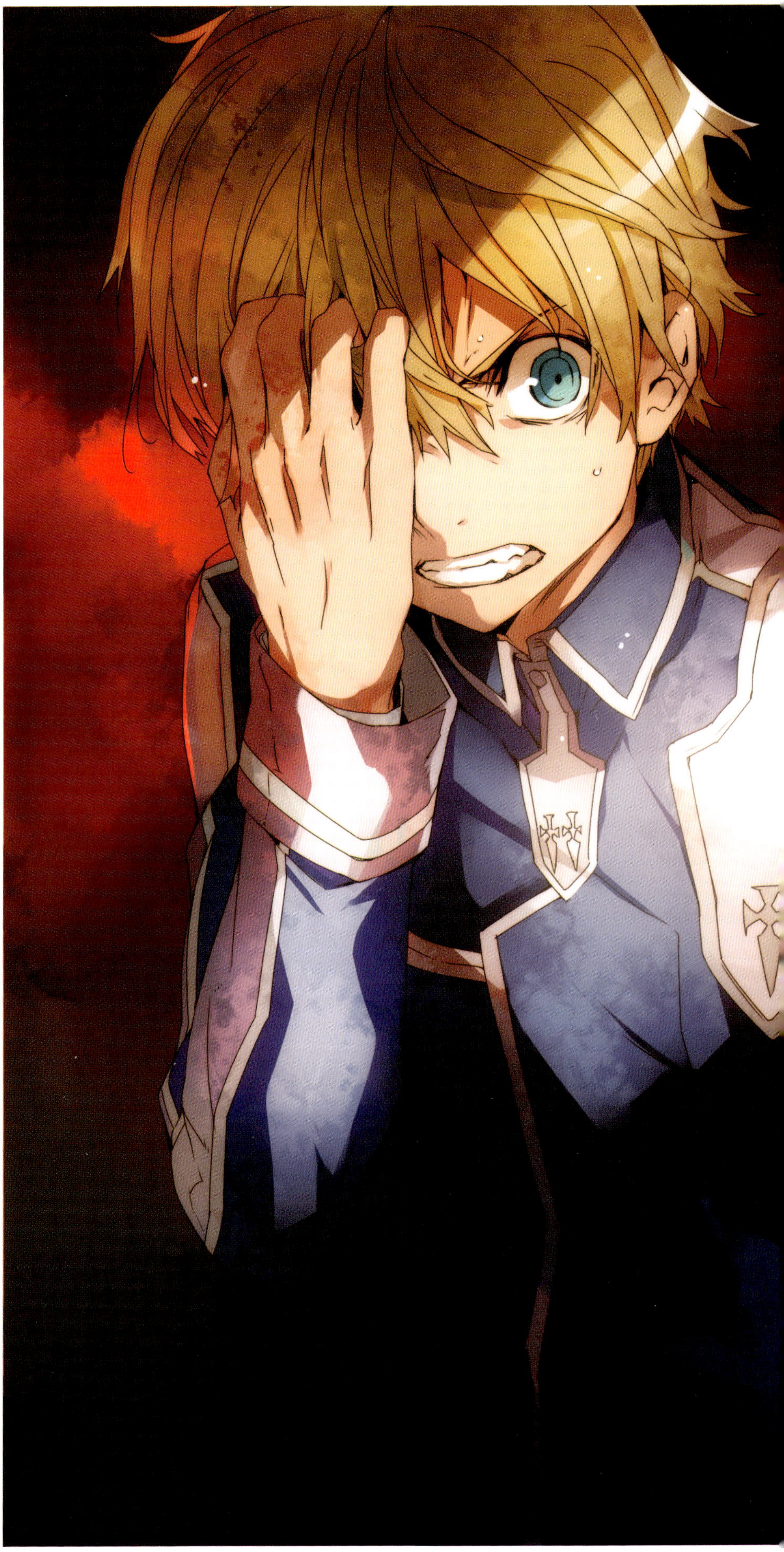

Dengeki Bunko
Sword Art Online 11: Alicization Turning
Illustration: December 2012

I remember really putting a lot of emotions into these expressions. I think I really drew upon the heat of the written scenes when finishing these images.

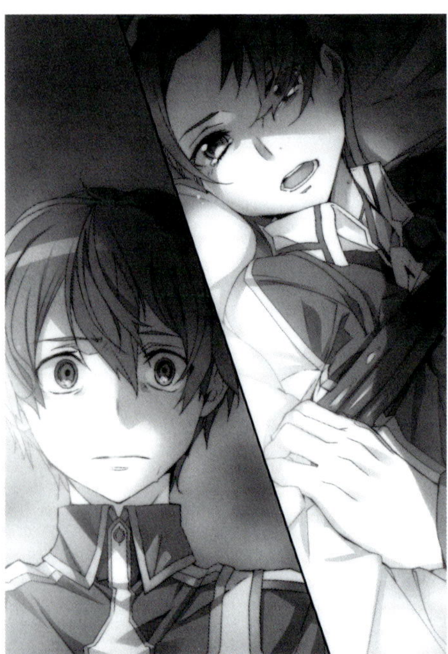

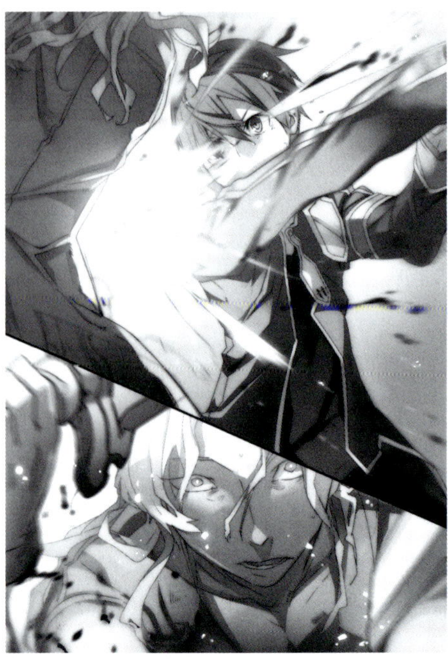

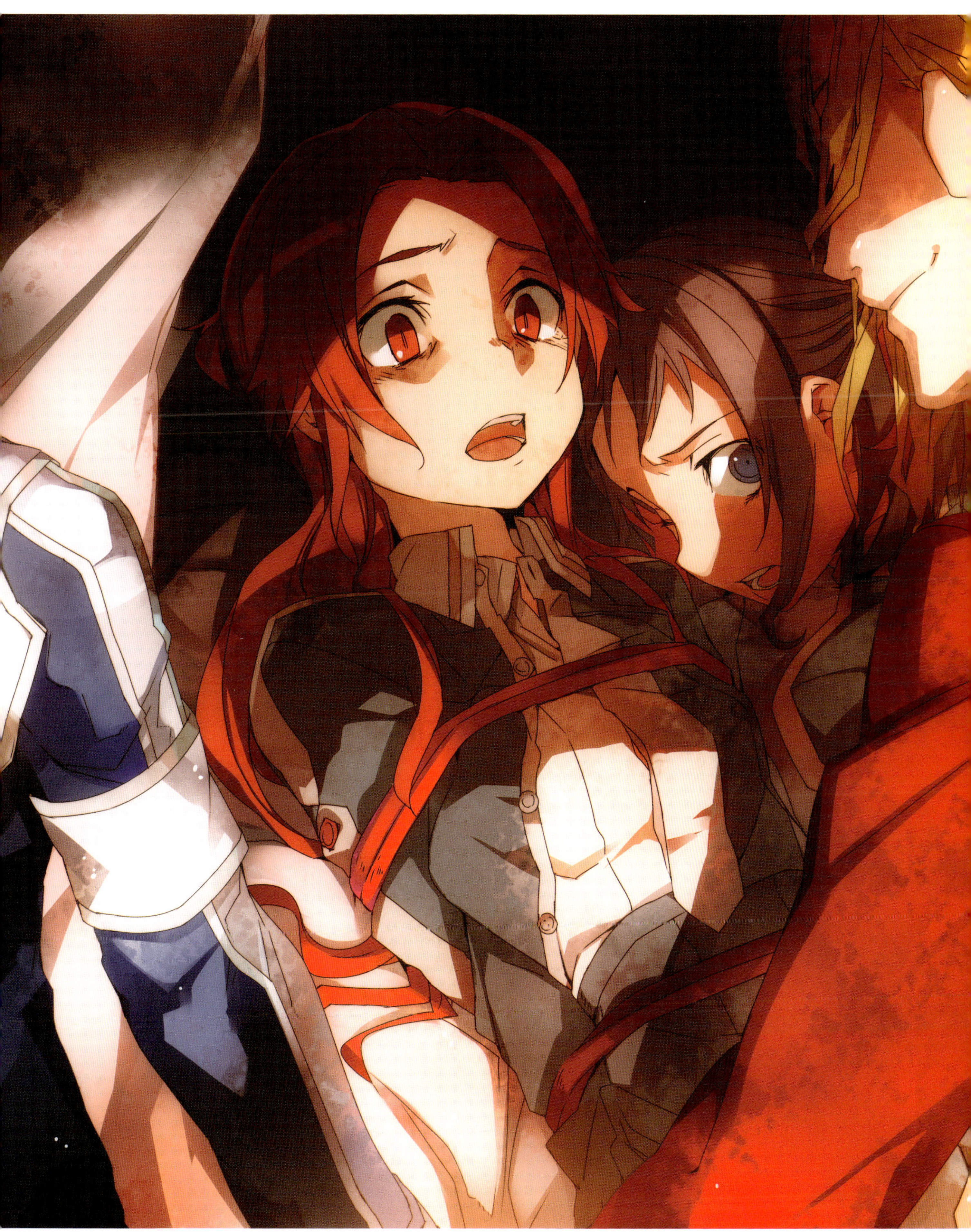

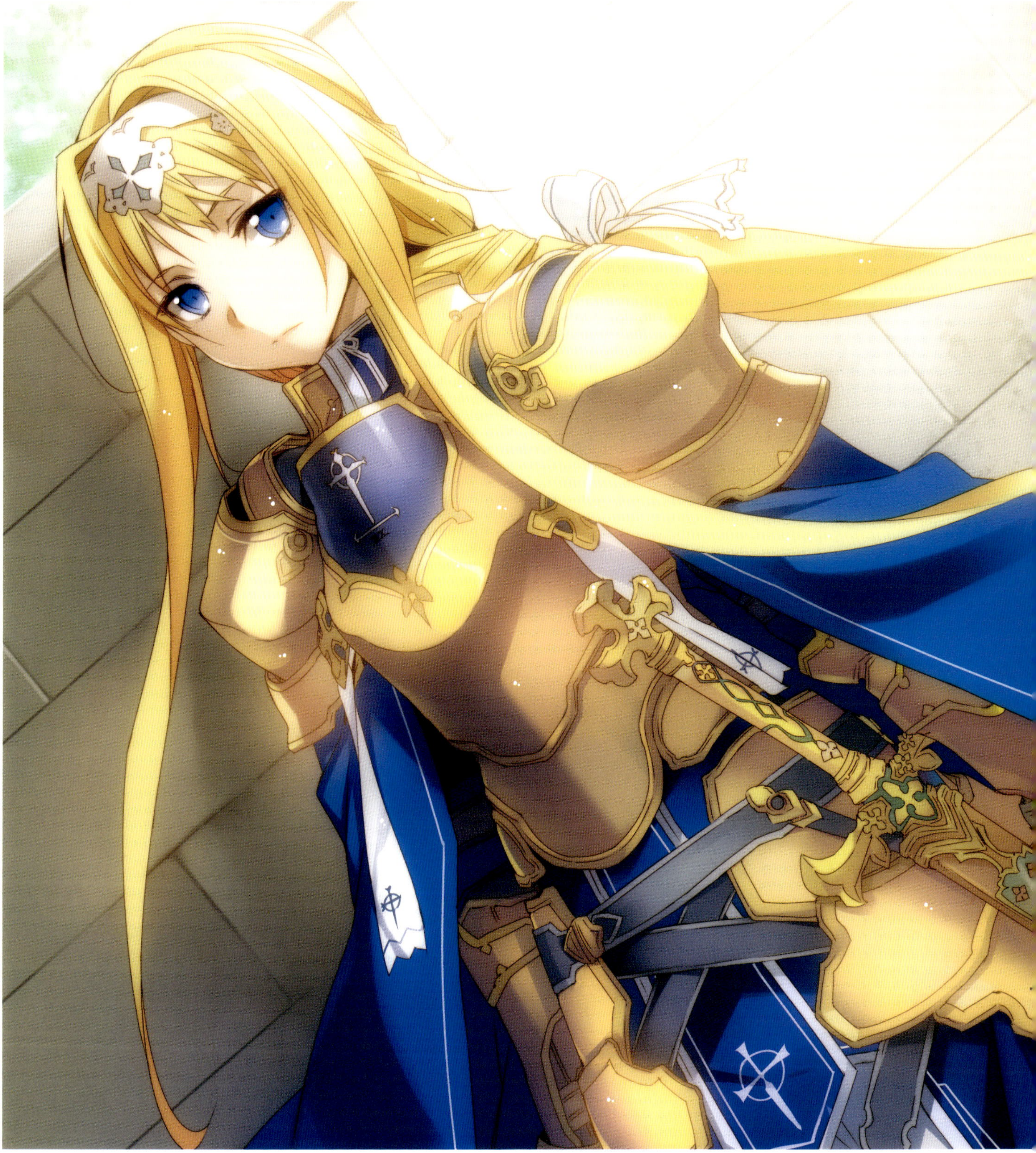

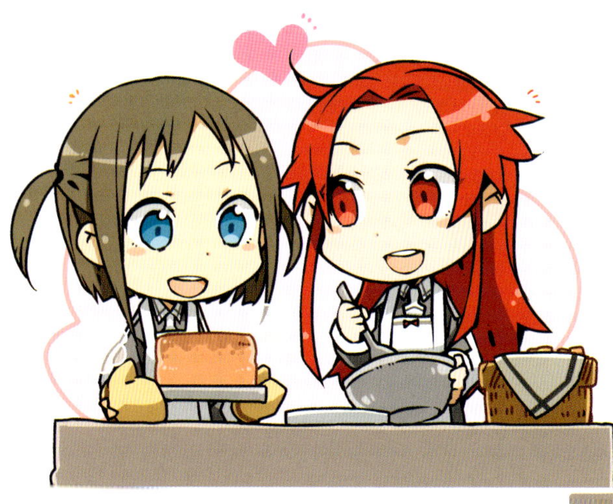

Dengeki Bunko
Sword Art Online 11: Alicization Turning
Back Cover: December 2012

Ronie and Tiese cooking.
They're having a lot of fun.

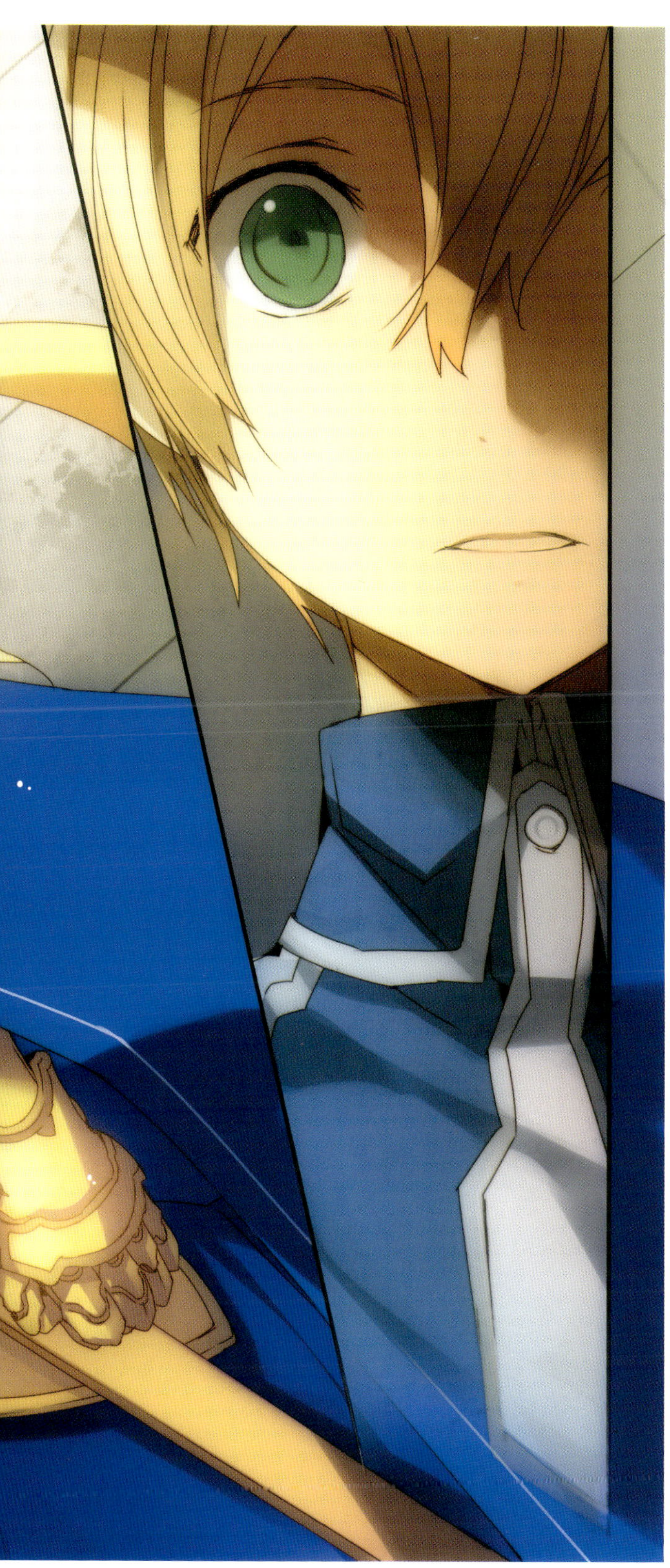

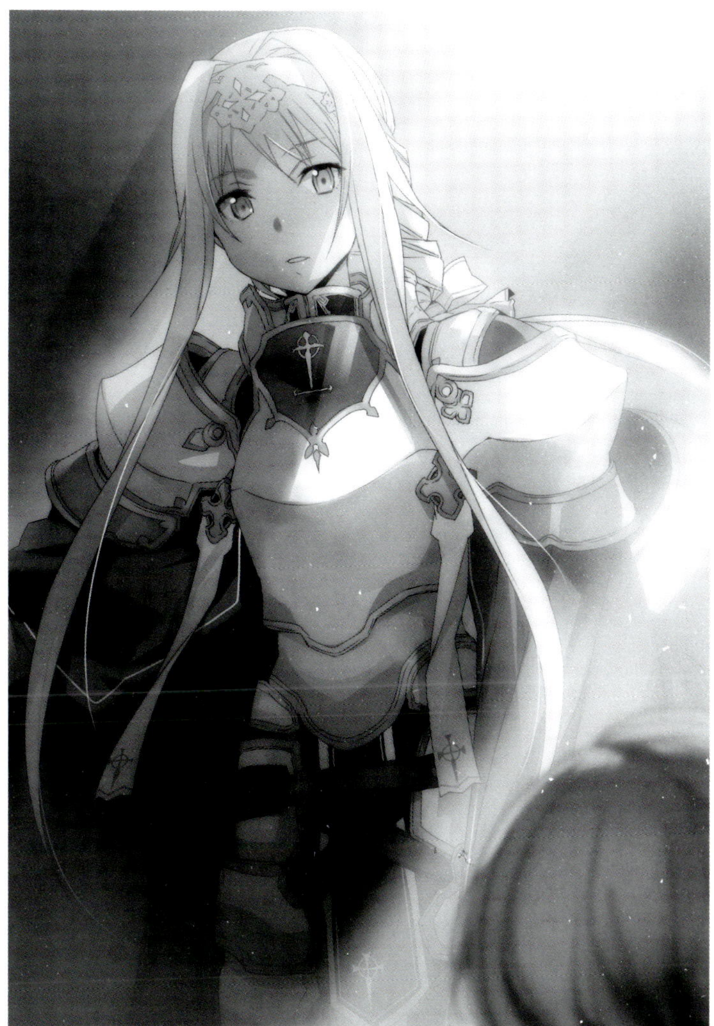

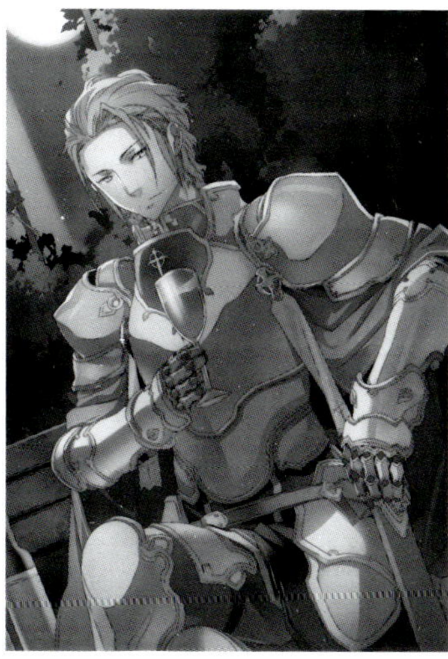

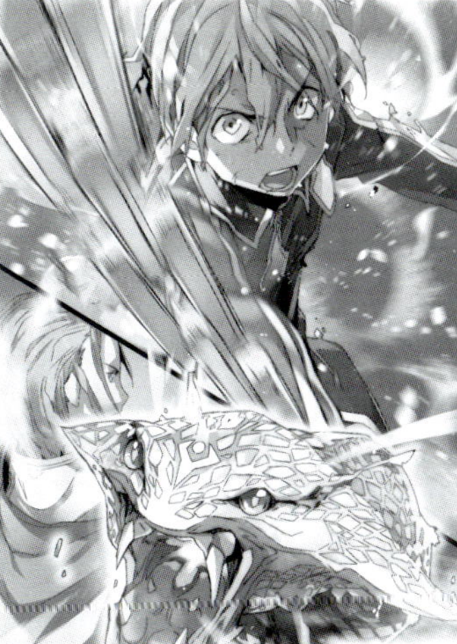

Dengeki Bunko
Sword Art Online 11: Alicization Turning
Frontispiece: December 2012

Alice's reintroduction. I used her armor as the basis for all the Integrity Knights' armor after her, so this illustration really captures a snapshot of the amount of work I set up for myself later. Drawing armor is really hard! I'm sorry, animators!

Dengeki Bunko
Sword Art Online 11: Alicization Turning
Illustration: December 2012

Kinda feels like it would be really uncomfortable for Eldrie to cross his legs like that in a full suit of armor, but let's not sweat the details. I hadn't designed the Administrator yet at this point. It looks like I was thinking of more cowlicky hair, I guess.

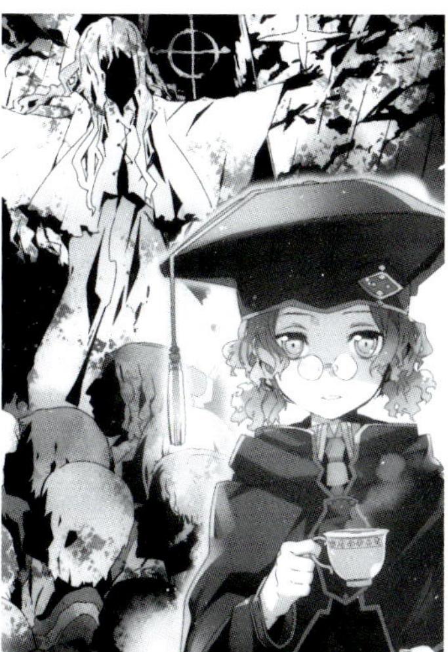

SWORD ART ONLINE media mix 1

A section comprised of various pieces done outside of the main novels. These provide ample opportunity for scenarios you wouldn't see in the novels, so there's a great volume of situations found here.

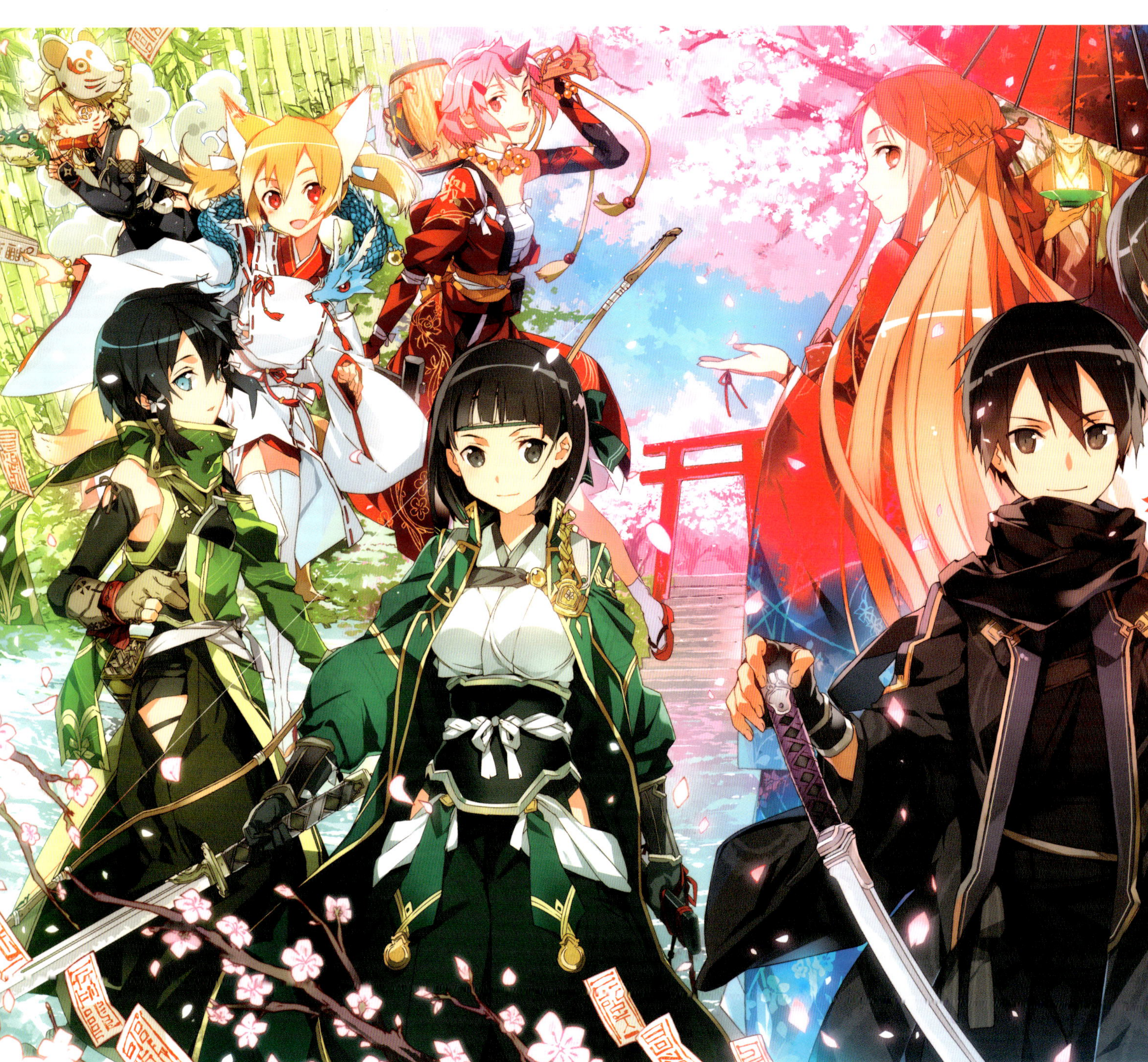

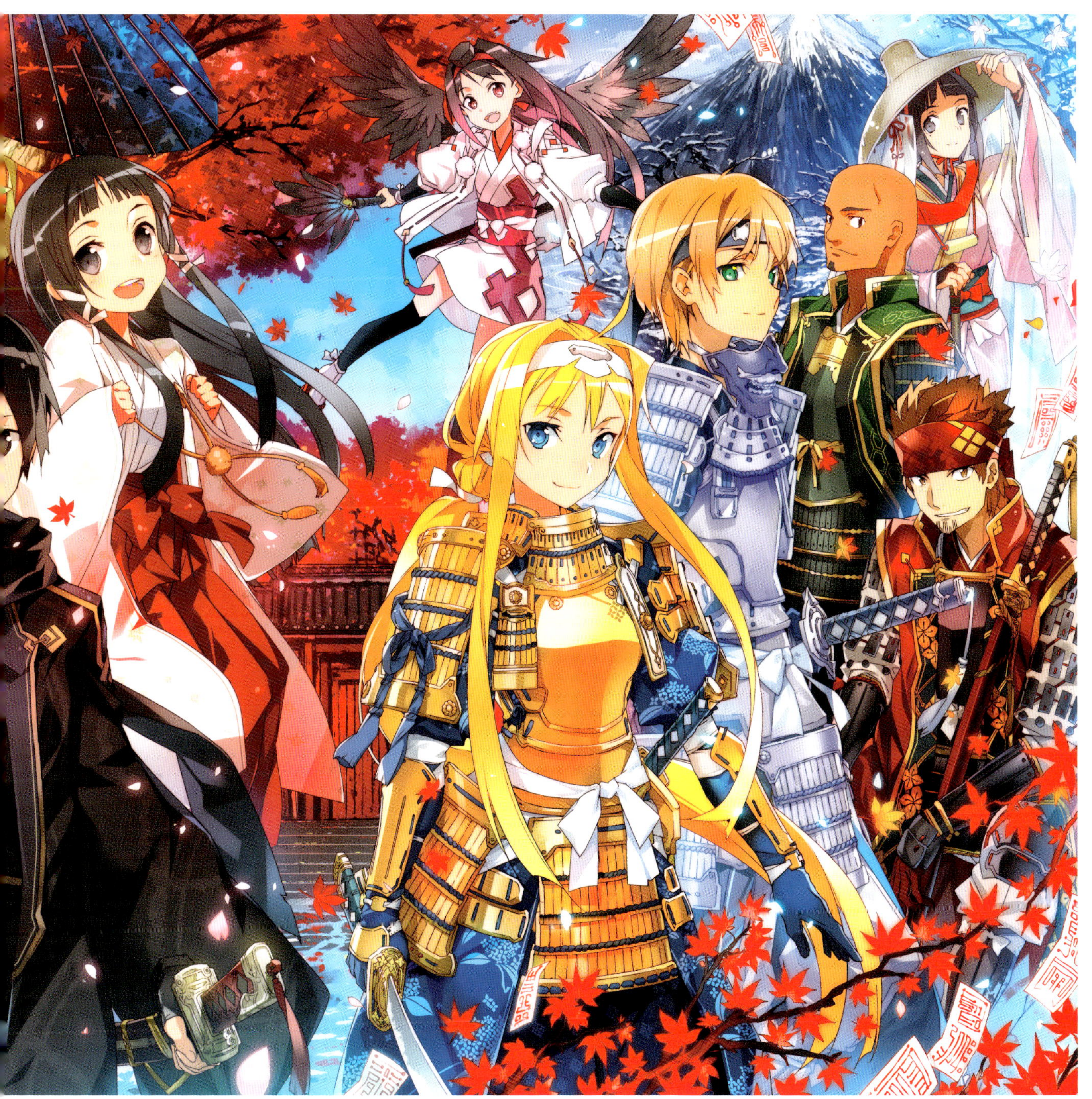

***Dengeki Bunko Magazine*, Vol. 42-44**

Three-Part Combination Poster: February–June 2015

A poster series that spanned three issues of *Dengeki Bunko Magazine*. They gave me free reign to draw this series with whatever setting and composition I wanted. *SAO* in a traditional Japanese design was an idea I'd always wanted to try, so this was great fun. I was thinking up all kinds of character details for them, so if you sense a kind of story behind them and their professions, my mission was successful.

Dengeki Bunko Magazine*, Vol. 41
Cover: December 2014

This is nice and simple, since magazine covers get plastered with all kinds of text on top. Boy, that's a really dangerous angle on Asuna's skirt!

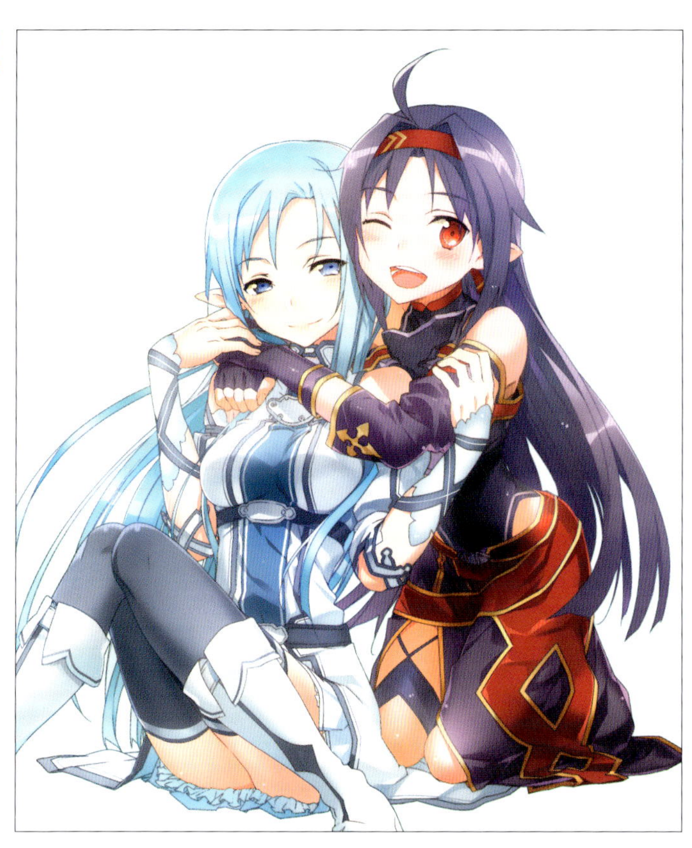

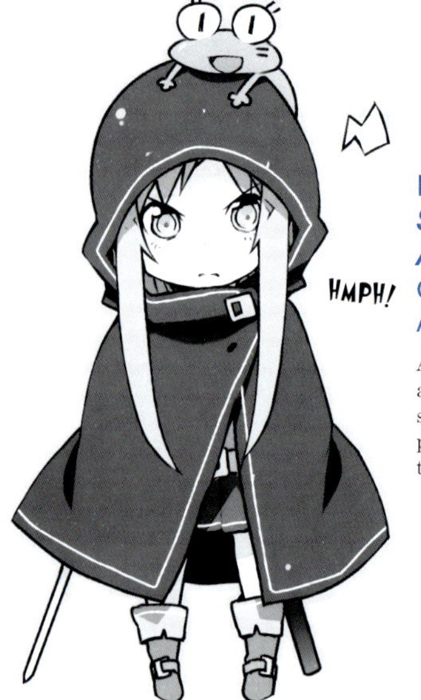

Dengeki Comics Next
***Sword Art Online 11: Sword Art Online Progressive*, Vol. 1**
Celebratory Illustration: August 2013

Asuna's a pretty soft character now, but at the start of Progressive, she was really spiky and angry. That was great, too! I'm pretty sure my comment to go along with this illustration said as much.

Dengeki Comics
***Sword Art Online: Fairy Dance*, Vol. 2**
Celebratory Illustration: August 2013

***Text:* "Congrats on the Volume 2 release!"**
***Bubble:* "Yay!"**
"2!" Looking at it now, there's way too much detail crammed around those fingers. Hard to parse!

Dengeki Comics
***Sword Art Online: Fairy Dance*, Vol. 1**
Celebratory Illustration: October 2012

***Top:* "Volume release celebration!"**
***Bottom:* "Congratulations!"**
When I get the chance to draw Suguha how I want, I feel like I go for the real girl more often than Leafa.

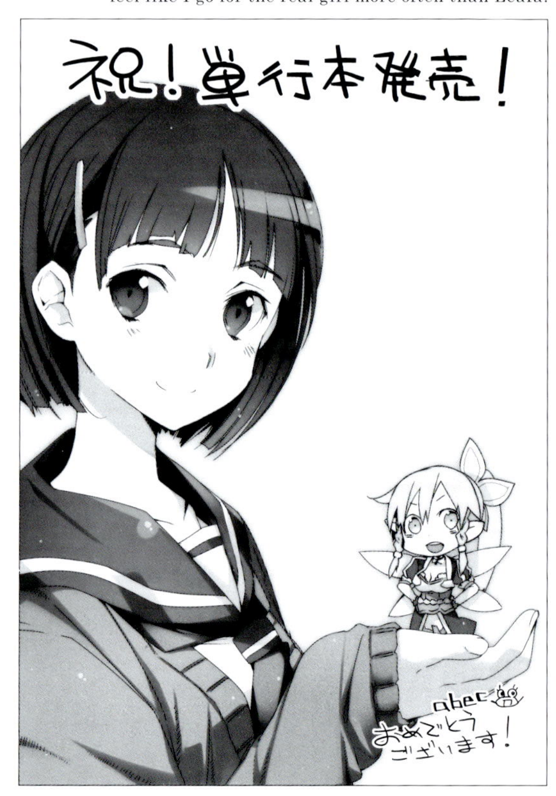

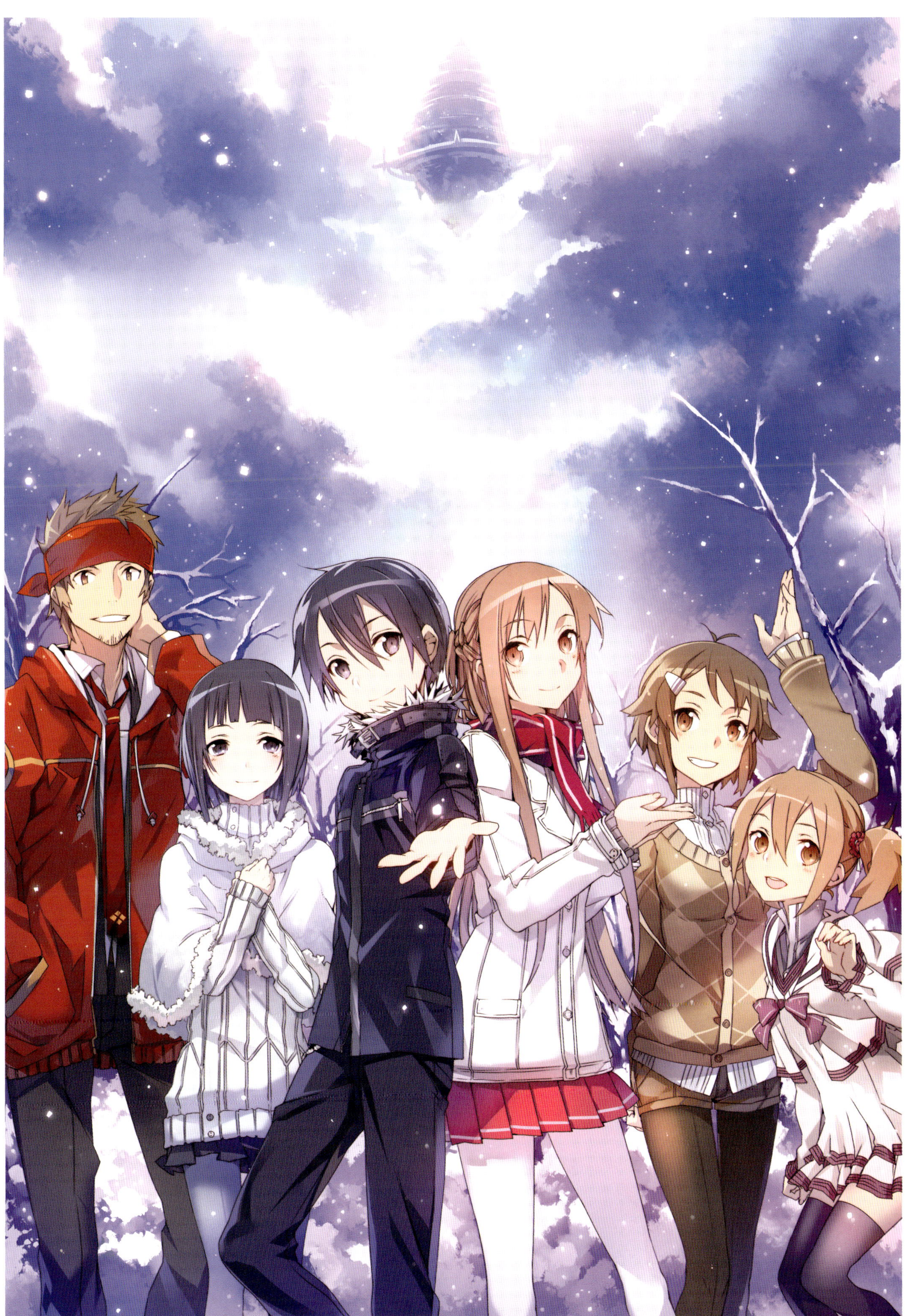

Dengeki Bunko 20th Anniversary Celebration
Dengeki Bunko Exhibit: Winter
Famous Scene Collection, Winter: December 2013

This is a selection of characters who fought in Aincrad, which is why Sachi is there. I knew she was a popular character, so I had a feeling that the Sachi fans would love this one. If I drew it again, I'd probably include Argo, but she didn't take the spotlight until later.

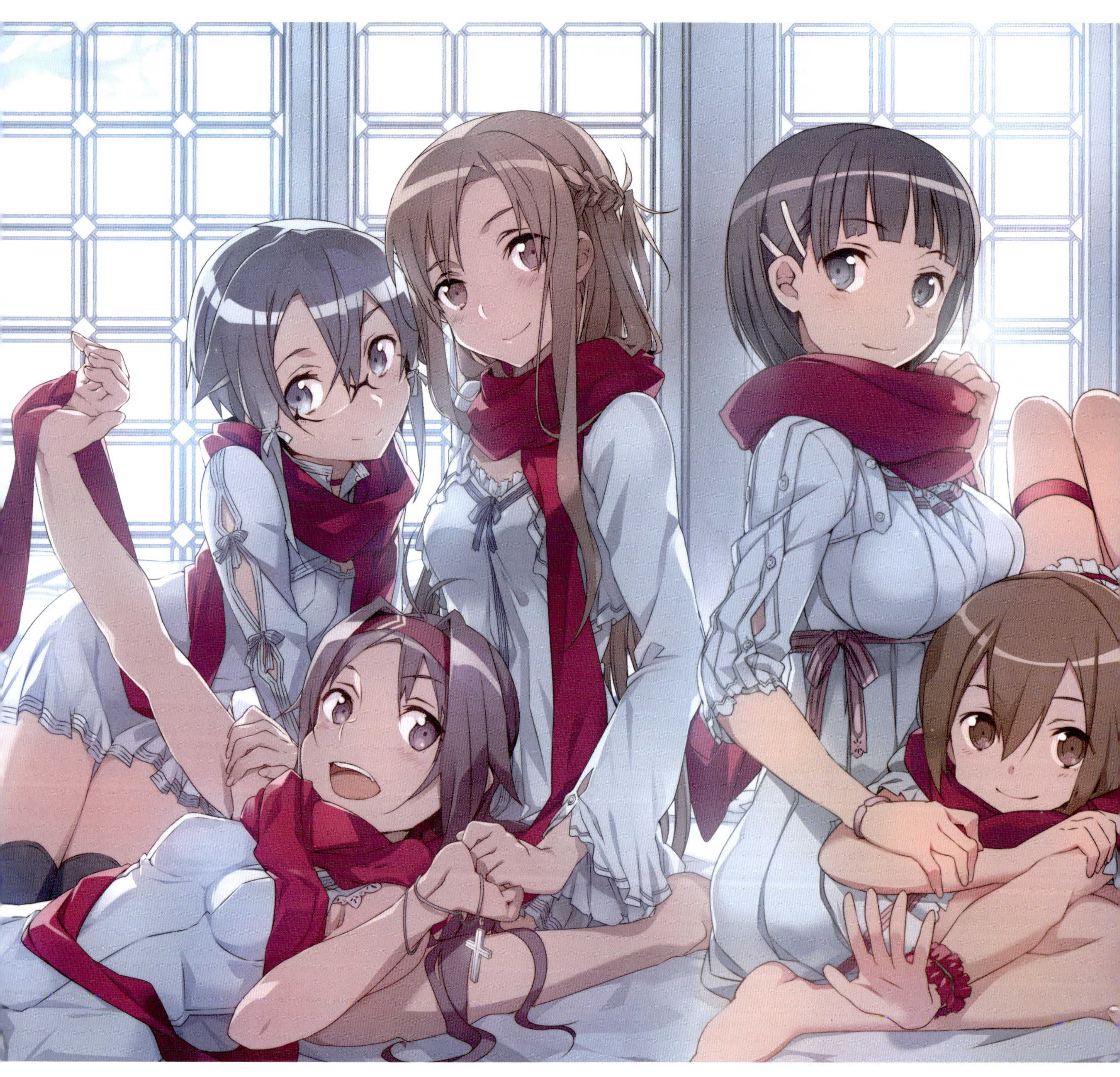

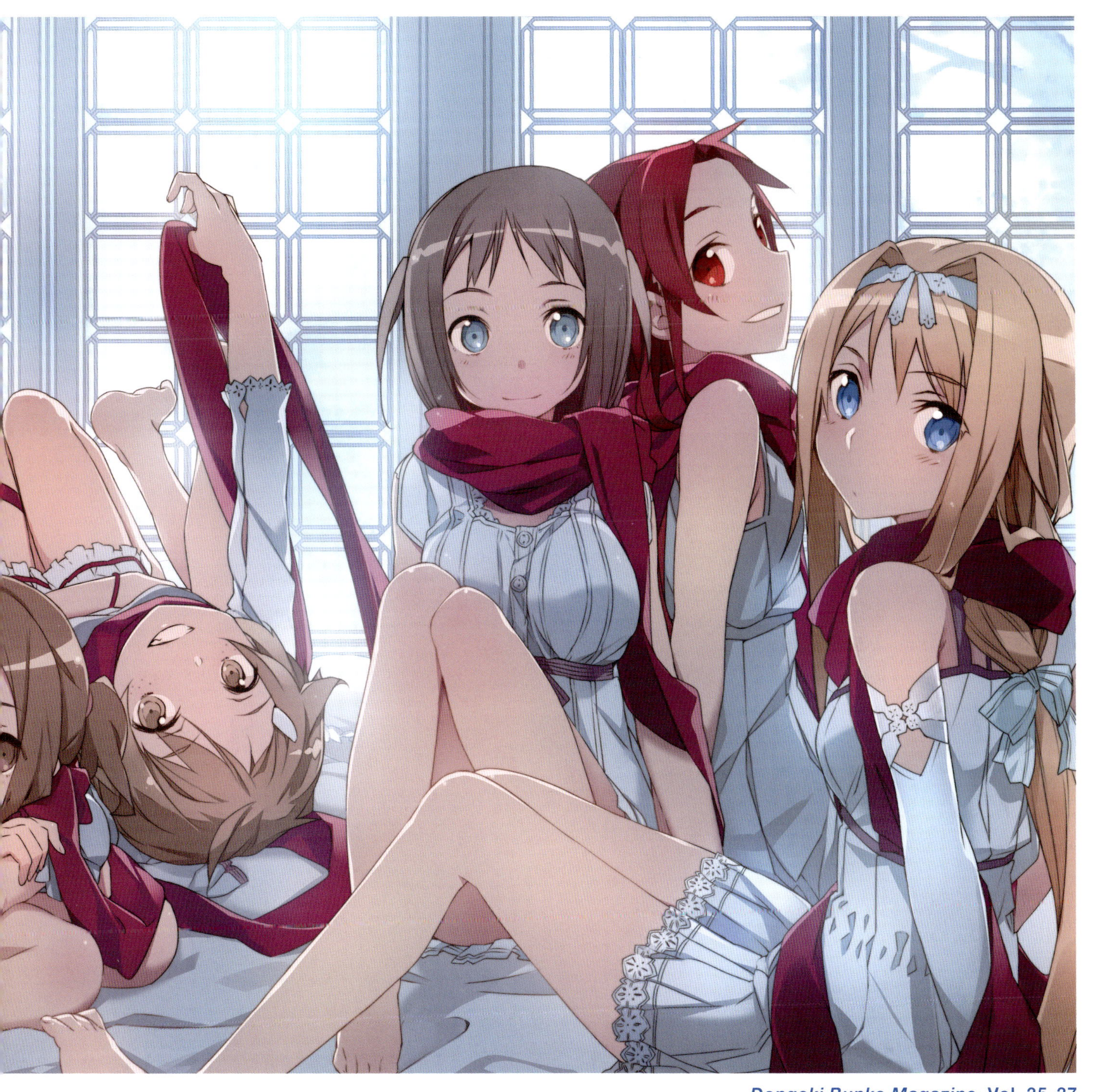

***Dengeki Bunko Magazine*, Vol. 35-37**
Three-Part Combination Poster: December 2013–April 2014

This was the second set of three consecutive posters, I think? The concept is actually fairly close to the cover of this book, I suppose. The idea is that they're all wearing one very long muffler.

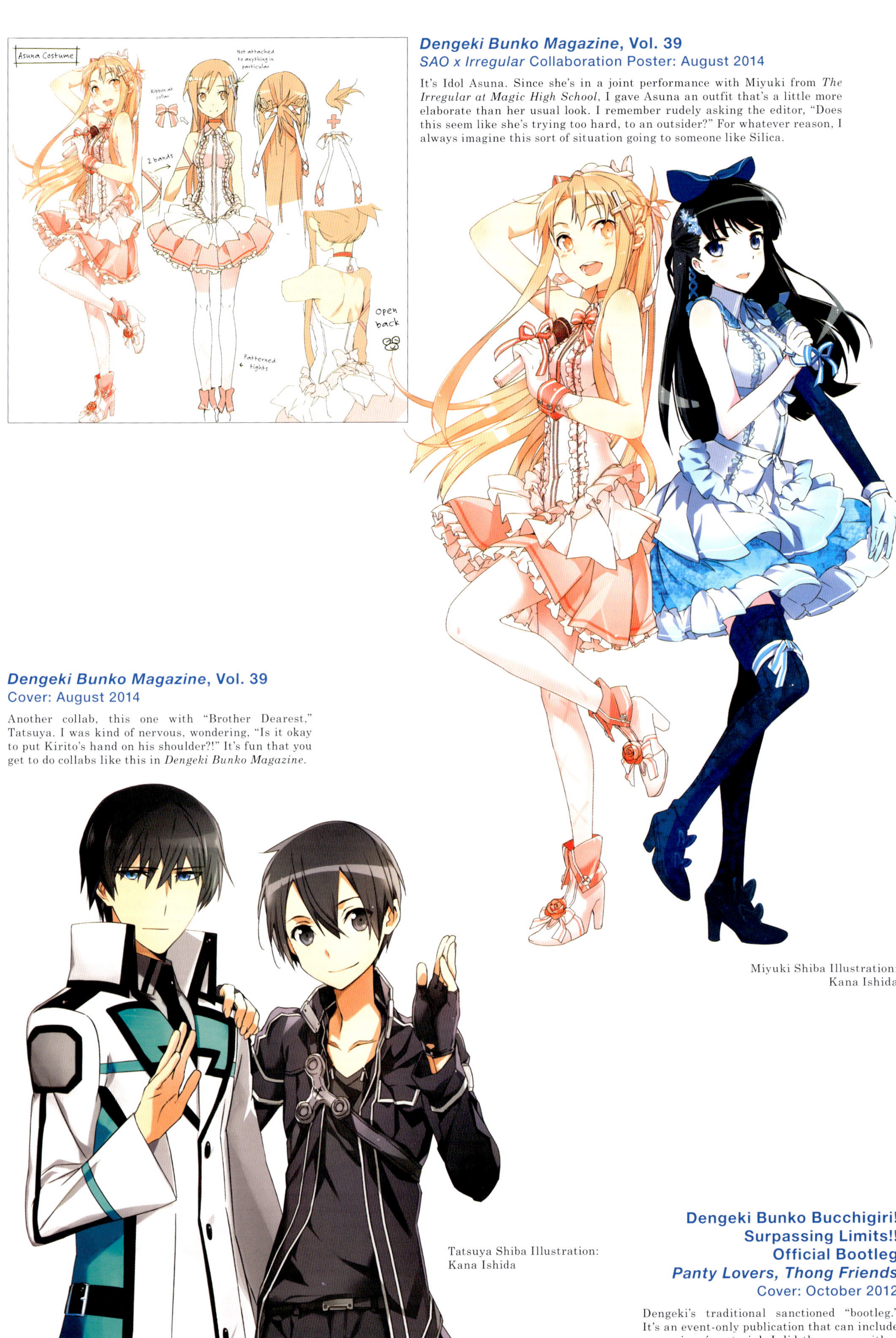

Dengeki Bunko Magazine, Vol. 39

SAO x Irregular Collaboration Poster: August 2014

It's Idol Asuna. Since she's in a joint performance with Miyuki from *The Irregular at Magic High School*, I gave Asuna an outfit that's a little more elaborate than her usual look. I remember rudely asking the editor, "Does this seem like she's trying too hard, to an outsider?" For whatever reason, I always imagine this sort of situation going to someone like Silica.

Miyuki Shiba Illustration: Kana Ishida

Dengeki Bunko Magazine, Vol. 39

Cover: August 2014

Another collab, this one with "Brother Dearest," Tatsuya. I was kind of nervous, wondering, "Is it okay to put Kirito's hand on his shoulder?!" It's fun that you get to do collabs like this in *Dengeki Bunko Magazine*.

Tatsuya Shiba Illustration: Kana Ishida

Dengeki Bunko Bucchigiri! Surpassing Limits!! Official Bootleg *Panty Lovers, Thong Friends*

Cover: October 2012

Dengeki's traditional sanctioned "bootleg." It's an event-only publication that can include some risqué material. I did the cover, with a string thong theme, but I knew I didn't want to go overboard with it. The result looks more like regular panties and not very thong-y.

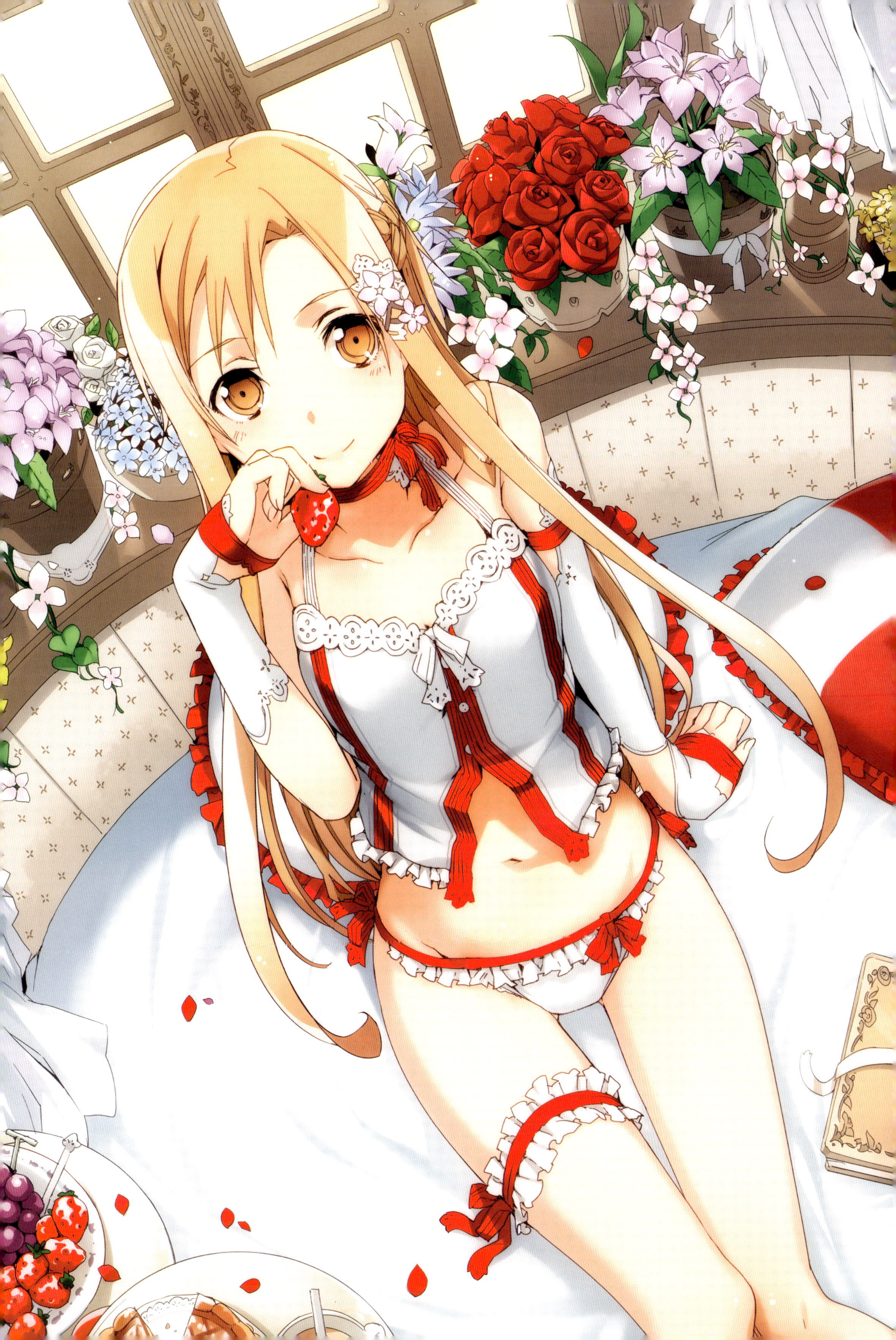

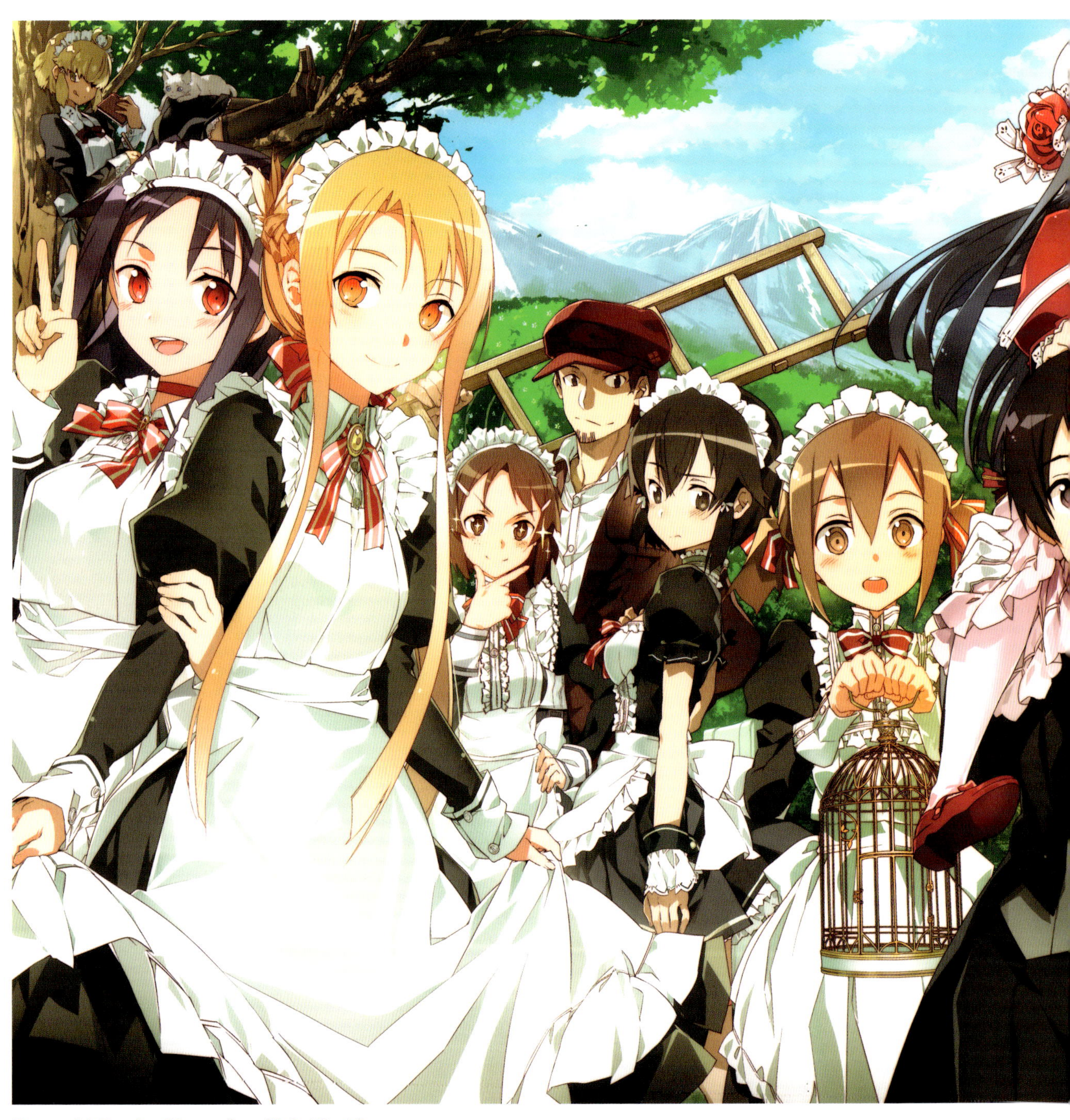

***Dengeki Bunko Magazine*, Vol. 46–48**
Three-Part Combination Poster: October 2015–February 2016

As you can see, the theme is maids. At first, I was thinking of having the AI characters be the clients, with the players as the servants. But I couldn't overcome my desire to draw maid Alice and butler Eugeo, so only the administrative AIs got the nod. A family of Yui, Cardinal, and Administrator would probably be pretty entertaining.

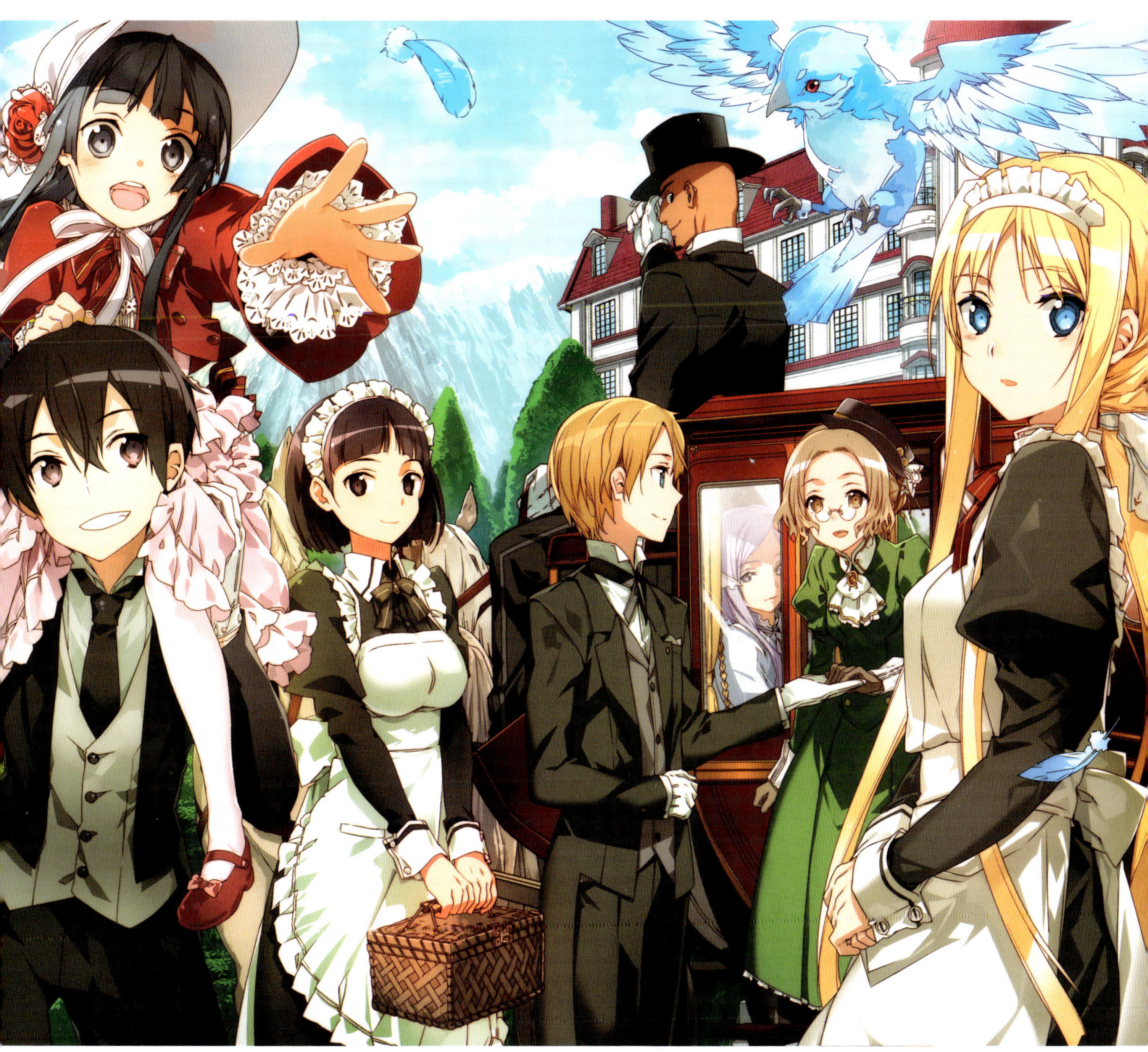

SWORD ART ONLINE
Alicization Rising

The volume where Kirito and Eugeo head for the top floor of Central Cathedral. There are many illustrations of them facing off against the Integrity Knights in this book.

Dengeki Bunko
Sword Art Online 12: Alicization Rising
Cover: April 2013

I actually forgot that I had a rough cover design that featured Fanatio. The one with Linel and Fizel was chosen instead, and the background design was meant to evoke a set of stairs.

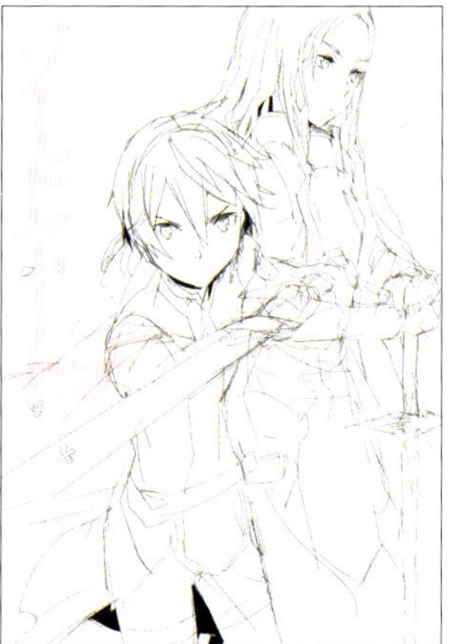

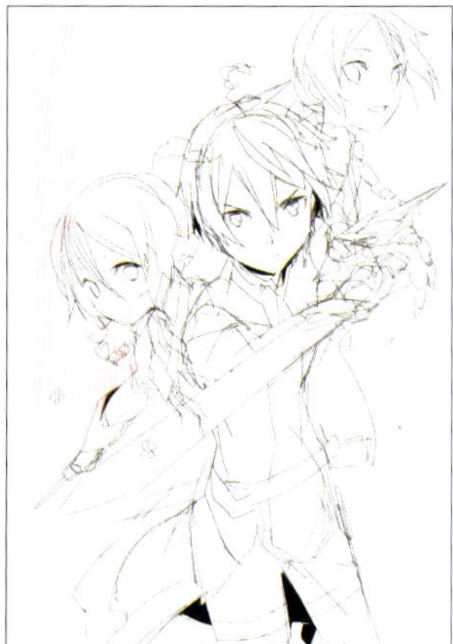

Alternate Cover Sketches

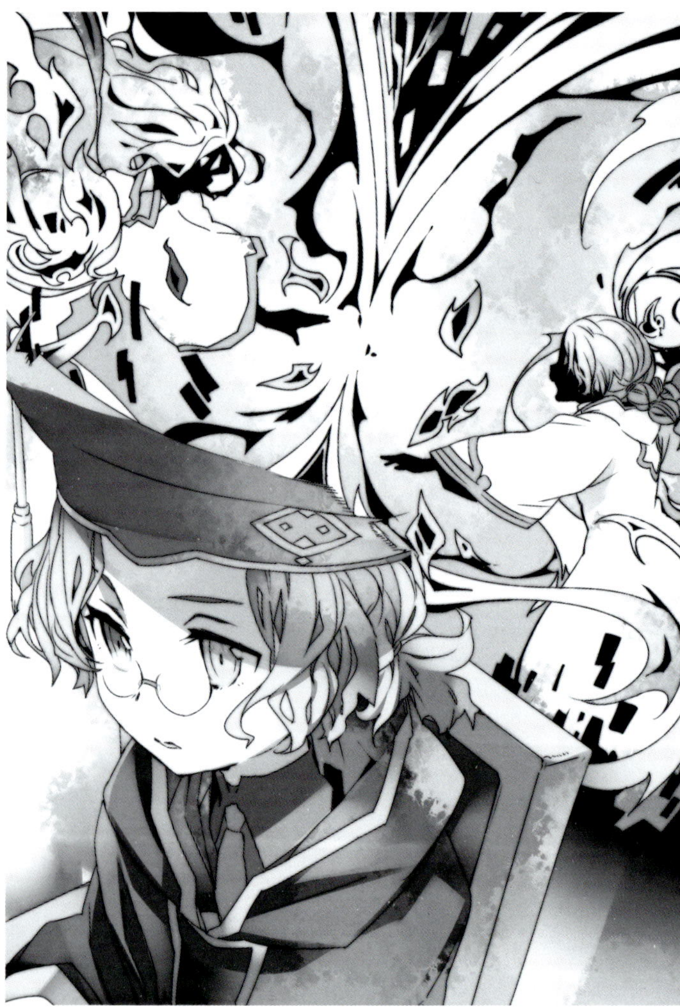

Dengeki Bunko
Sword Art Online 12: Alicization Rising
Illustration: April 2013

Two pieces that single out Cardinal. Once again, the hair in the scene depicting Administrator isn't the way she looks eventually, because I hadn't designed her yet.

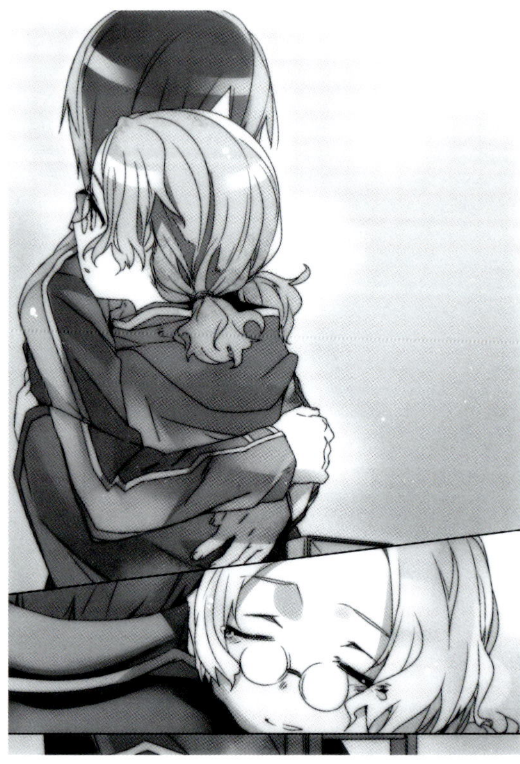

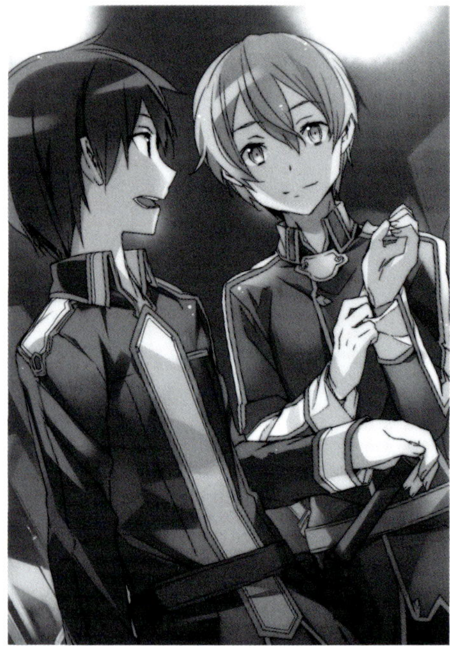

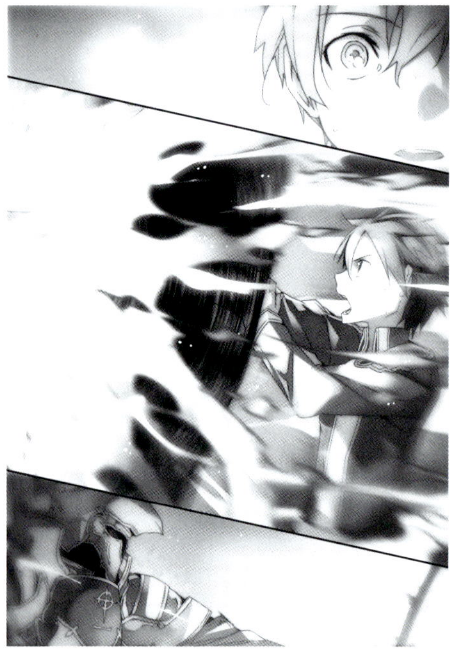

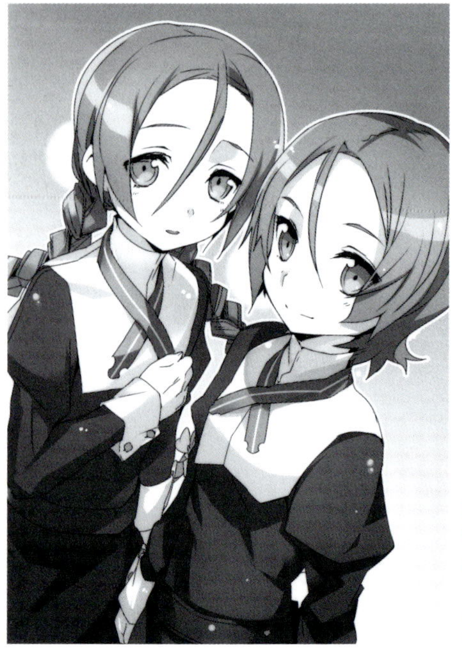

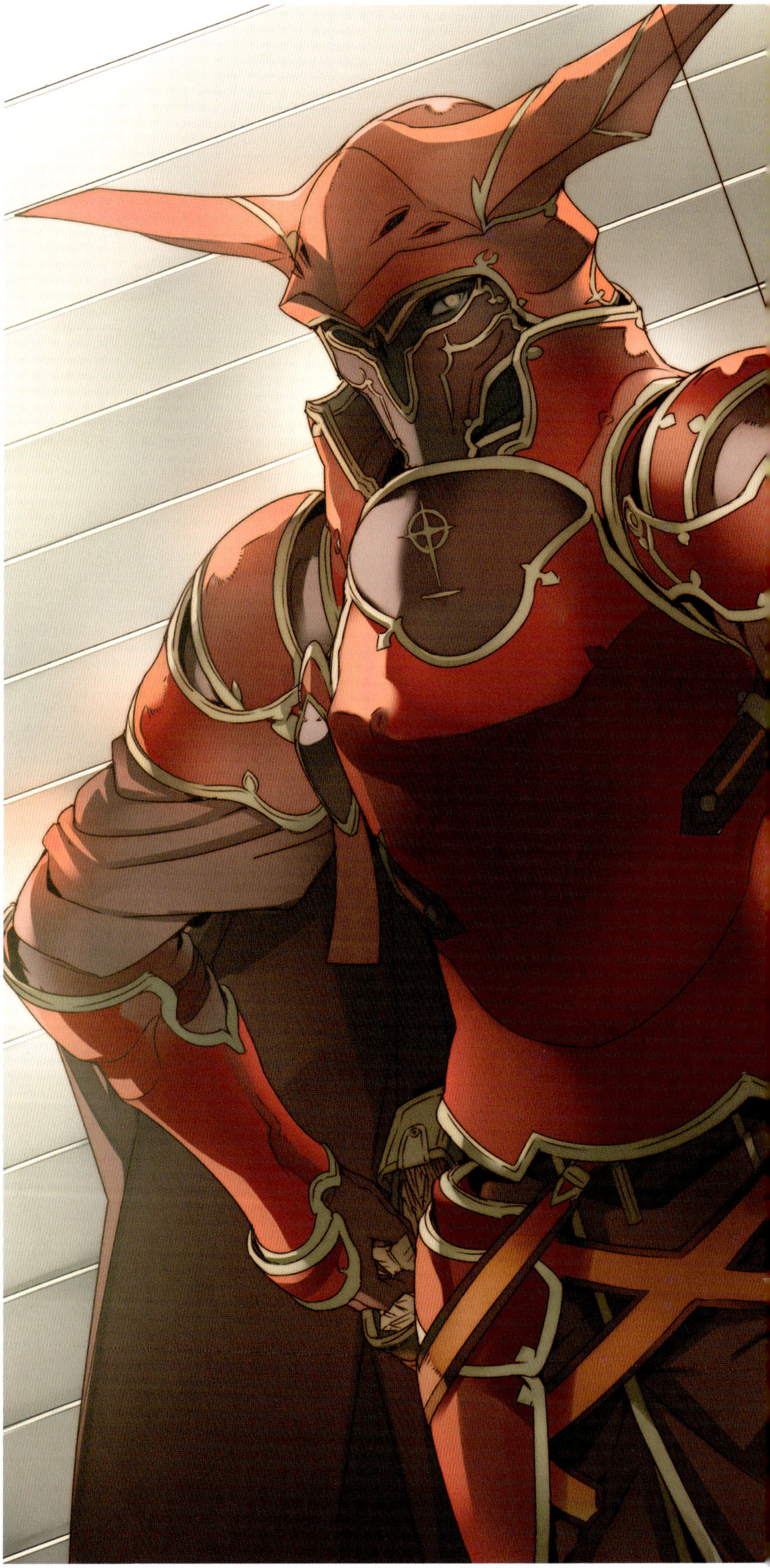

Dengeki Bunko
Sword Art Online 12: Alicization Rising
Illustration: April 2013

New duds for Eugeo and Kirito. I thought about giving them a design that mimicked the Integrity Knights, but opted to retain the style of their elite disciple uniforms. Also, if not for their placement on the cover, this would have been the first introduction to Linel and Fizel.

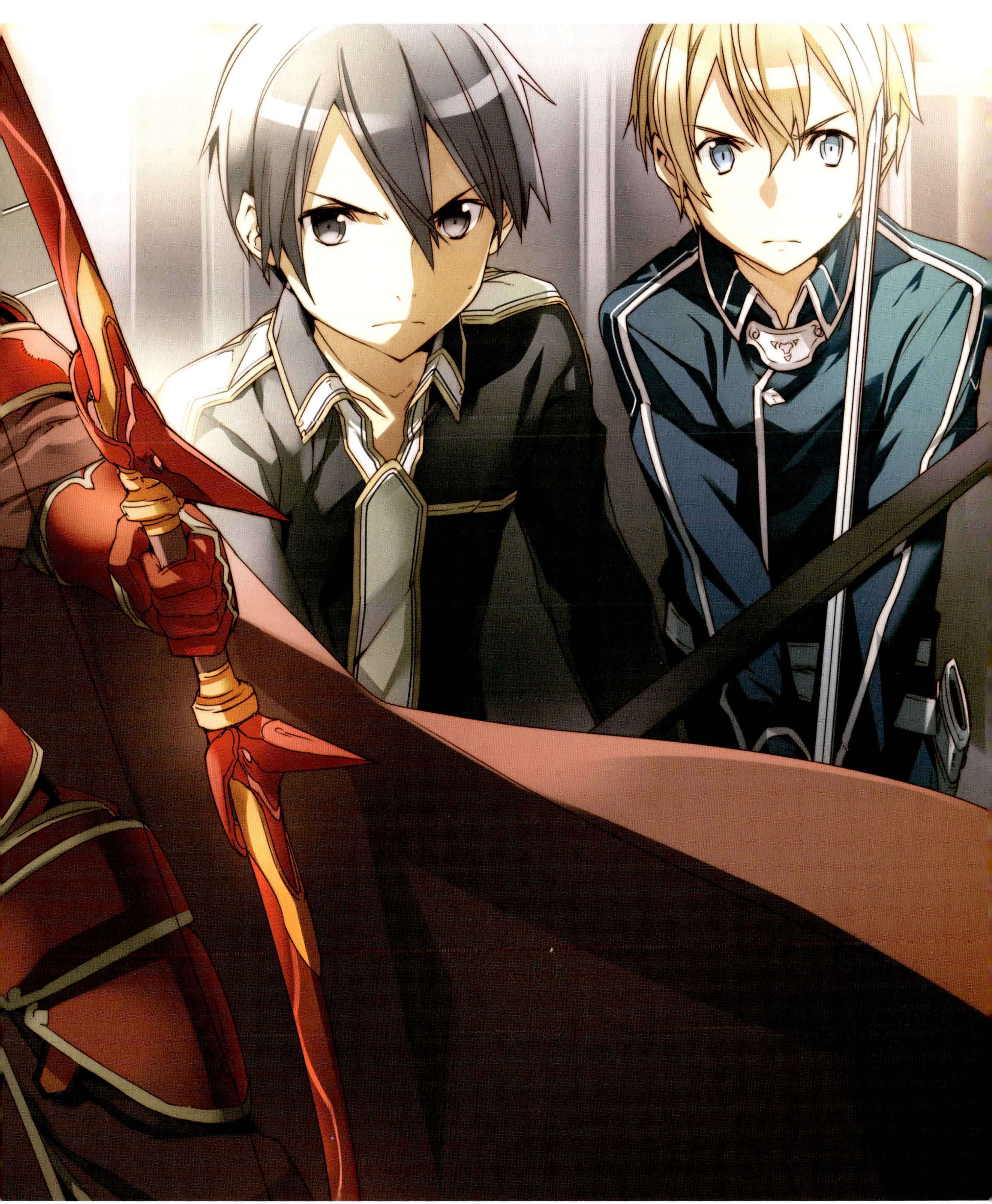

Dengeki Bunko

Sword Art Online 12: Alicization Rising

Frontispiece: April 2013

I was just thinking that Deusolbert's bow was likely to get caught on his armor, when I realized in a panic that I drew him without his armpit guard on the left side! While writing this comment, I quickly looked it up, and my original rough design and anime design had a guard there. As often happens, when I was drawing the piece, I thought, "Maybe I should do this instead," and changed the design, then forgot all about it. And if you're a birdbrain like me, you'll go and draw something directly based on the rough design after that, so there are multiple designs out there. I'm so sorry about that. When you're drawing him, just draw whichever version you like.

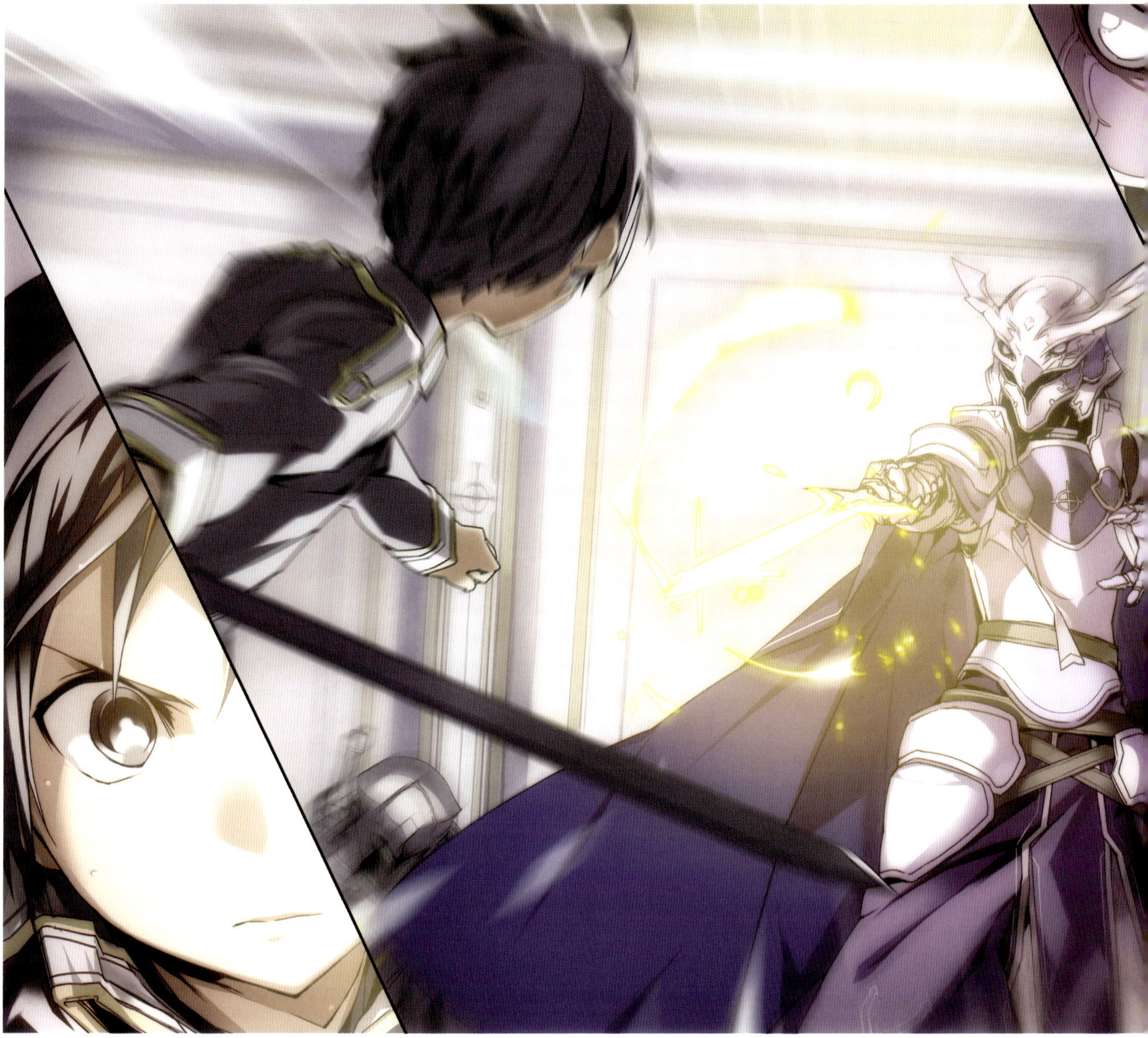

Dengeki Bunko, *Sword Art Online 12: Alicization Rising*
Frontispiece: April 2013

Pointing a sword at the camera is tricky, because it makes the blade look small. It's hard to capture at a glance. But if you pull the camera out too far, there isn't enough impact for the small size of the book. So instead, I've got them facing each other, but with a perspective that doesn't quite match. In the book, there's the gutter in the middle, so sometimes you might not even notice these things.

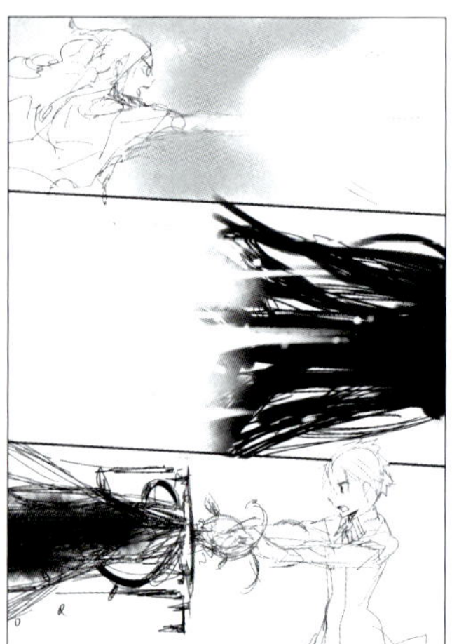

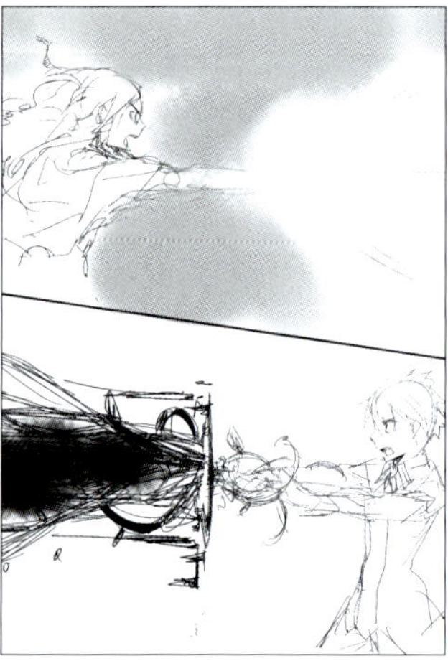

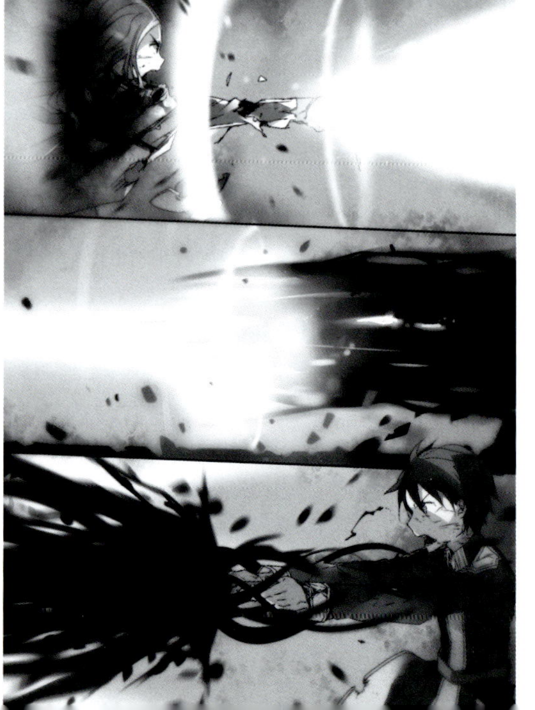

Dengeki Bunko
Sword Art Online 12: Alicization Rising
Illustration: April 2013

I'm pretty sure I went with a clean thirds structure on this one in order to avoid overlapping the composition with the piece where Deusolbert is spraying fire.

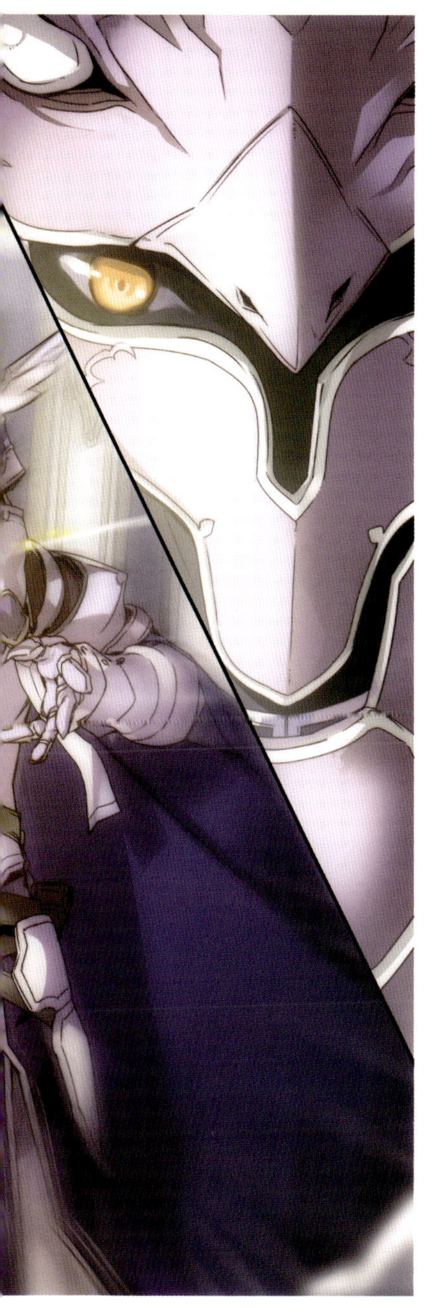

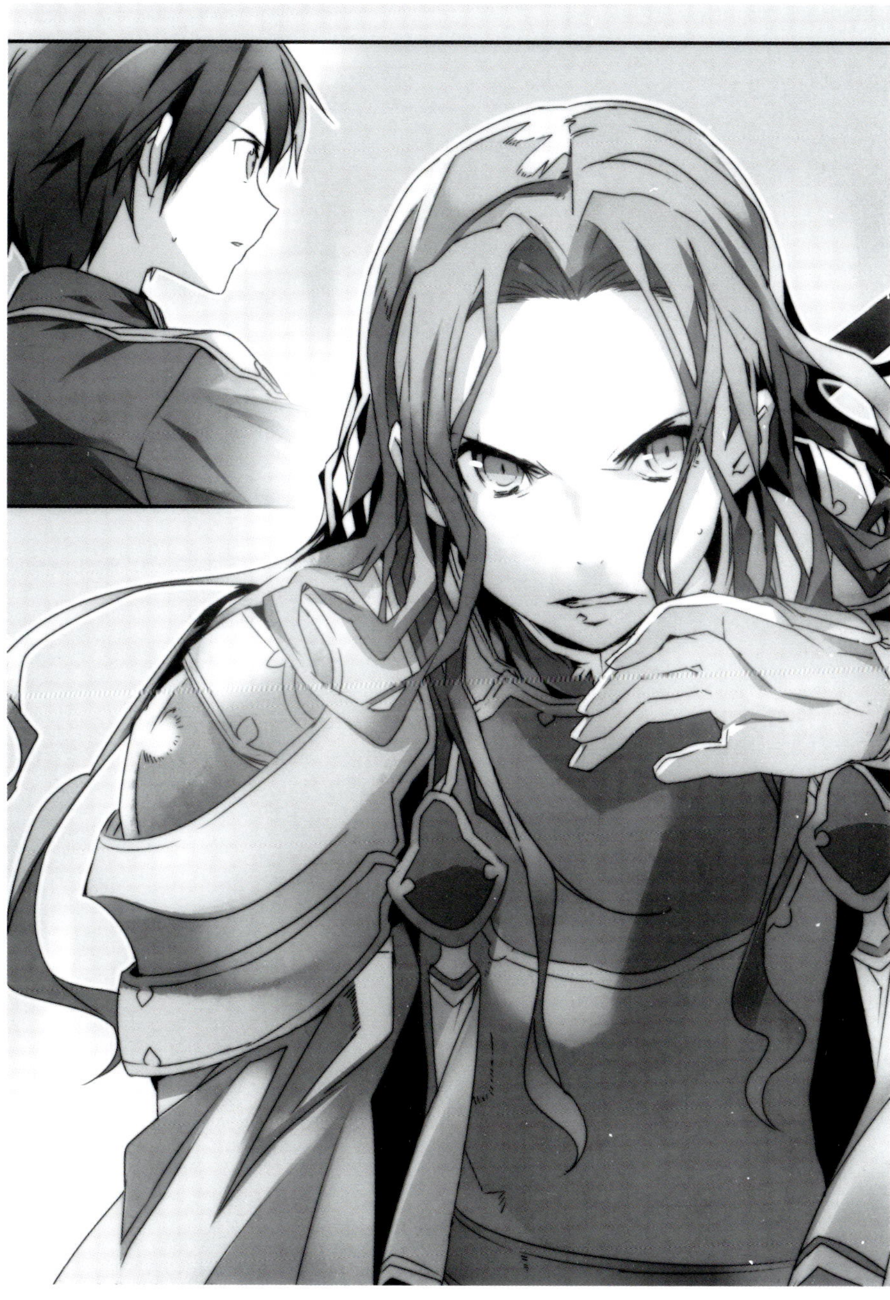

Dengeki Bunko
Sword Art Online 12: Alicization Rising
Illustration: April 2013

I wonder how she got all that hair into a helmet.

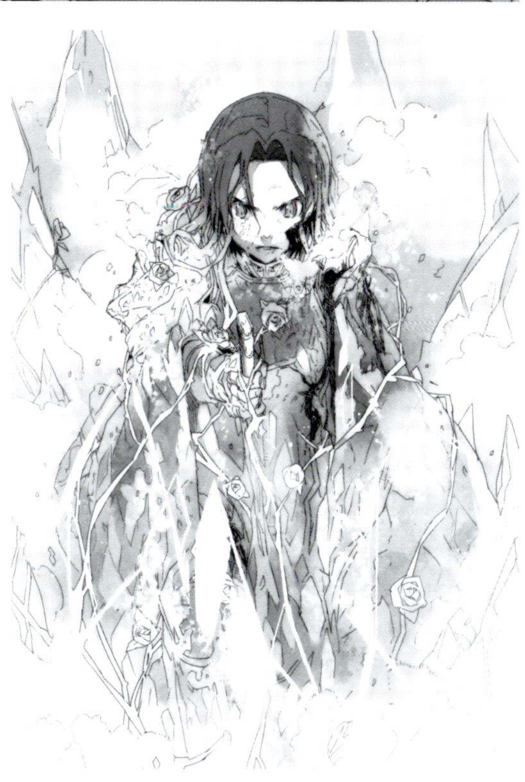

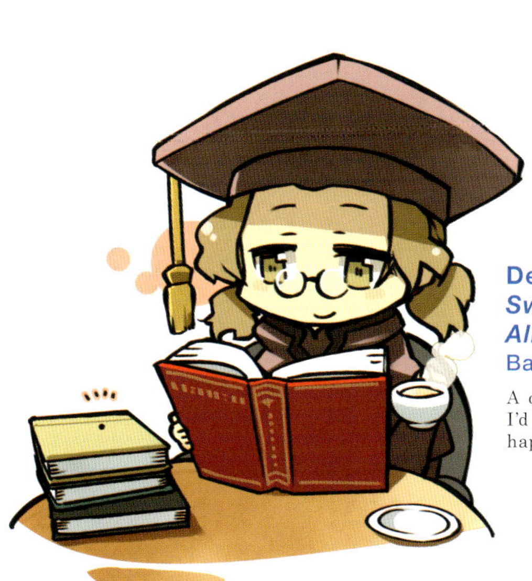

Dengeki Bunko
Sword Art Online 12: Alicization Rising
Back Cover: April 2013

A cut of Cardinal and Charlotte. I'd like to see them living together happily in the future.

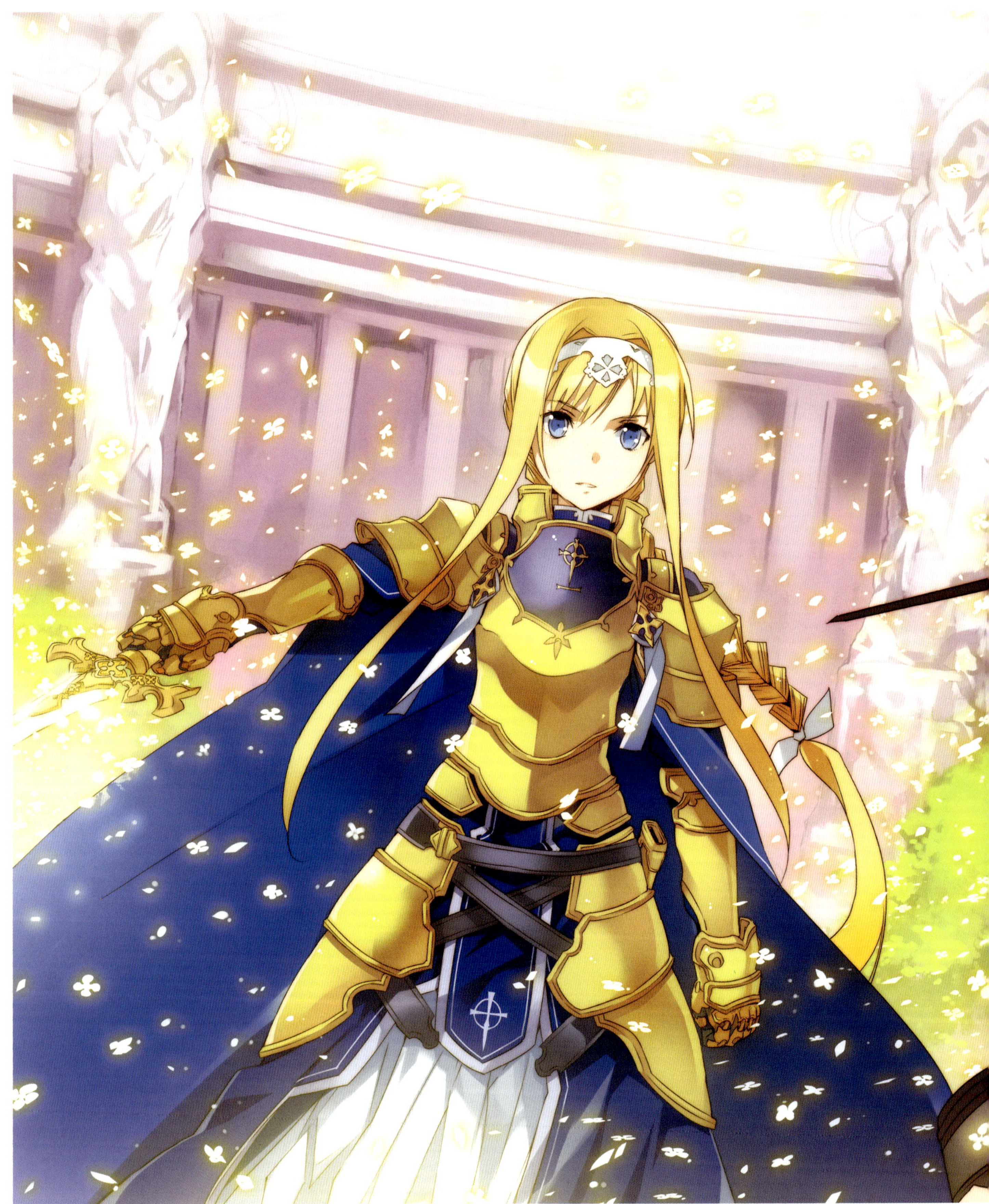

Dengeki Bunko
Sword Art Online 12: Alicization Rising
Frontispiece: April 2013

The Alice showdown. All three of these frontispiece spreads have been Integrity Knight confrontations.

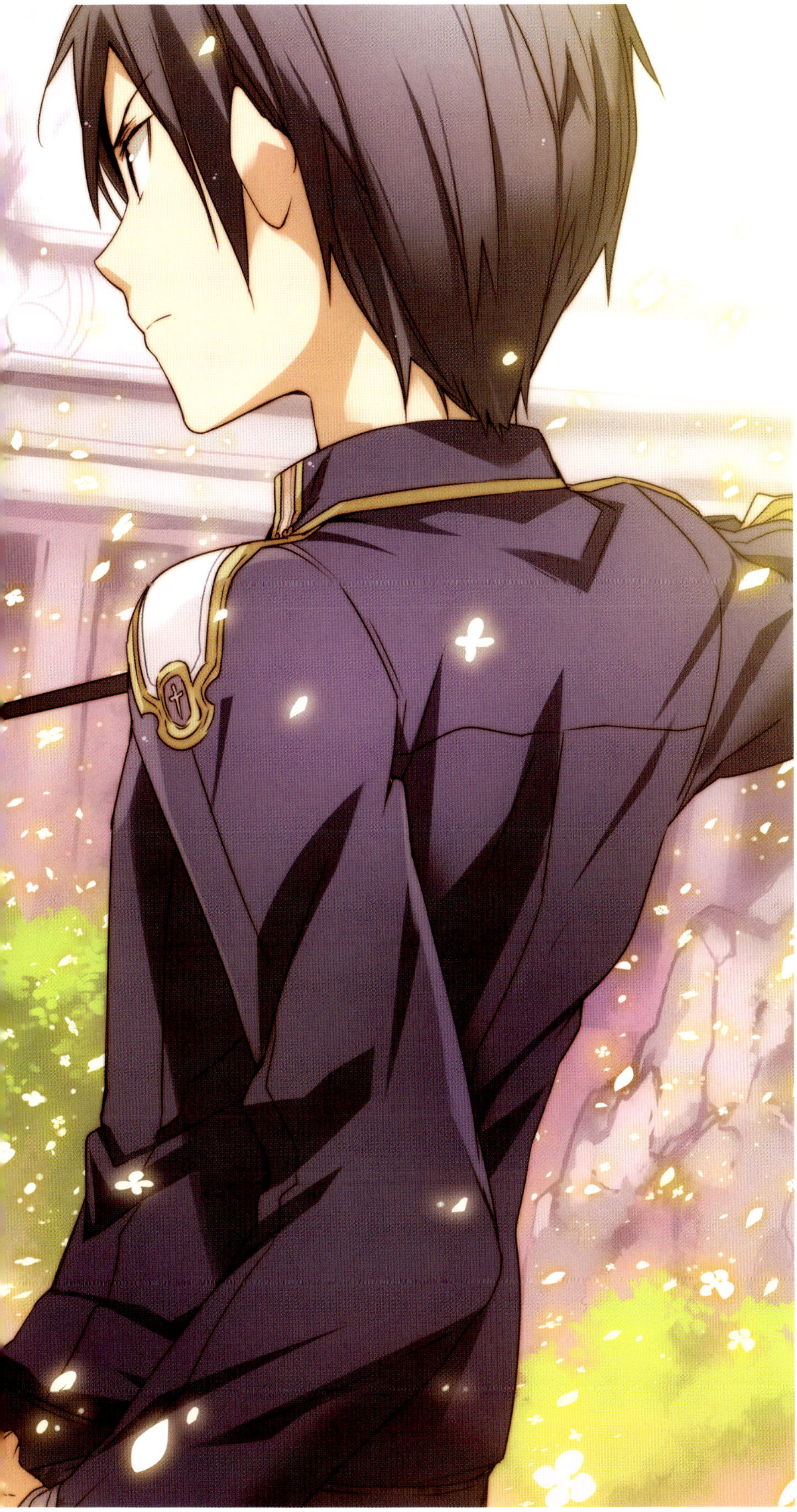

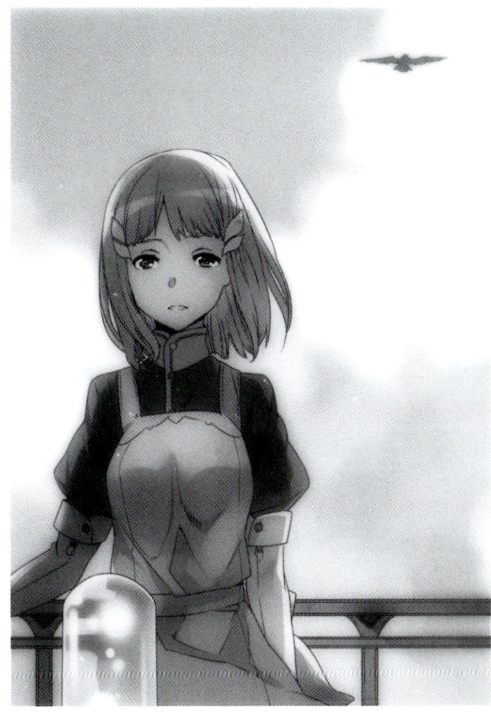

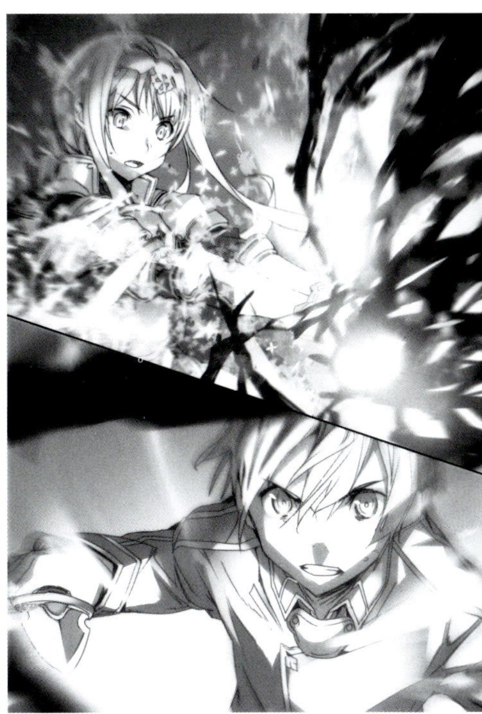

Dengeki Bunko
Sword Art Online 12: Alicization Rising
Illustration: April 2013

I remember not having time to design the Operator separately, so this illustration was basically right from scratch. This sometimes happens with characters who don't seem likely to have more scenes, and then I start to panic when they appear more often later on.

SWORD ART ONLINE

Alicization dividing

A volume where Eugeo and Kirito get split apart and head upward separately. It's also a volume that goes deep into Alice's story.

Dengeki Bunko
Sword Art Online 13: Alicization Dividing
Cover: August 2013

I really like this cover because of the momentum it has and the particular contrast of blues. The background is meant to evoke a wall being broken through.

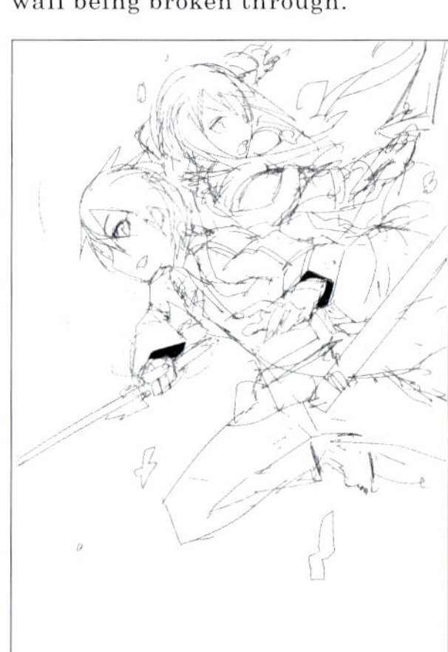

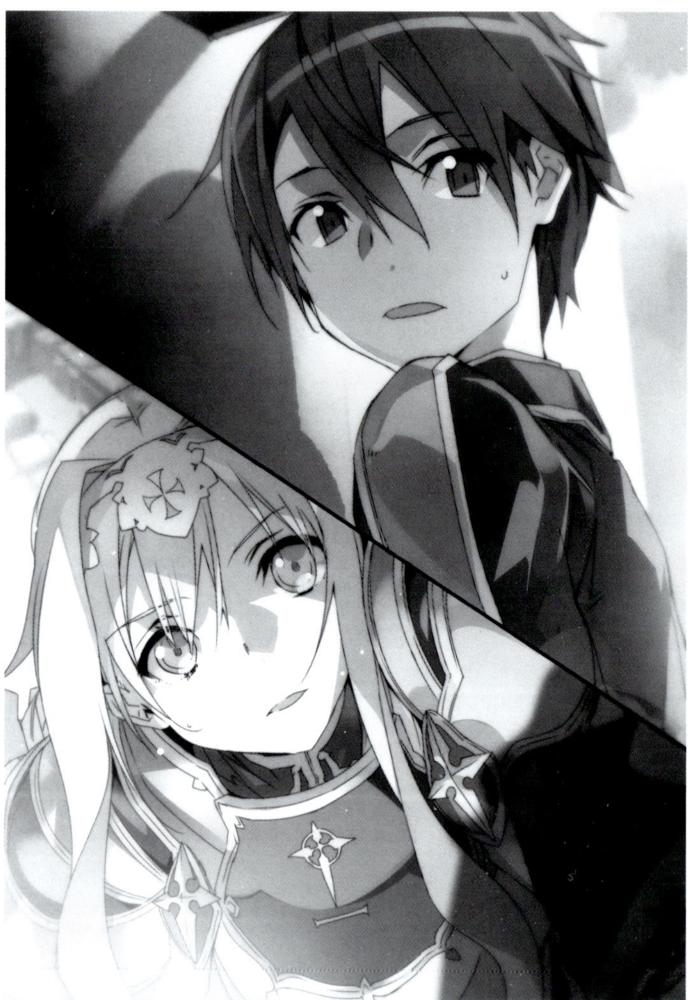

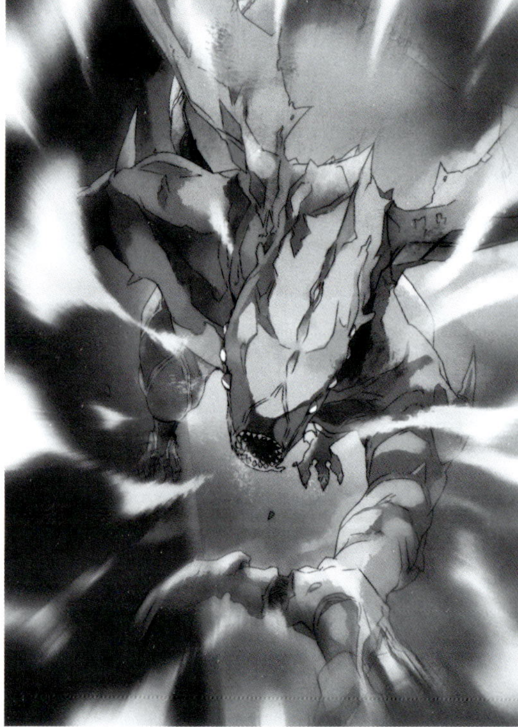

Dengeki Bunko
Sword Art Online 13: Alicization Dividing
Illustration: August 2013

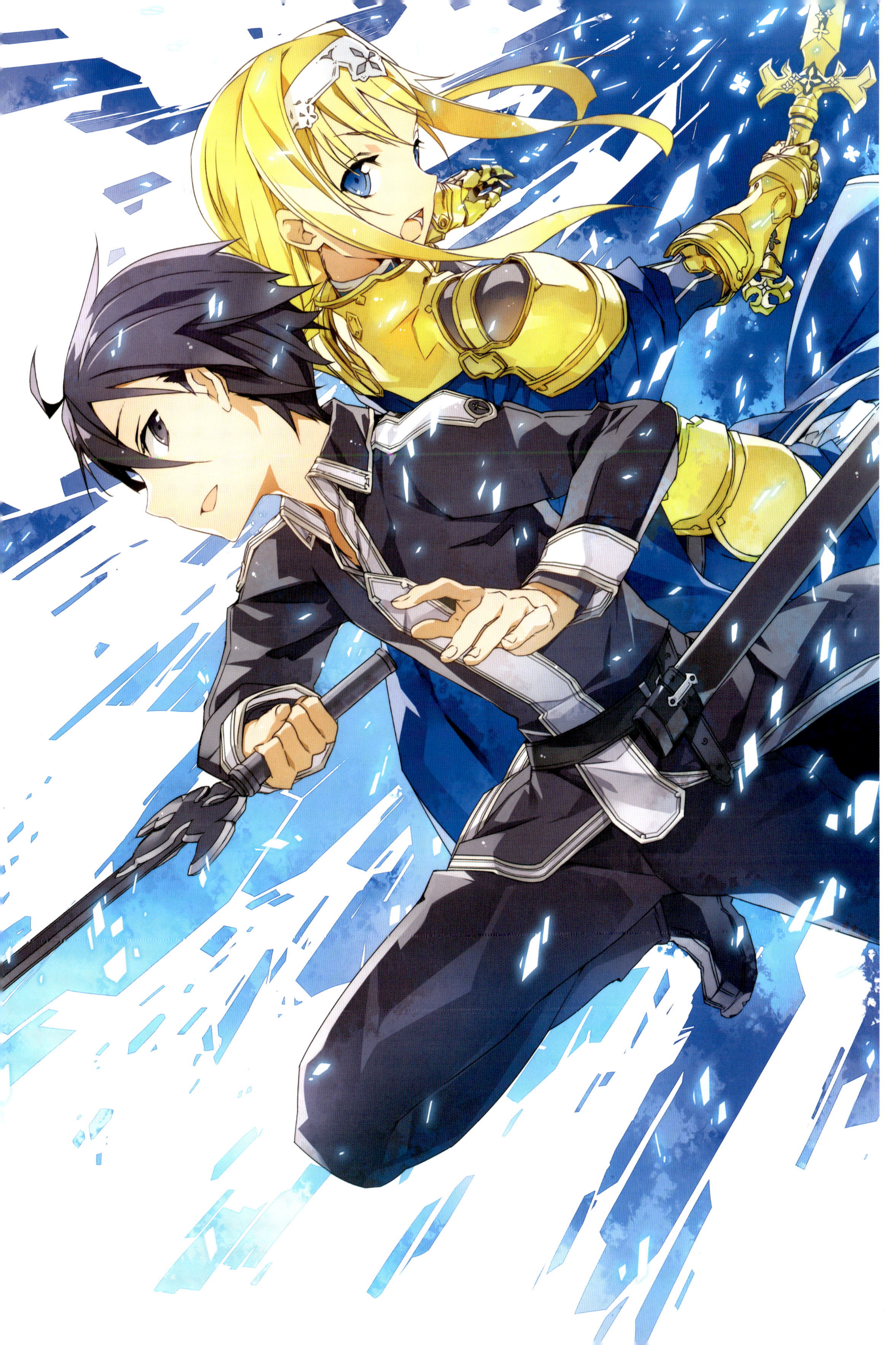

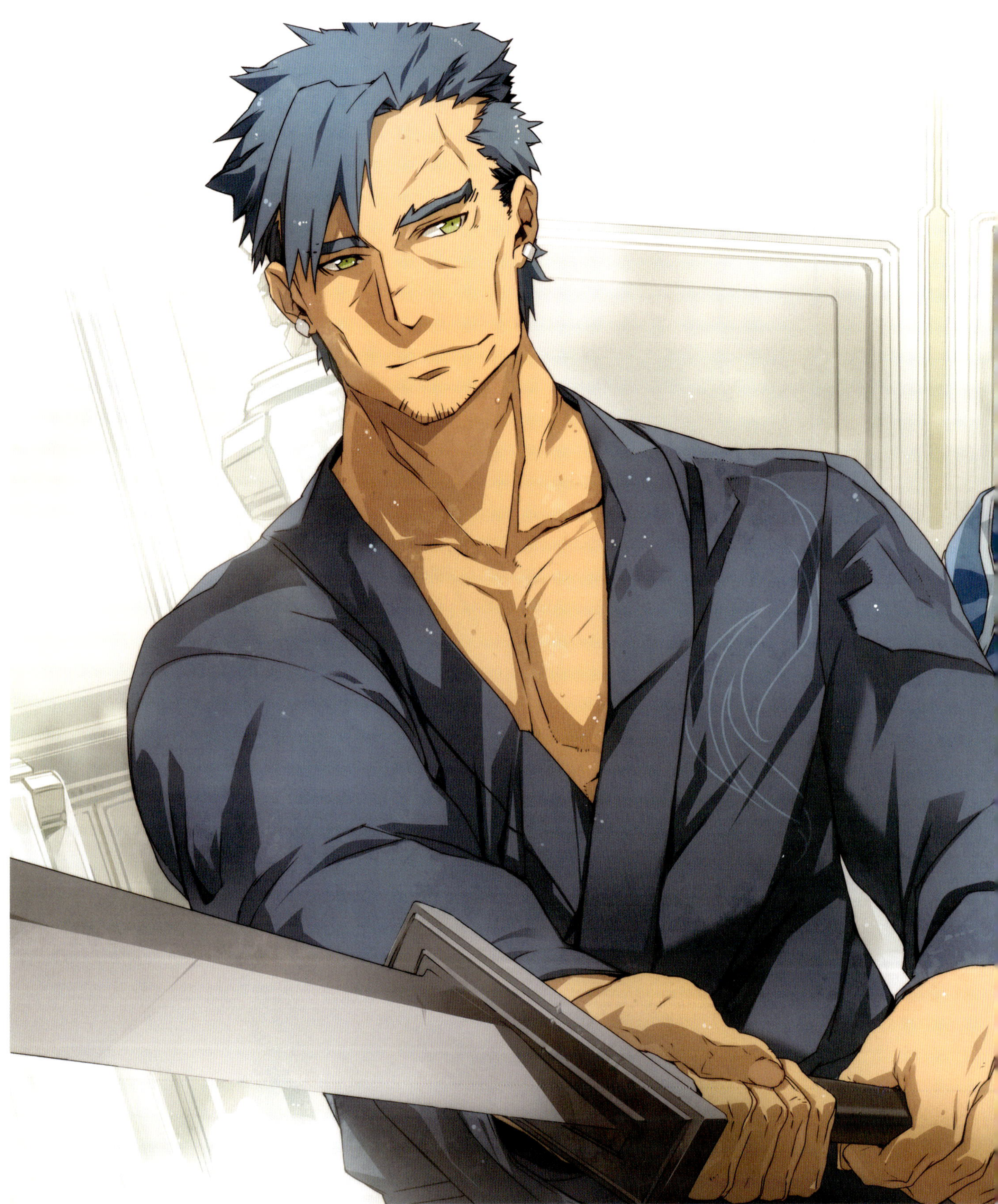

Dengeki Bunko
Sword Art Online 13: Alicization Dividing
Frontispiece: August 2013

Eugeo and Bercouli, facing off. A pair that shares a quiet, powerful bond.

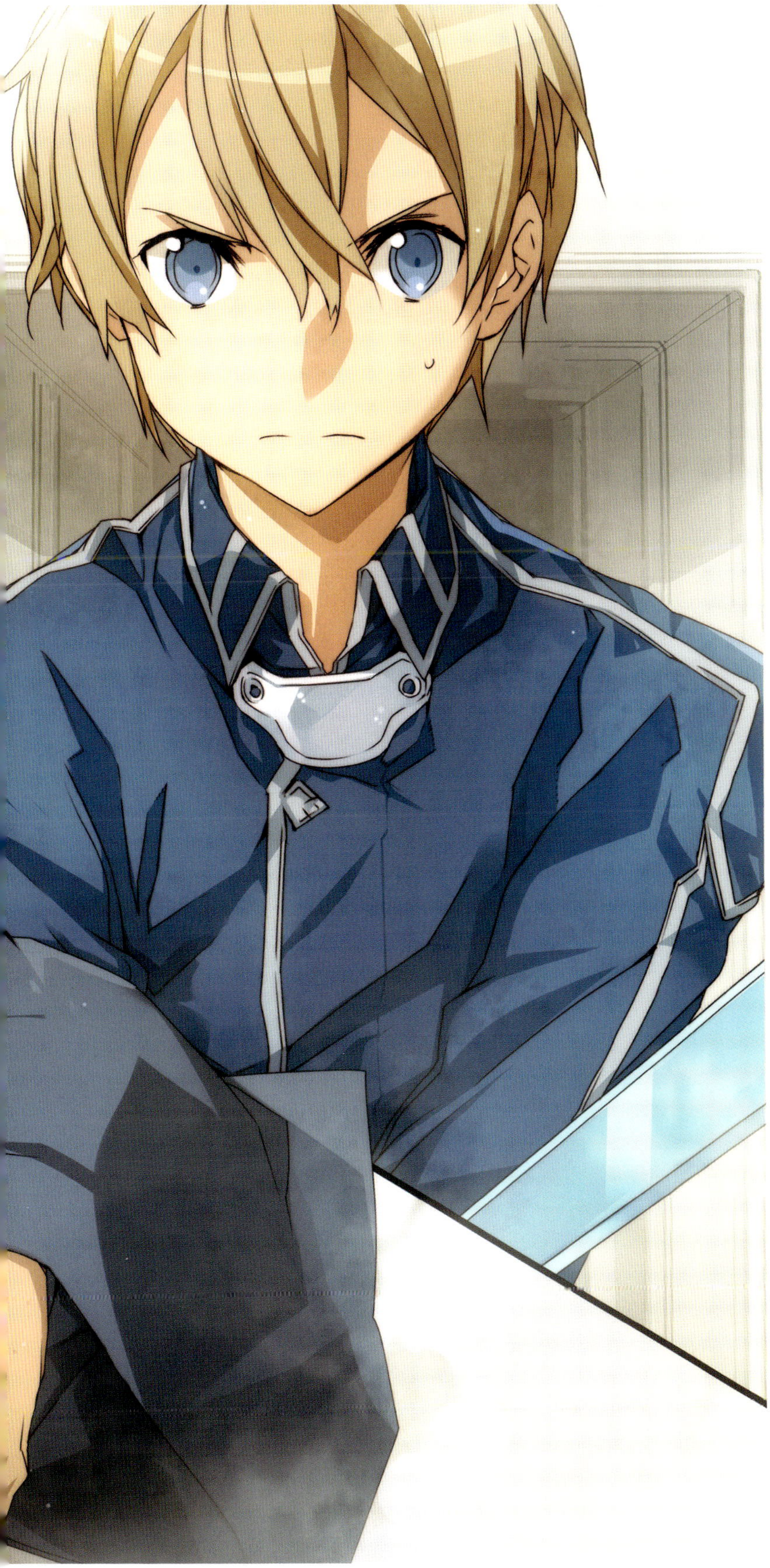

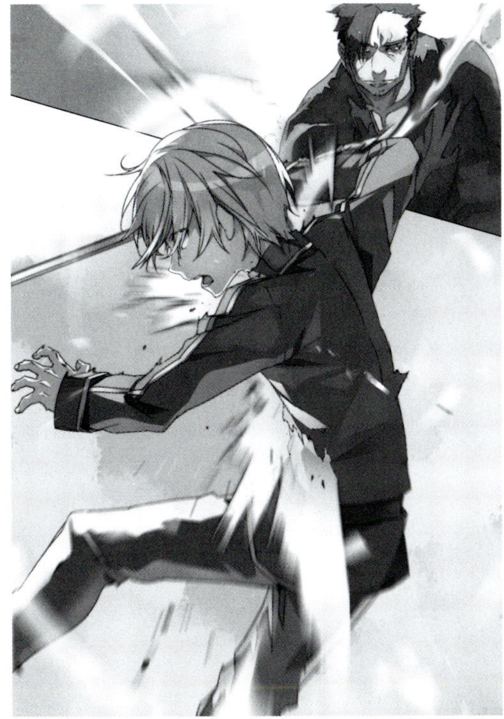

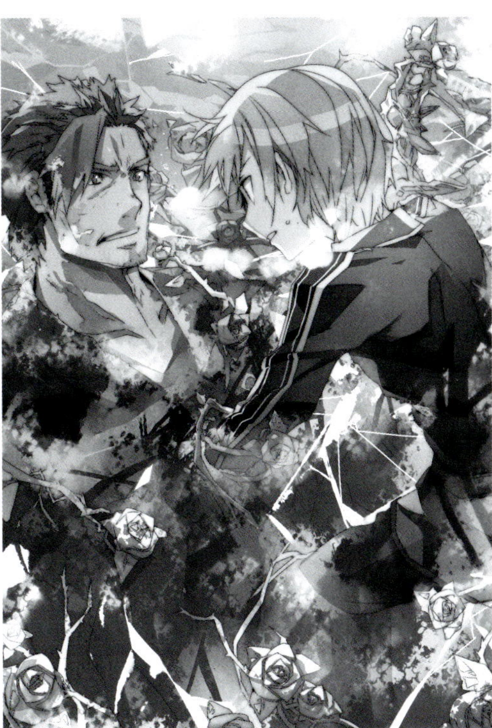

Dengoki Bunko
Sword Art Online 13: Alicization Dividing
Illustration: August 2013

I really like both of these illustrations. Especially Bercouli's slashing attack with the Time-Splitting Sword. So cool!

Dengeki Bunko
Sword Art Online 13: Alicization Dividing
Back Cover: August 2013

Text: Reality / Fantasy
Fan service. This is fan service.

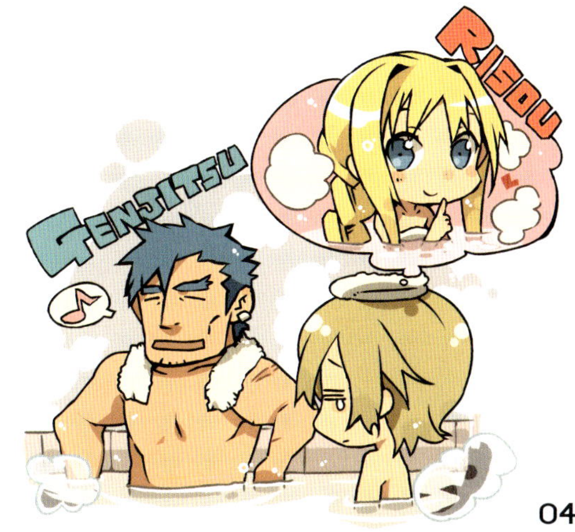

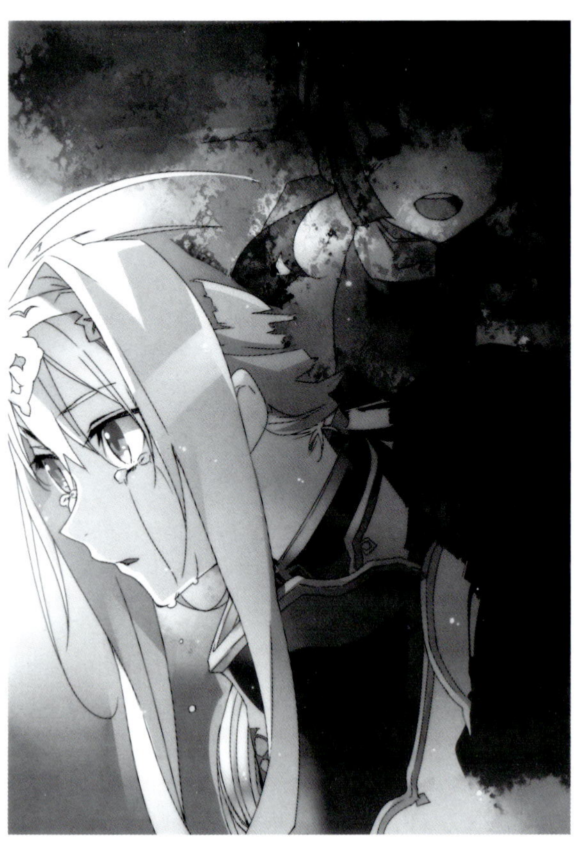

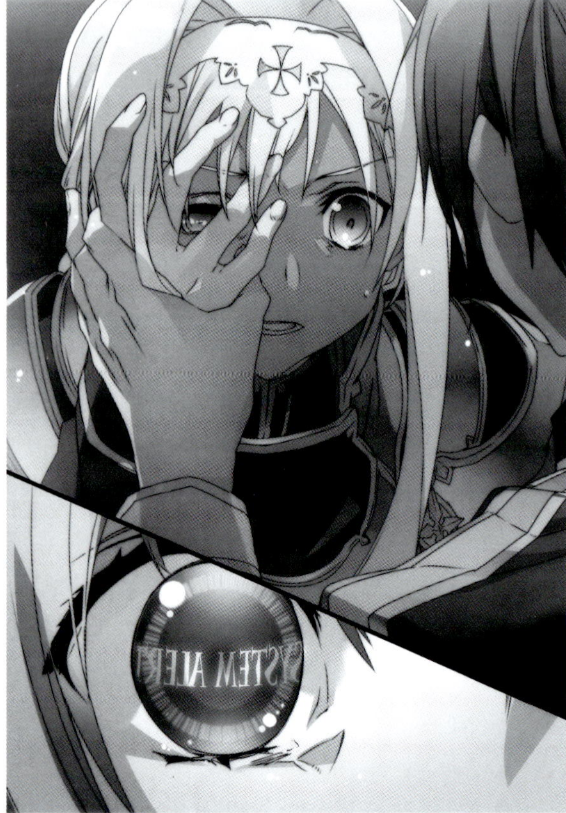

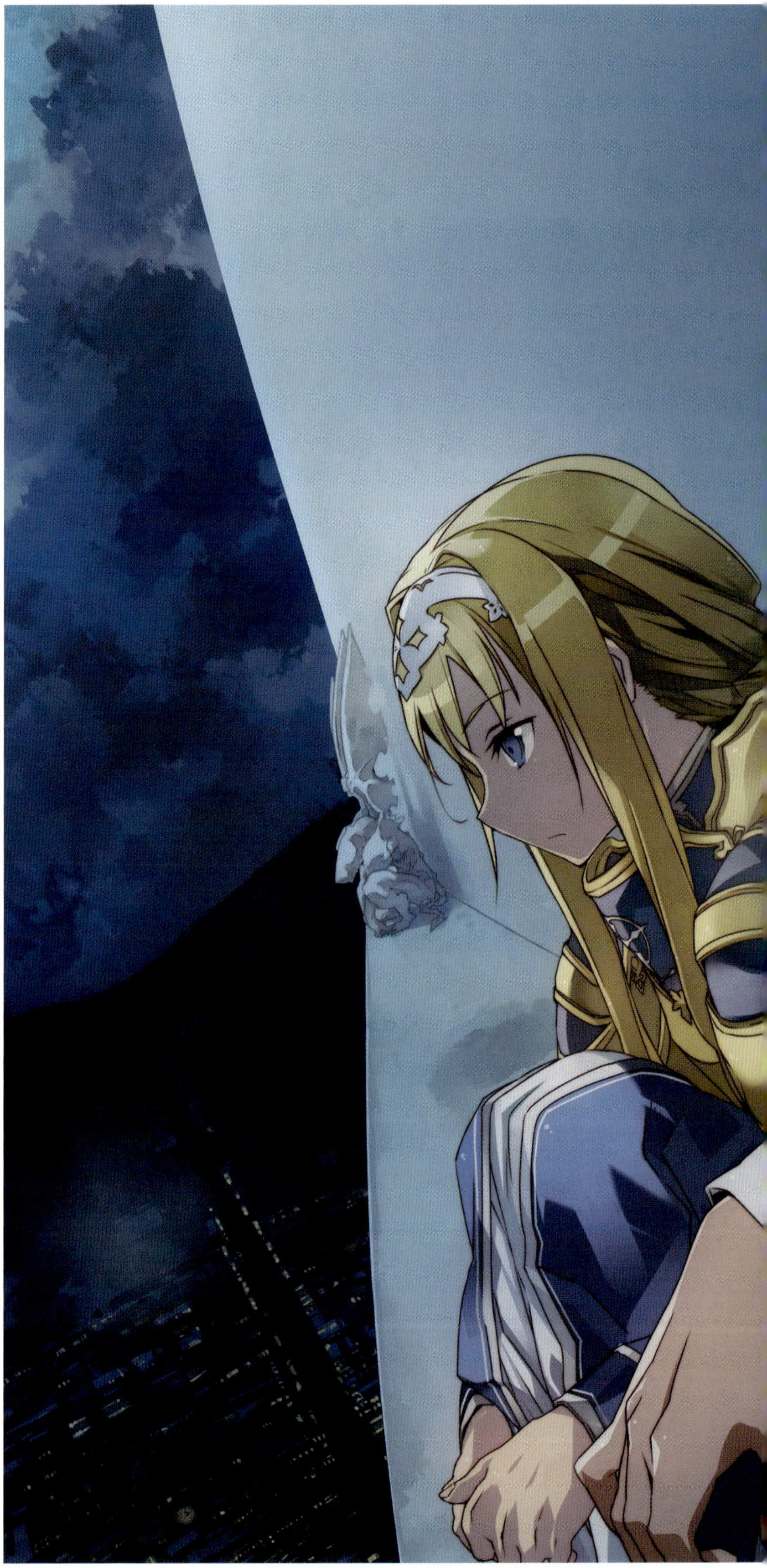

Dengeki Bunko
Sword Art Online 13: Alicization Dividing
Illustration: August 2013

I like all of Alice's expressions. I think that the scenes where her emotions are really leaping from the page, you can tell that I was drawing with a lot of momentum.

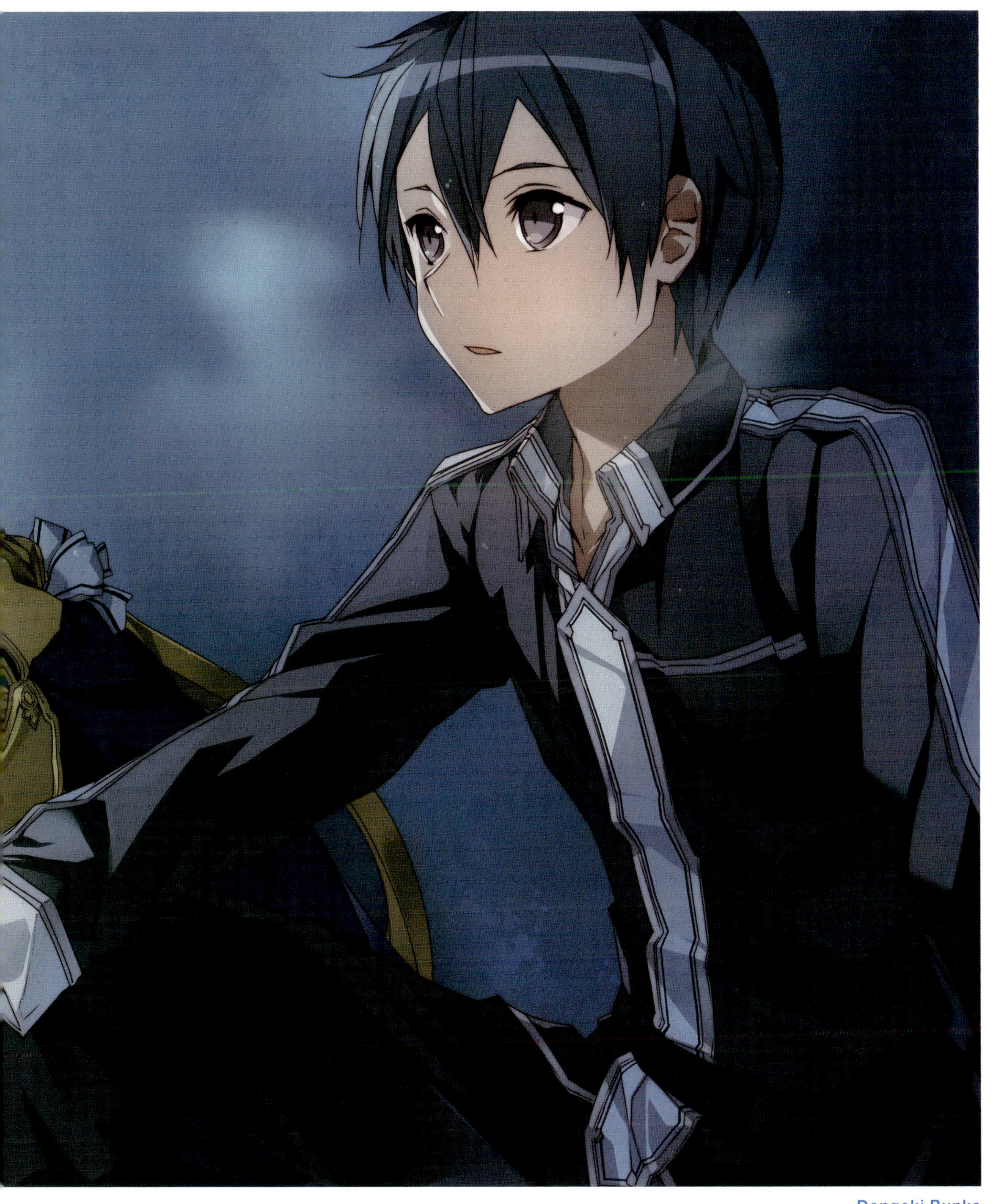

Dengeki Bunko
Sword Art Online 13: Alicization Dividing
Frontispiece: August 2013

It's difficult to provide a sense of scale with a building that's totally flat on all sides. When there's lots of decoration and detail, the visual information helps you put it into perspective. Although that has its own difficulties.

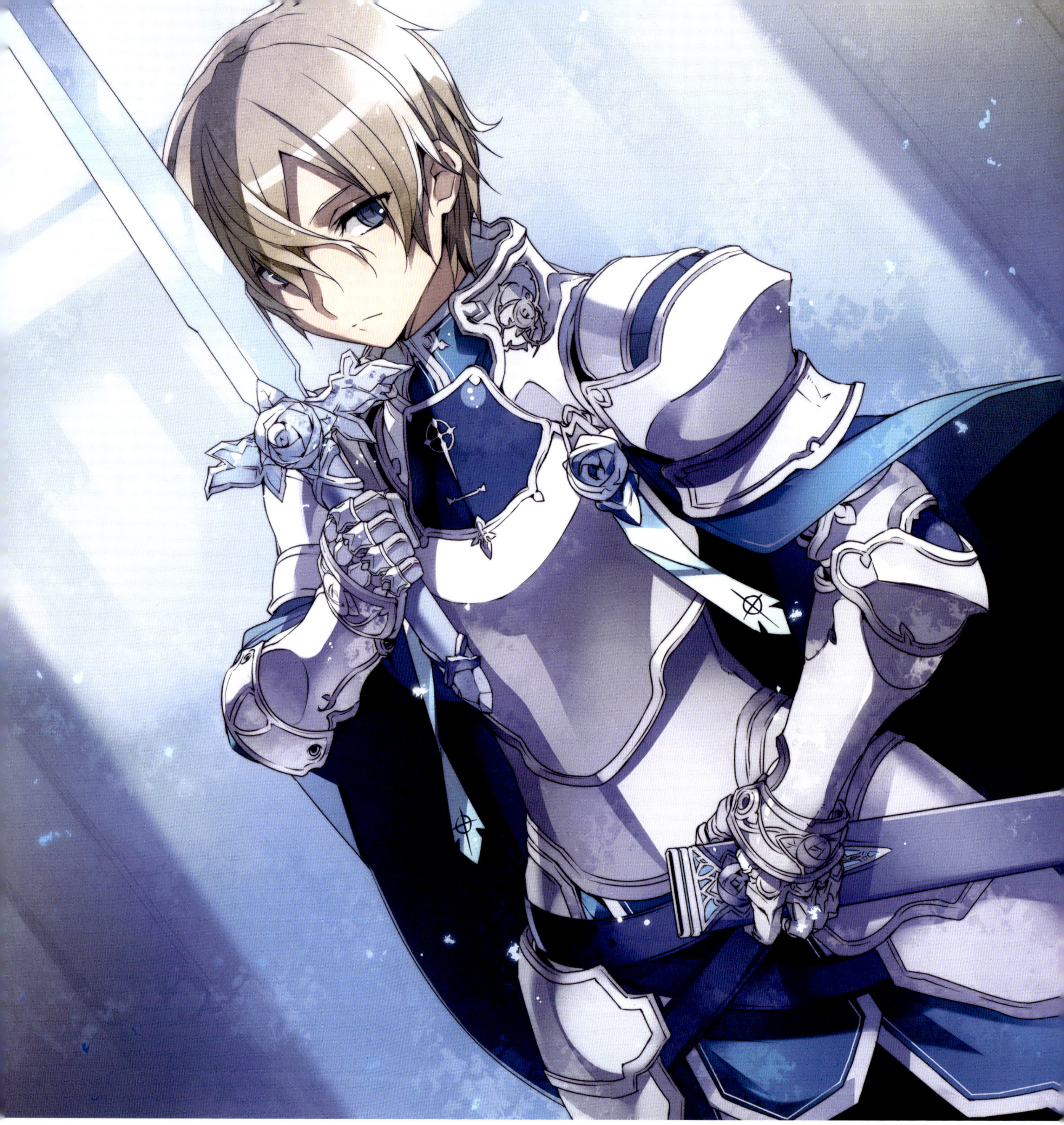

Dengeki Bunko
Sword Art Online 13: Alicization Dividing
Illustration: August 2013

I really like my illustration of Chudelkin. I wanted to give it that feeling of meat shaking on a super-slow-mo video.

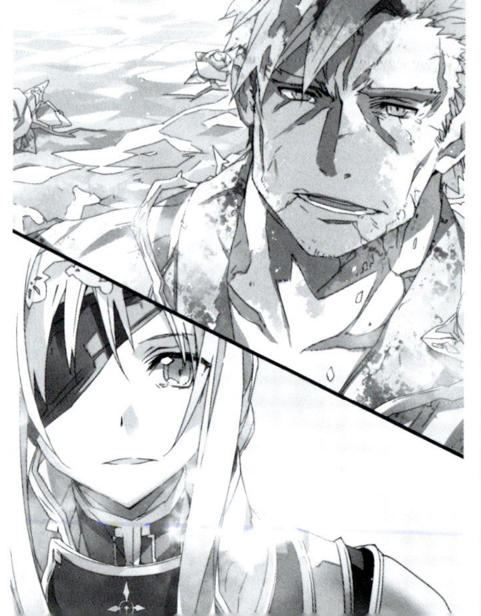

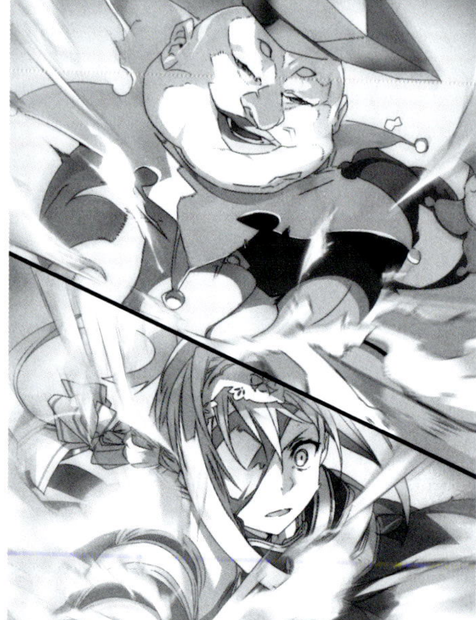

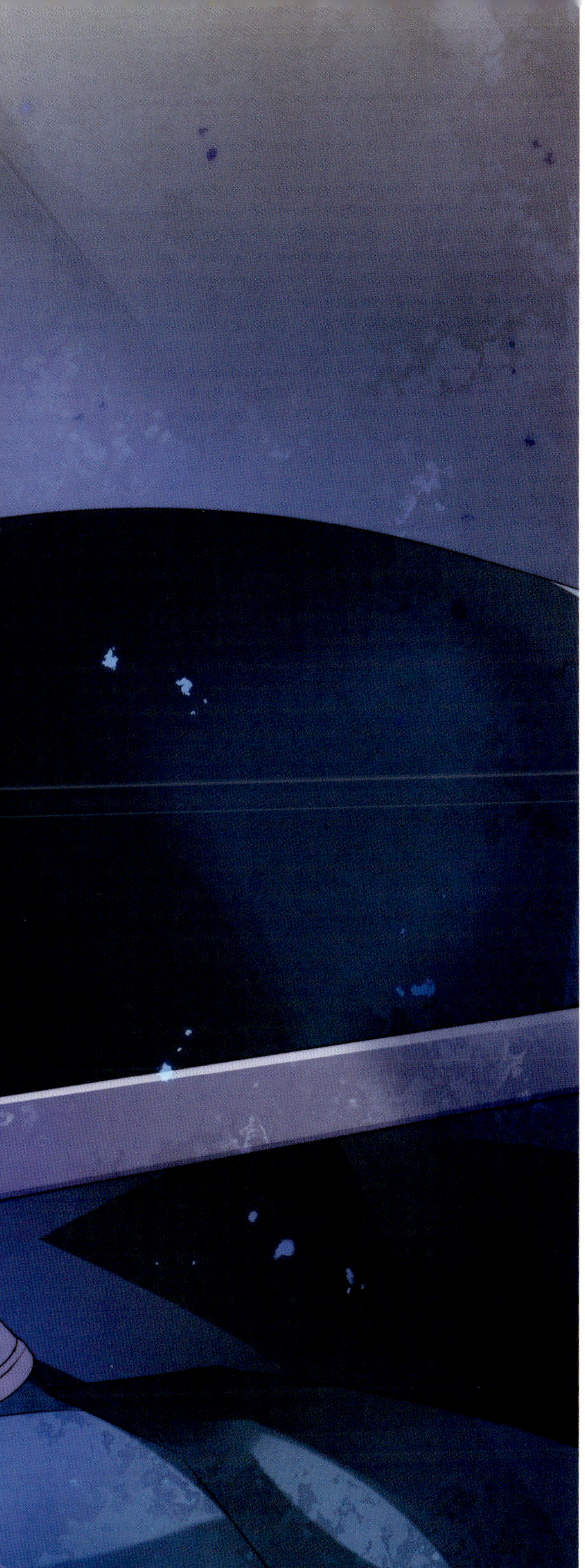

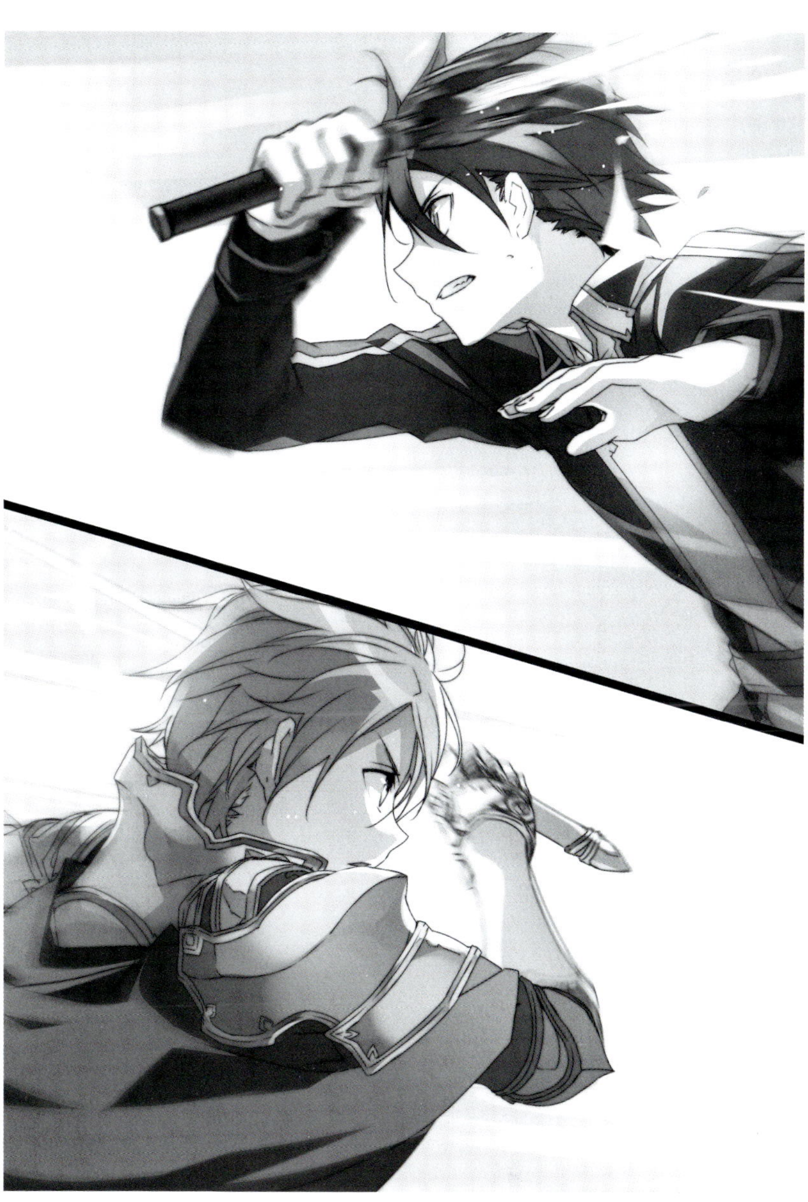

Dengeki Bunko
Sword Art Online 13: Alicization Dividing
Frontispiece: August 2013

Eugeo the Integrity Knight. I kind of felt like he was the sharpest of anyone in that Integrity Knight armor. I think he looks great, what about you?

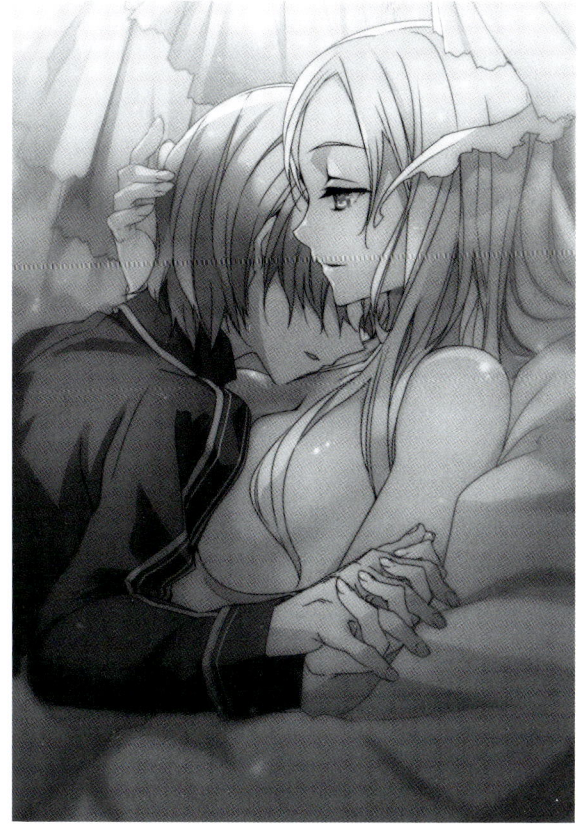

Dengeki Bunko
Sword Art Online 13: Alicization Dividing
Illustration: August 2013

I can't blame him. You know? He's a growing boy.

SWORD ART ONLINE

Alicization Uniting

The volume that closes out the Human Realm story of the Alicization arc and ends a chapter in the story of Kirito and Eugeo.

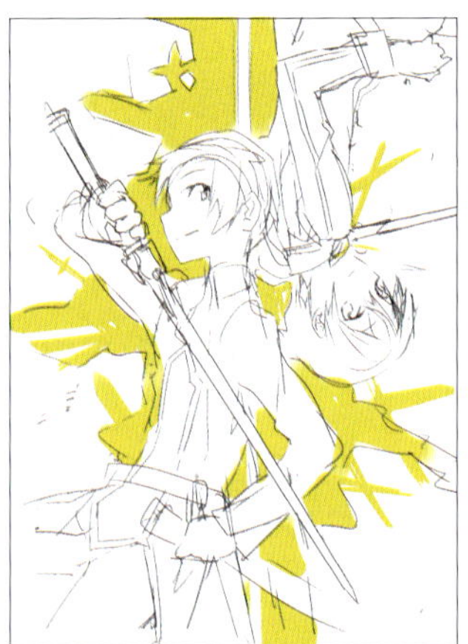

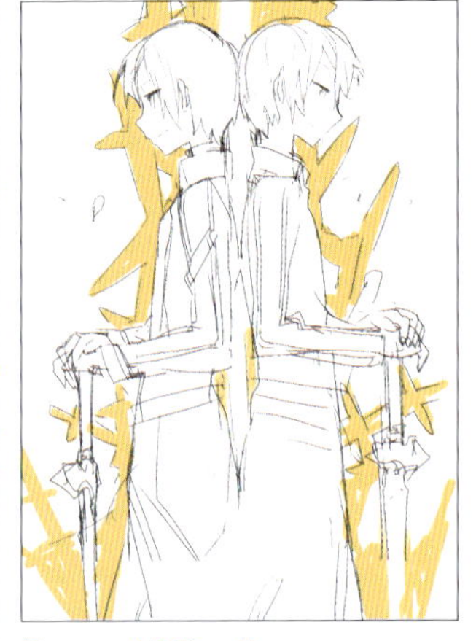

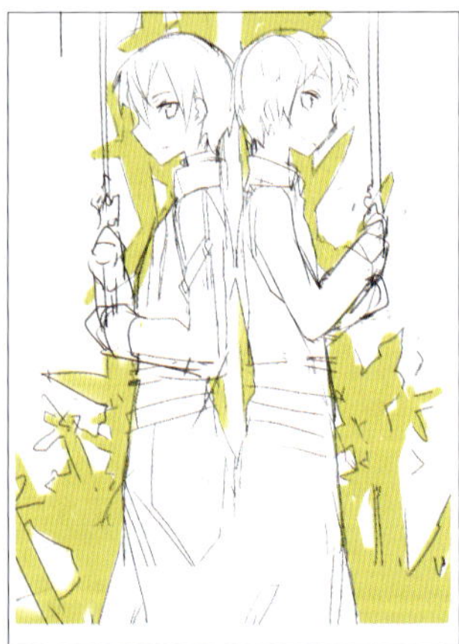

Alternate Cover Sketches

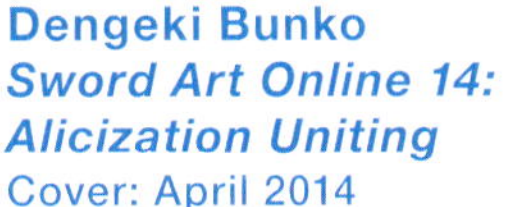

Dengeki Bunko
Sword Art Online 14: Alicization Uniting
Cover: April 2014

The cover, of course, is Eugeo and Kirito. The background is the swords from the sword golems, with a memory crystal hidden behind them. In the original edition, it was cut off, so you could barely see them. I wonder if anyone noticed.

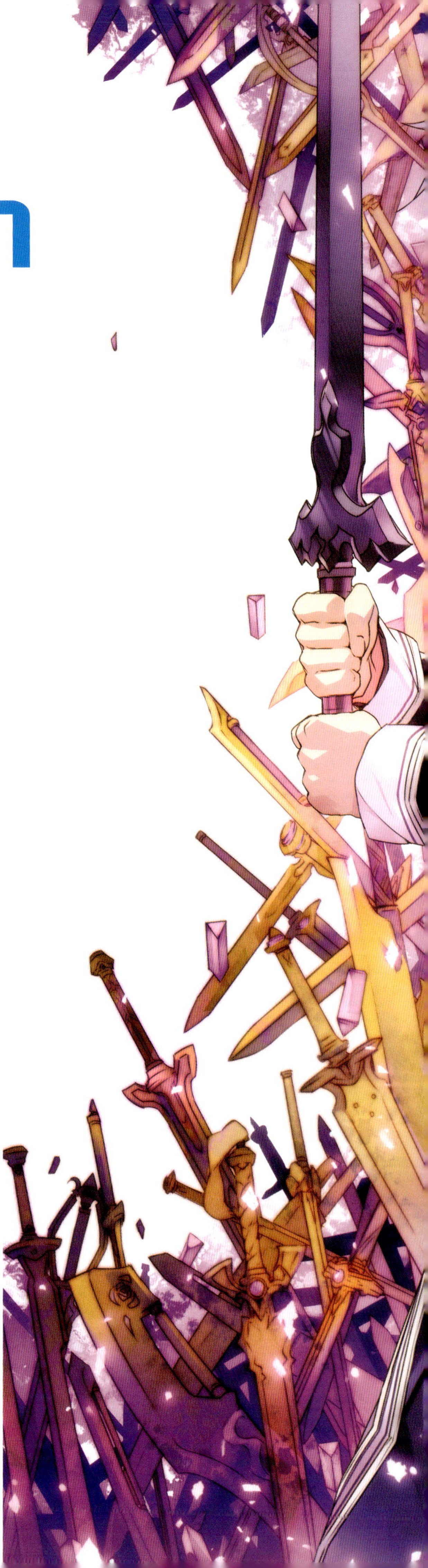

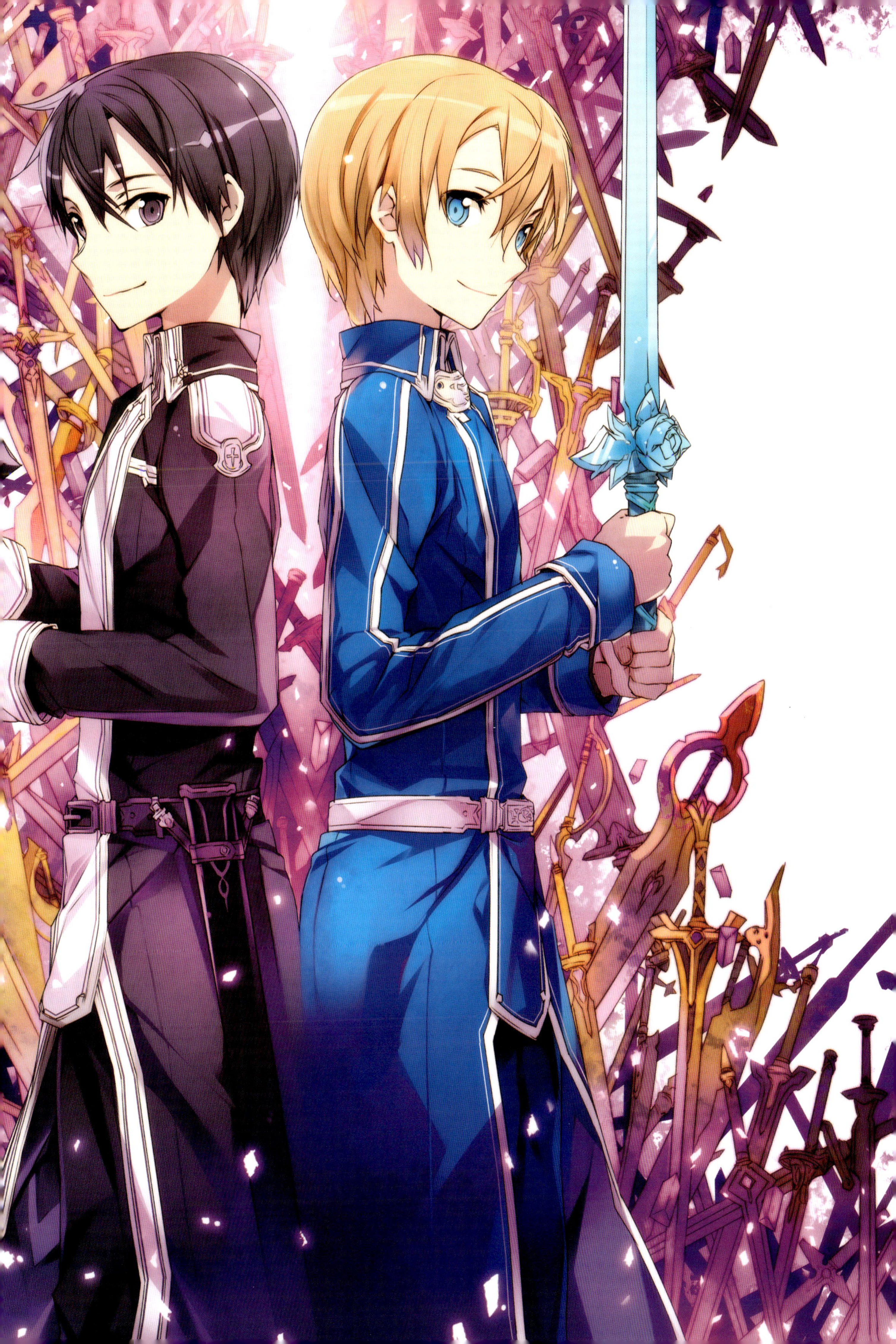

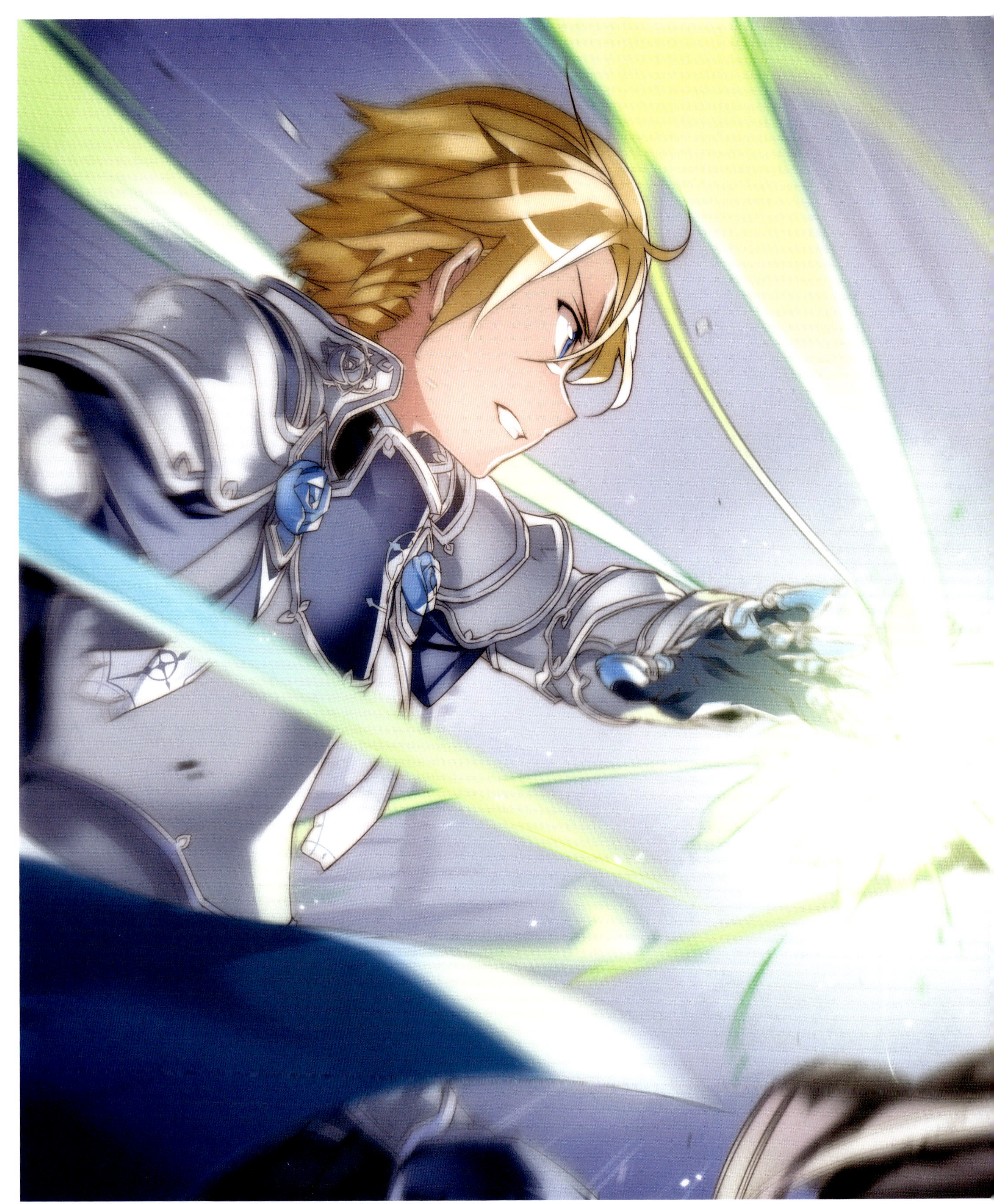

Dengeki Bunko
Sword Art Online 14: Alicization Uniting
Frontispiece: April 2014

Kirito and Eugeo locked in battle. I definitely feel like this one is underwhelming without the text on top.

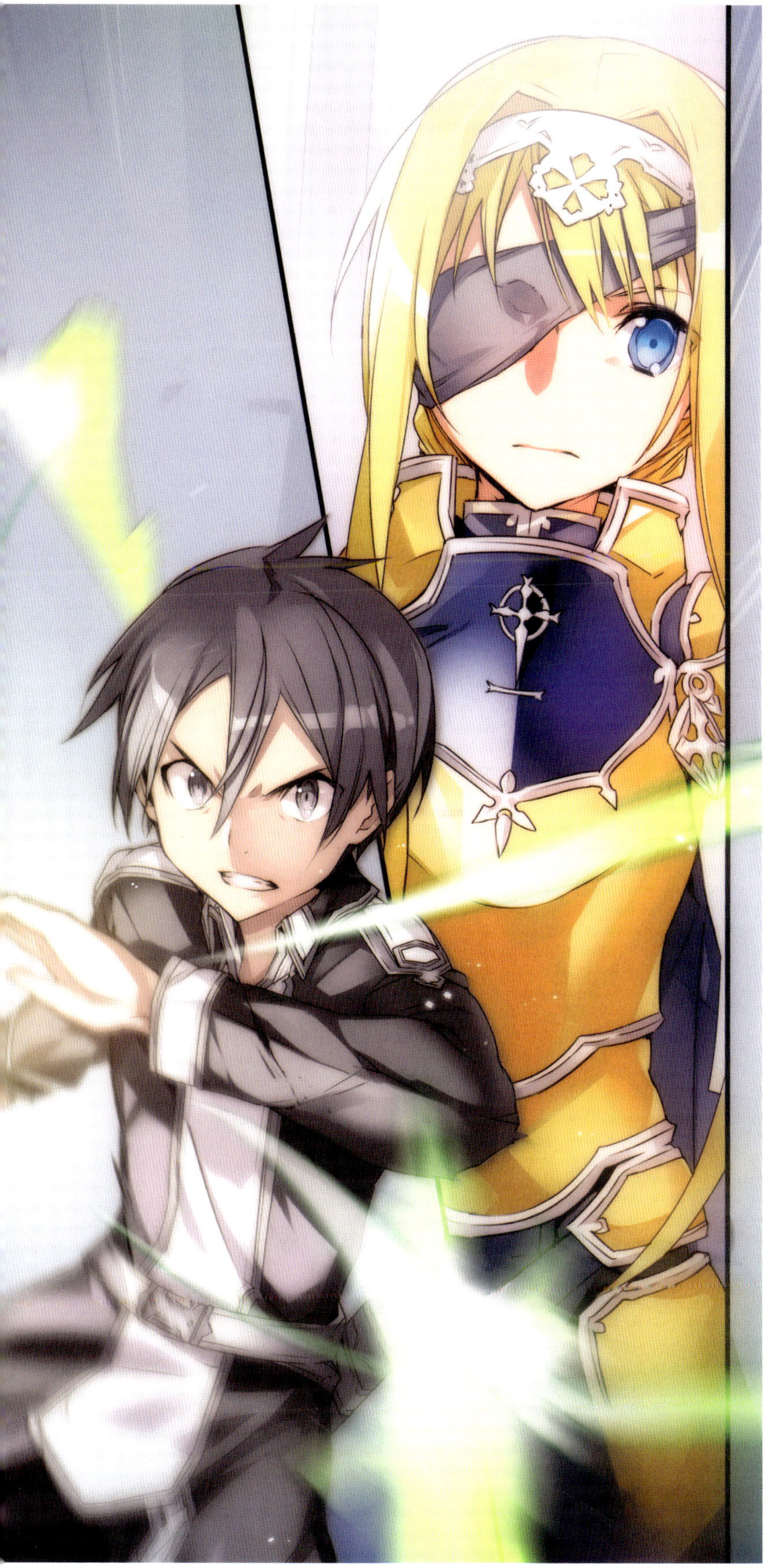

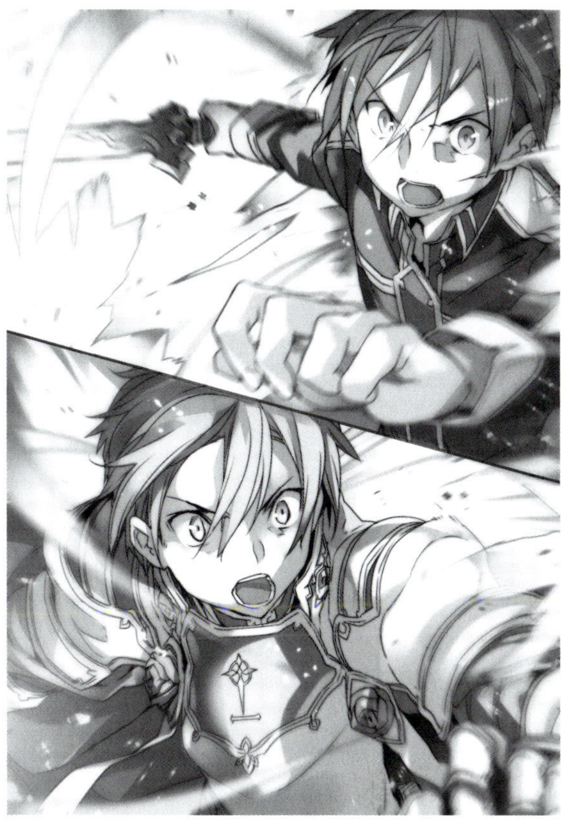

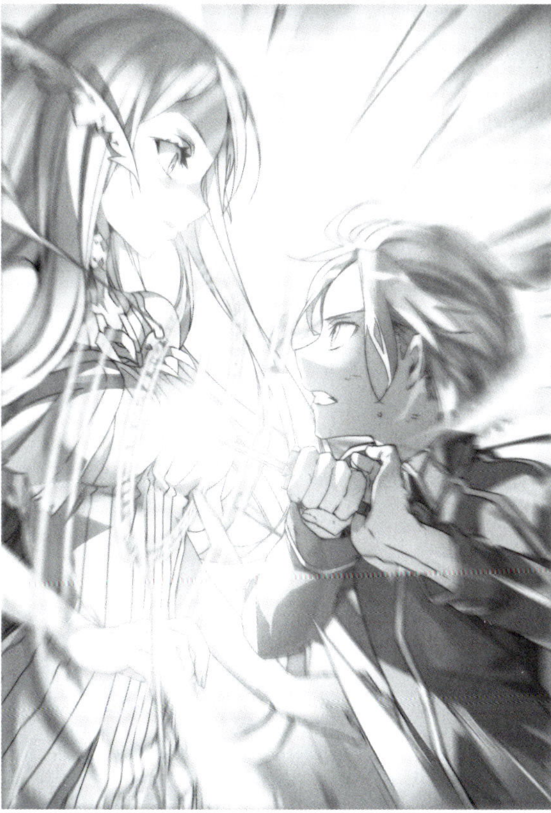

Dengeki Bunko
Sword Art Online 14: Alicization Uniting
Illustration: April 2014

It's more or less the same scene as the color illustration, and their poses are similar, but I think the intensity is a little denser here. I like the black-and-white piece better.

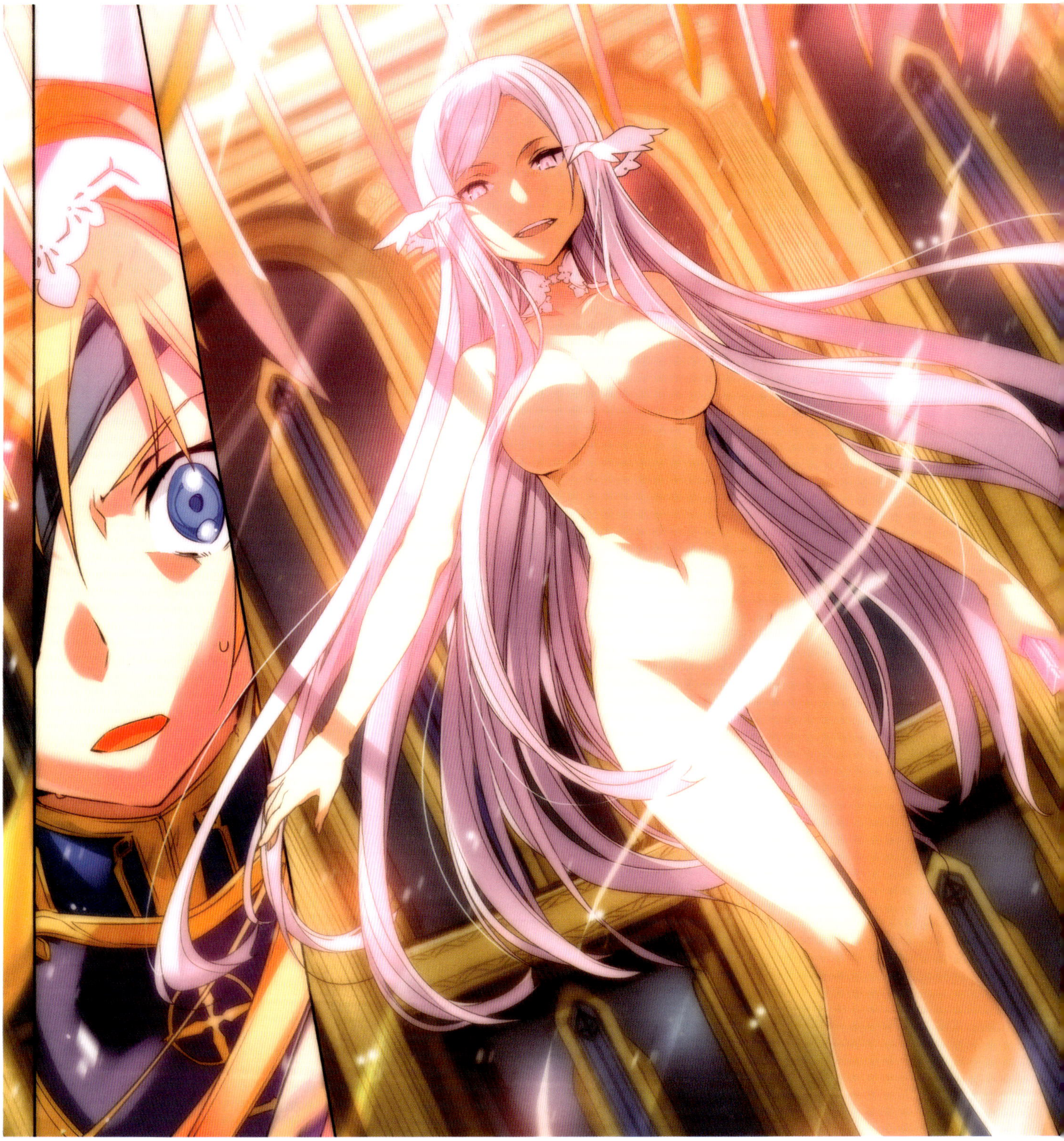

Dengeki Bunko

Sword Art Online 14: Alicization Uniting

Frontispiecc: April 2014

When I turned this piece in, I realized the background didn't match the description in the text, and I had to quickly fix it up (crying all the while). At last, we see the totally nude Administrator. Did you guys see the anime? It was unbelievable, she was actually naked the whole time.

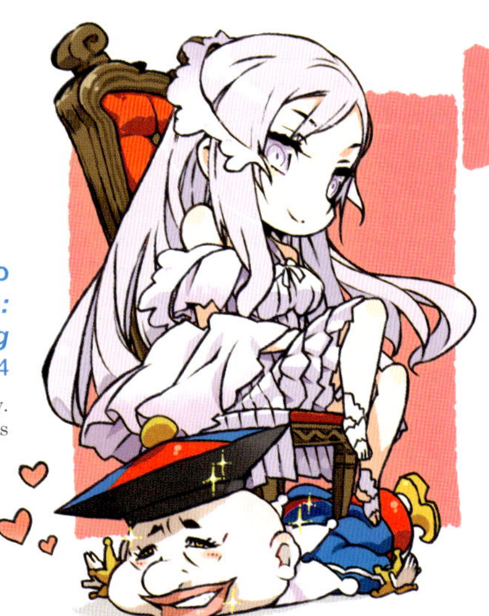

Dengeki Bunko

Sword Art Online 14: Alicization Uniting

Back Cover: April 2014

Chudelkin looks very happy. The important part is that she's not directly sitting on him.

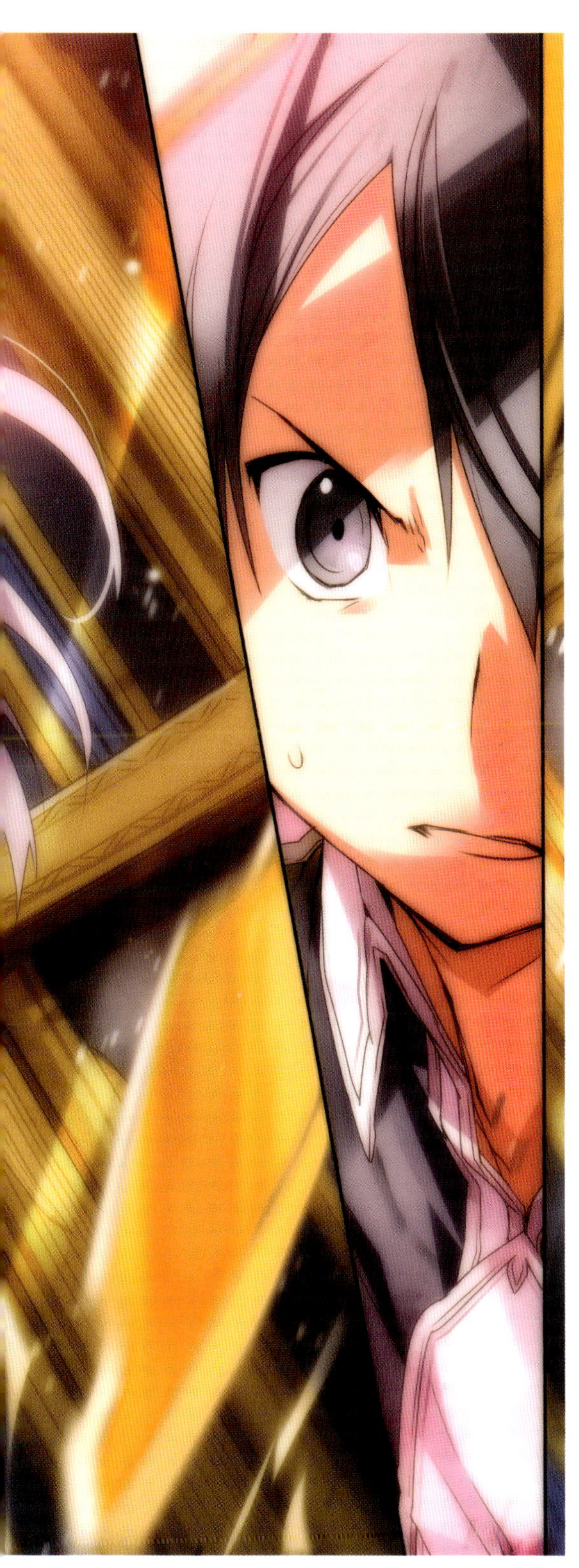
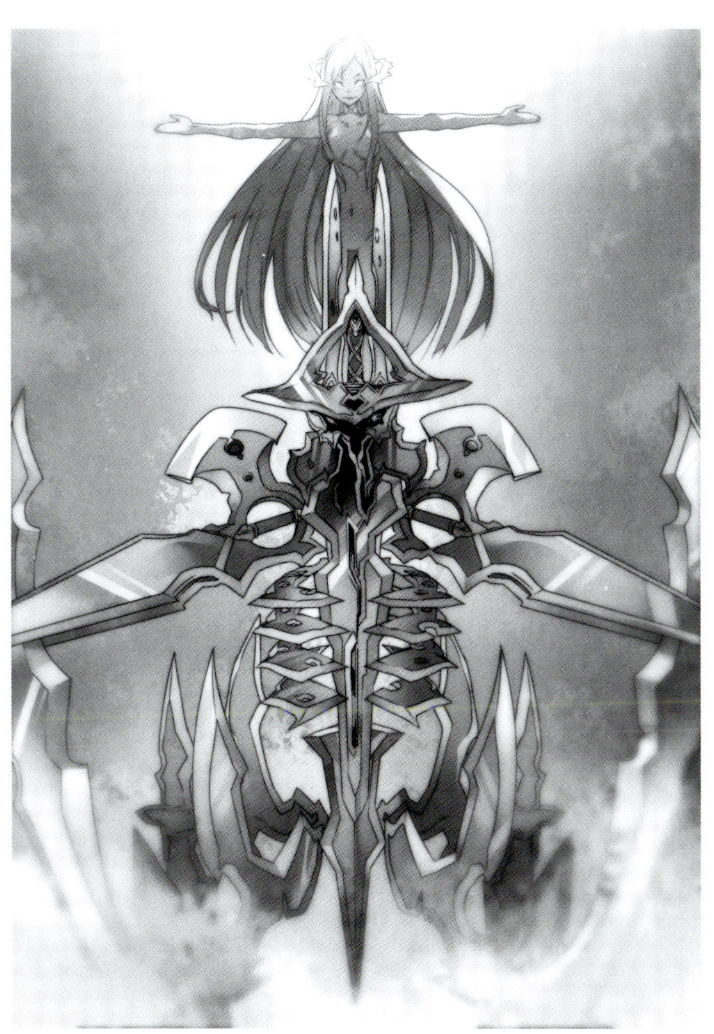
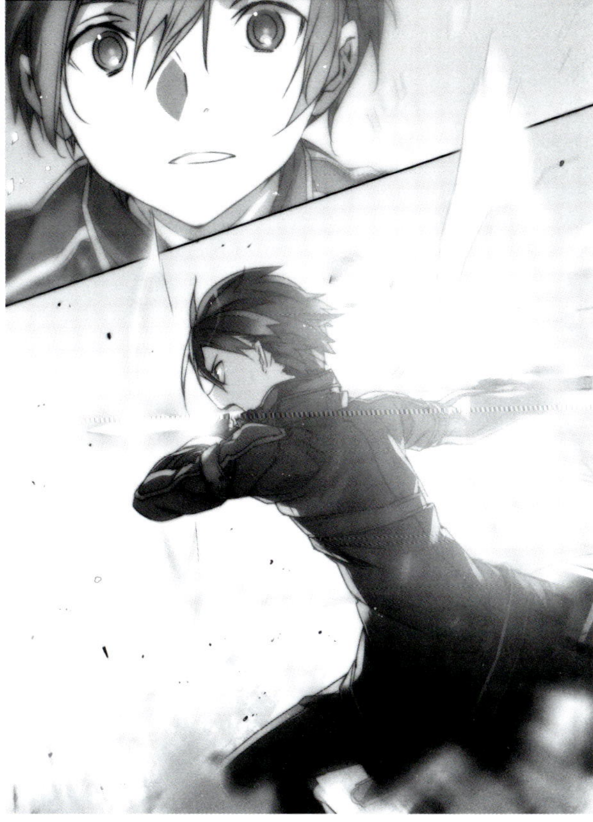
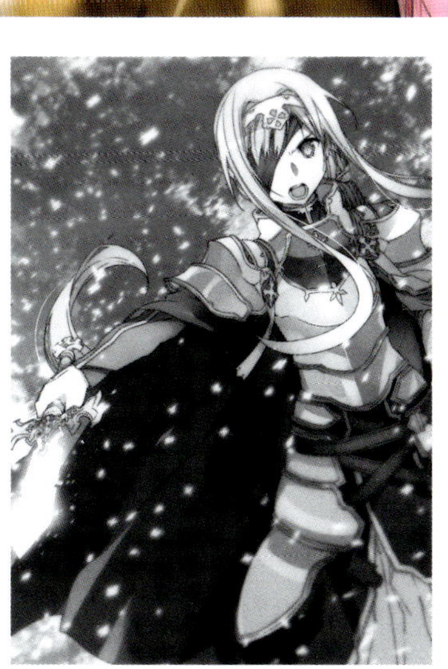
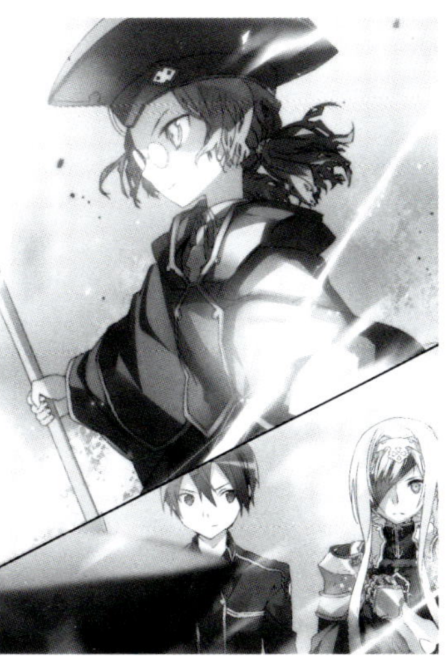

Dengeki Bunko

Sword Art Online 14: Alicization Uniting

Illustration: April 2014

I received a design for the sword golems from Kawahara-sensei, and that's what I drew this one from. I kind of like Administrator standing on top with her arms outstretched.

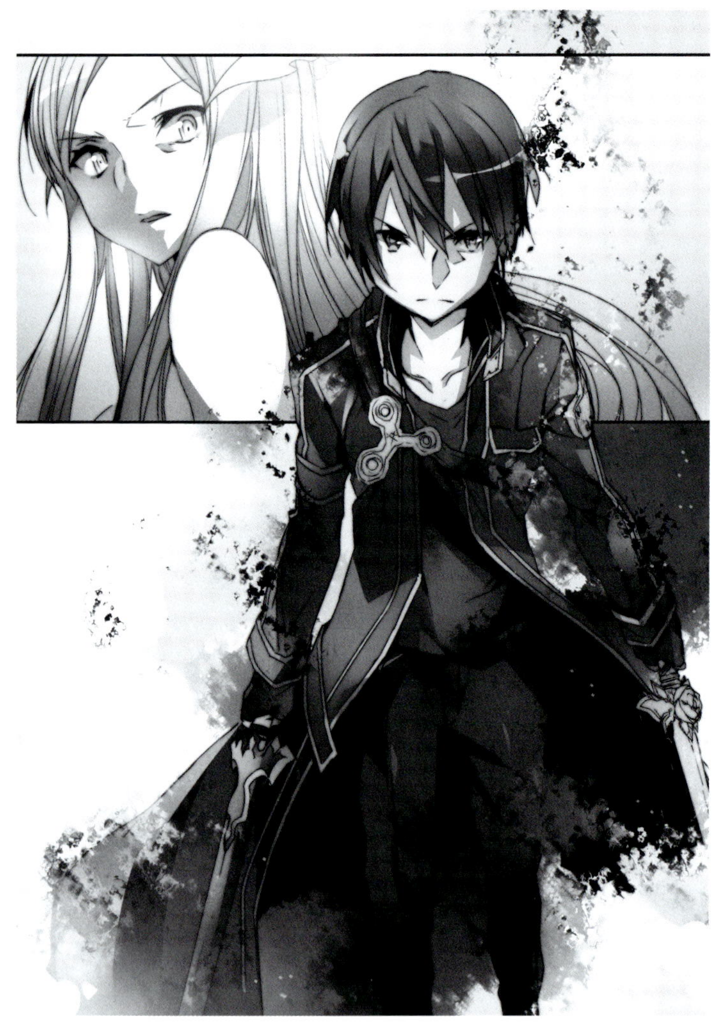

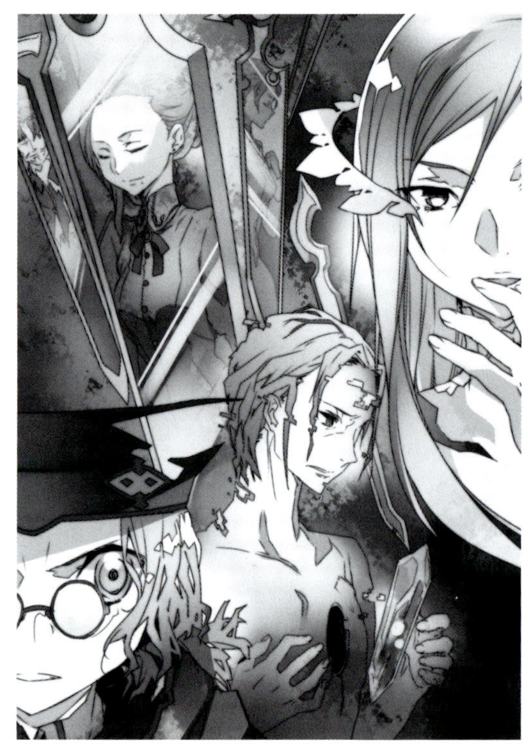

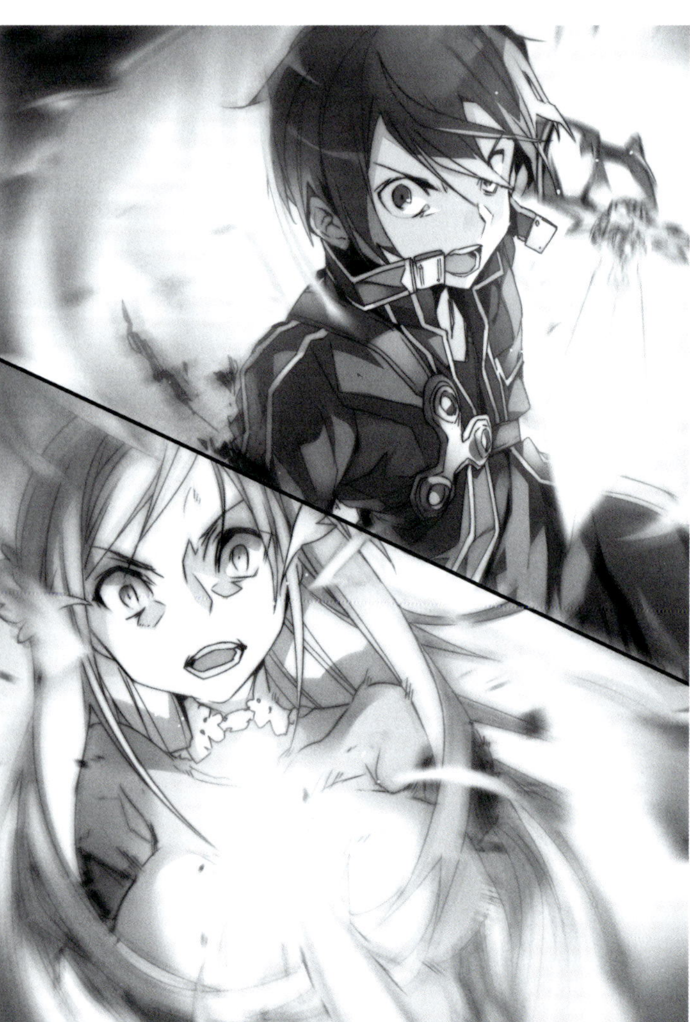

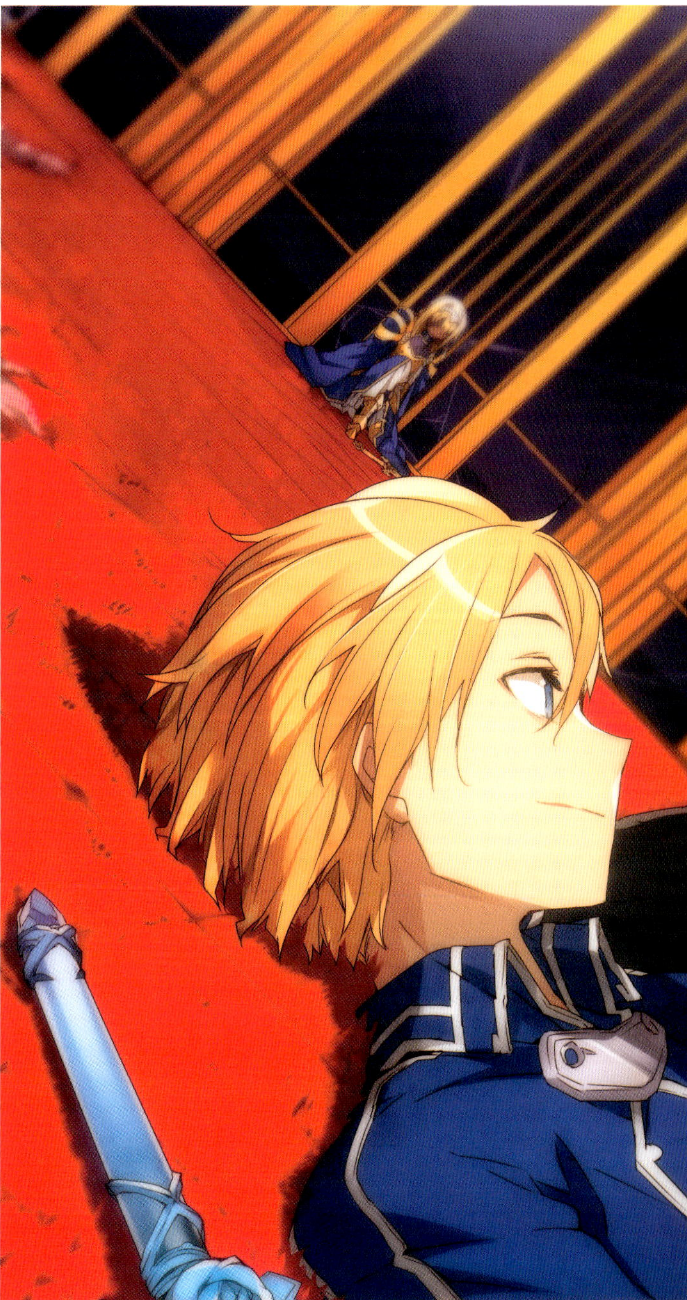

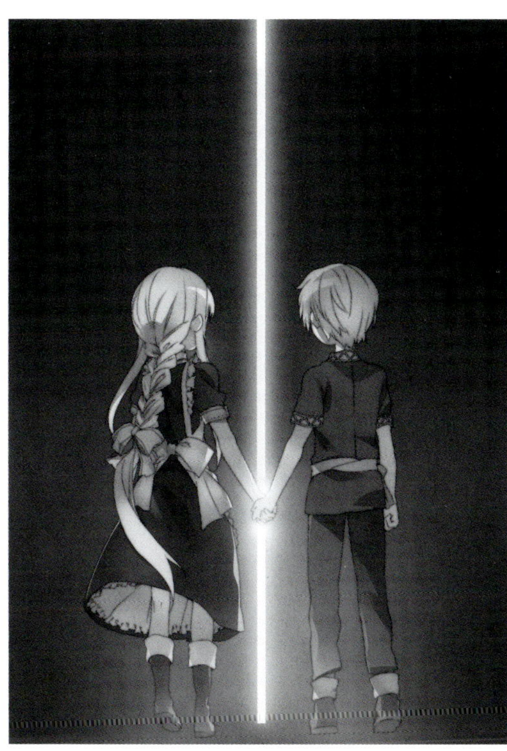

Dengeki Bunko
Sword Art Online 14: Alicization Uniting
Illustration: April 2014

The piece of Eugeo and Alice echoes the book cover. You'd think it had been ages since I drew Kirito in his Aincrad style, but it didn't feel that way, because I do licensed versions of that look all the time.

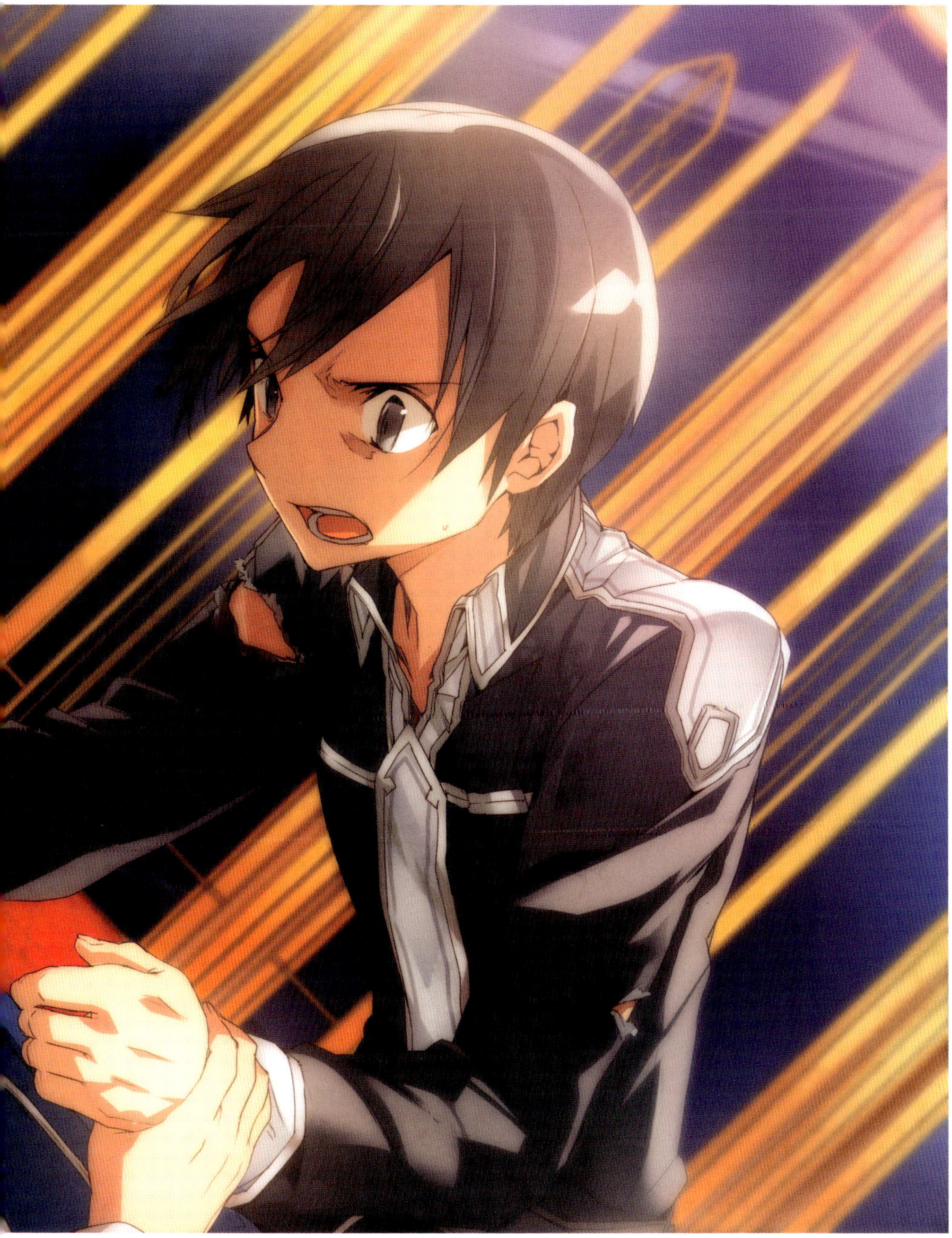

Dengeki Bunko
Sword Art Online 14: Alicization Uniting
Frontispiece: April 2014

Is this too much of a spoiler to put at the front of the book? But sometimes, they put in color illustrations that are a misdirect, so part of me thought maybe people wouldn't believe it the first time.

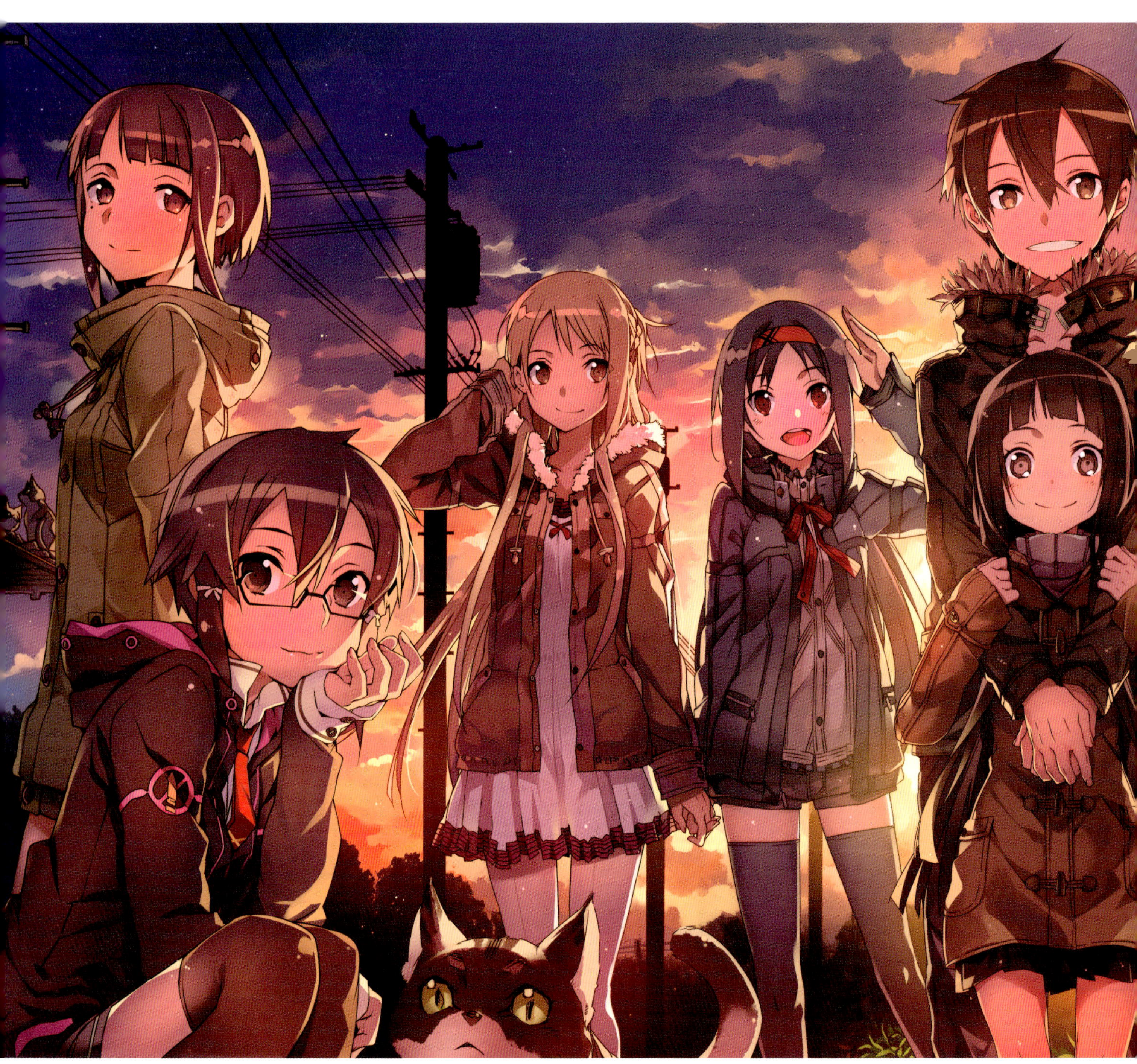

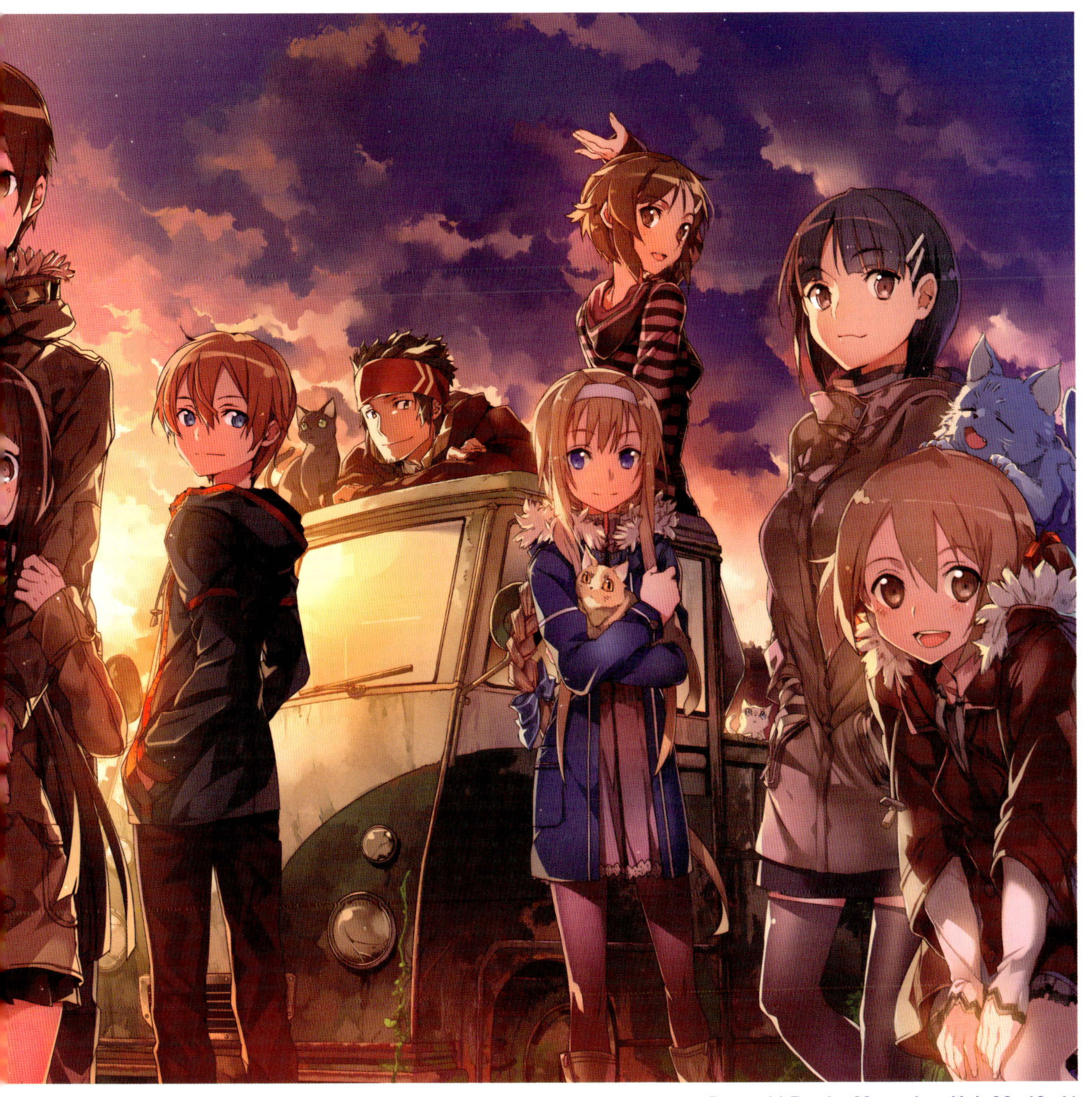

***Dengeki Bunko Magazine*, Vol. 38, 40, 41**
Three-Part Combination Poster: June–December 2014

SAO characters accompanied by sunset and cats. In this three-part poster series, I made the cutoff from the first and second poster land between Asuna and Yuuki, so you couldn't tell whose hand she was holding at first. Well, people figured it out! I really liked this series of posters, because I got to draw situations you'd never get to see in the original story. Also, Pina turned into a cat.

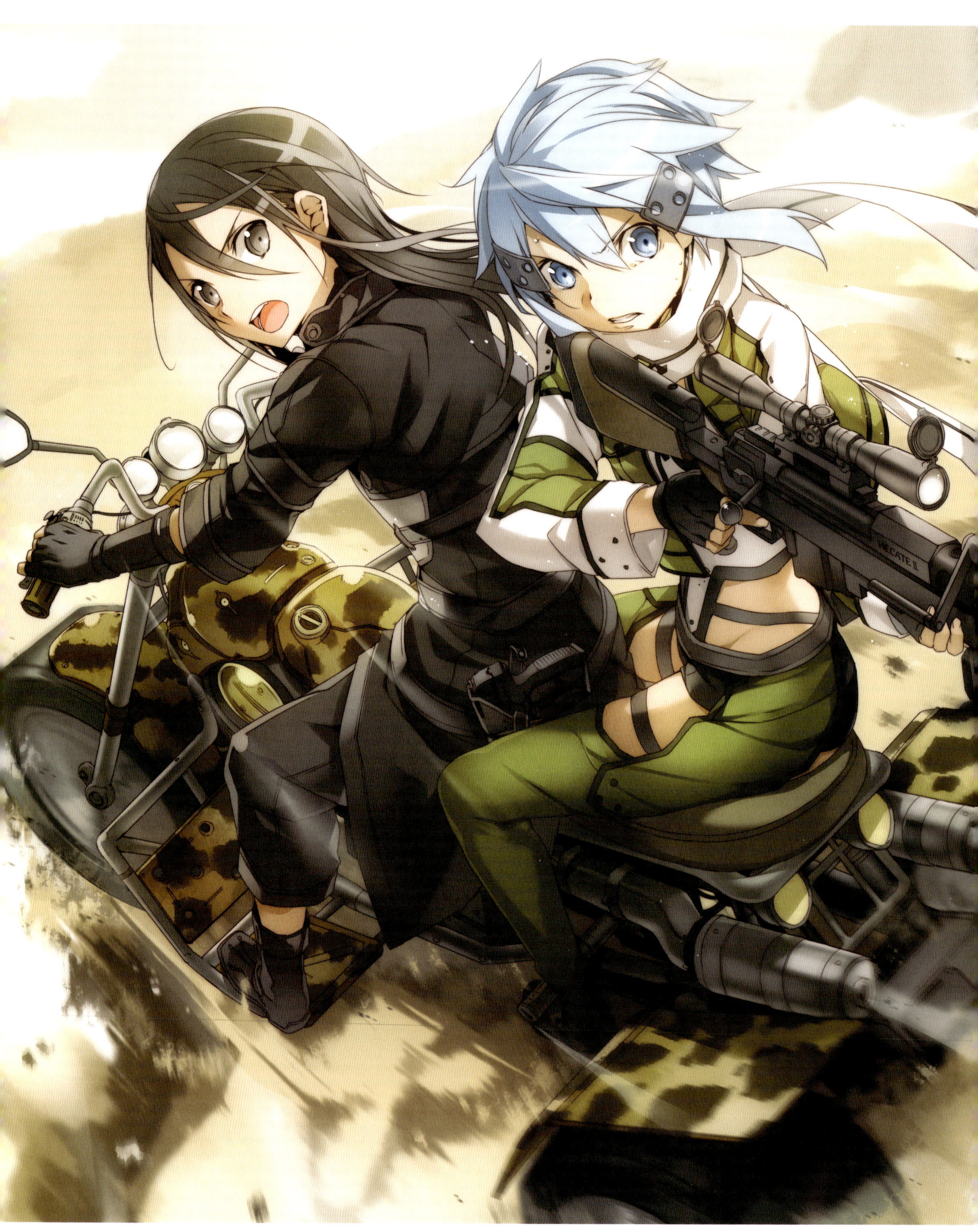
HECATE II

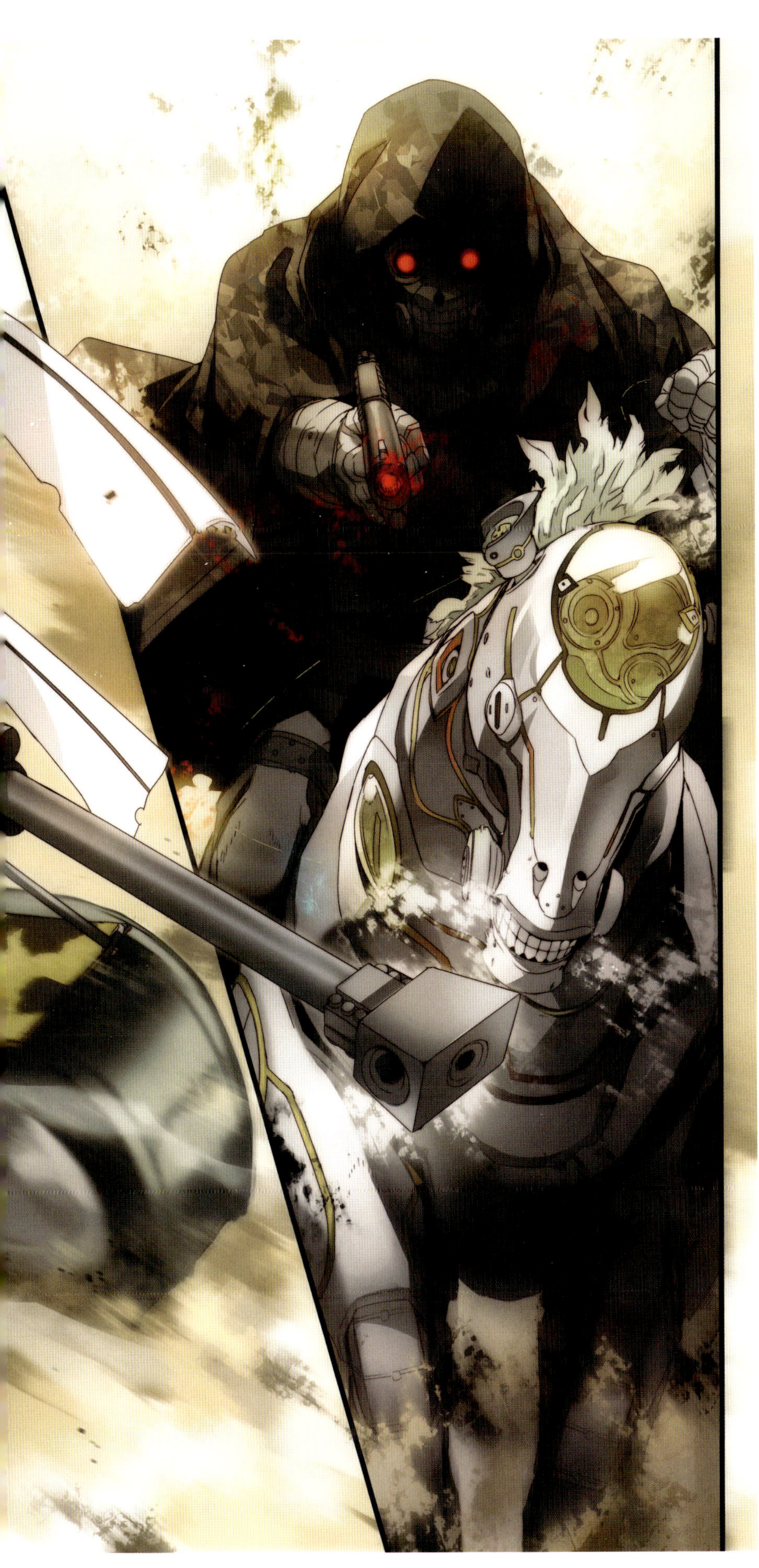

Dengeki Bunko
20th Anniversary Celebration
Dengeki Bunko Exhibit
Famous Scene Collection: August 2013

This project was about drawing scenes from the novels that didn't get illustrated before. It's hard enough to draw guns, but the trike, too?! Way too hard! Hopefully it comes across as tense and exciting.

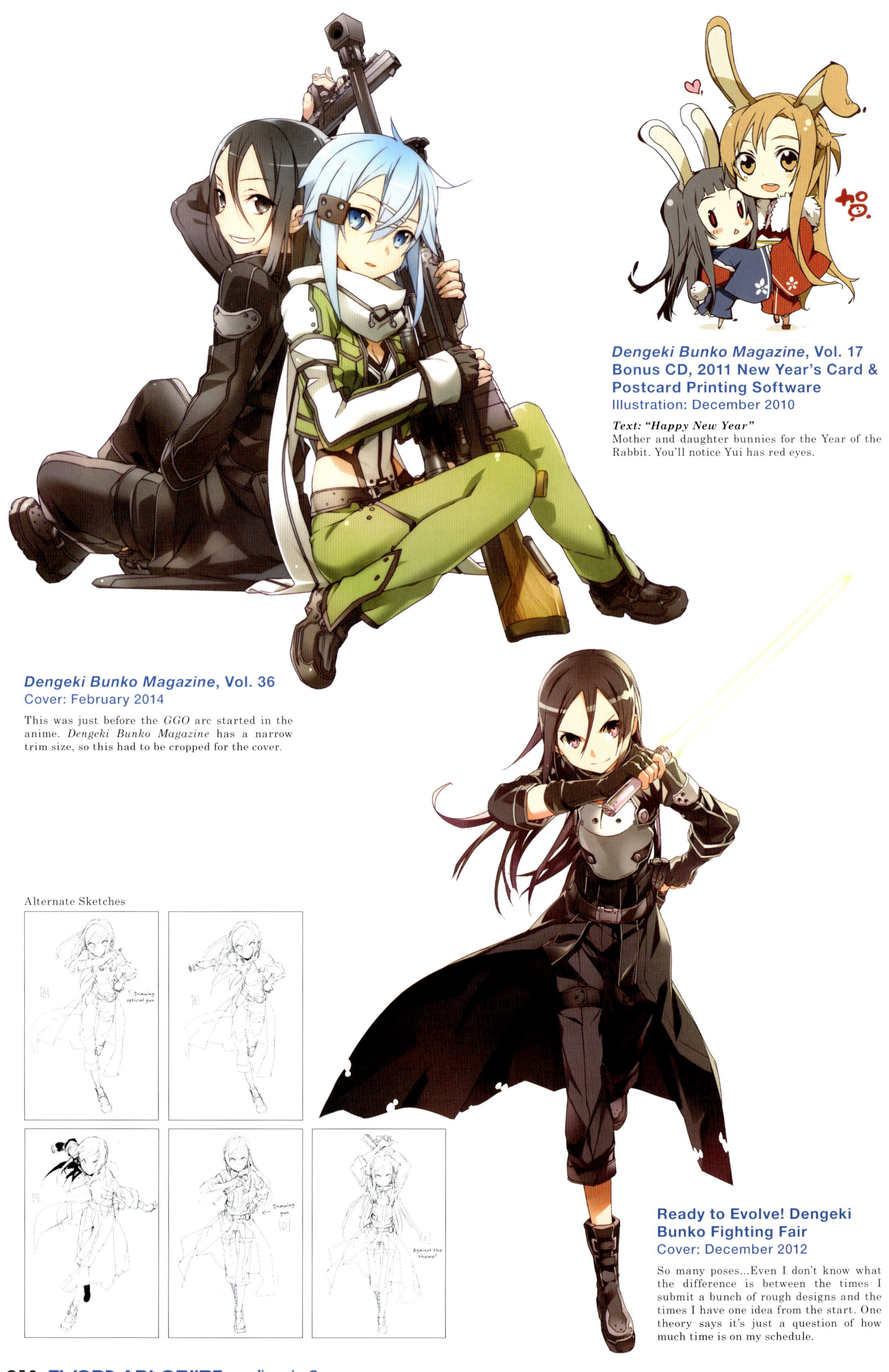

Dengeki Bunko Magazine, Vol. 17 Bonus CD, 2011 New Year's Card & Postcard Printing Software
Illustration: December 2010

Text: "Happy New Year"
Mother and daughter bunnies for the Year of the Rabbit. You'll notice Yui has red eyes.

Dengeki Bunko Magazine, Vol. 36
Cover: February 2014

This was just before the *GGO* arc started in the anime. *Dengeki Bunko Magazine* has a narrow trim size, so this had to be cropped for the cover.

Alternate Sketches

Ready to Evolve! Dengeki Bunko Fighting Fair
Cover: December 2012

So many poses...Even I don't know what the difference is between the times I submit a bunch of rough designs and the times I have one idea from the start. One theory says it's just a question of how much time is on my schedule.

Alternate Sketches

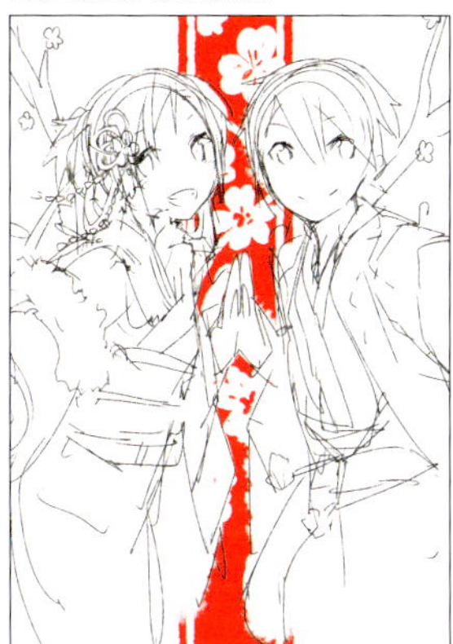

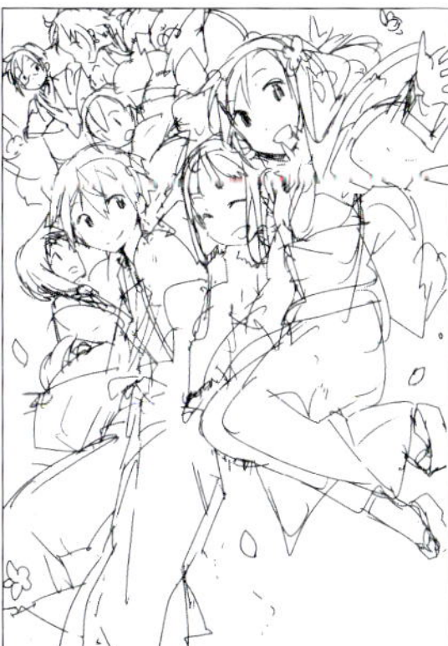

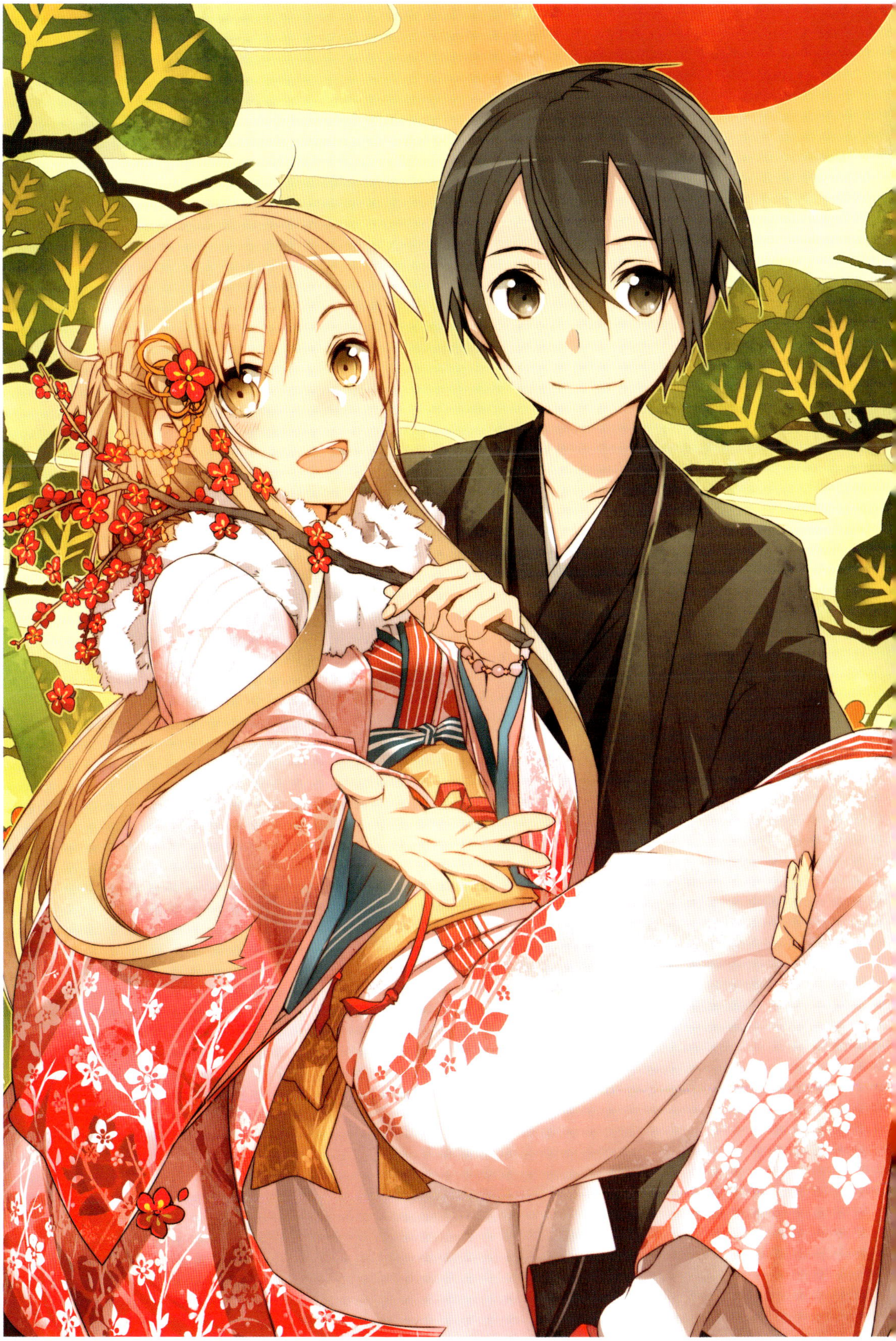

Yomiuri Shimbun, National Morning Edition
Promotional Illustration: January 2014

An illustration that was, stunningly enough, run on an entire page of the *Yomiuri Shimbun* on January 1st. I remember feeling incredible pressure when they told me how much it cost. I think the busier alternate sketch would have been too much like the usual thing.

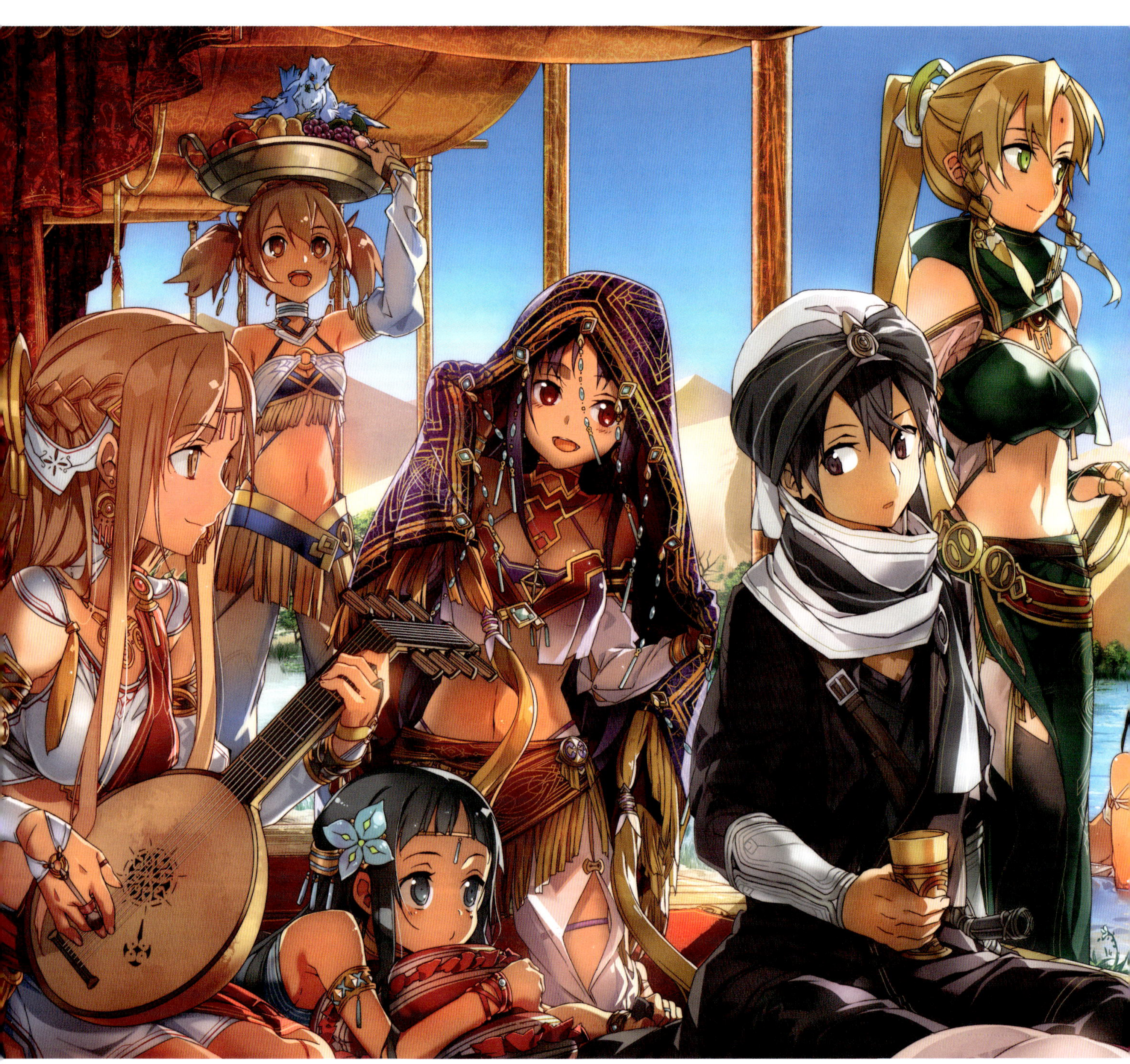

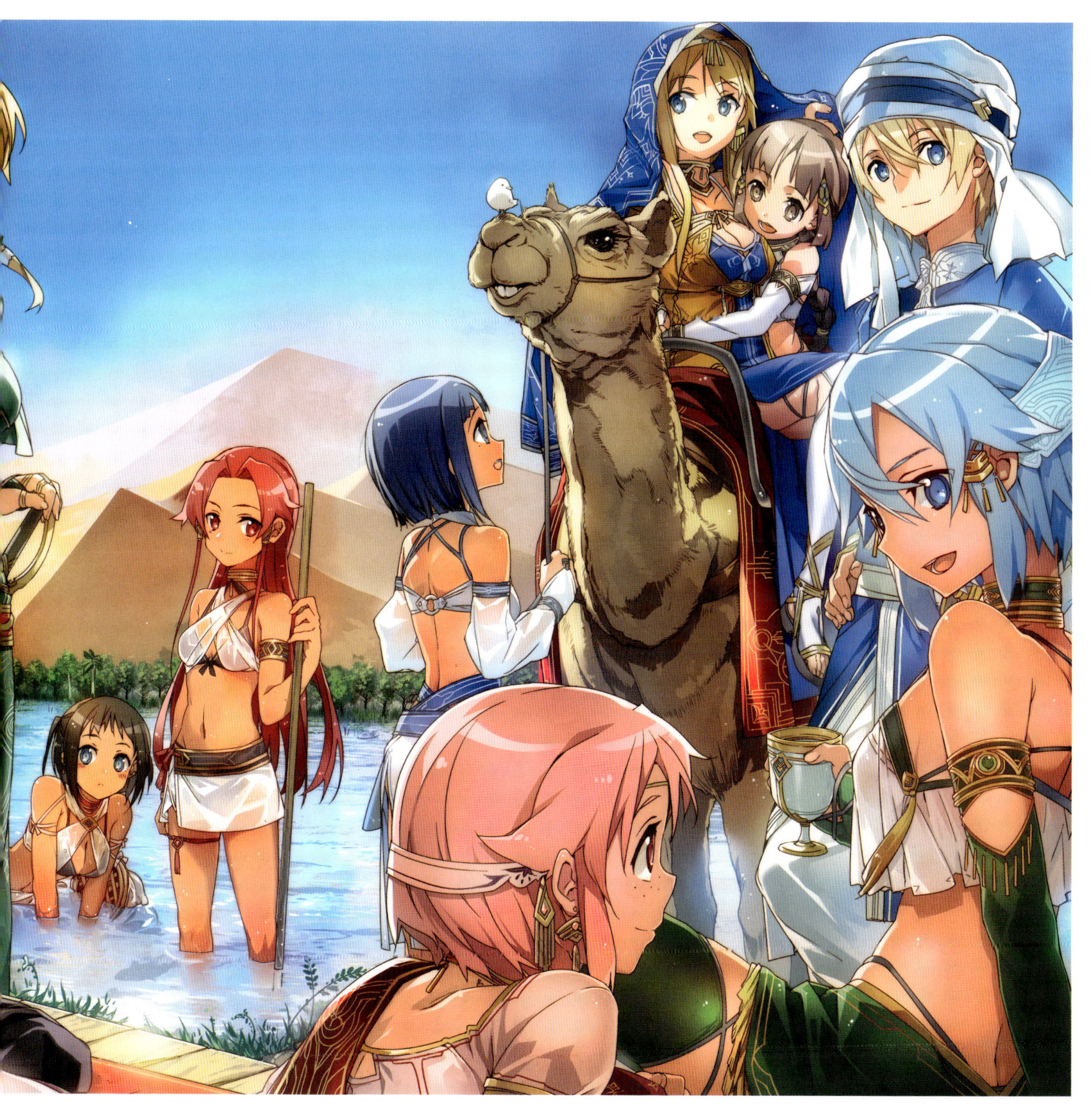

Dengeki Bunko Magazine, Vol. 49–51

Three-Part Combination Poster: April–August 2016

A three-part poster series depicting Arabian-style *SAO*. I think my favorite detail is the low-key obnoxious expression on that camel. Alice might be riding the camel, but rest assured that it is not Amayori reborn or anything.

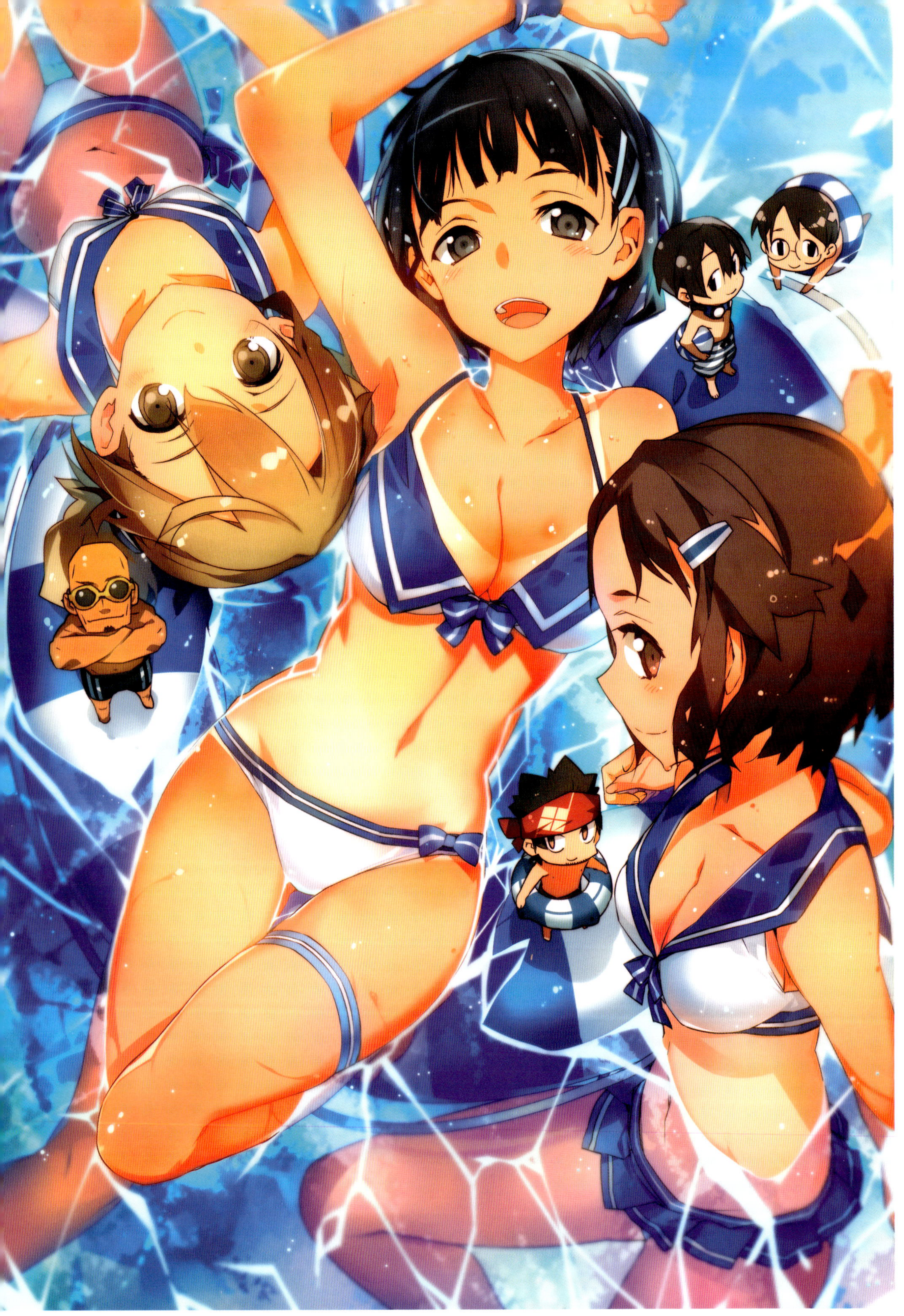

Dengeki Bunko 3,000 Titles Celebration! Official Bootleg, *Dengeki Girls Swimsuit Festival!*
Cover: October 2015

Since this was another "bootleg," I included Suguha with the "More Scenes" girls. I wanted to draw some tan lines, so I figured that making it a sailor-type swimsuit wouldn't be too risqué. Well, I may have overdone it. Some of you might not have even noticed that the guys are in the picture as super-deformed chibi characters.

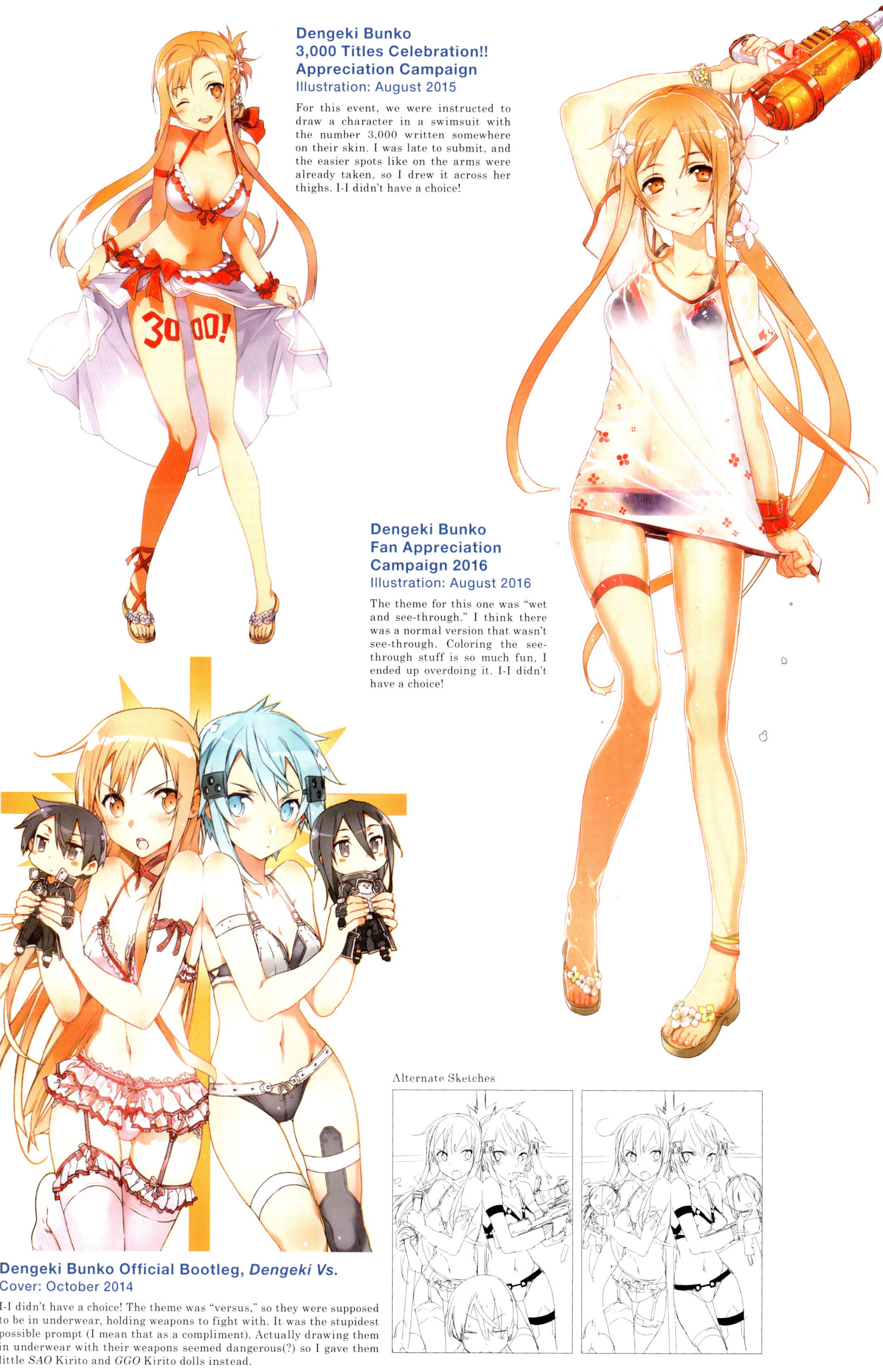

Dengeki Bunko 3,000 Titles Celebration!! Appreciation Campaign

Illustration: August 2015

For this event, we were instructed to draw a character in a swimsuit with the number 3,000 written somewhere on their skin. I was late to submit, and the easier spots like on the arms were already taken, so I drew it across her thighs. I-I didn't have a choice!

Dengeki Bunko Fan Appreciation Campaign 2016

Illustration: August 2016

The theme for this one was "wet and see-through." I think there was a normal version that wasn't see-through. Coloring the see-through stuff is so much fun, I ended up overdoing it. I-I didn't have a choice!

Dengeki Bunko Official Bootleg, *Dengeki Vs.*

Cover: October 2014

I-I didn't have a choice! The theme was "versus," so they were supposed to be in underwear, holding weapons to fight with. It was the stupidest possible prompt (I mean that as a compliment). Actually drawing them in underwear with their weapons seemed dangerous(?) so I gave them little *SAO* Kirito and *GGO* Kirito dolls instead.

Alternate Sketches

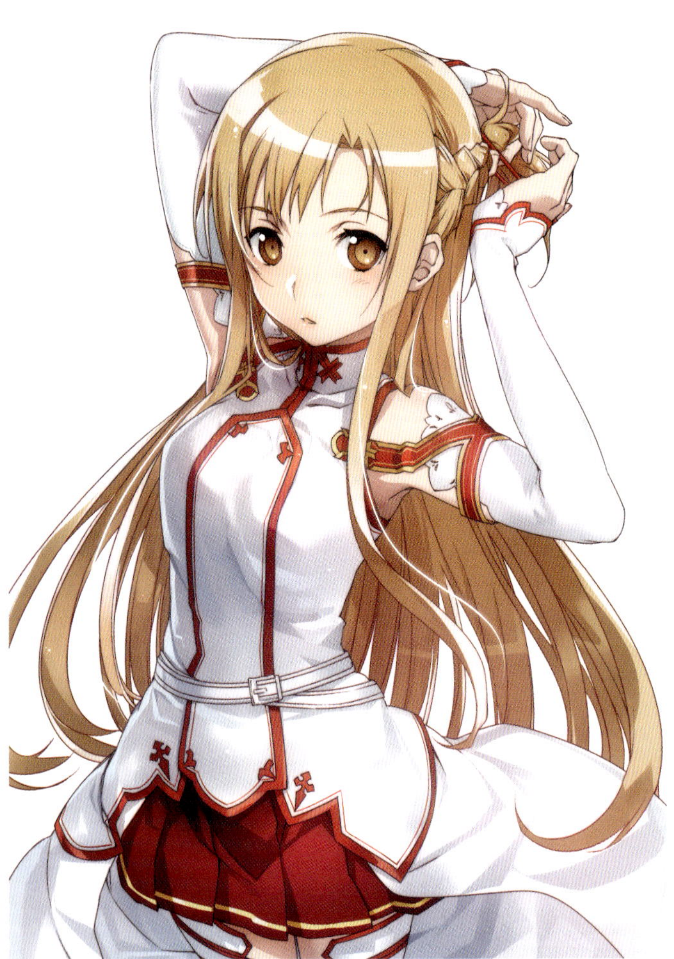

***Dengeki Bunko Magazine*, Vol. 55**
Character Book Vol. 2: Asuna
Cover: April 2017

Girls tying up their hair are cute. I always wanted to draw this pose.

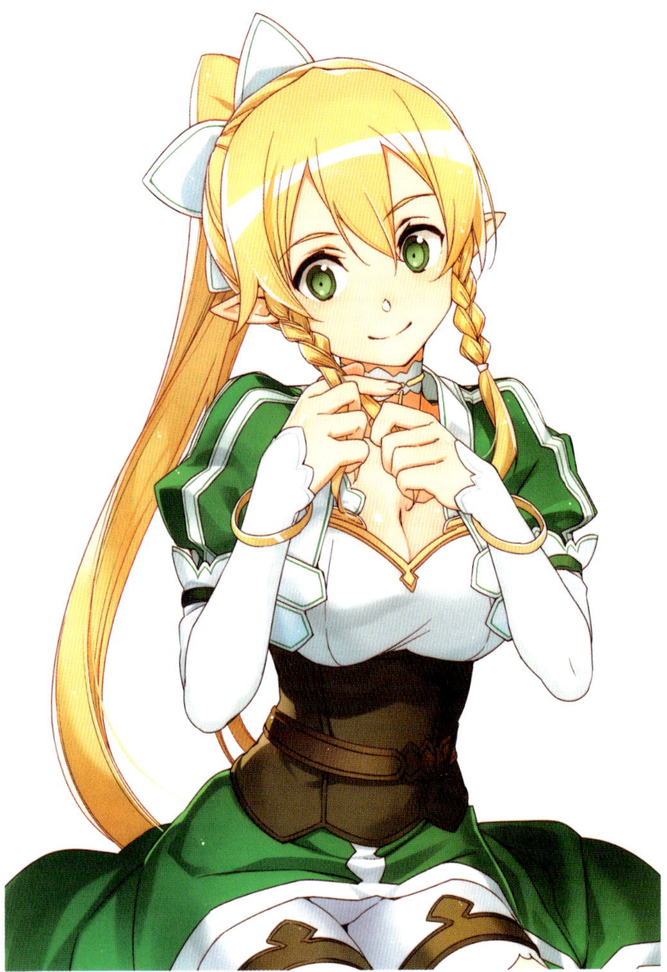

***Dengeki Bunko Magazine*, Vol. 56**
Character Book Vol. 3: Leafa
Cover: June 2017

First Asuna, now Leafa. I probably should have drawn her tying up her ponytail, but then she'd just be mirroring Asuna's pose, so I drew her doing the braids on the side instead.

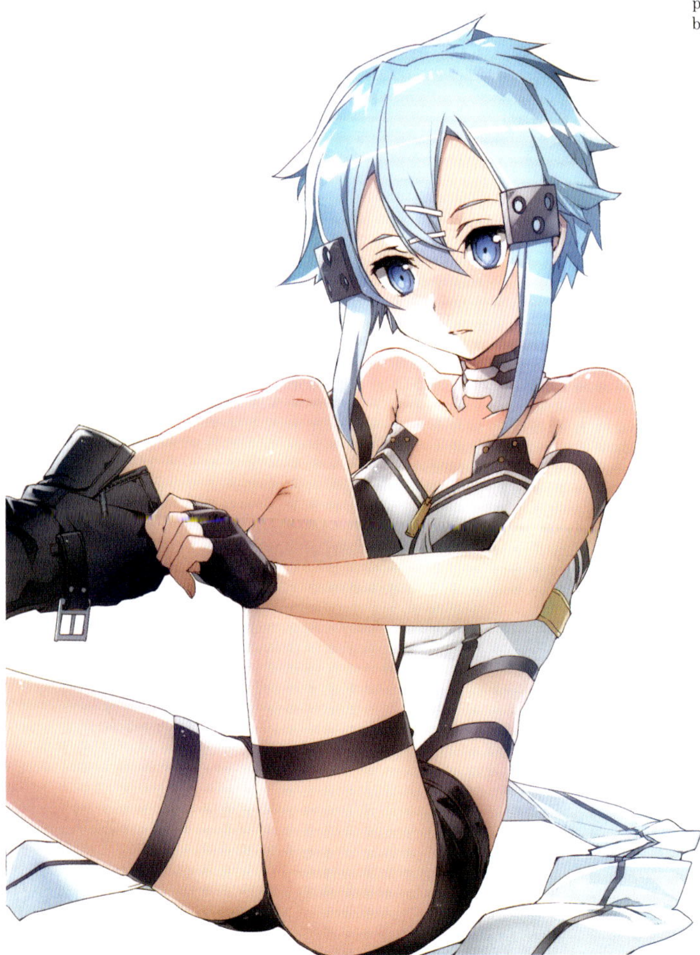

***Dengeki Bunko Magazine*, Vol. 57**
Character Book Vol. 4: Sinon
Cover: August 2017

After Asuna and Leafa, I wanted to draw her doing her hair too, but I gave up when she'd be mirroring Leafa. Instead, I kept up the theme of "getting ready" and had her putting on her boots. Without her muffler on top, she looks strangely exposed.

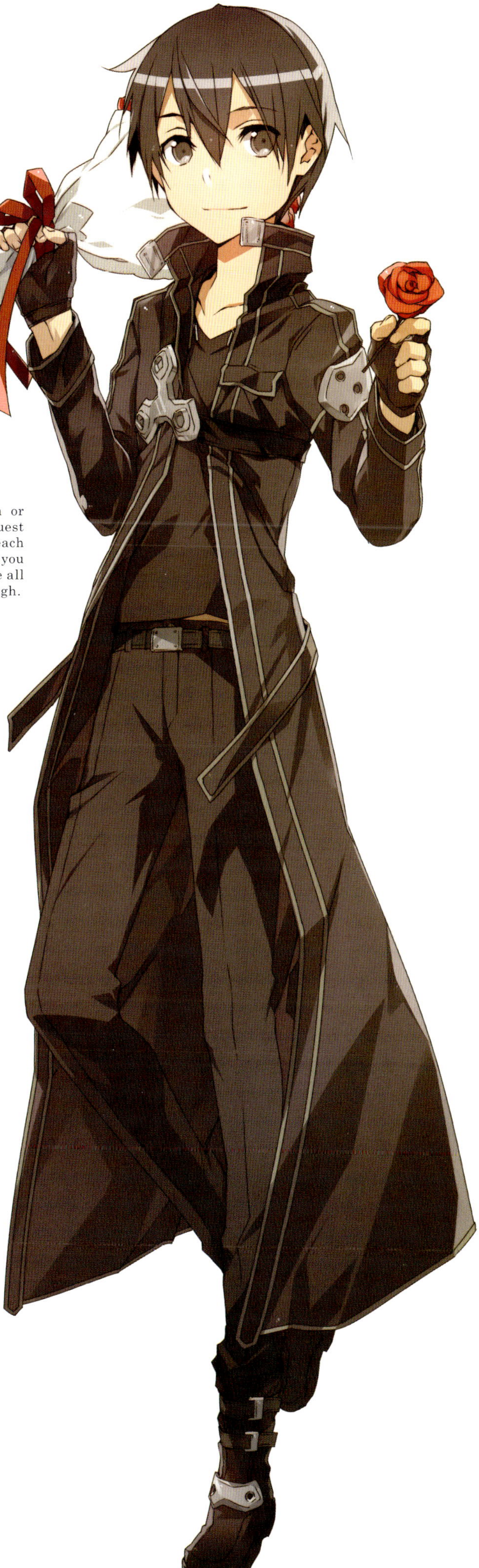

Dengeki Bunko 20th Anniversary Appreciation Project

Poster Illustration: August 2013

Dengeki Bunko always has some kind of campaign or event going on every year, and they'll always request one character illustration to use in promotions from each series. The male characters are rarely chosen, so when you do one, it sometimes creates funny results when they're all lined up. Usually it ends up being Asuna or Alice, though.

Alternate Sketches

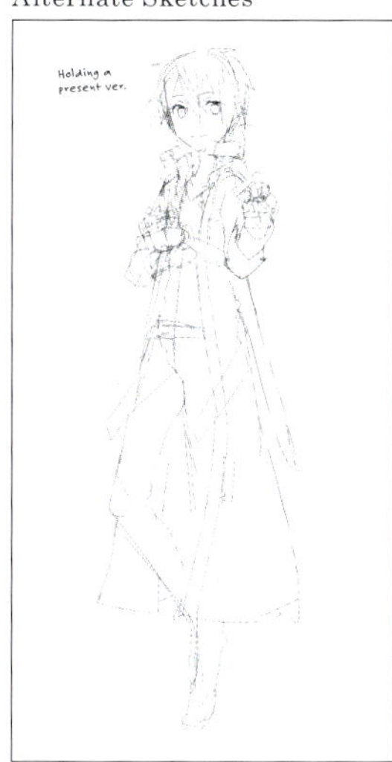

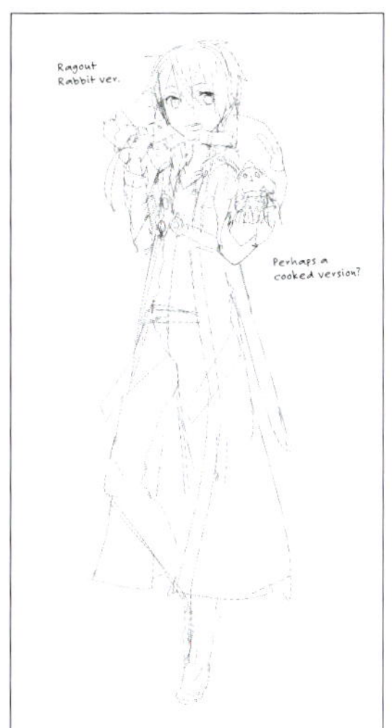

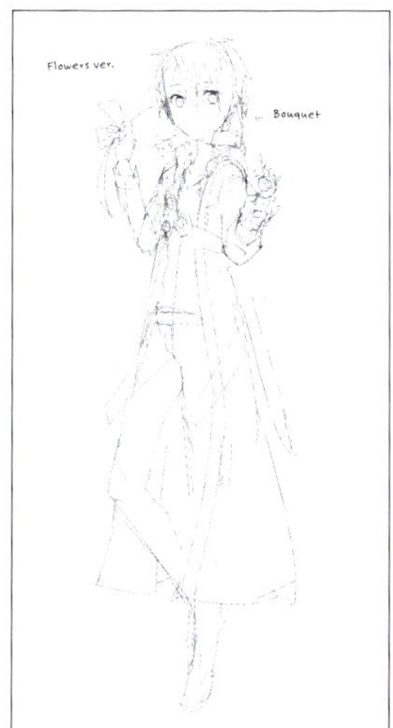

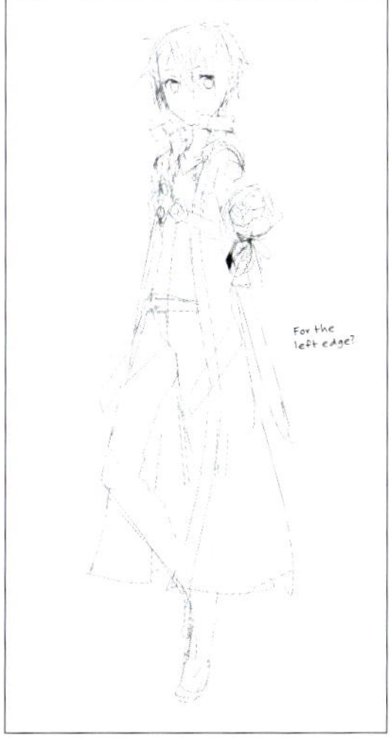

Sword Art Online
abec Artworks: Wanderers
Cover: March 2020

I thought about this one a whole lot and wanted to draw them all in white, in a different way than I've ever done before. I was worried that it might not look like an *SAO* art book on first glance. Thank you for picking it up anyway! For the character selection, I decided to limit it to those who appear in the Alicization and Progressive arcs, since that's what this book covers.

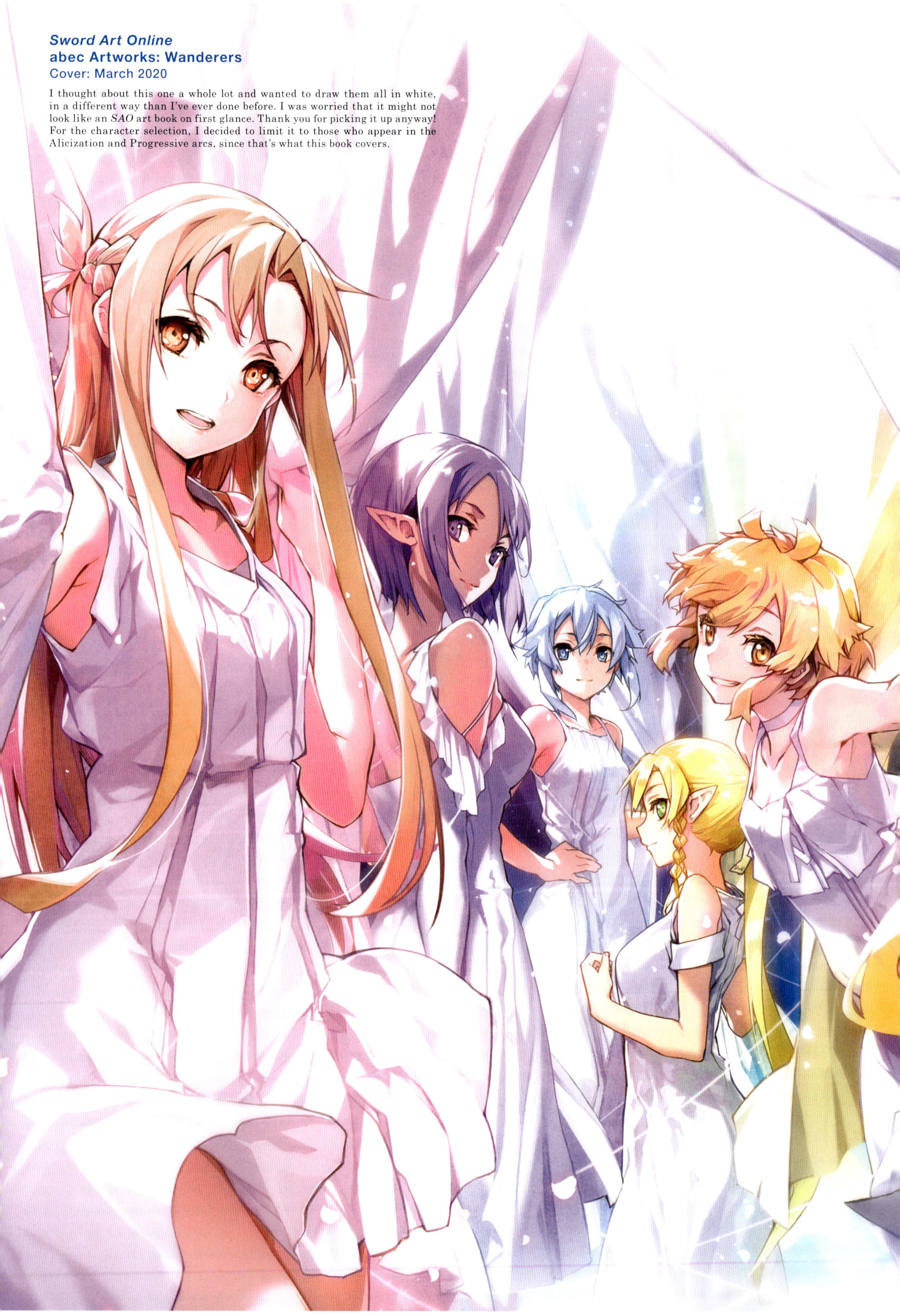

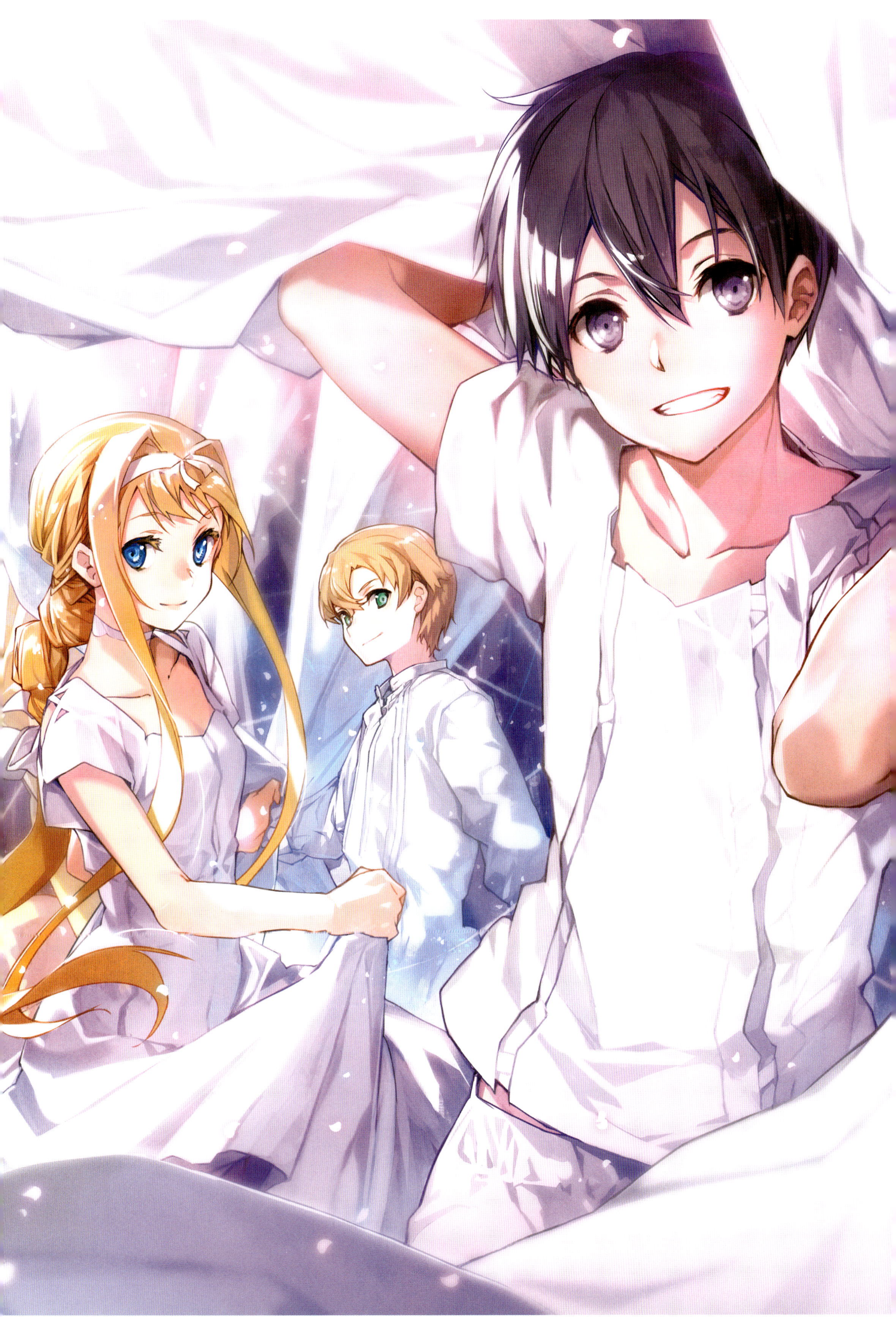

SWORD ART ONLINE

Alicization Invading

In this volume, it's half a year after the human realm arc. Alice, who's been taking care of Kirito while he's in a vegetative state, must now stand up to fight against an invasion from the Dark Territory.

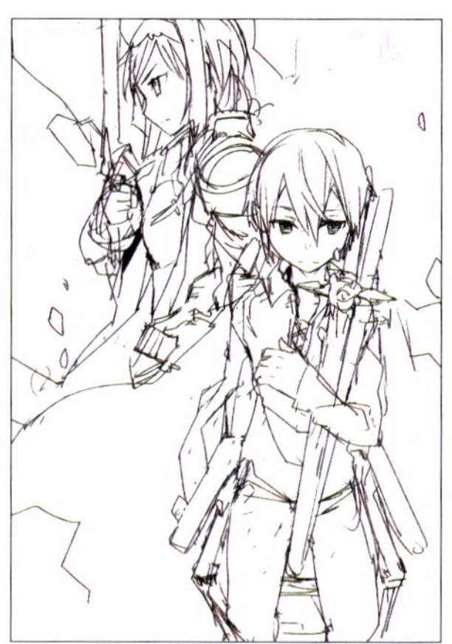

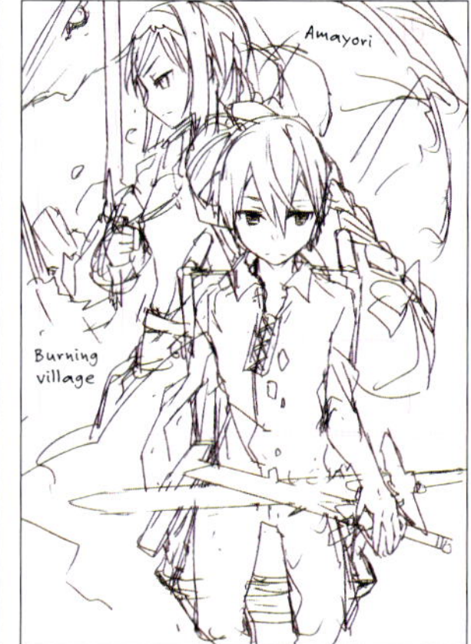

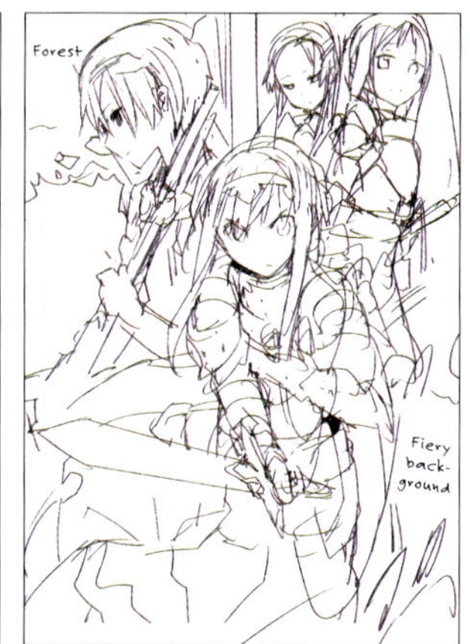

Alternate Cover Sketches

Dengeki Bunko
Sword Art Online 15: Alicization Invading
Cover: August 2014

This is the volume where I faced the dreaded "How can you put Kirito on the cover when he's barely present in the book?" conundrum. Still, the cover works as it is. Also, I'd already broken my rule in the previous volume that the layout must be characters in front of some silhouette-type background layer, so this time I just drew a full-on proper background.

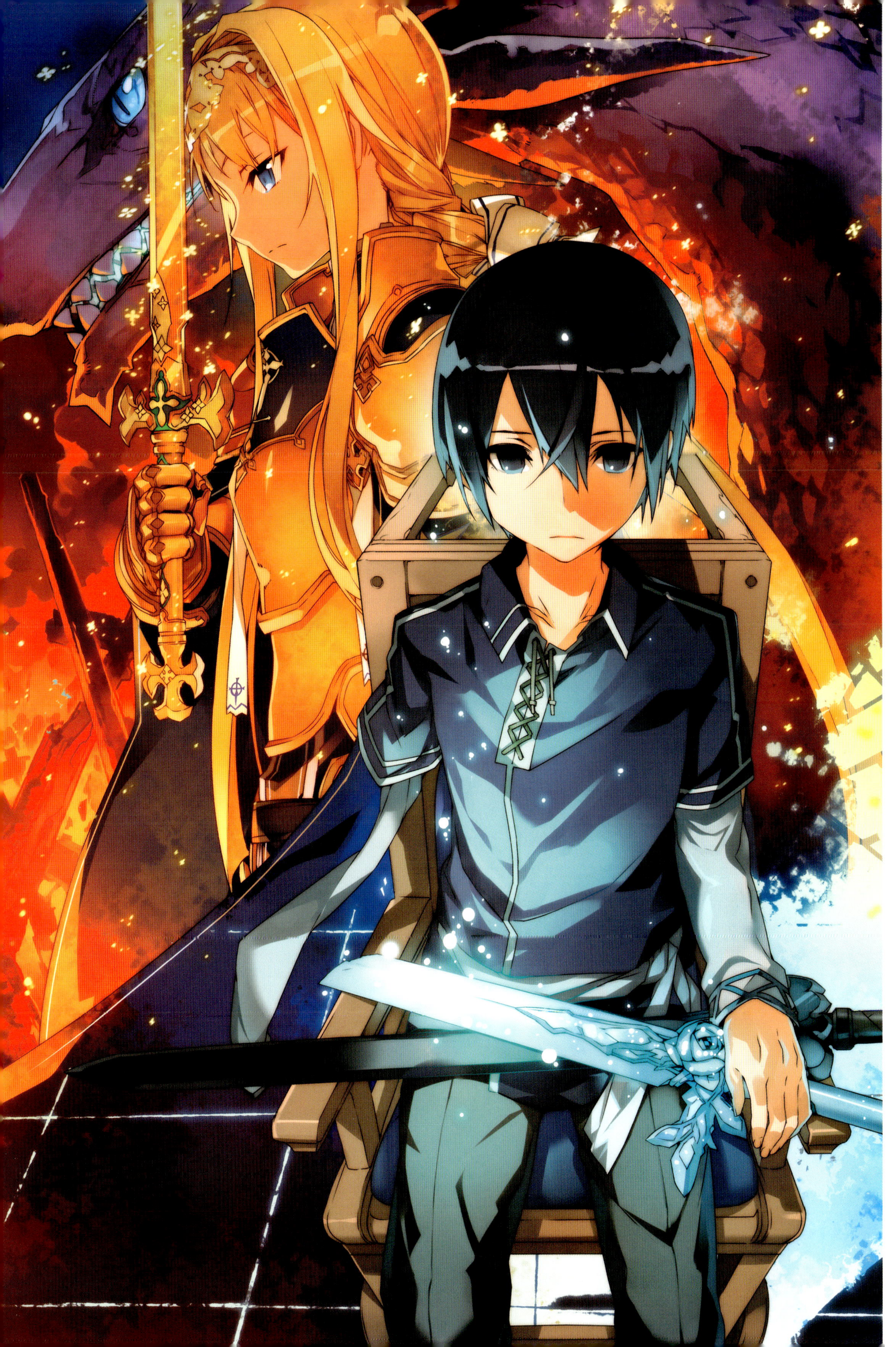

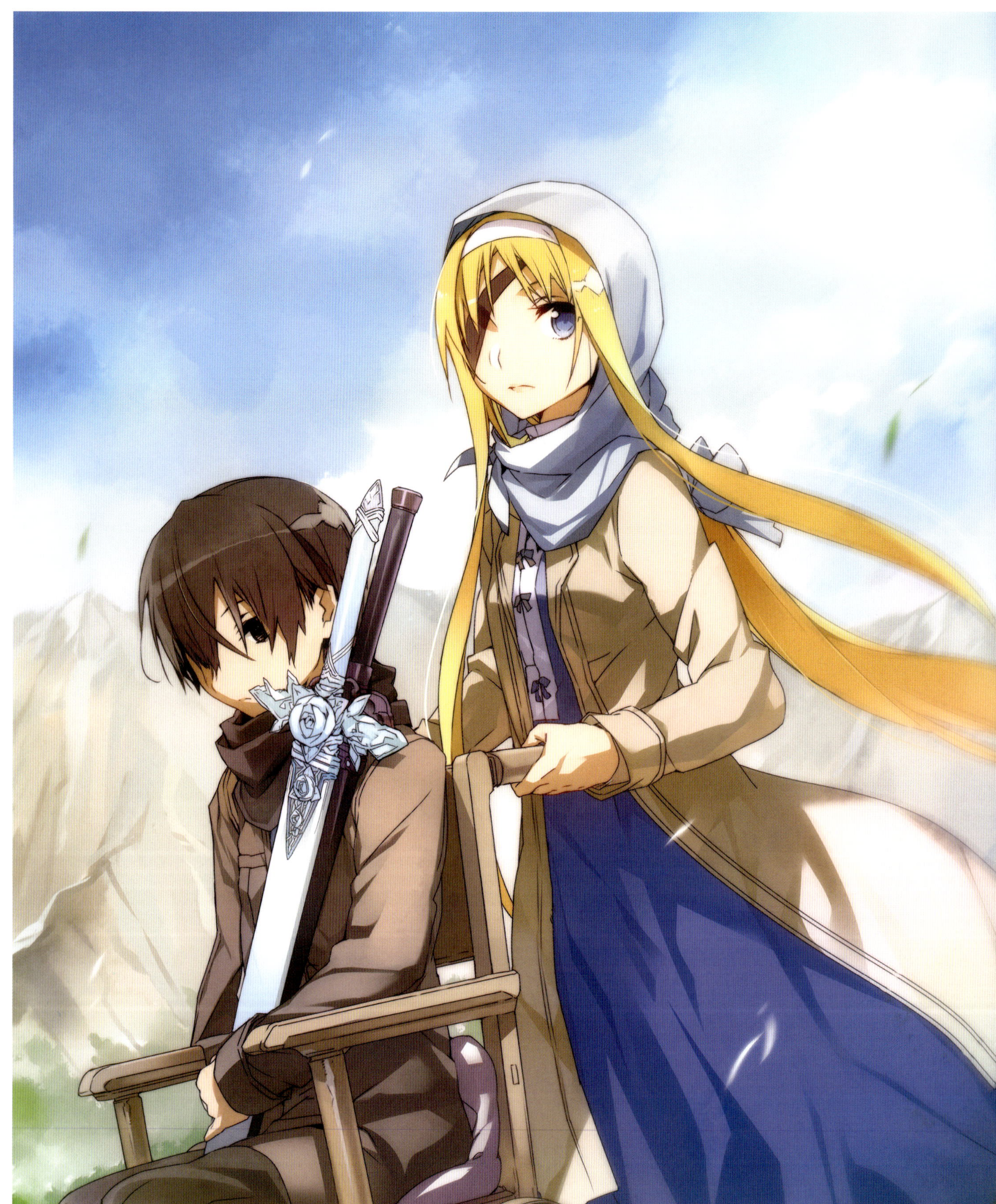

Dengeki Bunko
Sword Art Online 15: Alicization Invading
Frontispiece: August 2014

A caretaking scene. I wonder how well a wooden wheelchair works.

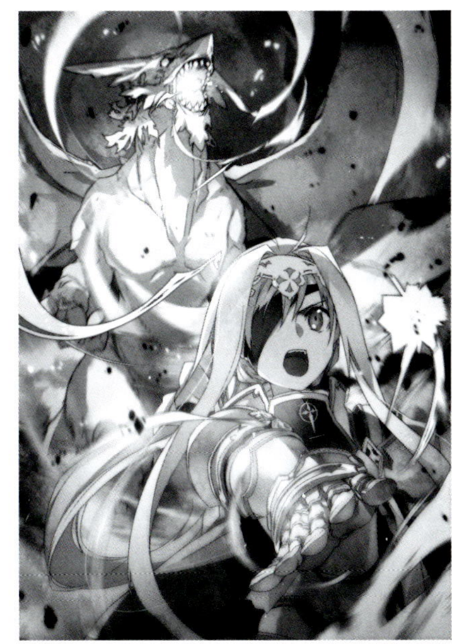

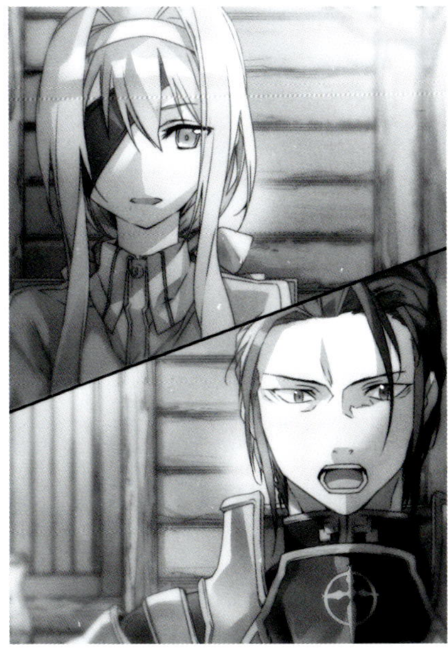

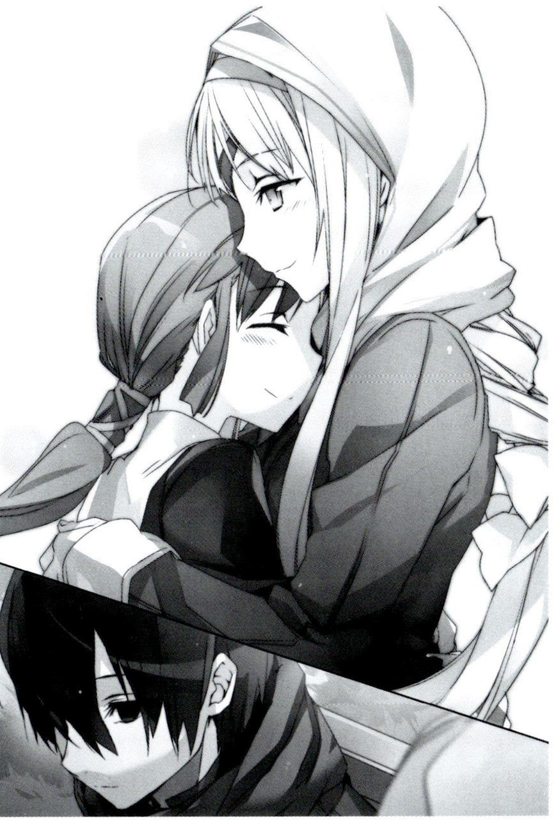

Dengeki Bunko
Sword Art Online 15: Alicization Invading
Illustration: August 2014

I really like that "Burn them all!" scene. You're supposed to be seeing her hand swing down with the order.

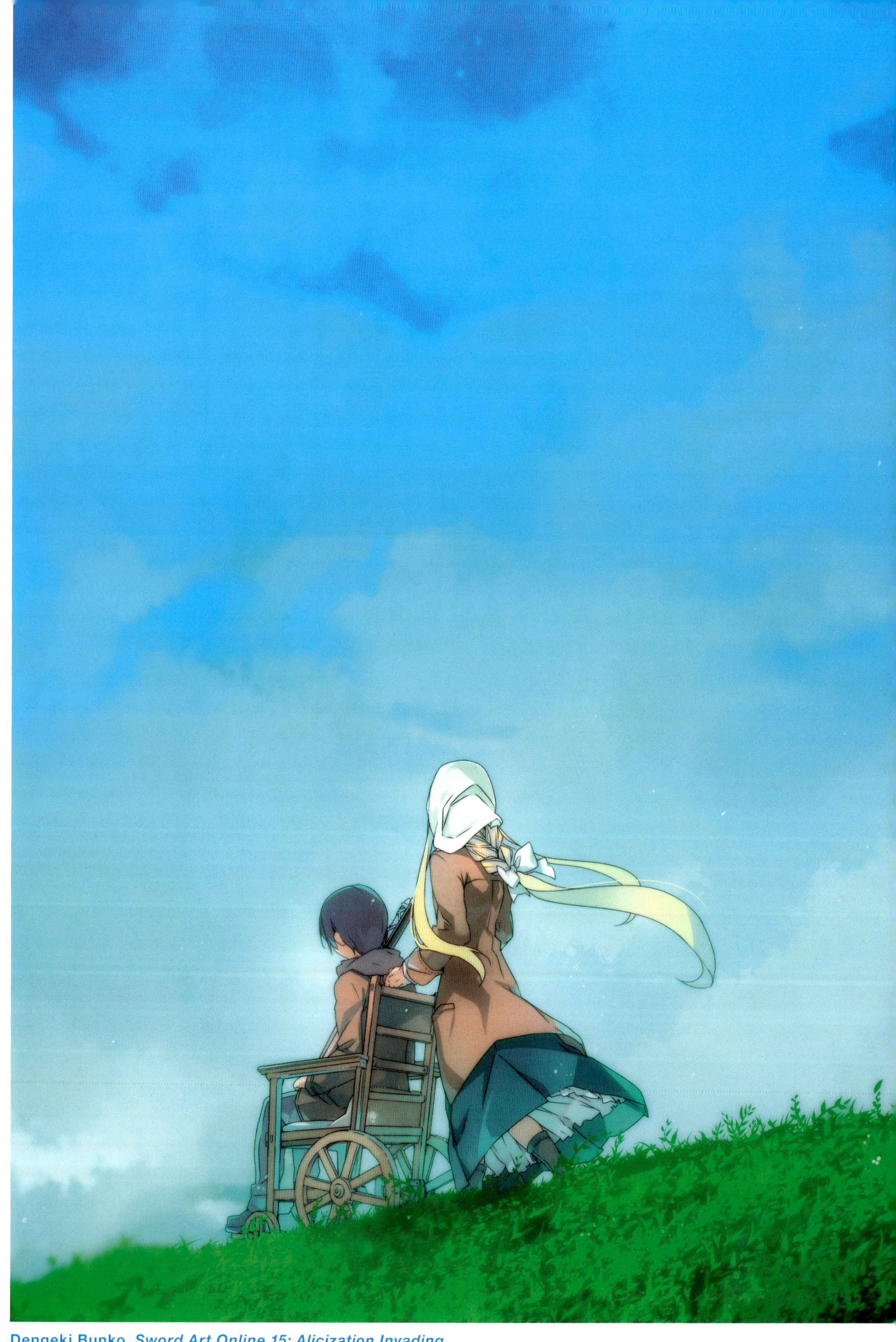

Dengeki Bunko, *Sword Art Online 15: Alicization Invading*
Frontispiece: August 2014

This is the same place I drew in the color illustration in the middle of Volume 9, *Alicization Beginning.*

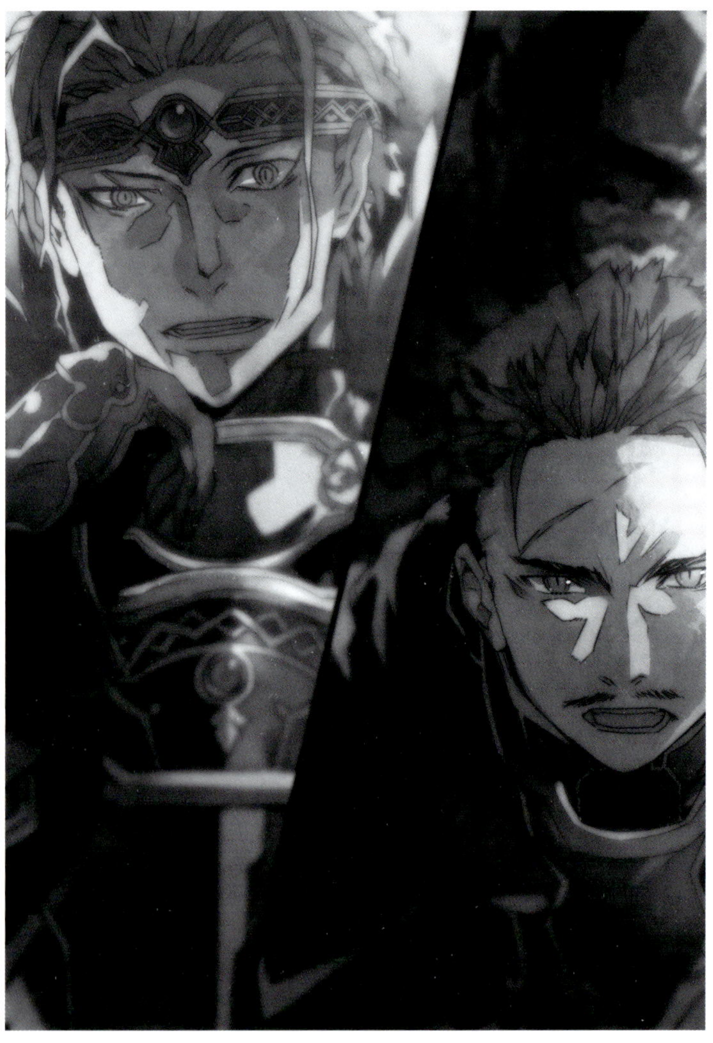

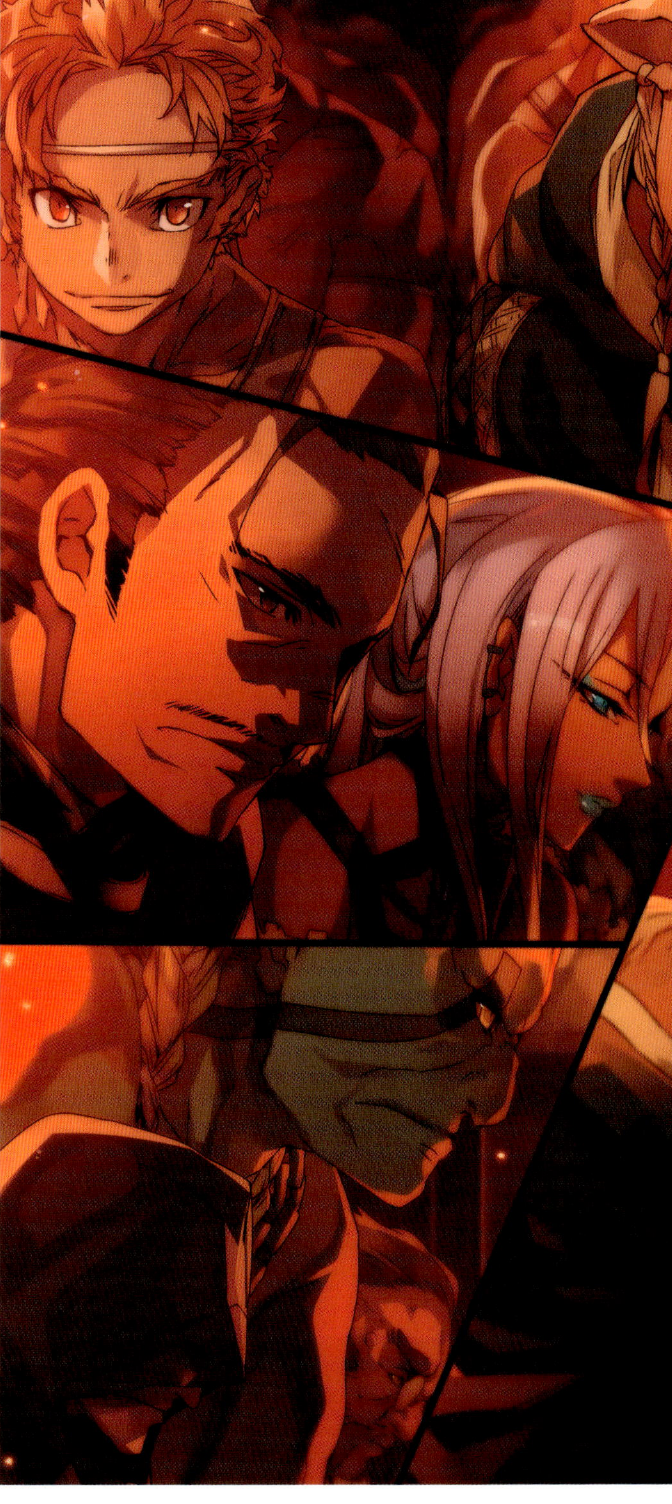

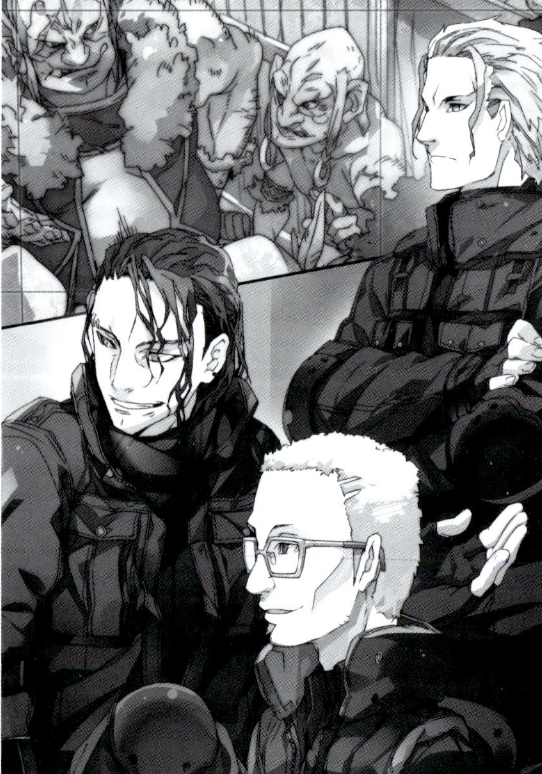

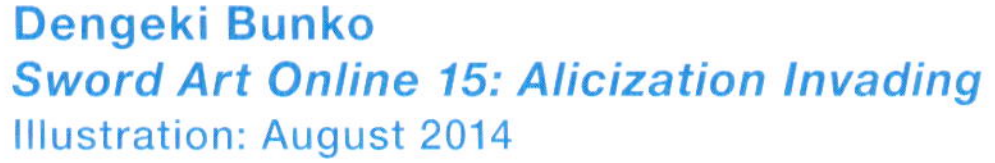

Dengeki Bunko
Sword Art Online 15: Alicization Invading
Illustration: August 2014

I've got this fun quirk where I find it easier to draw old guys than boys and girls, so I really enjoyed these pieces. I love scenes where you have just a bunch of older dudes hanging out, including goblins. Even if I'm the only one who loves them!

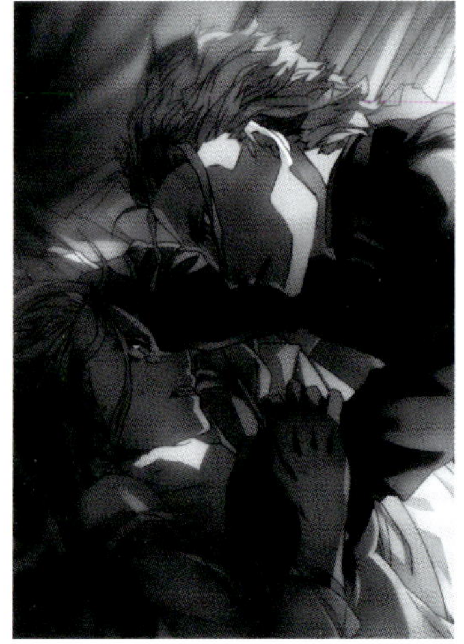

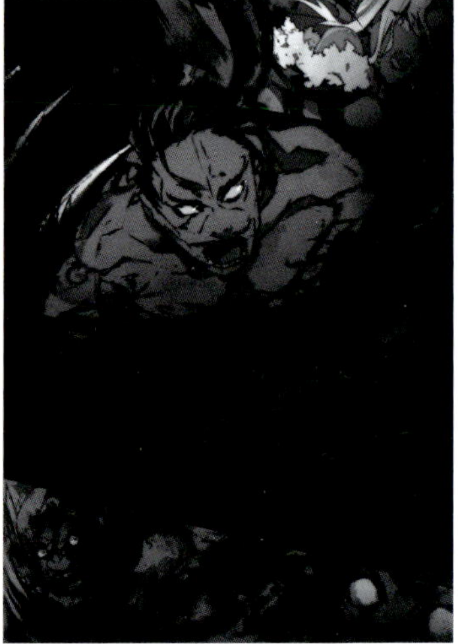

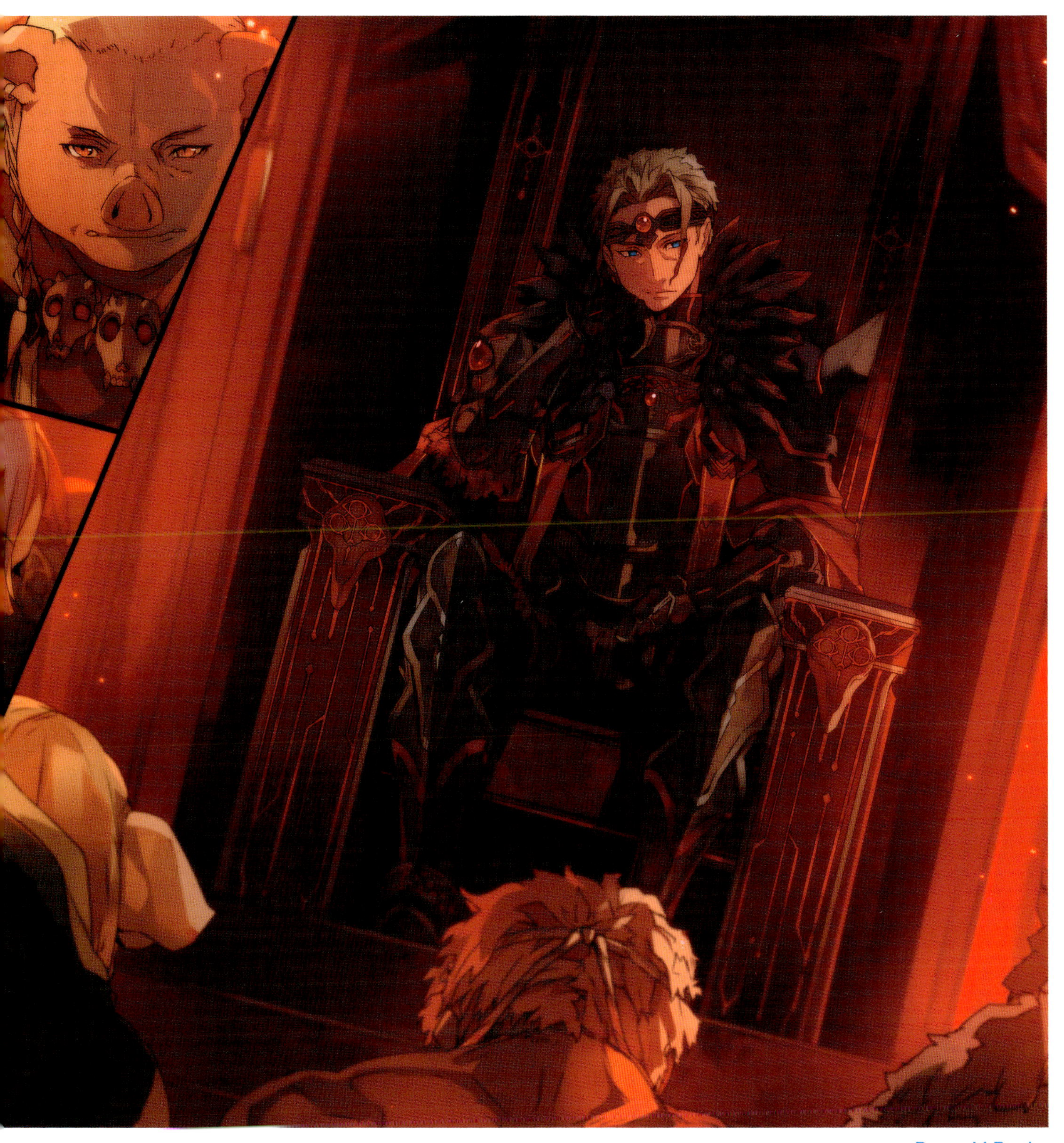

Dengeki Bunko
Sword Art Online 15: Alicization Invading
Frontispiece: August 2014

Throne room scene. I love scenes like this too, with all the army lords and such lined up.

Dengeki Bunko
Sword Art Online 15: Alicization Invading
Back Cover: August 2014

Left: "Moving in"
Center: "Howdy and Welcome! -Standby Village-"
Right: "Welcome"
The latest in the popular "More Scenes" series. Some would say it's an honor just to be a member.

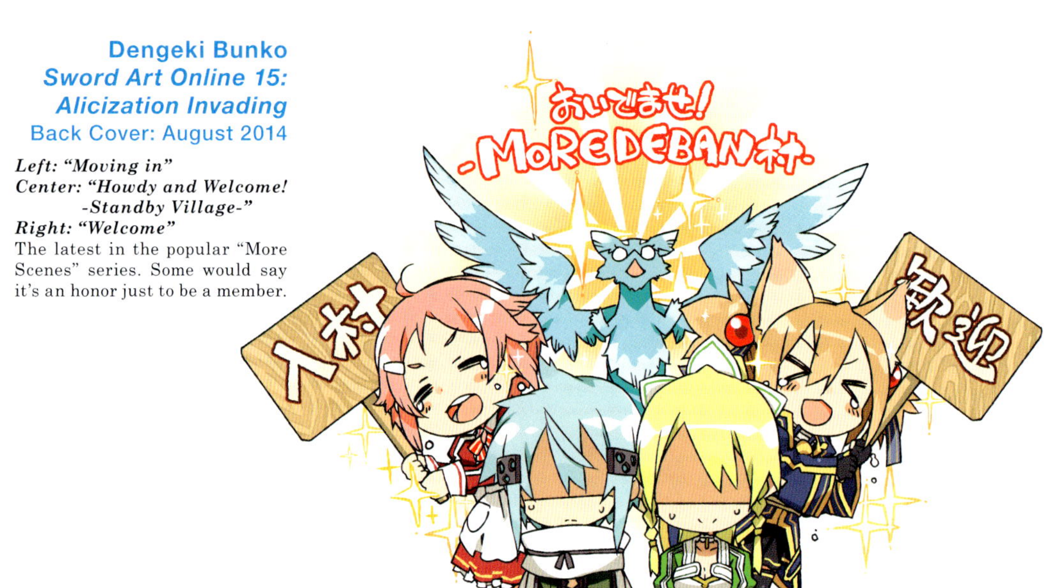

Dengeki Bunko
Sword Art Online 15: Alicization Invading
Frontispiece: August 2014

Alice meets up with the guardian army. Being surrounded by these warriors dressed in their terrifying, complicated armor makes you really appreciate what a lifesaver Bercouli is with his simple robe.

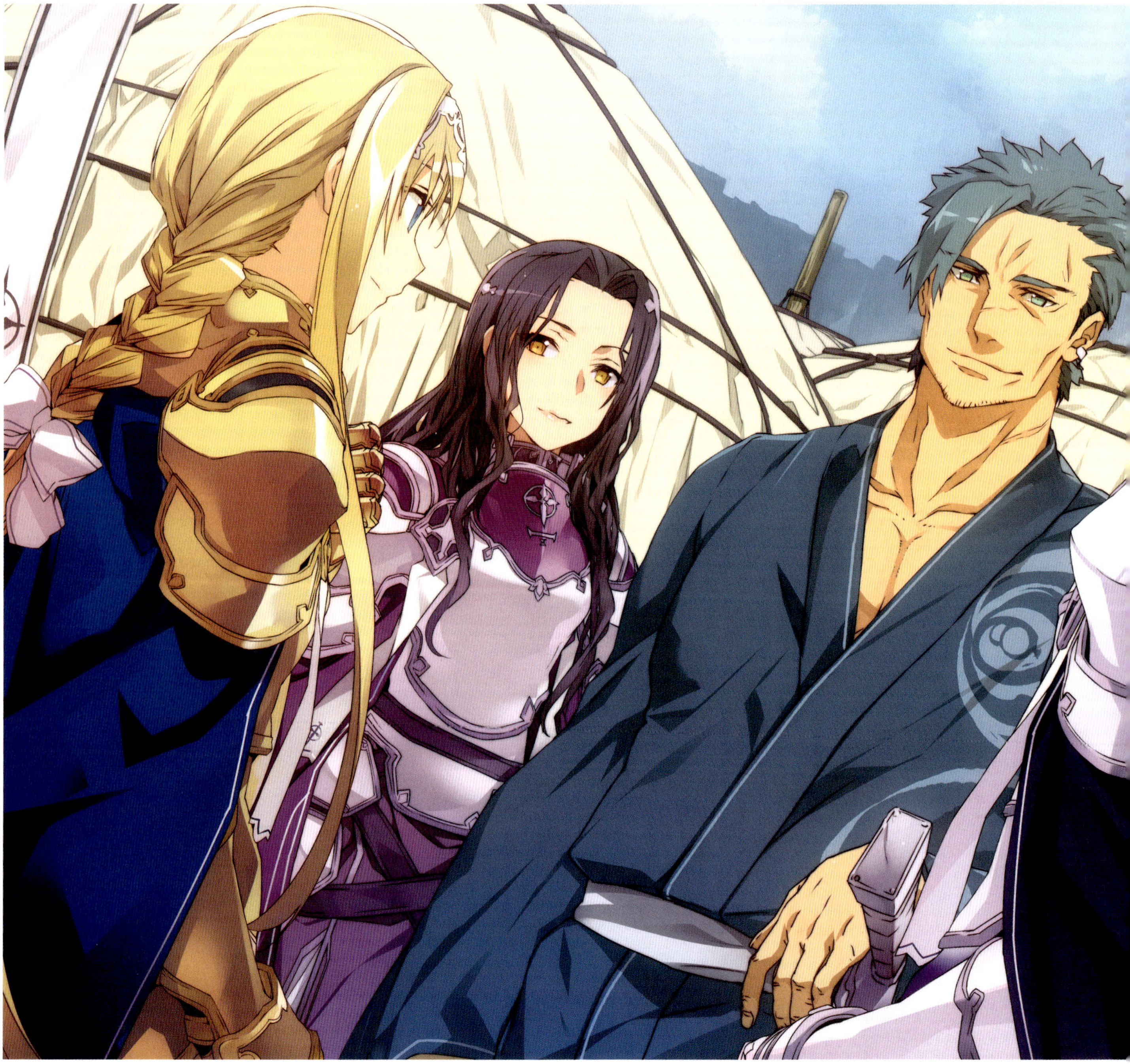

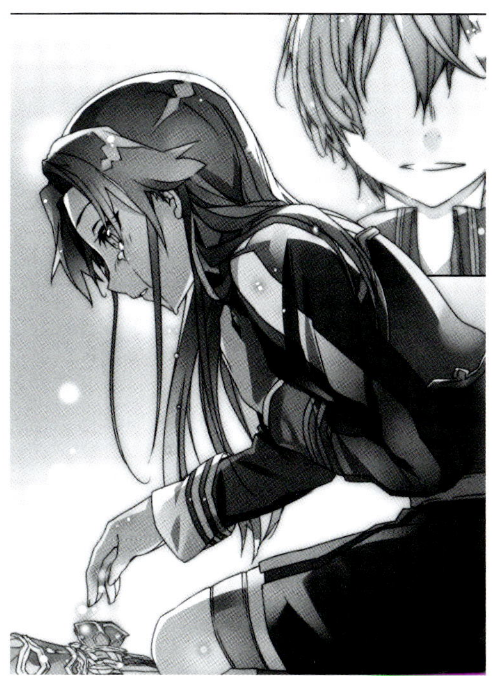
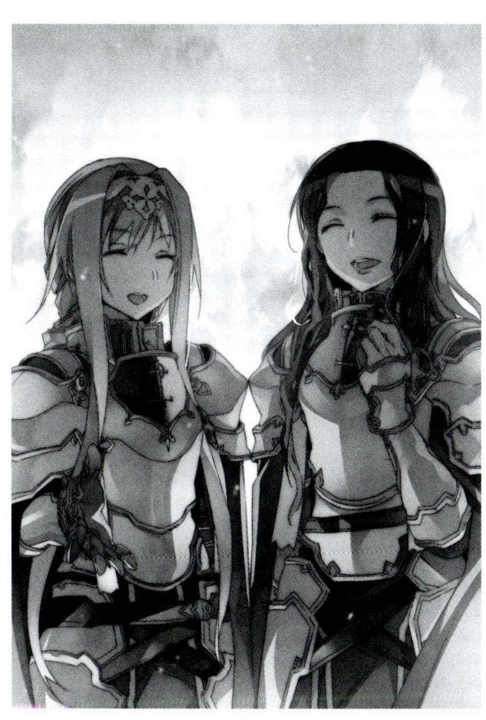
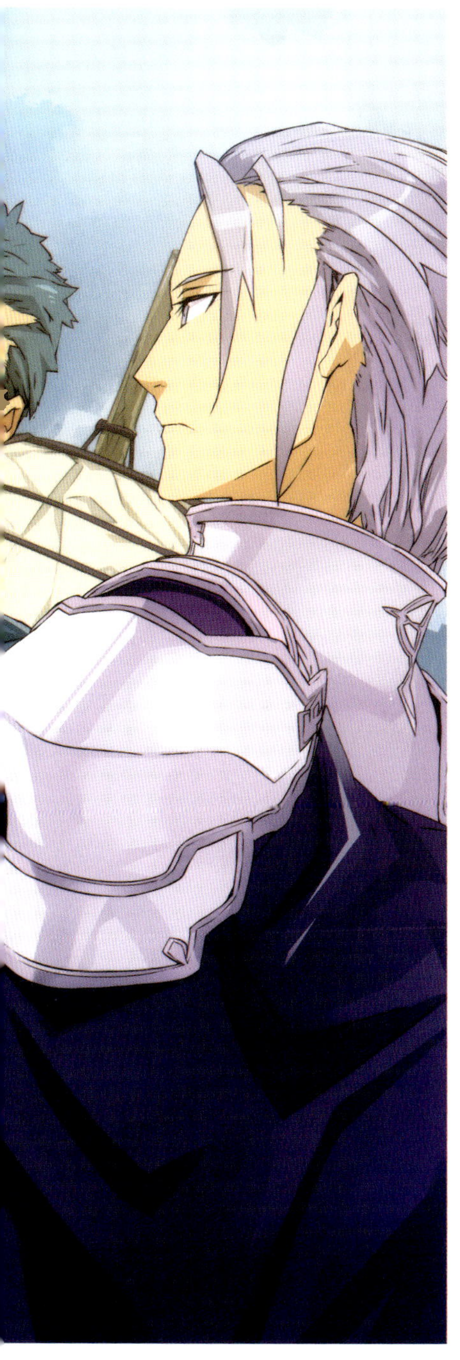
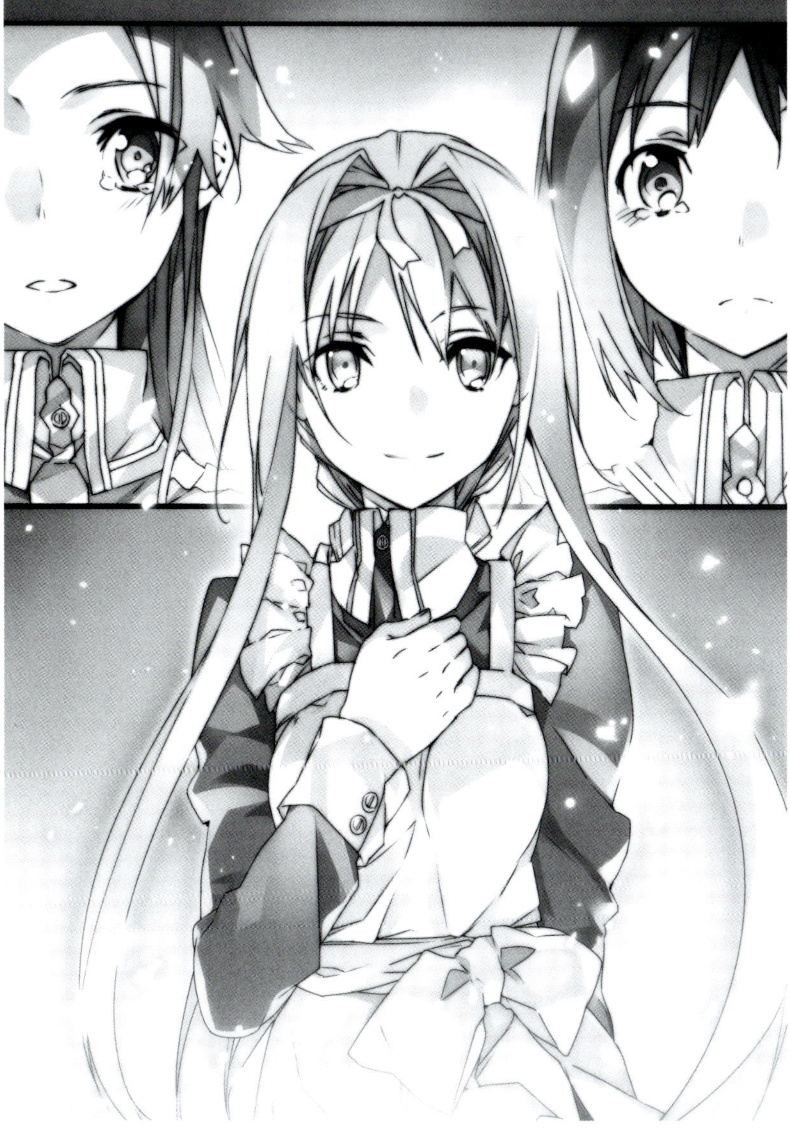

Dengeki Bunko
Sword Art Online 15: Alicization Invading
Illustration: August 2014

The scene where Alice changes how she looks and says, "Your body and appearance are entirely dependent on your heart," is one of my favorites.

SWORD ART ONLINE media mix 3

TV Animation, *Sword Art Online II*
Initial Key Visual: January 2014

This was the main visual we used to announce the second season of the anime, I think. I got really into it, and I like the way I handled the bullets in the background, and the general use of red.

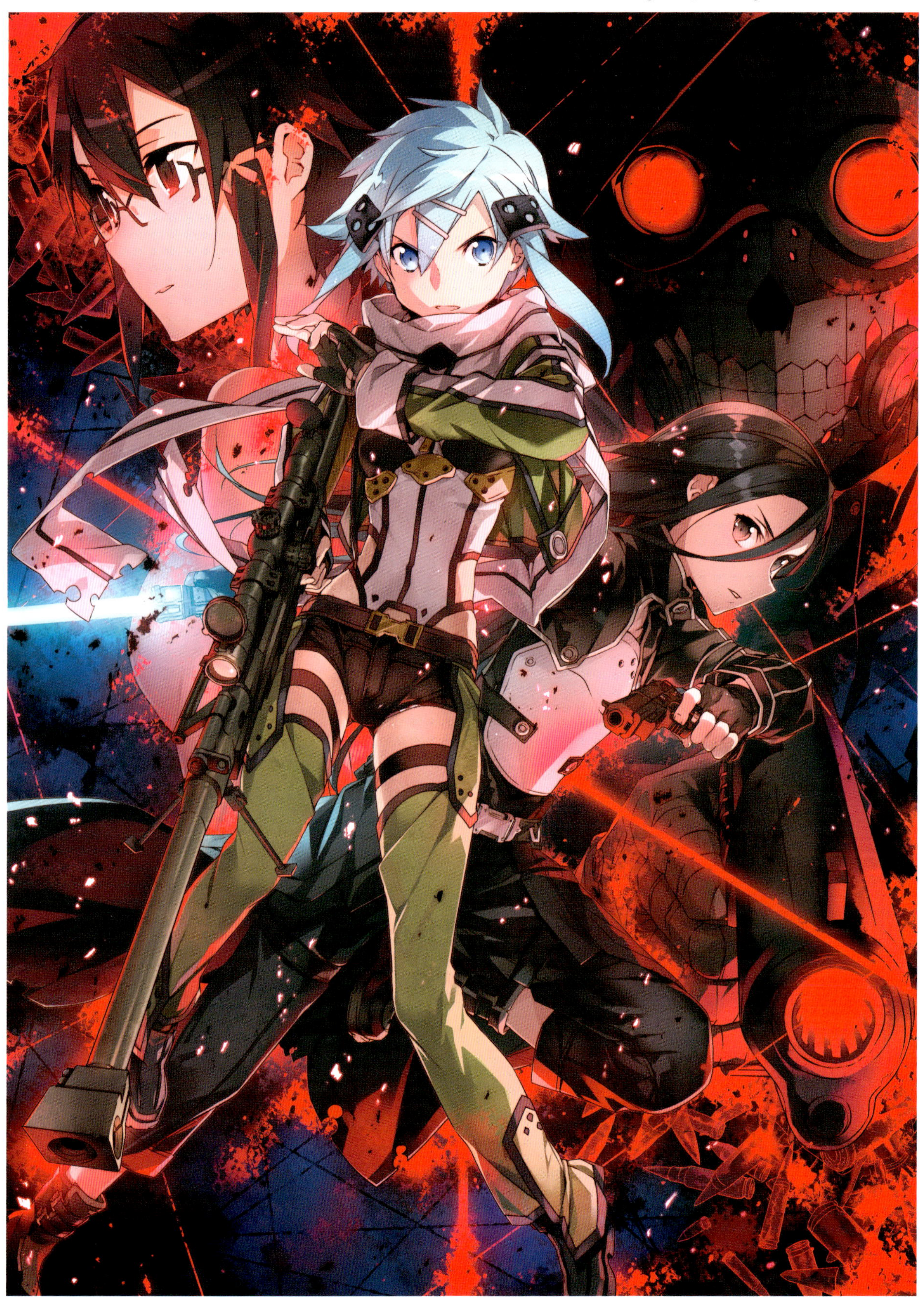

Mobile Game
Sword Art Online: Memory Defrag
Key Visual: August 2016

SAO has had a lot of games, but for the key visuals, they ask me to draw every character in full so they can be reused separately. It's a ton of work.

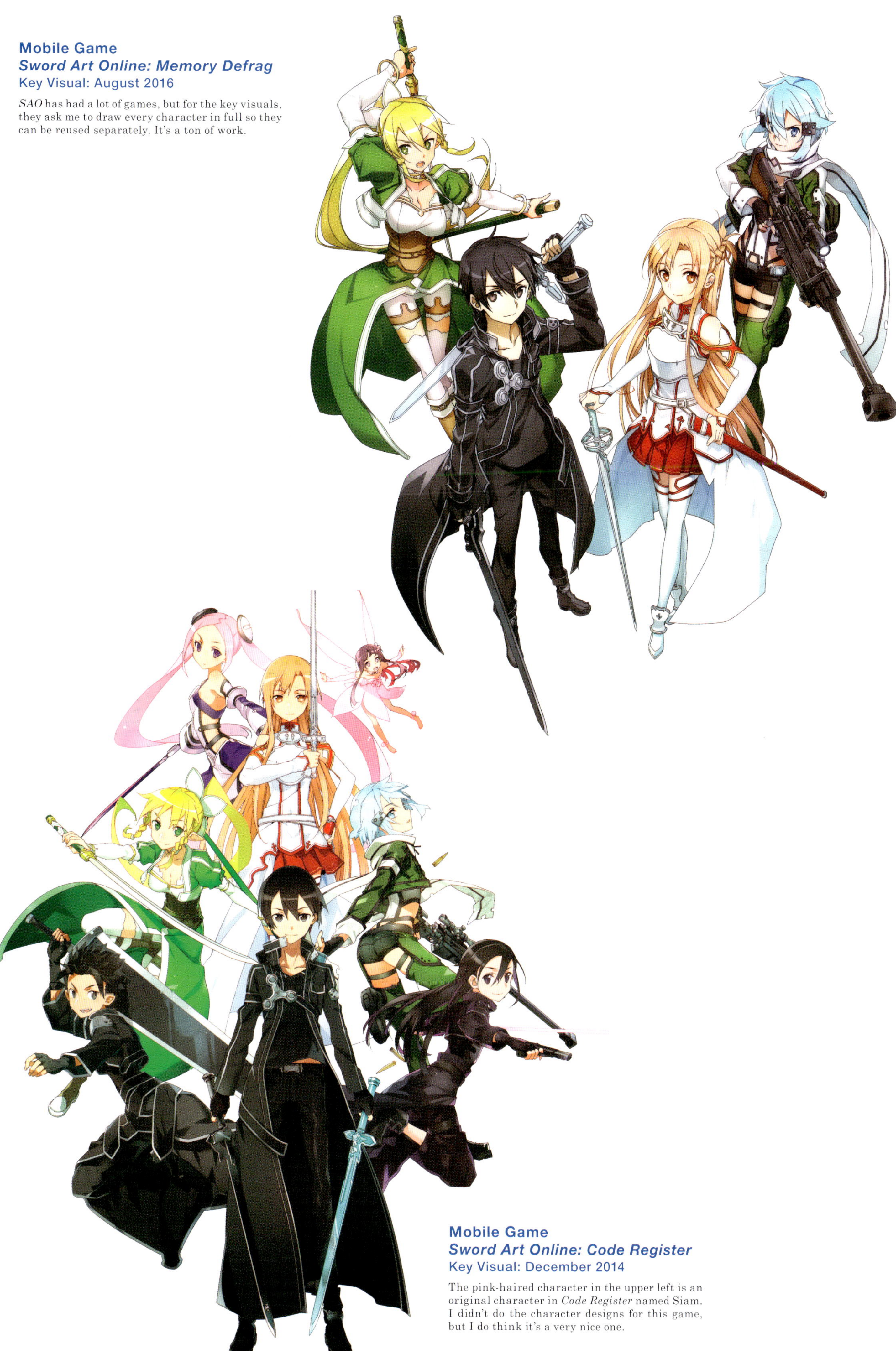

Mobile Game
Sword Art Online: Code Register
Key Visual: December 2014

The pink-haired character in the upper left is an original character in *Code Register* named Siam. I didn't do the character designs for this game, but I do think it's a very nice one.

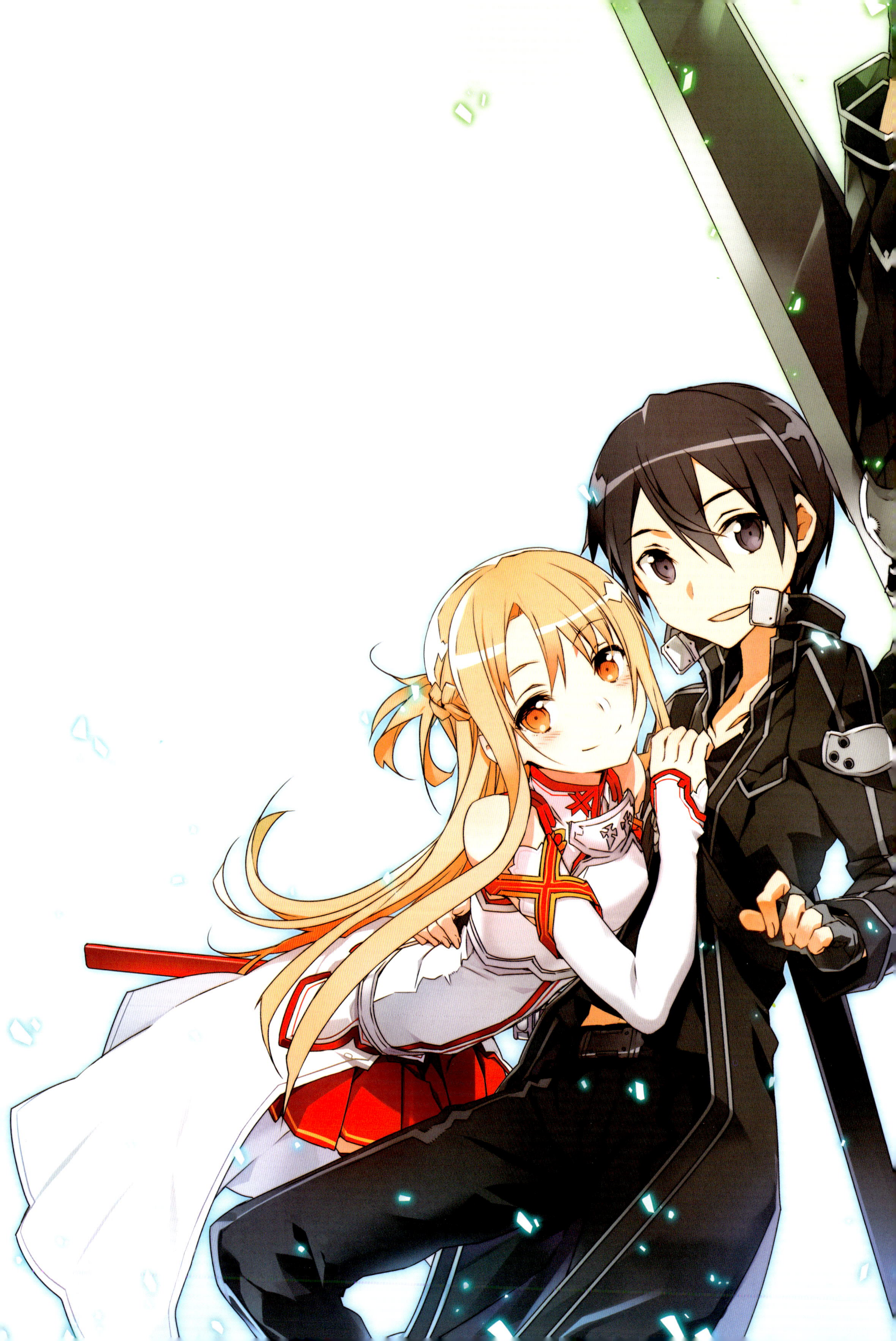

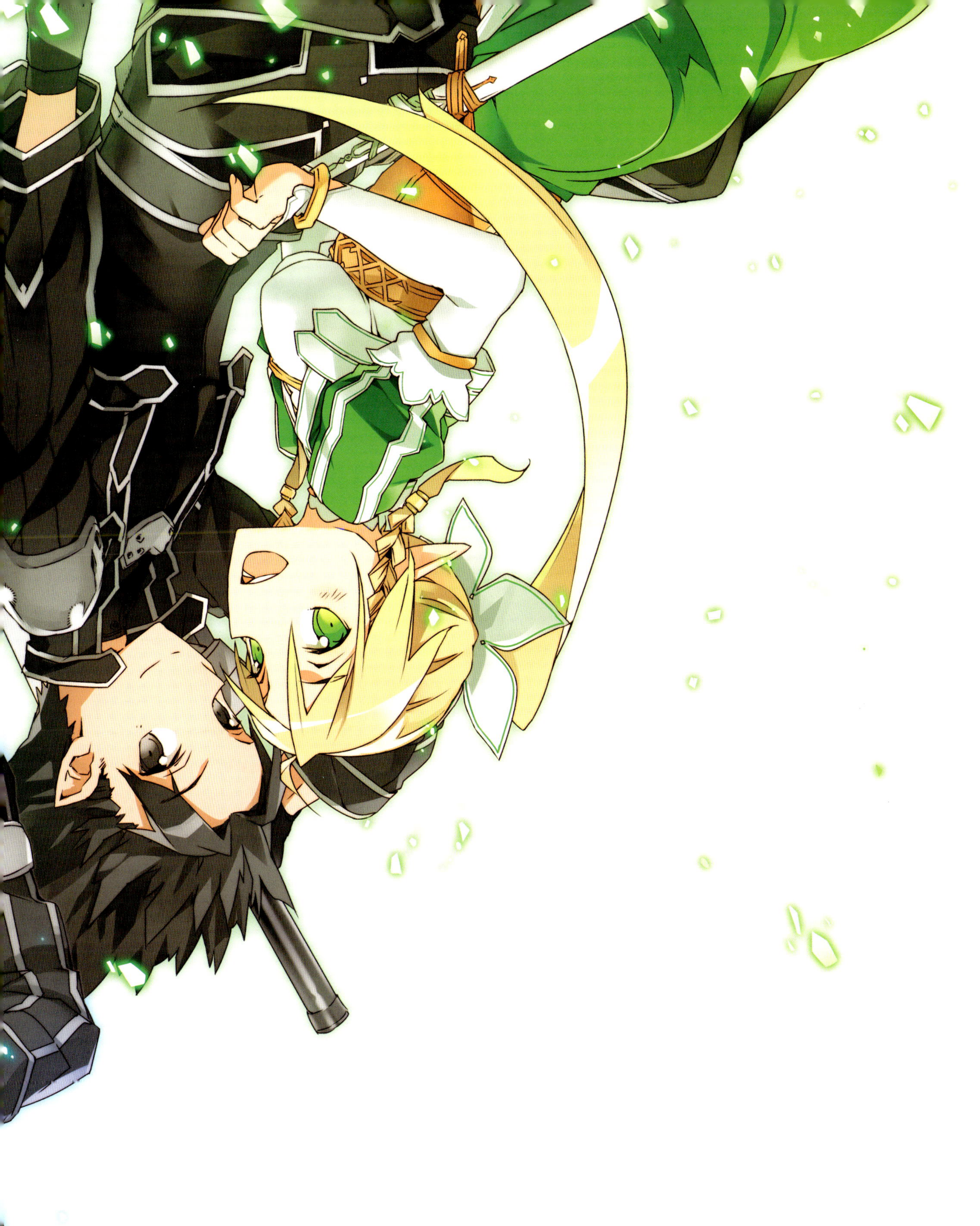

The Perfect Guide: Animation - Sword Art Online
Cover: June 2014

The official guidebook for the first season of the anime, which features quite a lot of animation designs, interviews, and such. For the cover, I drew Asuna, Kirito, and Leafa from the Aincrad and Fairy Dance arcs.

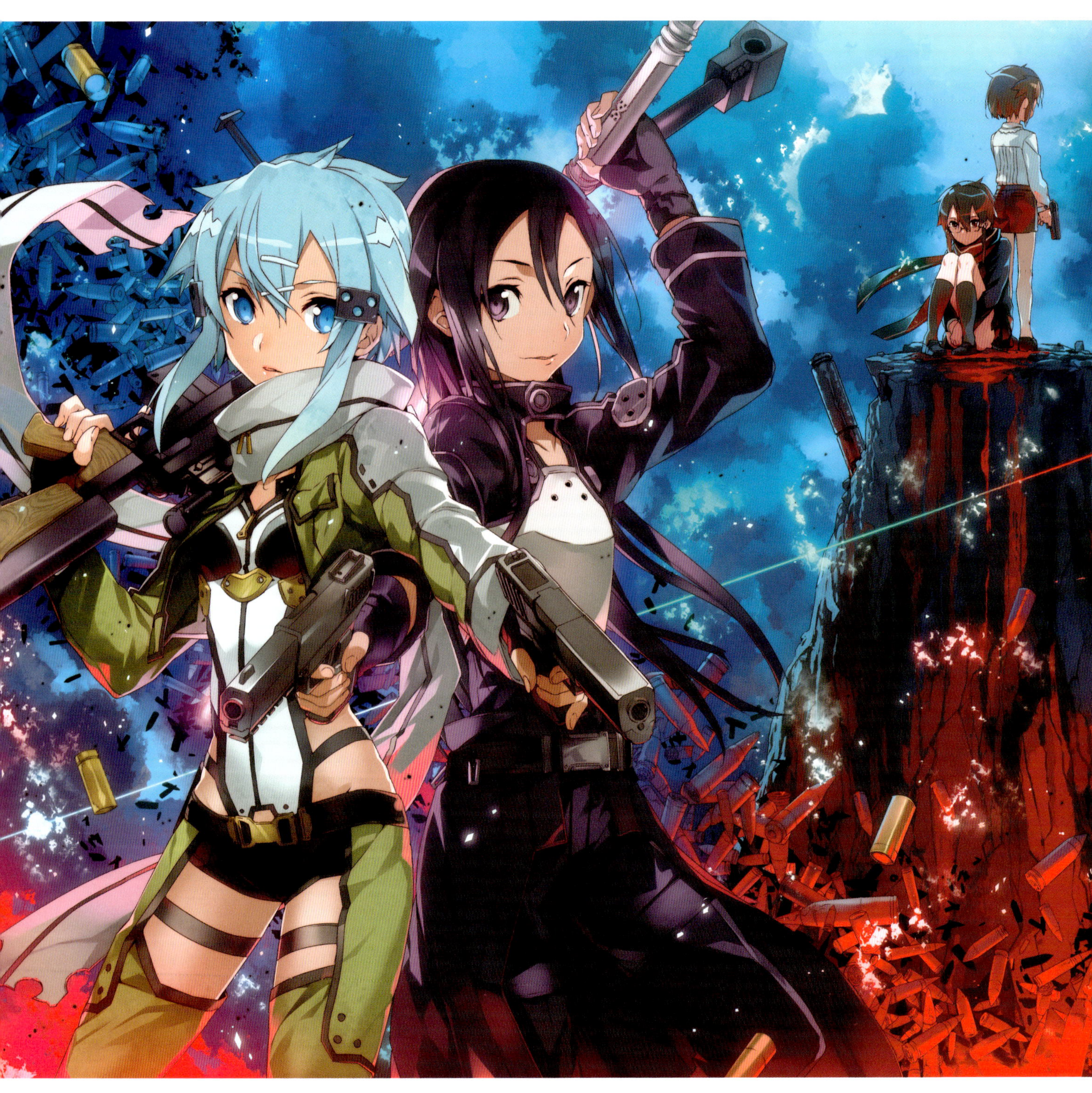

Alternate Sketches

Place logo and such here

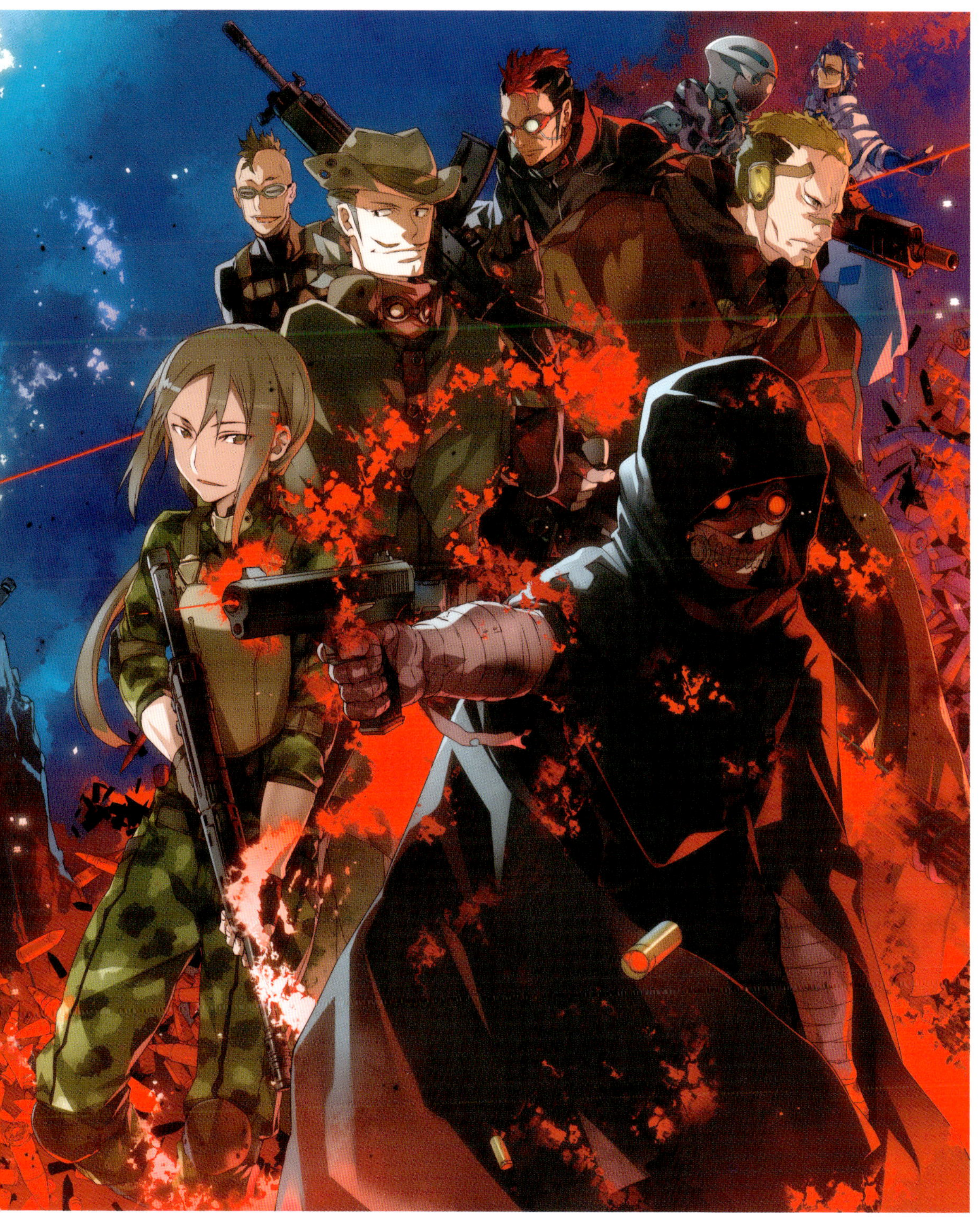

TV Animation, *Sword Art Online II* BD/DVD Vol. 1
Limited Edition "Phantom Bullet Arc" Box Illustration: October 2014

I wanted Shino in the center to be the only real-life person on the cover, so when you just put the avatars, it makes you think, "Hang on, the Gun Gale arc has fewer characters than I realized." In the end, I included a bunch of very minor characters.

TV Animation *Sword Art Online II* Second Cour OP Song: Haruka Tomatsu—"courage"
Limited Edition Jacket Illustration: December 2014

This illustration was for a CD jacket. Aided by Yuuki's popularity, it was very well received. I spent so much time looking at the right side that I completely forgot about Asuna looking away on the left.

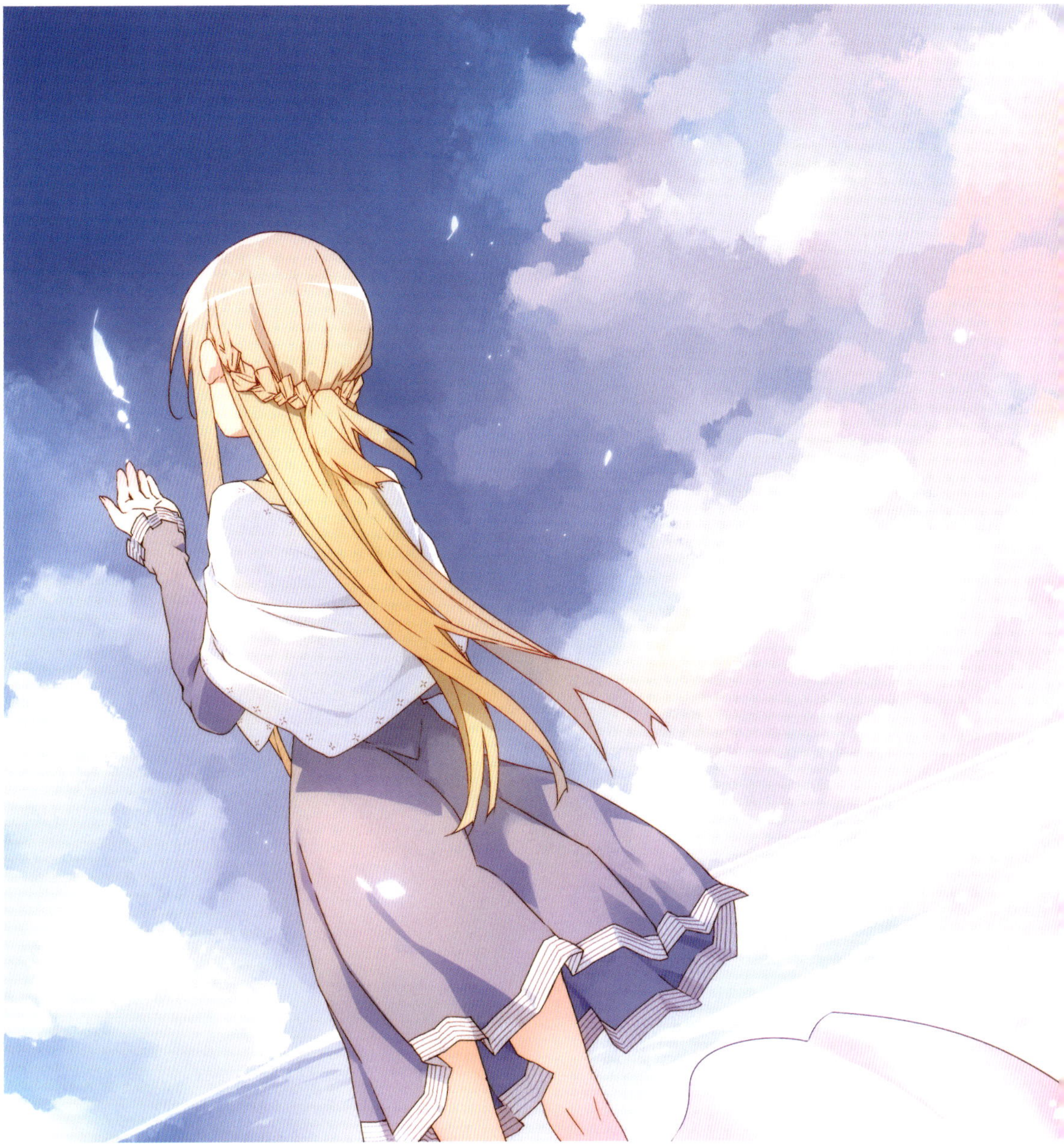

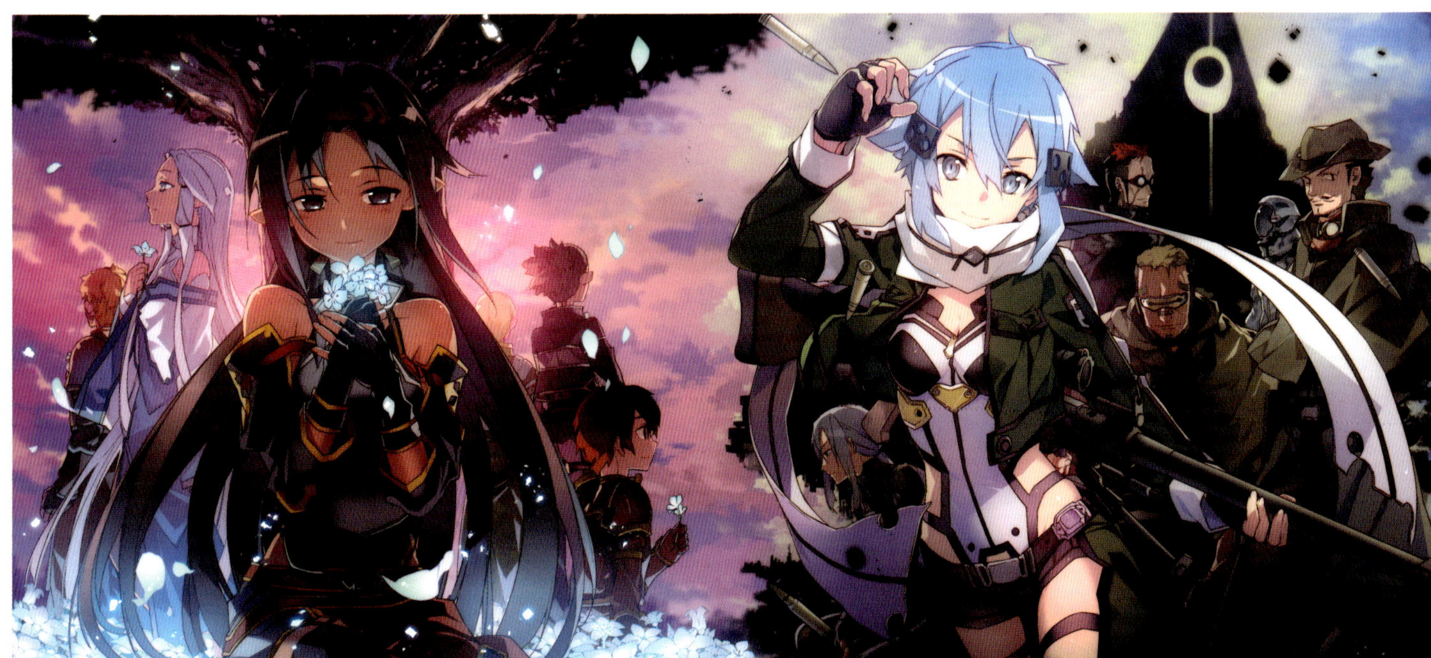

TV Animation Soundtrack, *Sword Art Online Music Collection*
Jacket Illustration: January 2016

This was a four-disc soundtrack for the anime. The illustration splits into four between the Aincrad, Fairy Dance, Phantom Bullet, and Mother's Rosary arcs, with the hope that you'd think about each of them as you go back and listen. Personally, I think it might be one of the best things I've ever drawn.

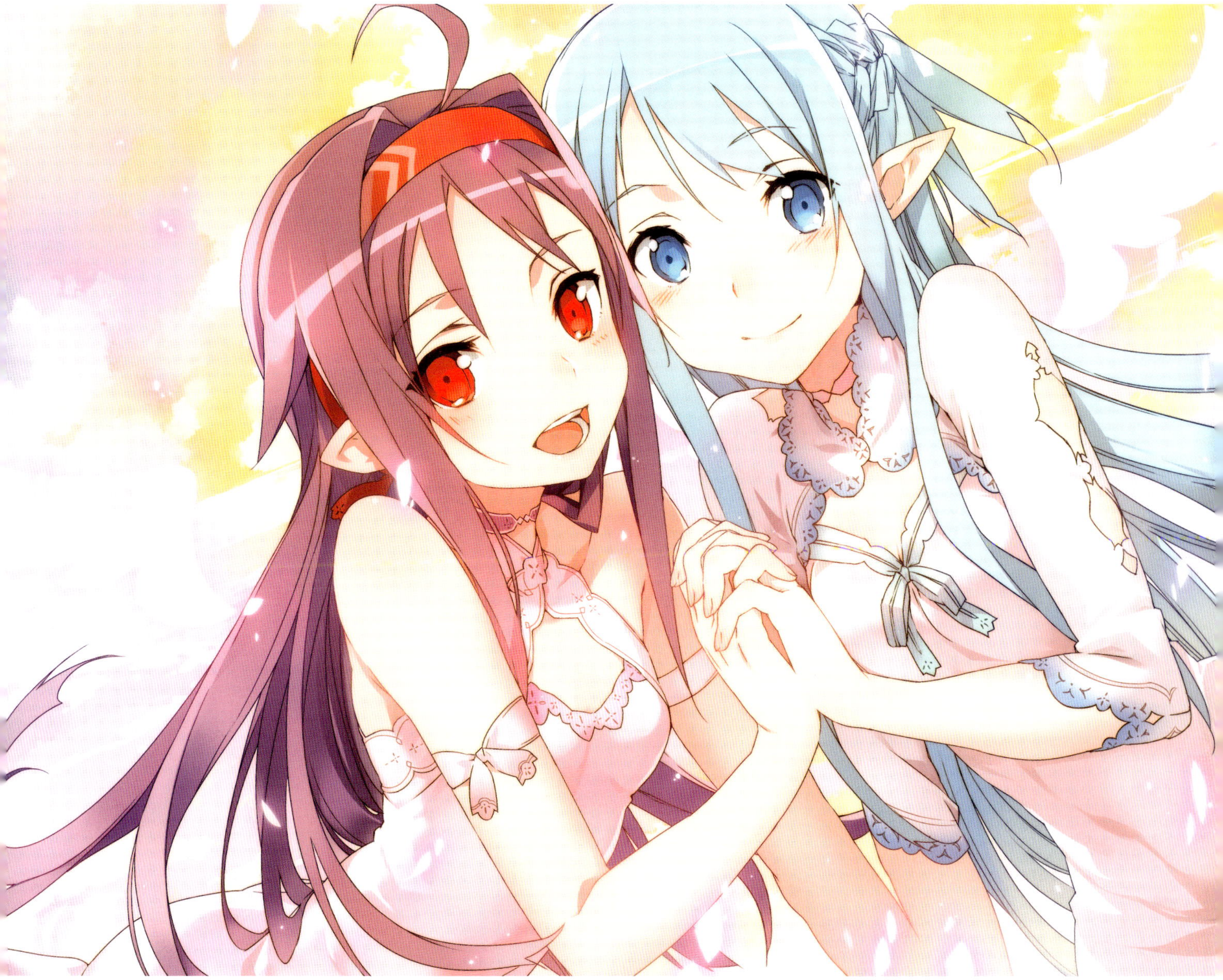

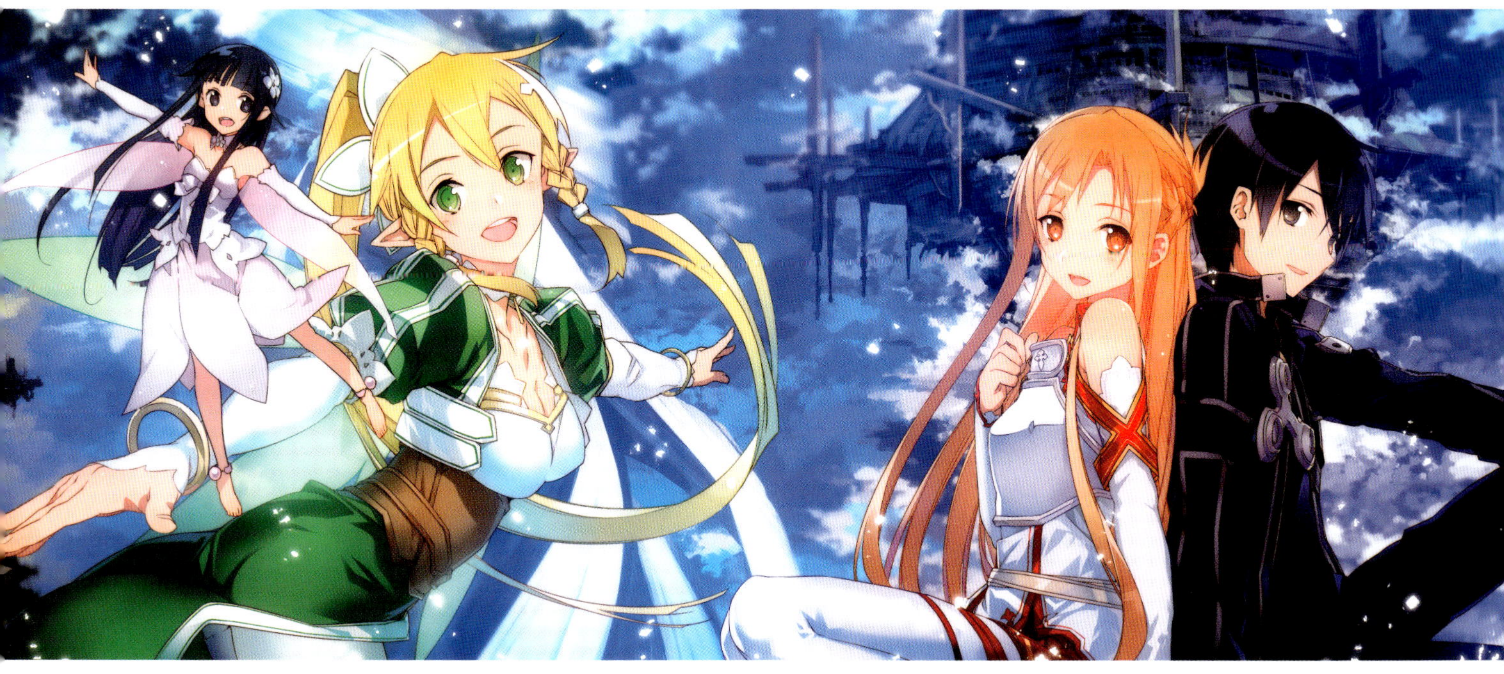

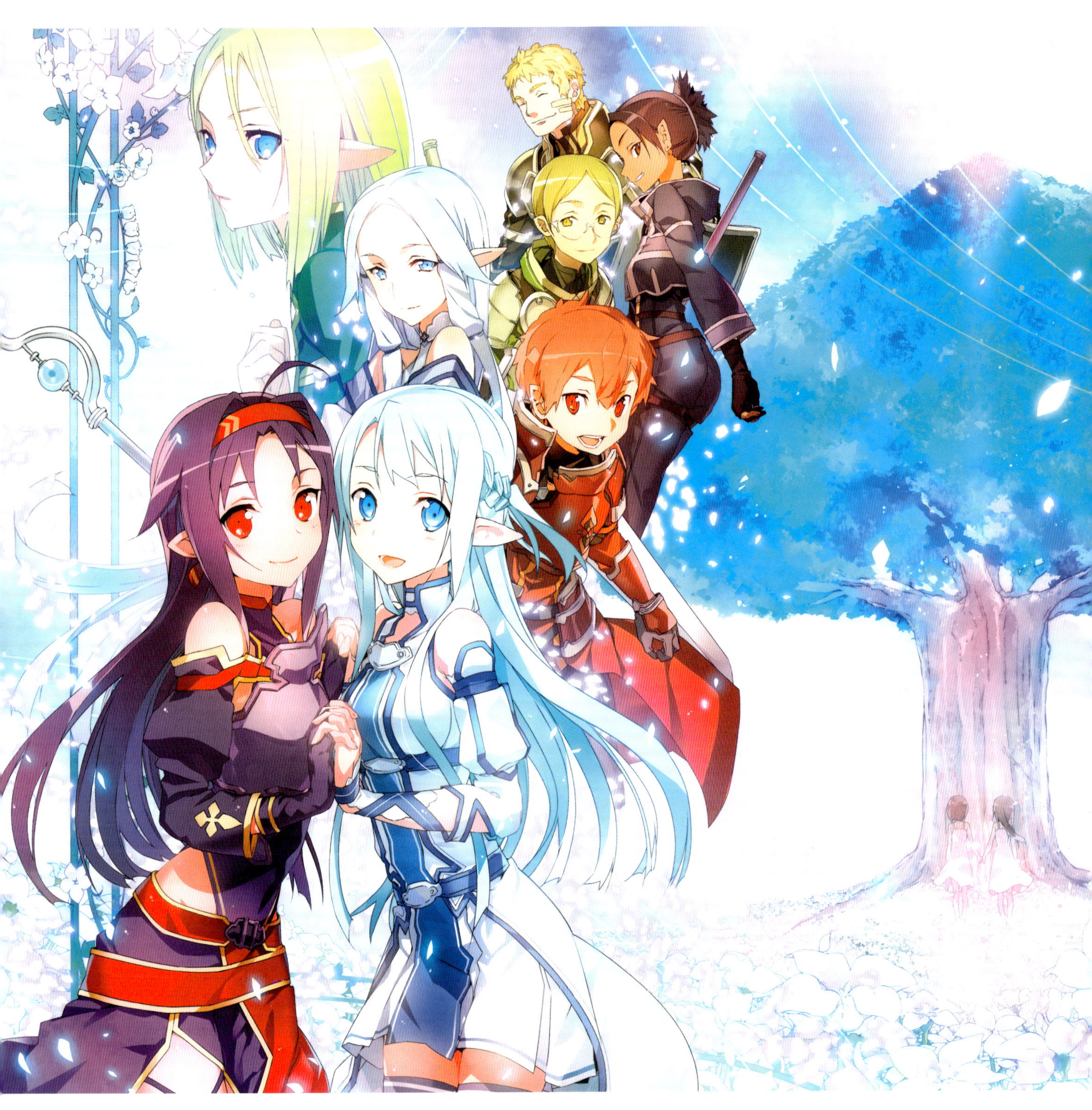

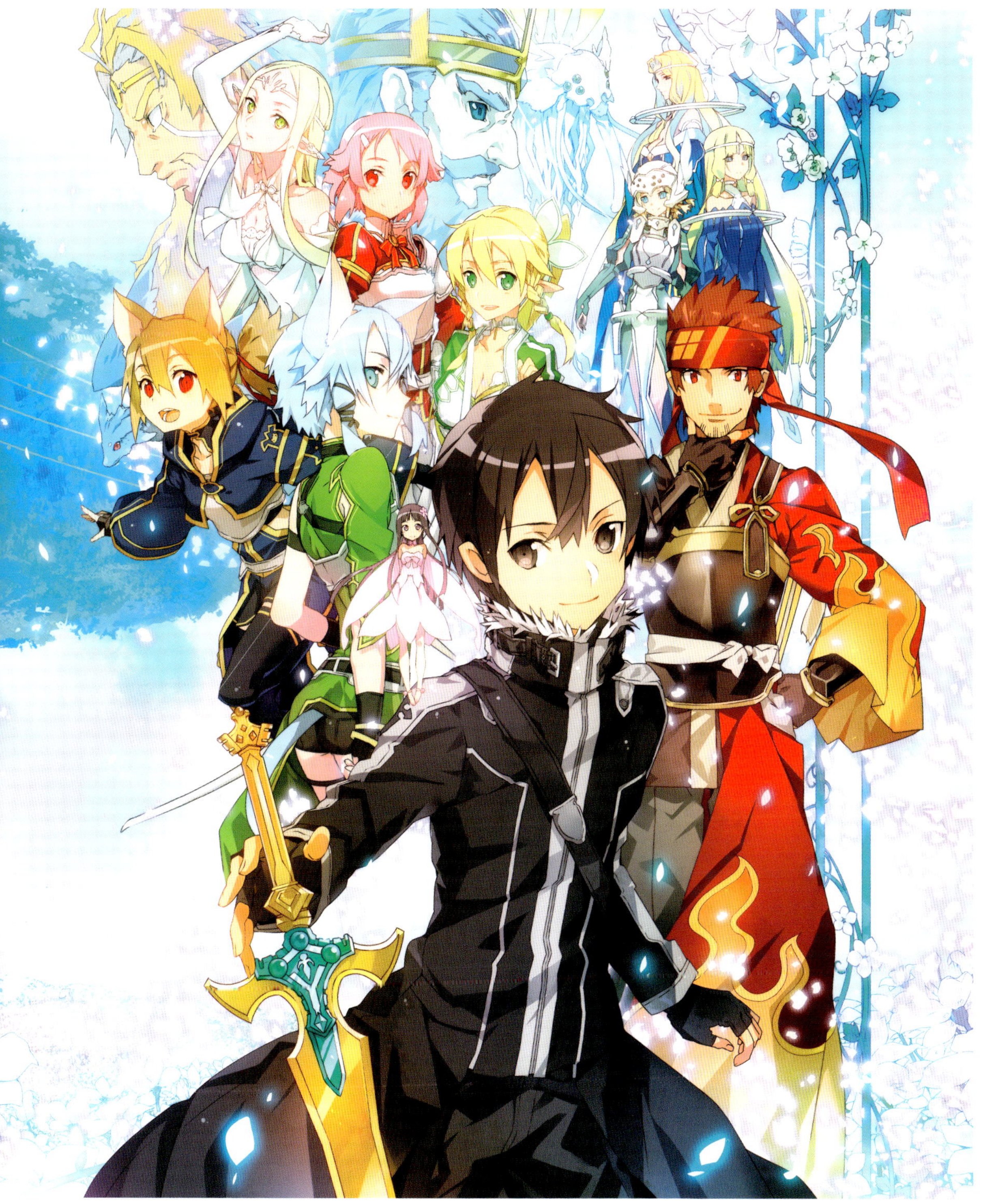

TV Animation, *Sword Art Online II* BD/DVD Vol. 6
Limited Edition "Calibur & Mother's Rosary Arc" Box Illustration: March 2015

The box illustration for the second half of the second season, covering the Calibur and Mother's Rosary arcs. A rather pastel-colored piece for the box set that mostly covers Mother's Rosary.

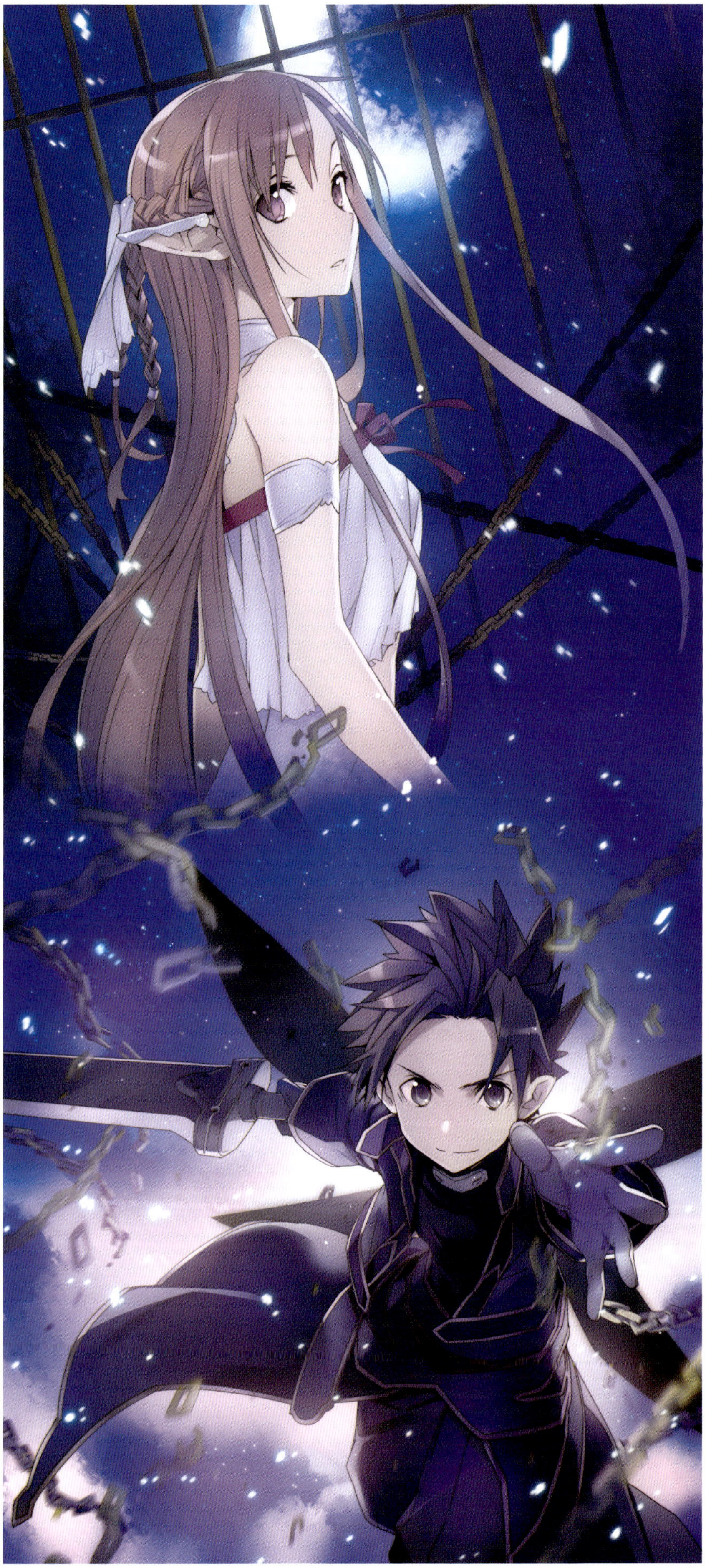

TV Animation, *Sword Art Online* Second Cour OP Song: Eir Aoi—"INNOCENCE"

Limited Edition Jacket Illustration: November 2012

Another CD cover. This one needed to work as two separate illustrations when folded, and one connected illustration when straightened out. It was very hard.

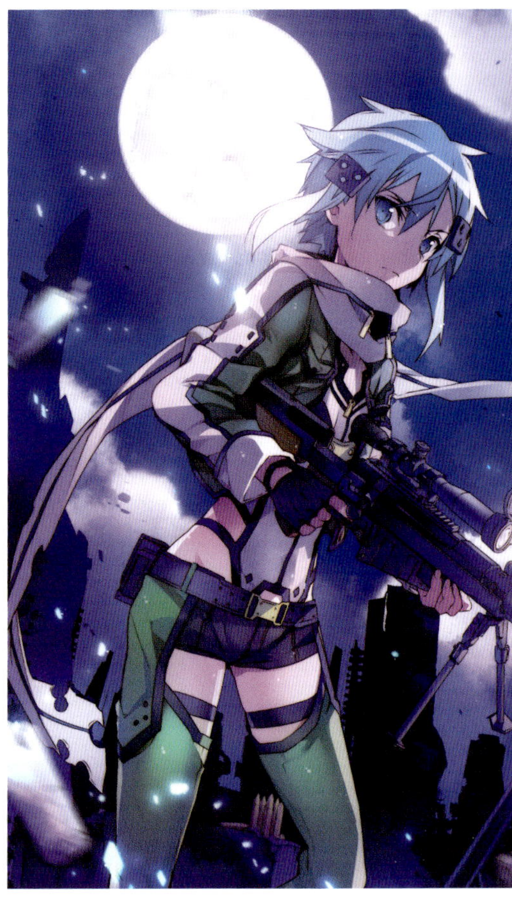

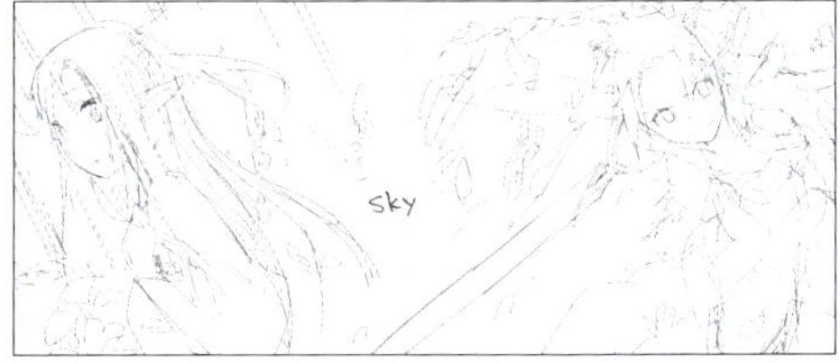

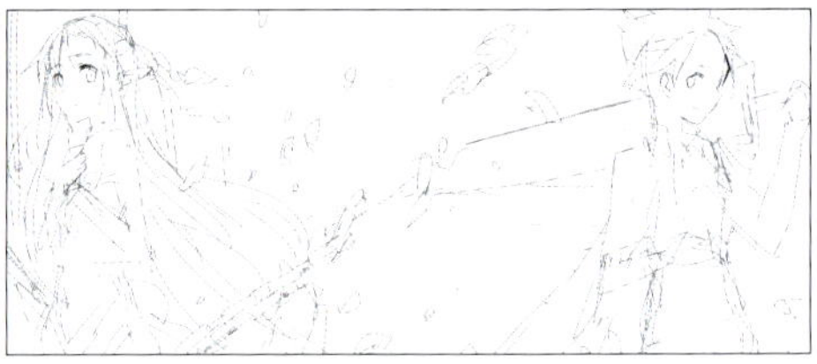

Alternate Sketches

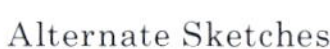

Alternate Sketches

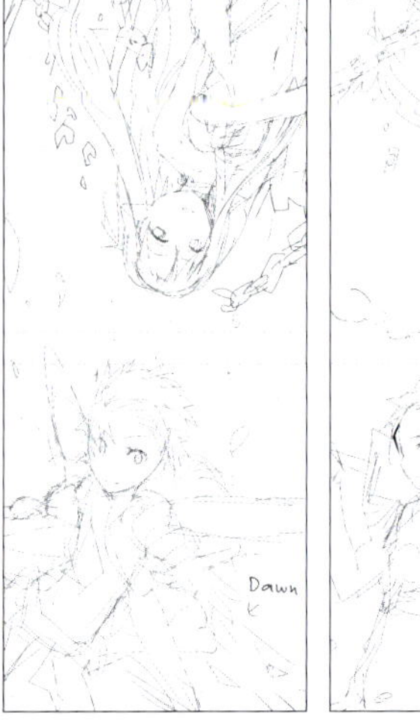

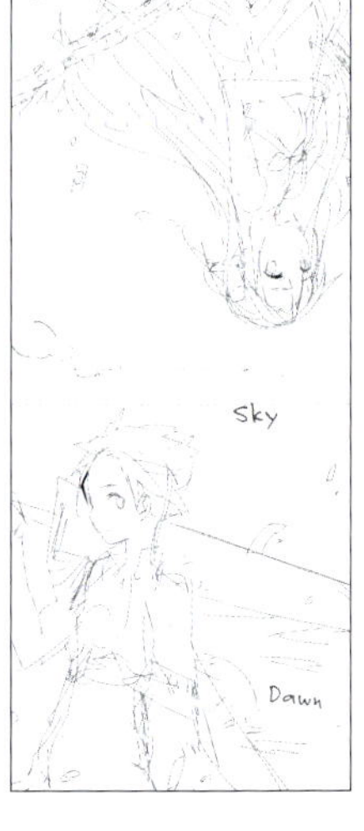

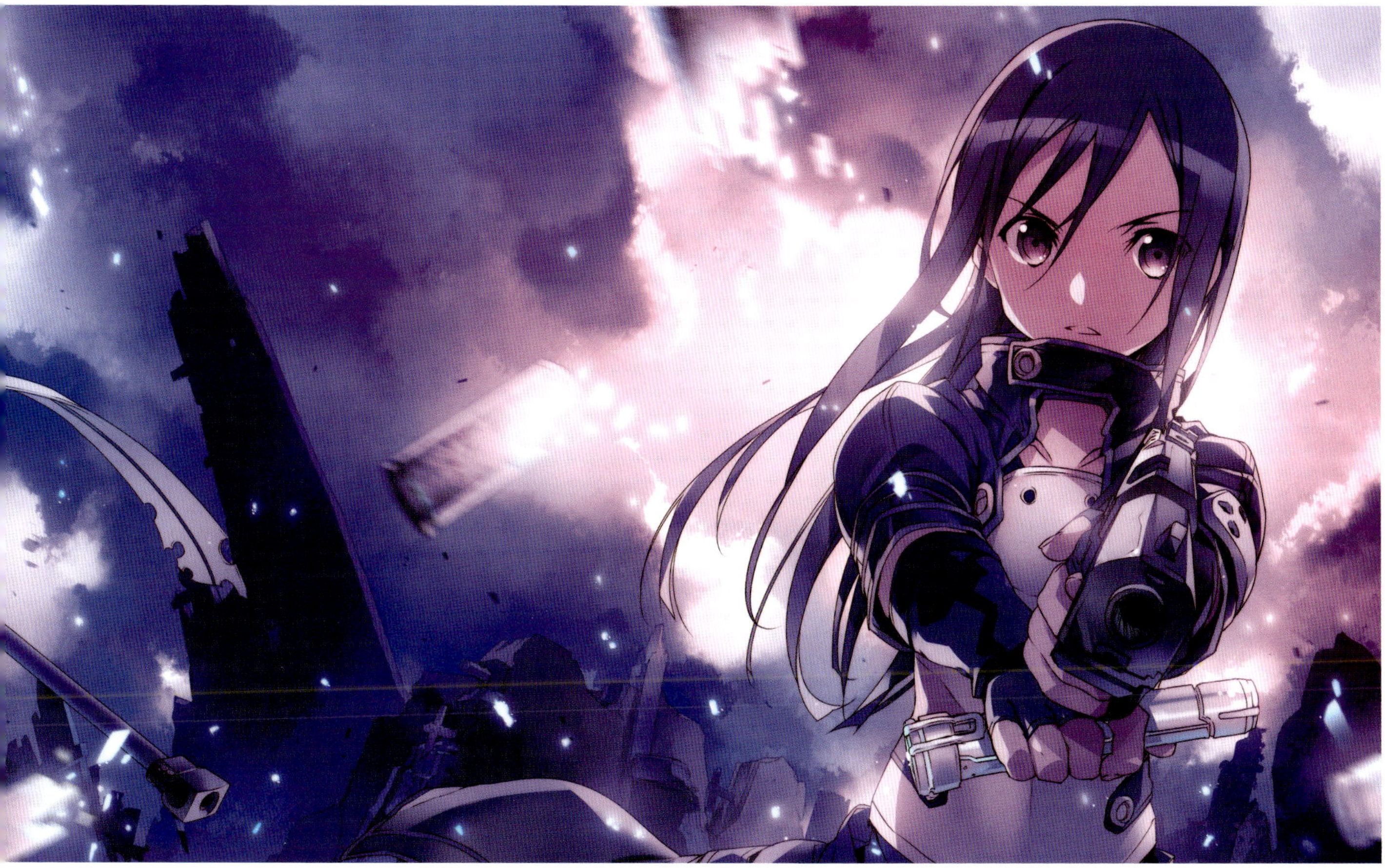

TV Animation, *Sword Art Online* First Cour OP Song: Eir Aoi—"IGNITE"

Limited Edition Jacket Illustration: August 2014

Another CD cover. The layout and color choice was meant to be similar to the jacket illustration on the previous page. My memory isn't entirely clear on whether or not it was because they were both Eir Aoi songs, or because her voice prompted me to go for this. I wonder why I did it.

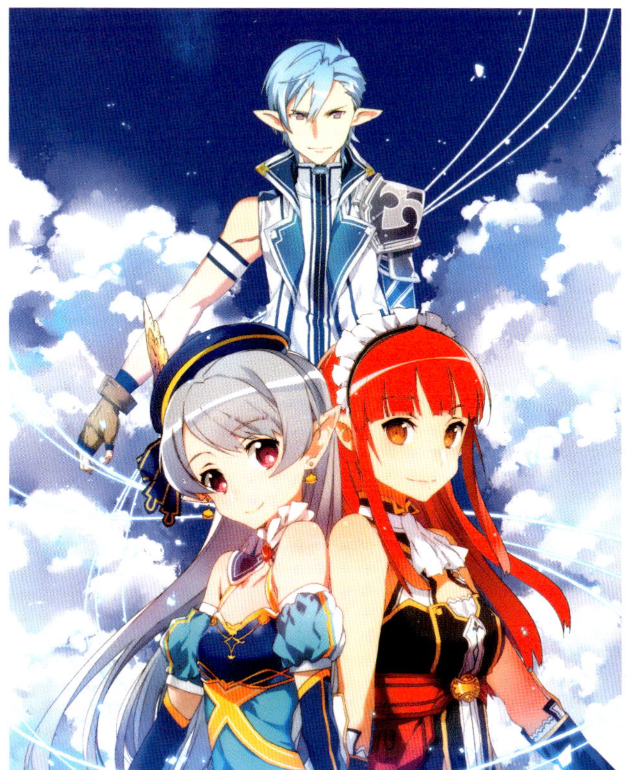

PS3/PS Vita Game
Sword Art Online: Lost Song
Limited Edition Box Rear Illustration: March 2015

I recall that the lines of light were meant to evoke the image of a musical staff. The games tend to have a lot of very delicately-designed characters, which makes them hard to draw.

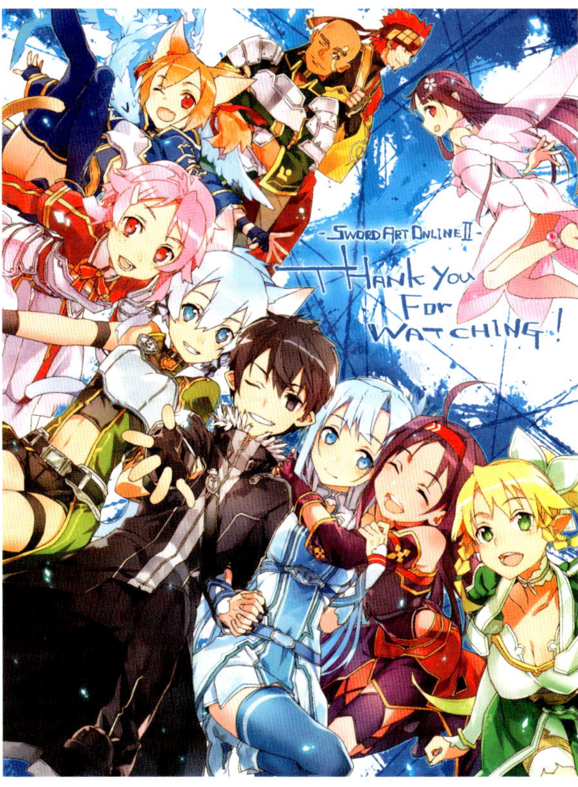

TV Animation
Sword Art Online II BD/DVD
Full Series Purchase Bonus Artwork: May 2015

I remember the instructions for this one were "all the main characters from Season 2 together." Naturally, the more characters there are, the more work it is to draw them all, so I definitely had a moment of "Where do you draw the line for 'main' characters?!"

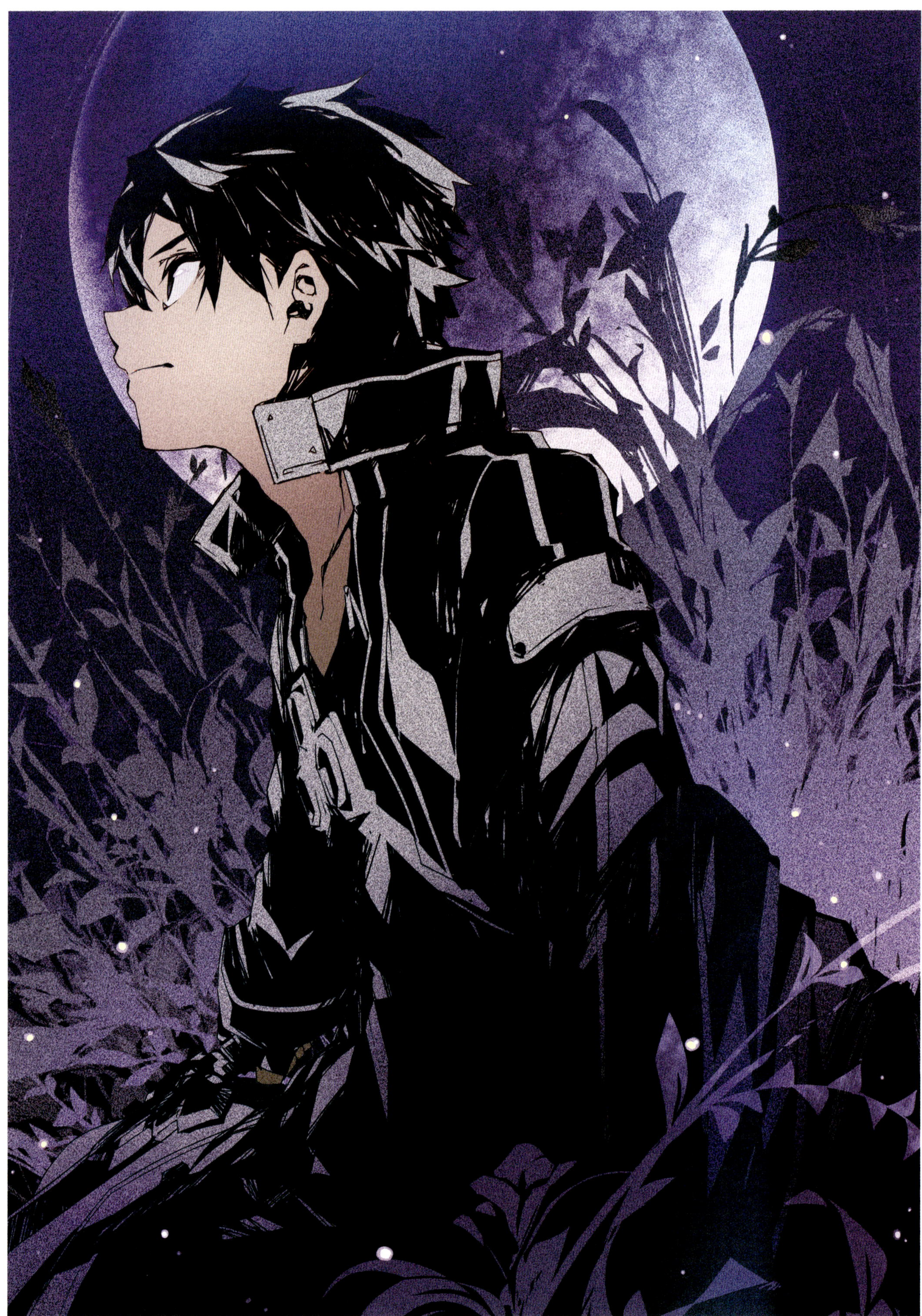

Never Commercially Published

A new illustration. It was a doodle I did with a red base that I ended up finishing with a field at night for the background. Based on where this was going in the book, I wish I'd stuck with the red color!

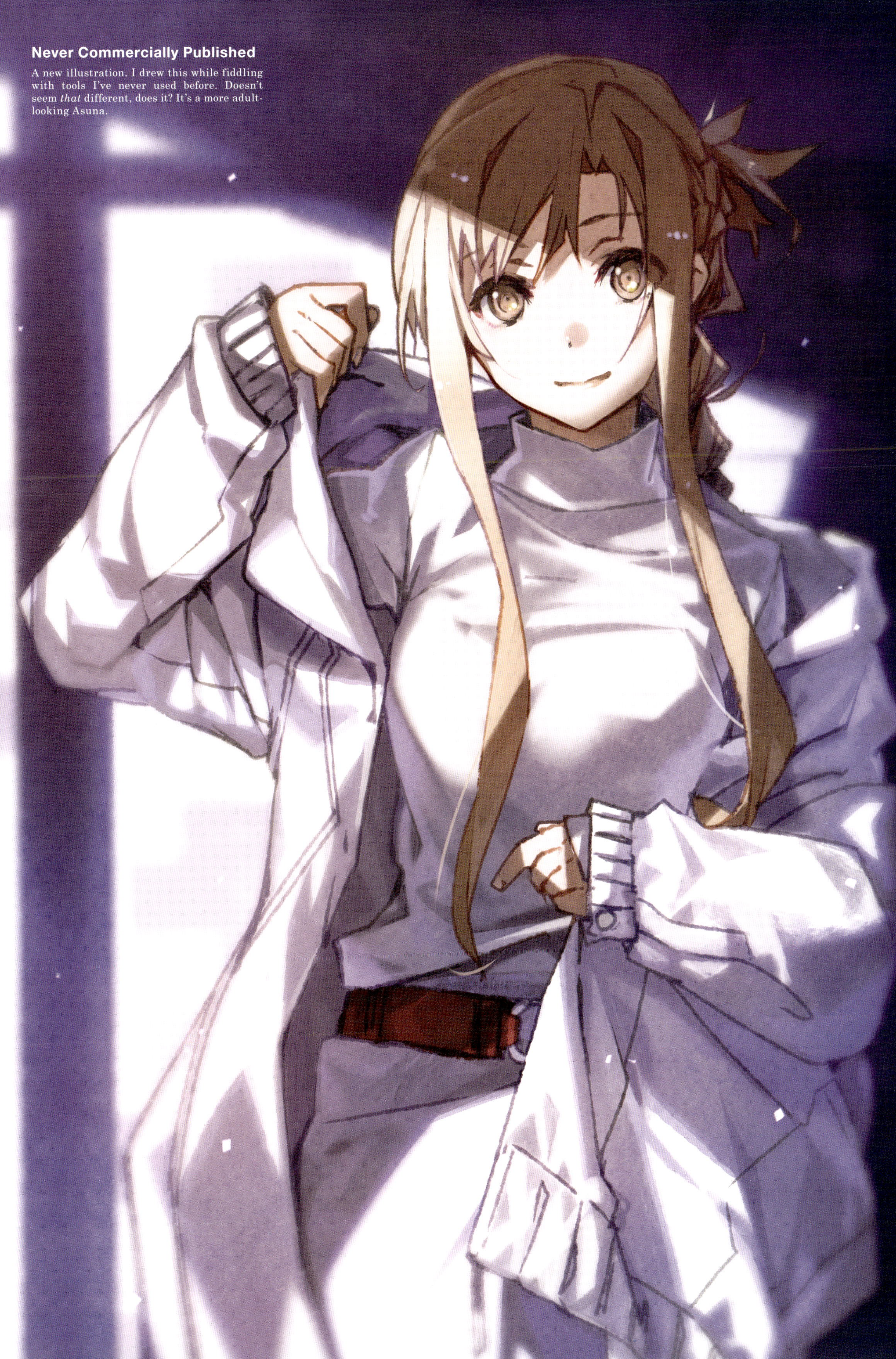

Never Commercially Published

A new illustration. I drew this while fiddling with tools I've never used before. Doesn't seem *that* different, does it? It's a more adult-looking Asuna.

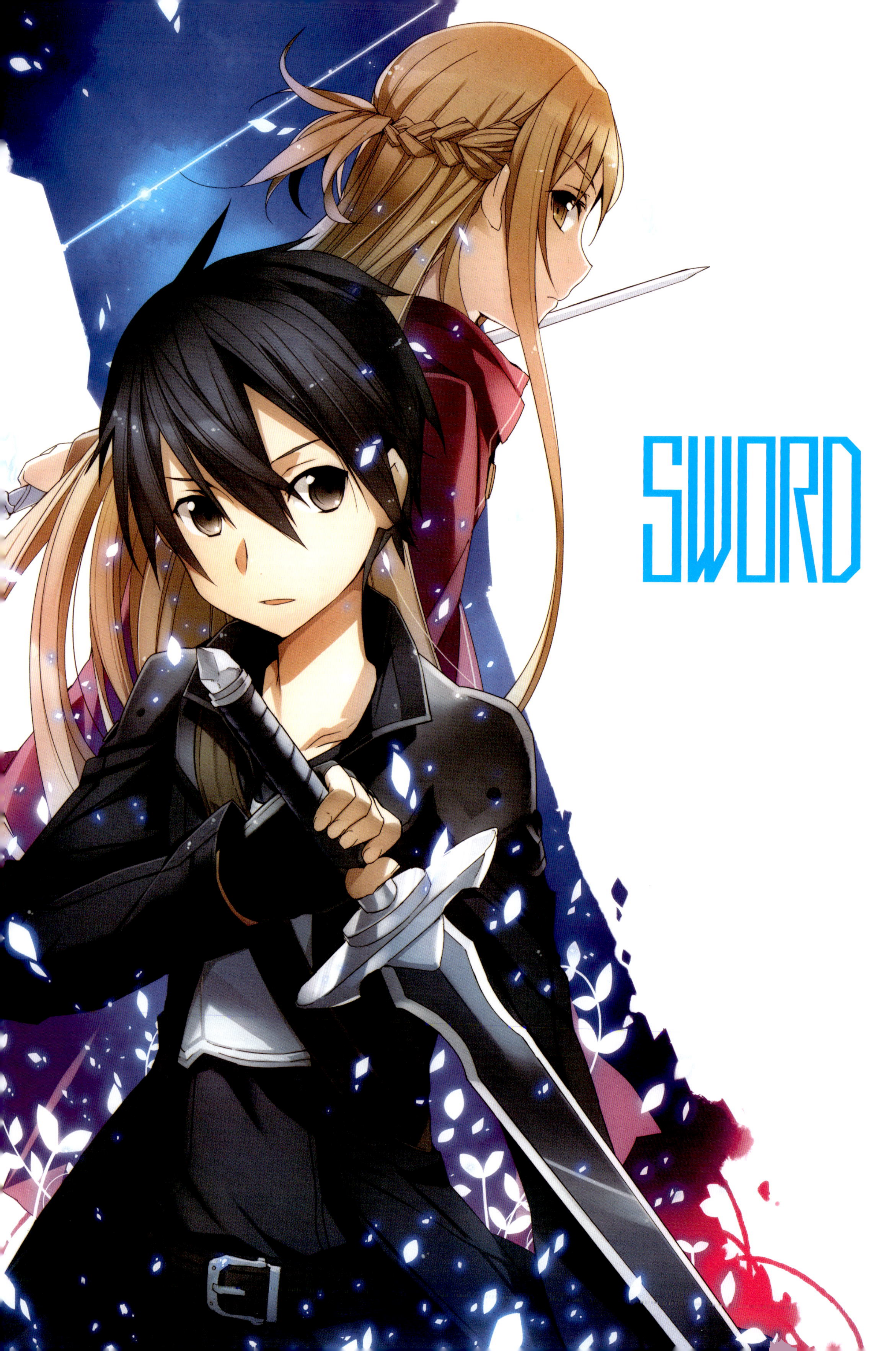
SWORD

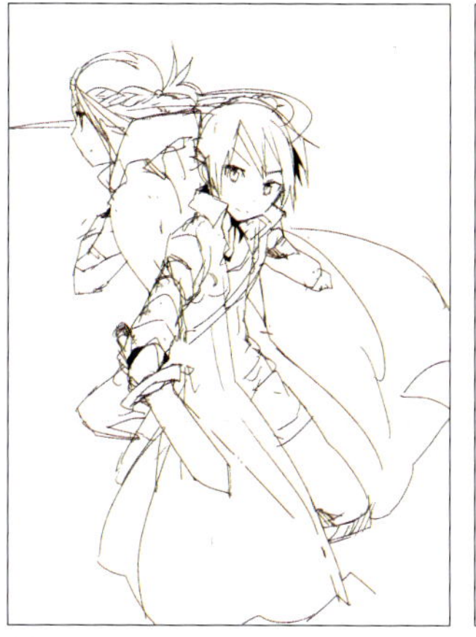
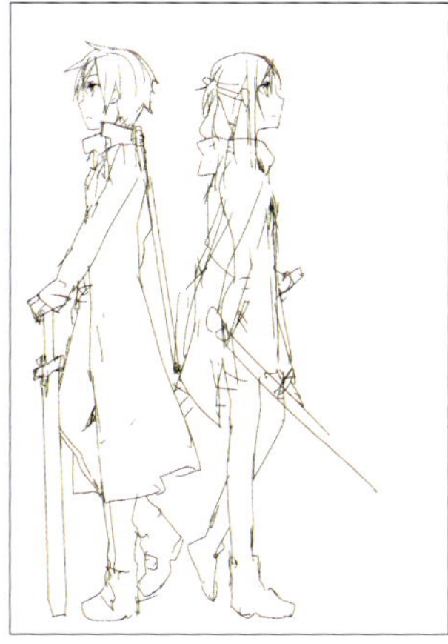
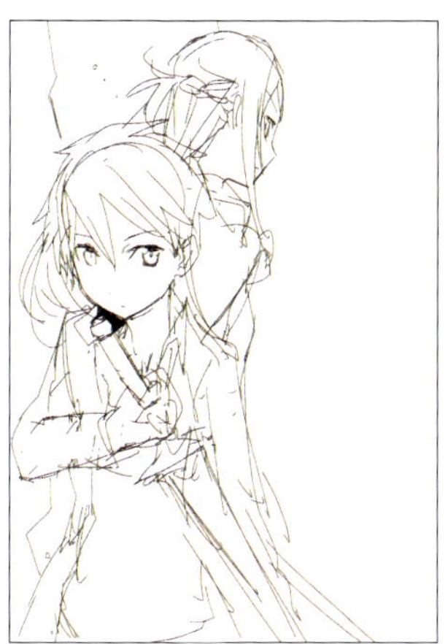

Alternate Cover Sketches

Dengeki Bunko
Sword Art Online Progressive 1
Cover: October 2012

The first volume cover of a new series forms the basis for everything after that, so it's common to have a number of variations.

001 ART ONLINE PROGRESSIVE

The Progressive series covers the entire story of Aincrad that got skipped over, one floor at a time. Will it actually finish while Kawahara-sensei and I are still alive...? The moment I heard about this series starting, I was certain that *SAO* was going to be my life's work. Hopefully I'll get to illustrate it all the way to the end!

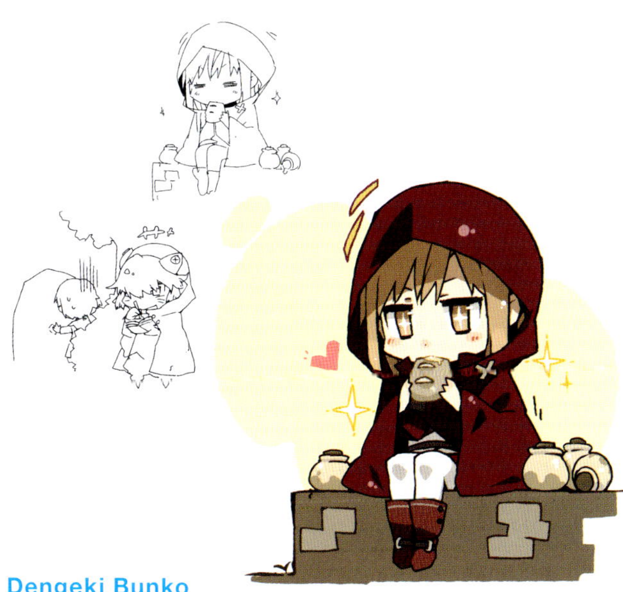

Dengeki Bunko
Sword Art Online Progressive 1
Back Cover: October 2012

Asuna eating bread with cream. A valuable slice of her thornier days.

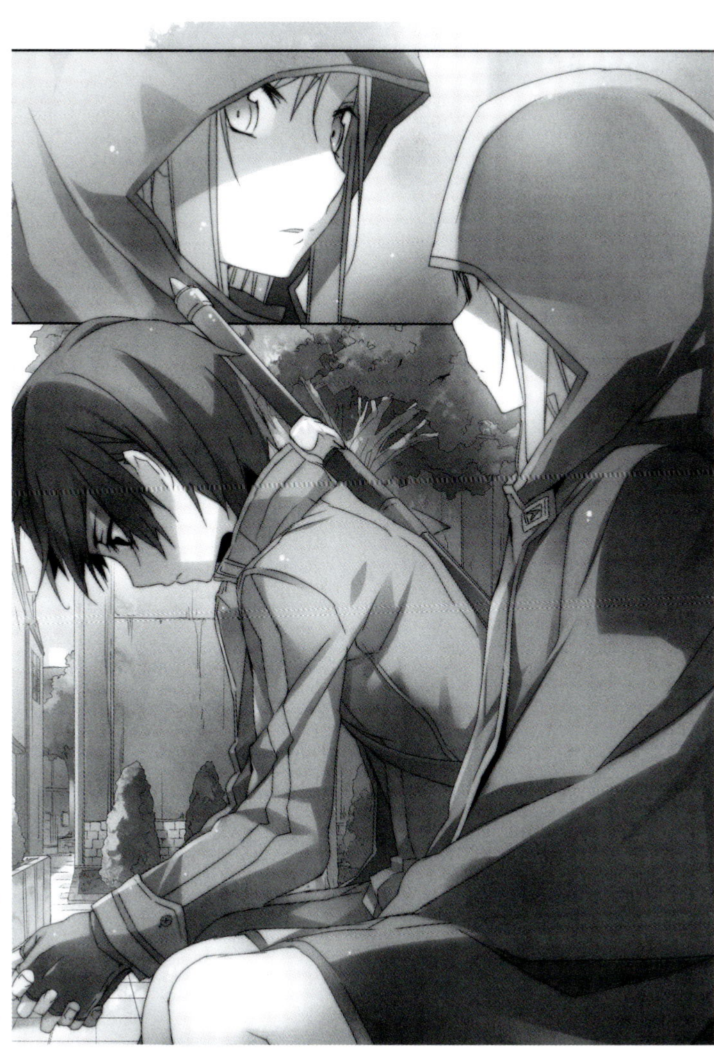

Dengeki Bunko
Sword Art Online Progressive 1
Illustration: October 2012

It's tough to capture starter equipment in art. If you try to make it look too good, it'll make it harder to design things later, but if you make them too simple, the picture looks weak.

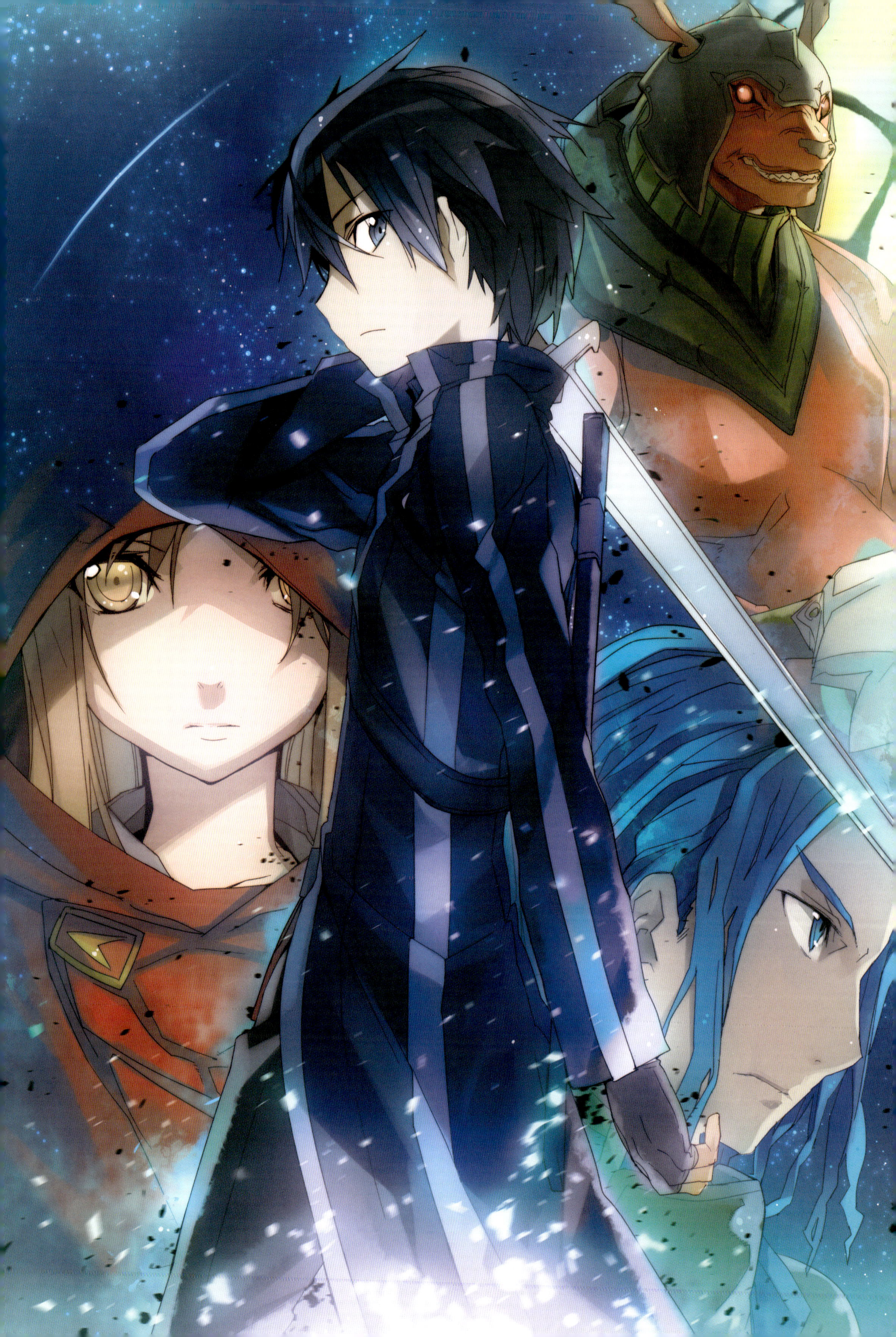

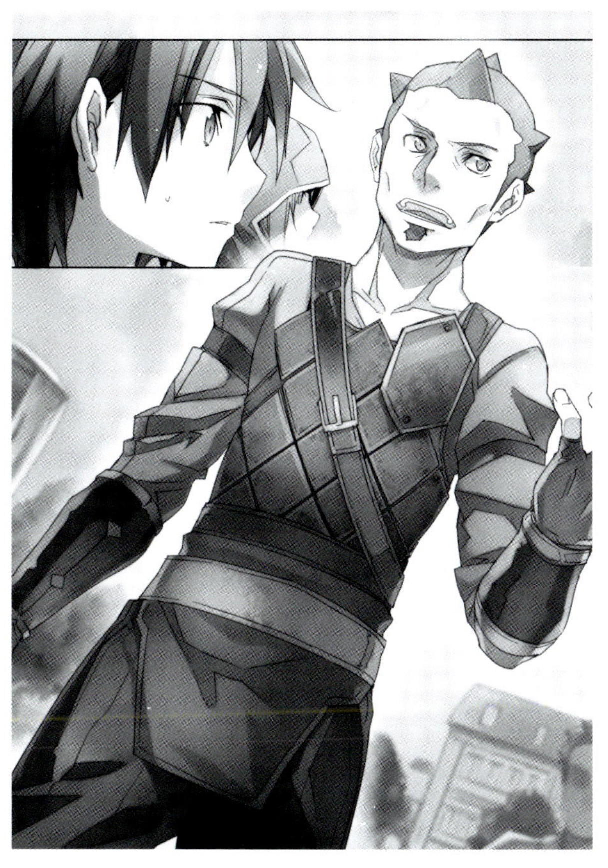

Dengeki Bunko
Sword Art Online
Progressive 1
Illustration: October 2012

Asuna in the bath. When I draw bathing and pool scenes, I typically sketch out the body below the water, then erase details as I do the water effects. It's a pretty annoying process.

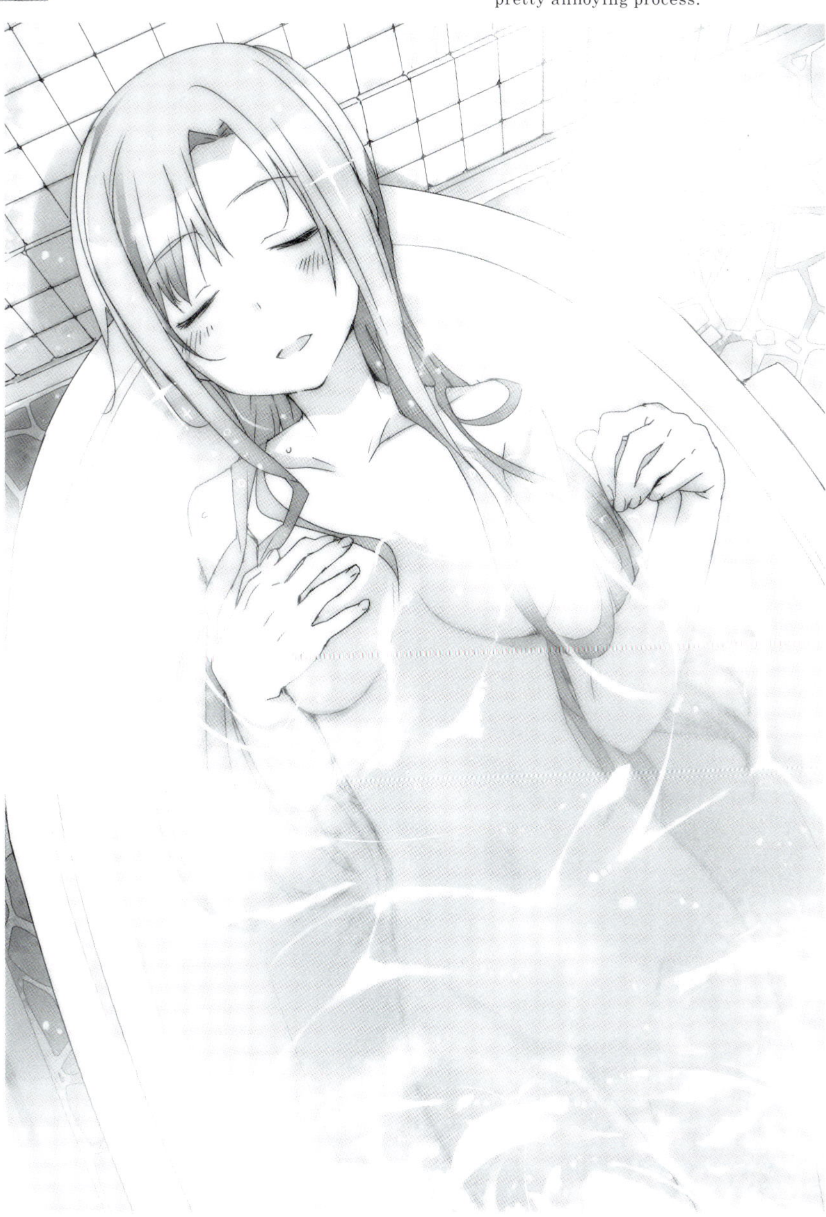

Dengeki Bunko
Sword Art Online
Progressive 1
Frontispiece: October 2012

The part of "Aria of a Starless Night" that was written as an original story for Episode 2 of the anime had already been serialized in the anime magazine, so this isn't really presented as a scene from the story, it's more of a general vibe for the book. Similar to the cover.

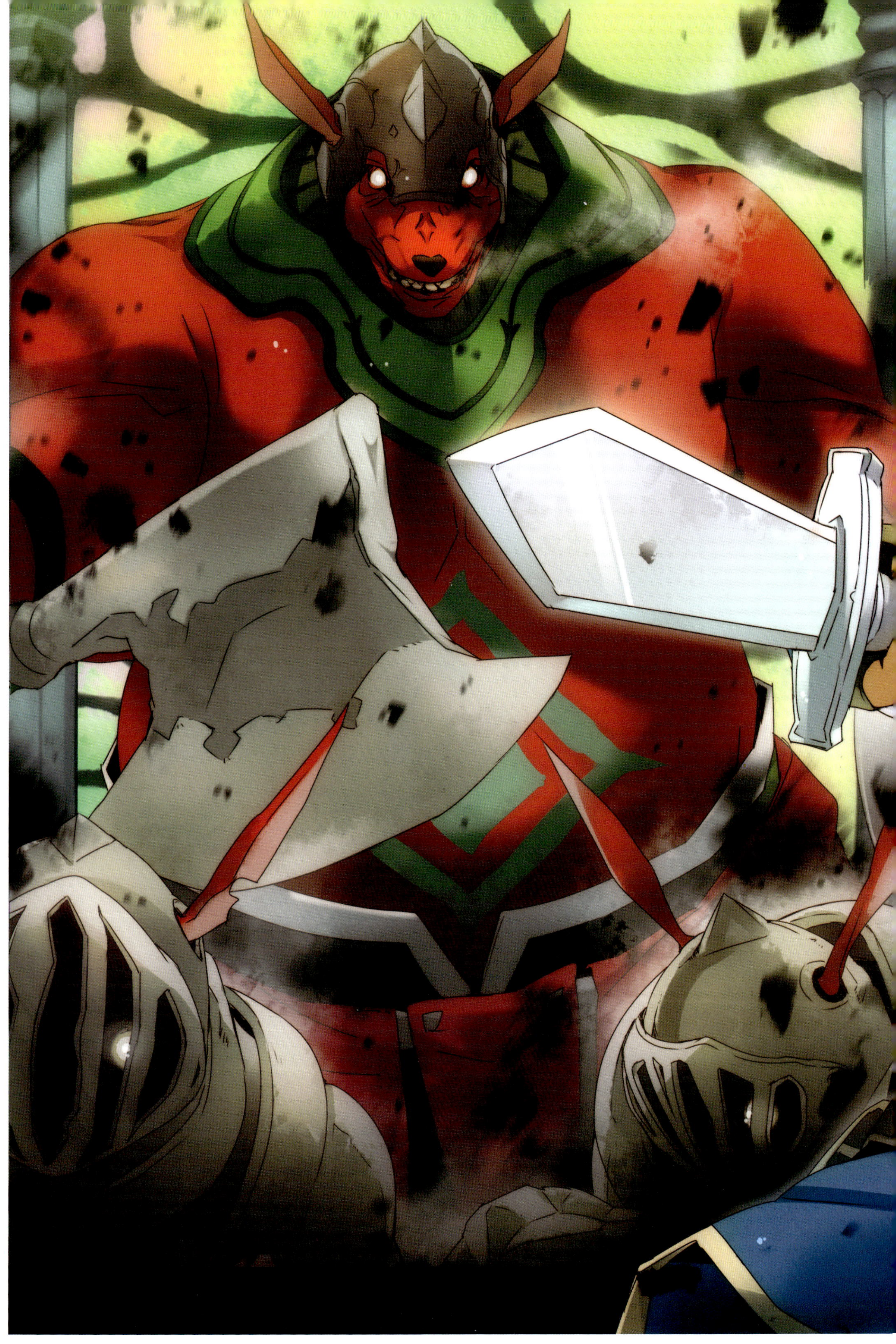

Dengeki Bunko, *Sword Art Online Progressive 1*
Frontispiece: October 2012

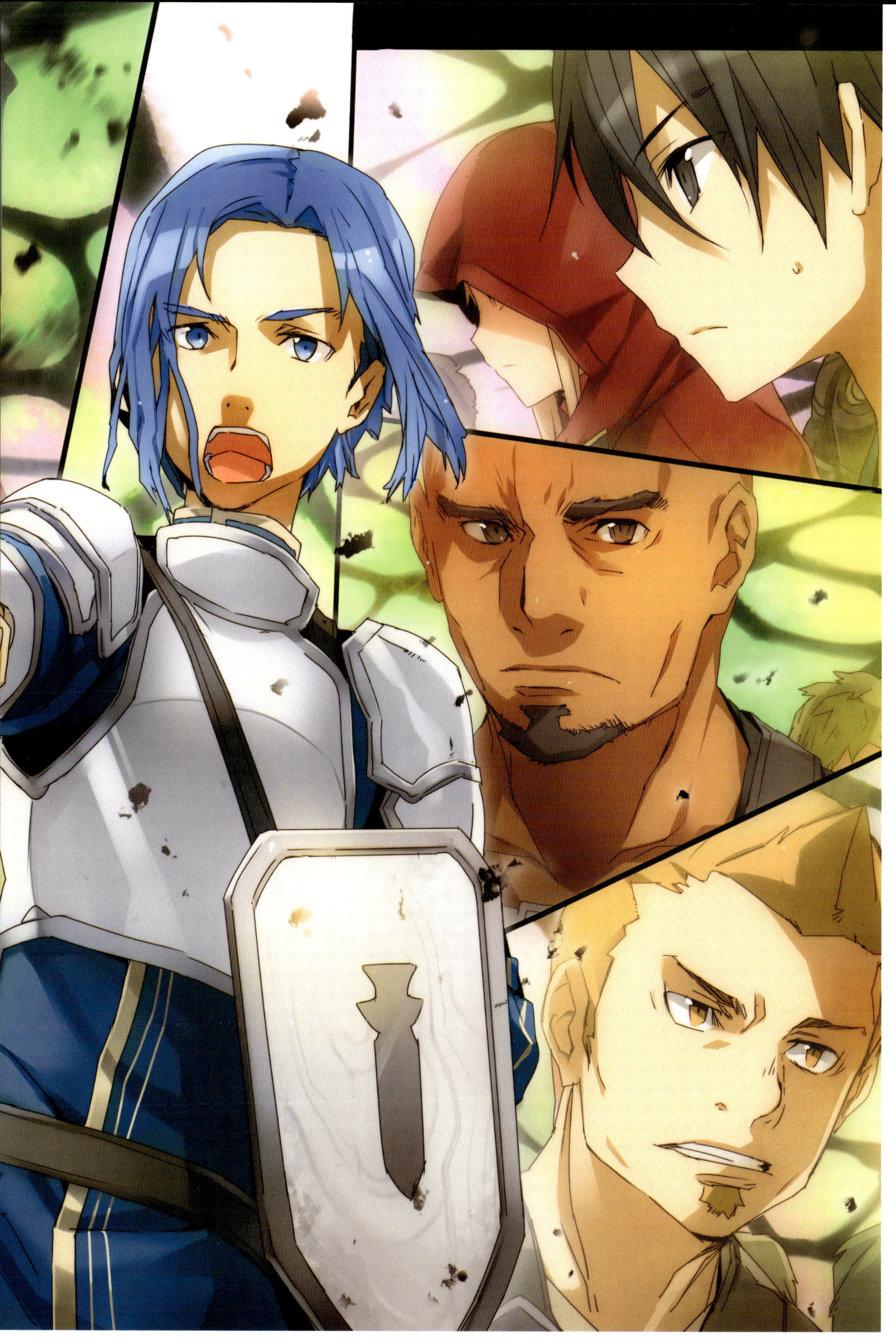

If the piece from page 94 is close to the cover, this one's more of a typical frontispiece, something that describes what's happening. For the kobold lord, I just used the design straight from the anime.

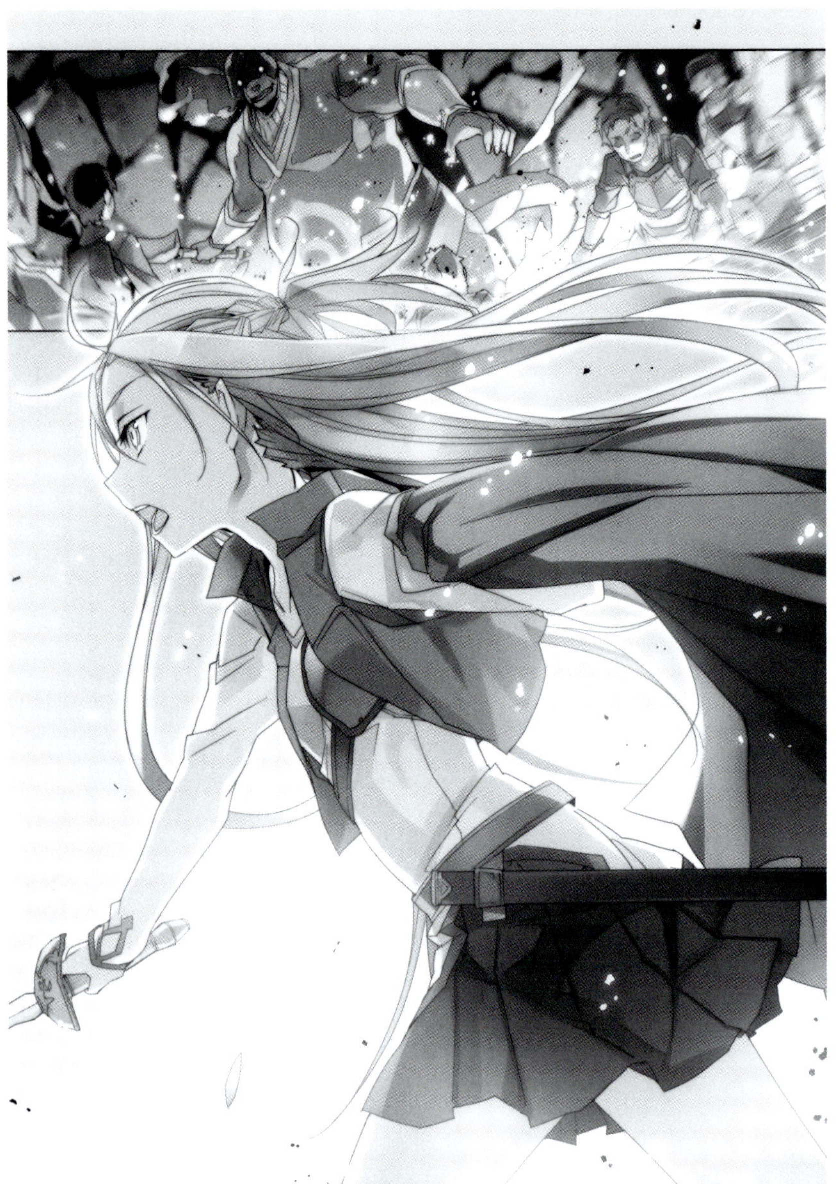

Dengeki Bunko
Sword Art Online Progressive 1
Frontispiece: October 2012

I like these scenes where they're watching something while hiding, because I get to draw her wearing the hood.

Dengeki Bunko
Sword Art Online Progressive 1
Illustration: October 2012

Even the story illustrations are all pretty serious and desperate.

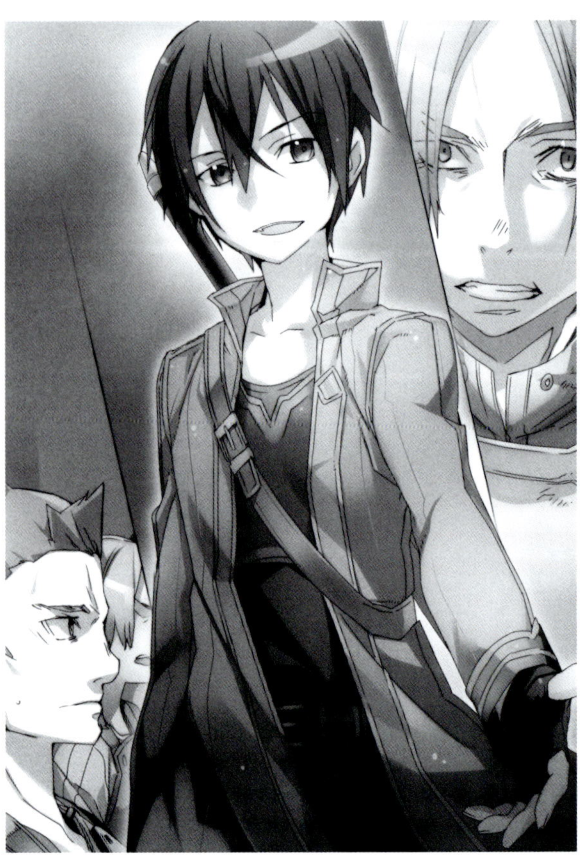

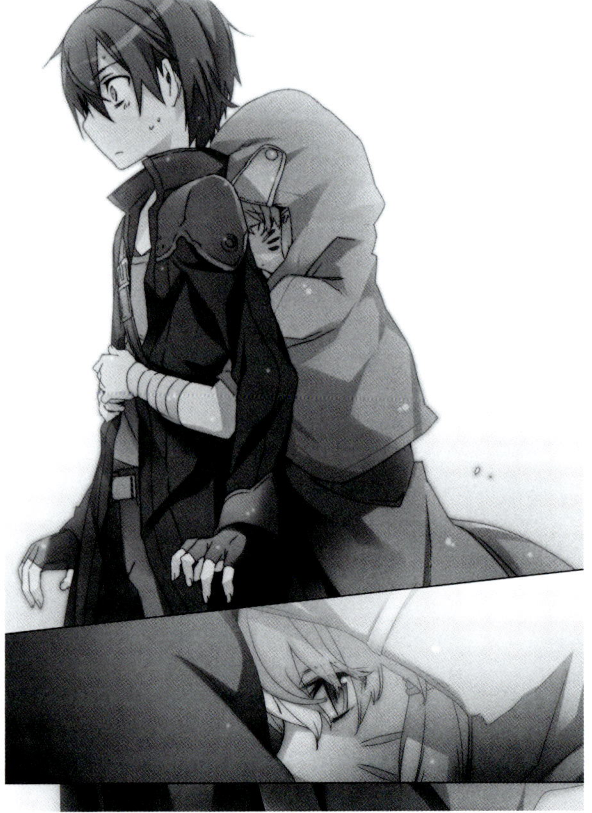

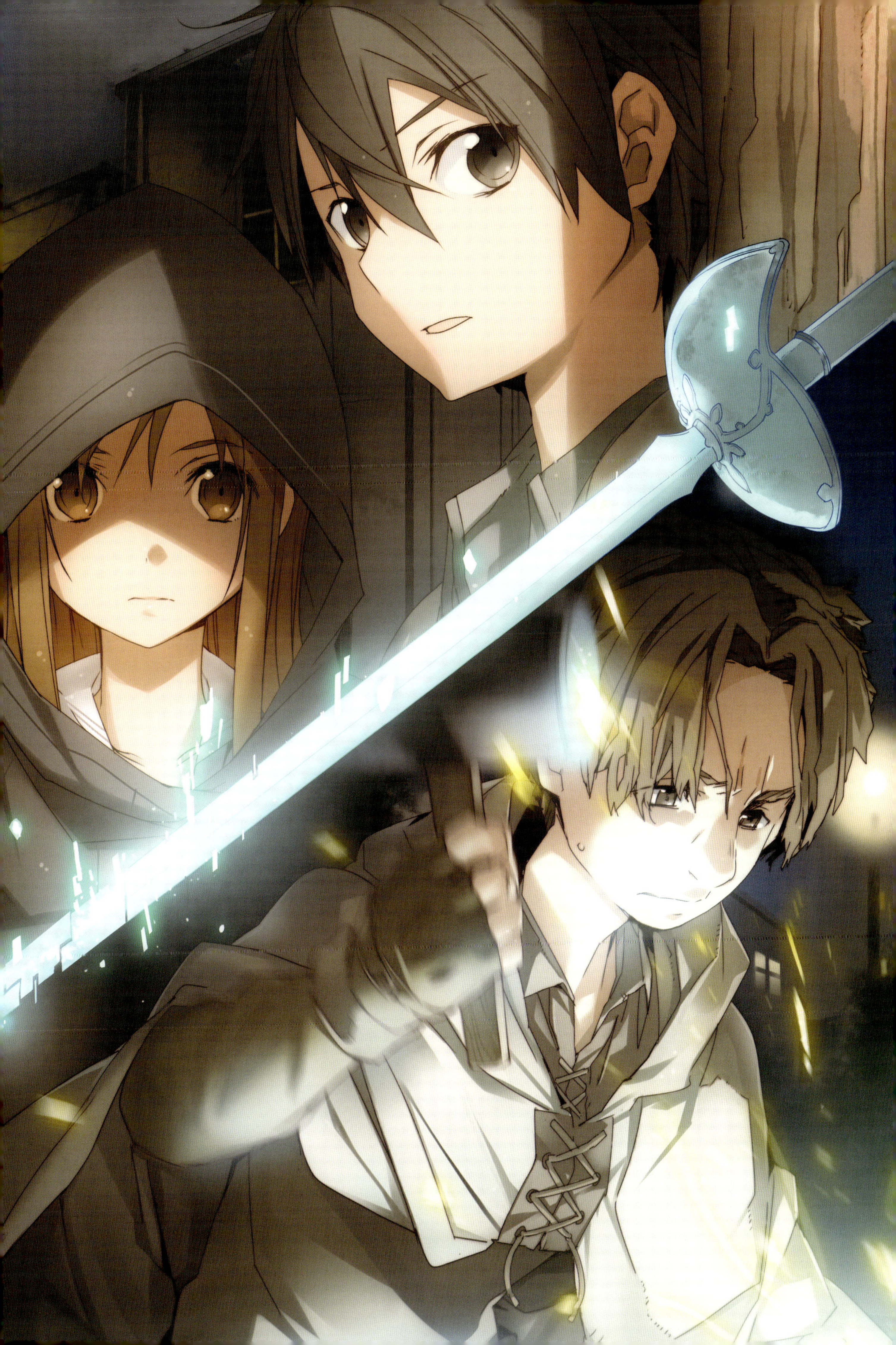

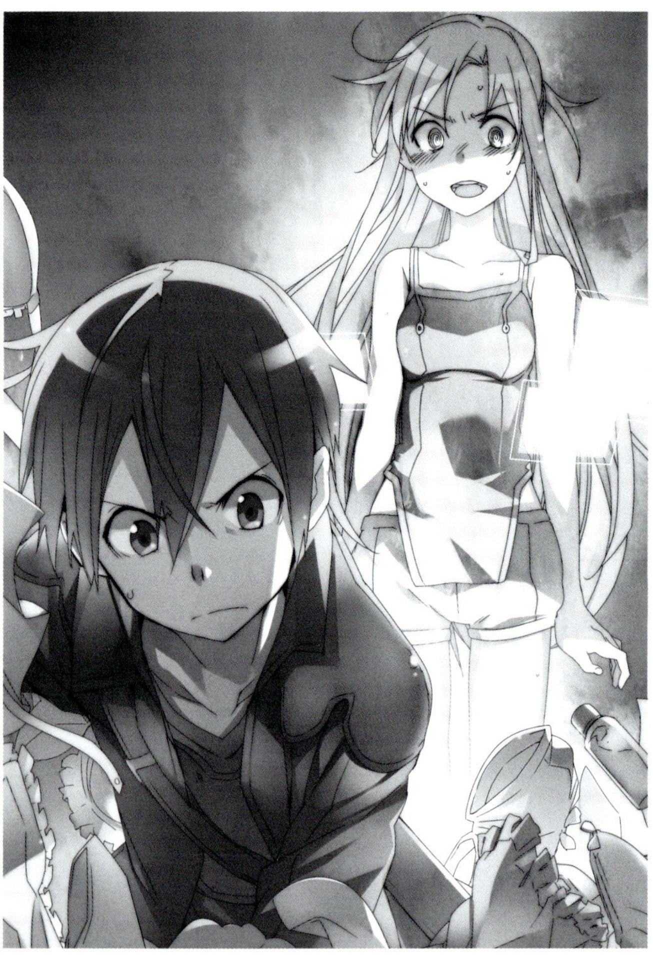

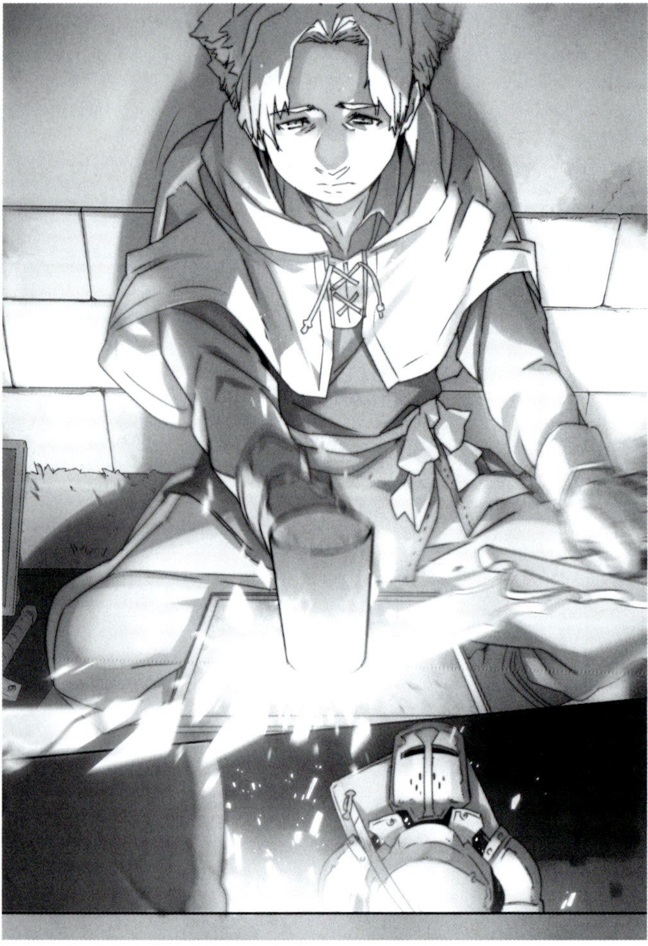

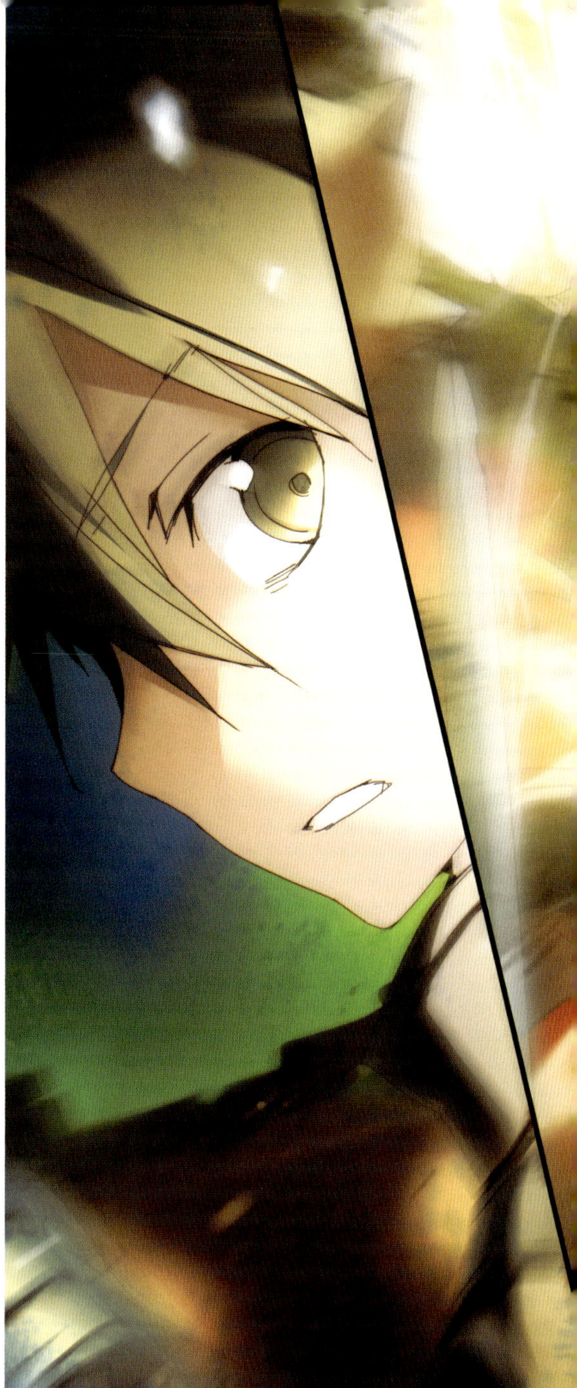

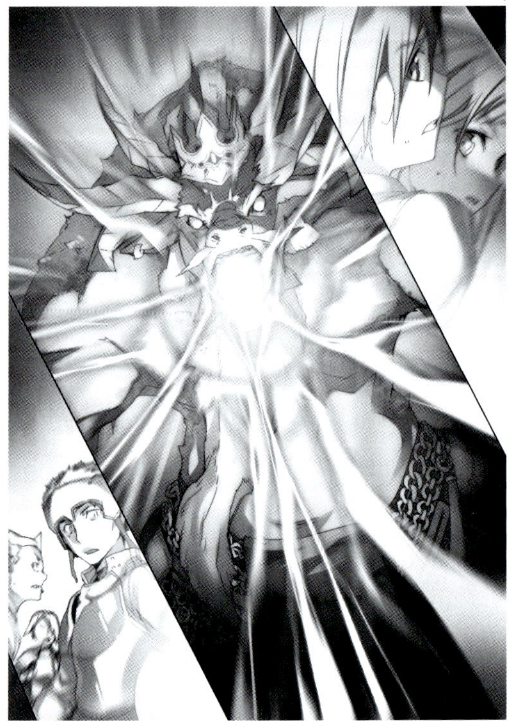

Dengeki Bunko
Sword Art Online Progressive 1
Illustration: October 2012

Kirito rifling through a pile of Asuna's belongings. One of the fun parts about Progressive is drawing lots of Asunas you don't always get to see.

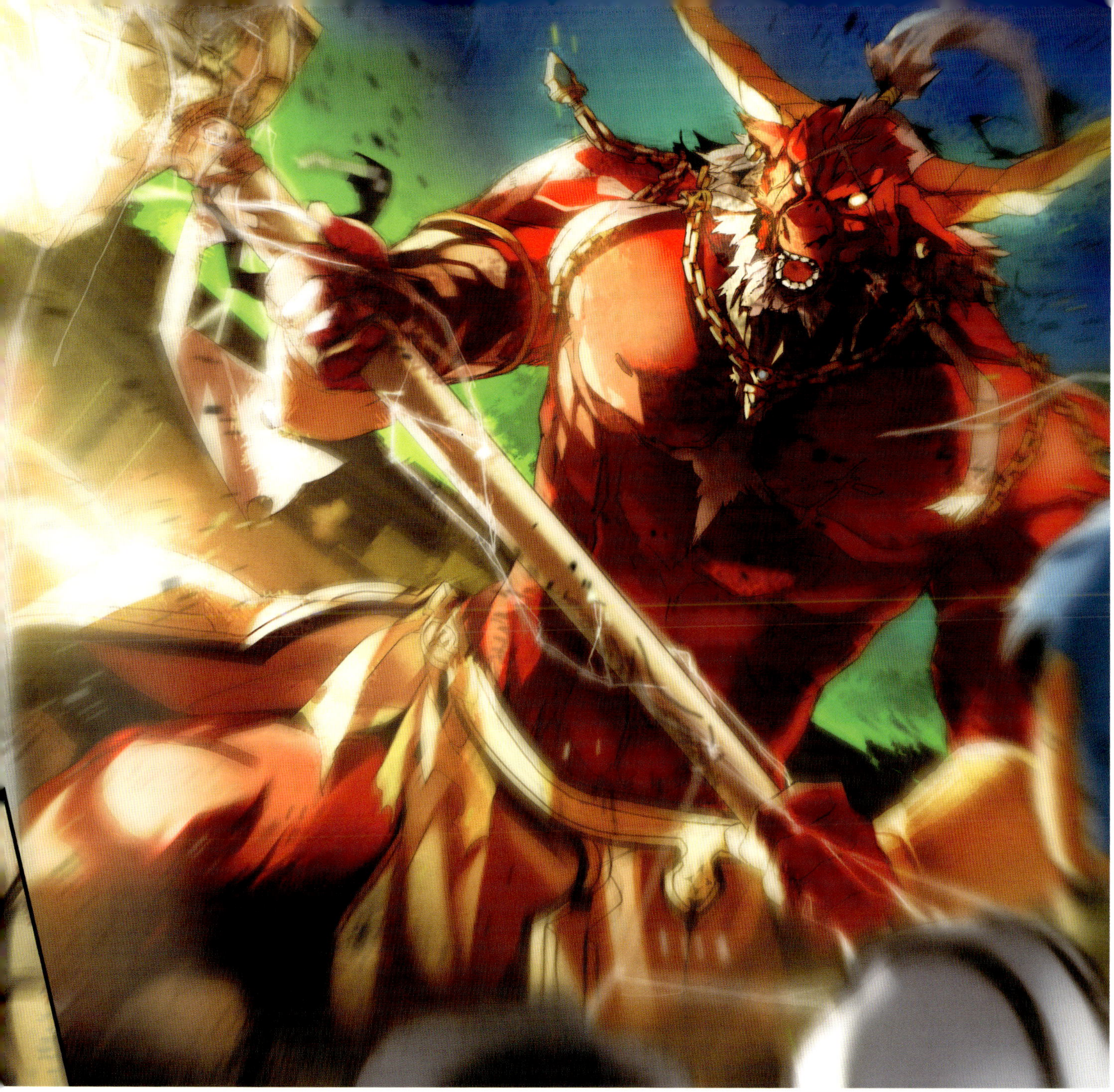

Dengeki Bunko
Sword Art Online Progressive 1
Frontispiece: October 2012

Boss fight. The game is deadly, and that death comes for you in the form of monsters. I really tried my best to make it feel serious and terrifying, but it's harder than you'd think.

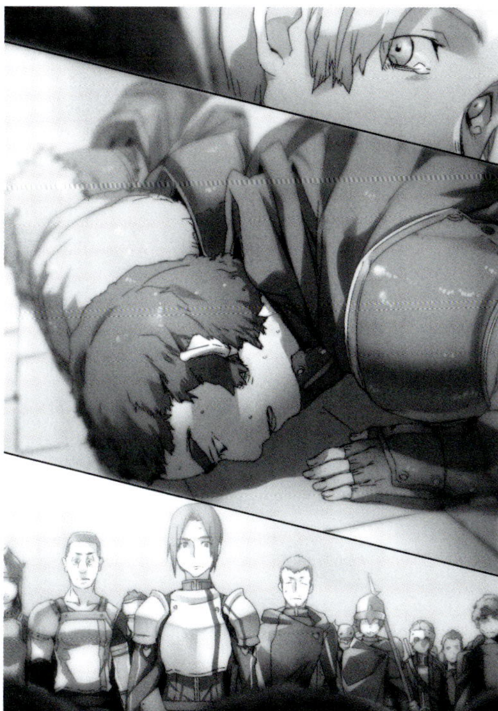

Dengeki Bunko
Sword Art Online Progressive 1
Illustration: October 2012

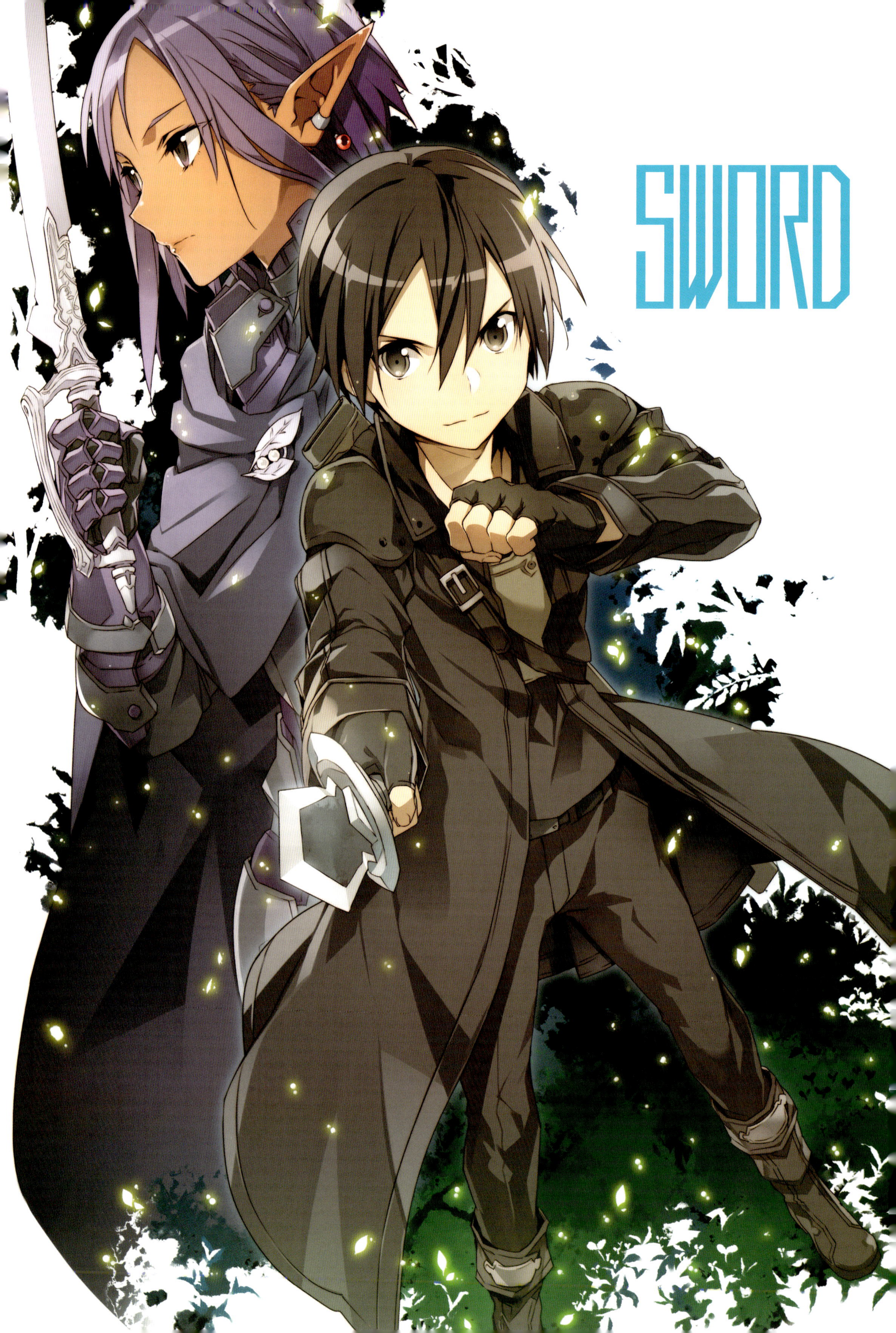
SWORD

ART ONLINE PROGRESSIVE 002

Volume 2 of Progressive, which covers the third floor and introduces Kizmel the NPC.

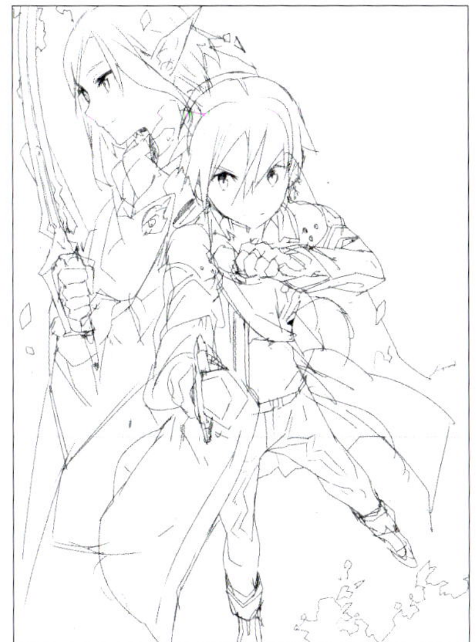

Dengeki Bunko
Sword Art Online Progressive 2
Cover: December 2013

The cover is Kizmel and Kirito. I really like Kizmel's side profile. It's very gallant.

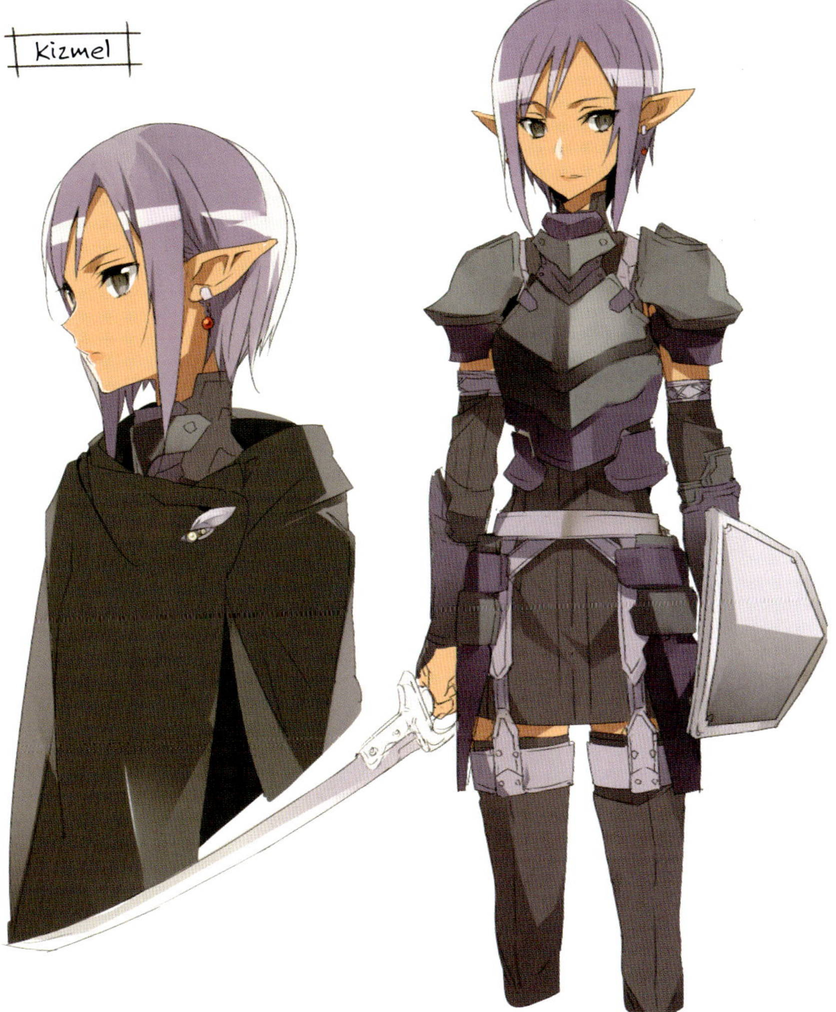

Dengeki Bunko, *Sword Art Online Progressive 2*
Character Design: December 2013

Kizmel the dark elf. I never thought I would be drawing a dark elf in the Aincrad setting. She's got a bit of a miniskirt on here. But there are shorts beneath it. At least, in my imagination.

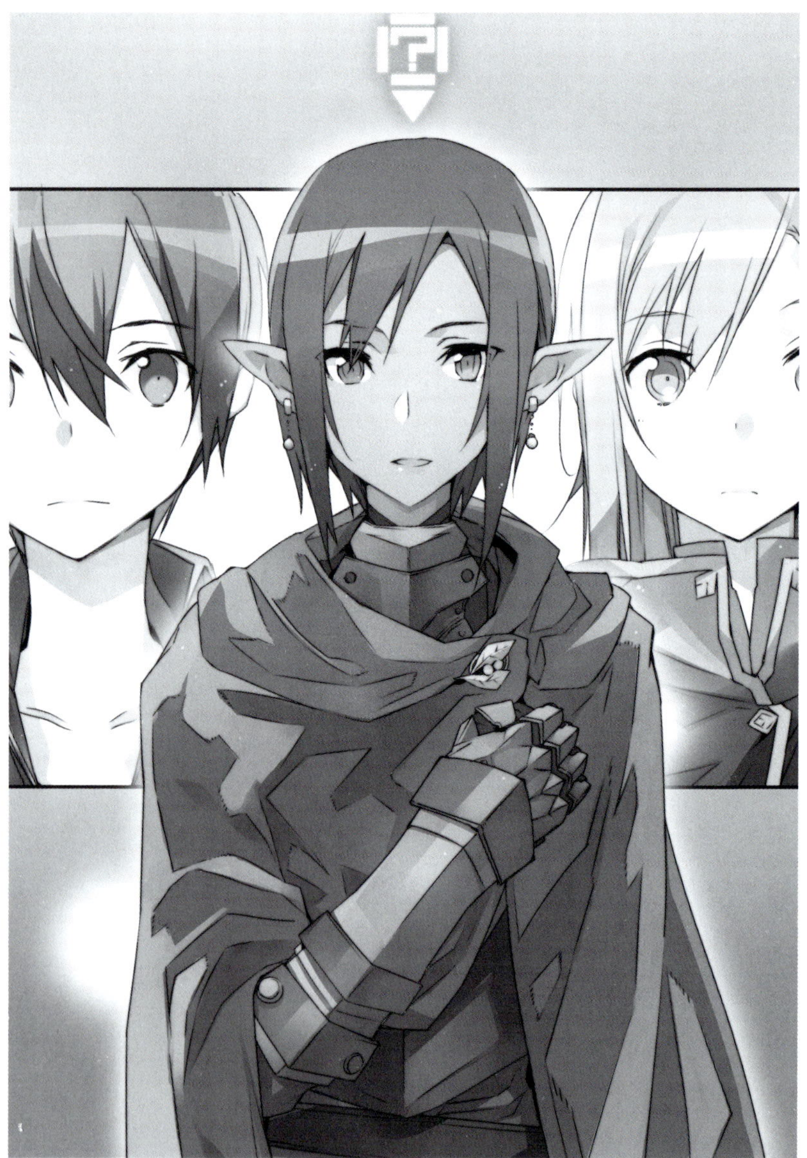

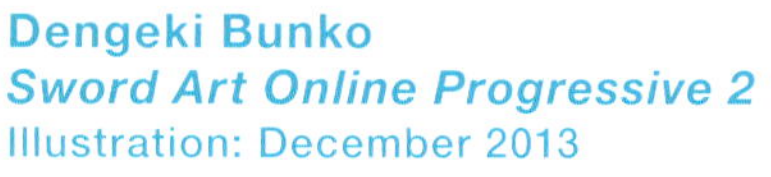

Dengeki Bunko
Sword Art Online Progressive 2
Illustration: December 2013

I thought about how I might distinguish NPCs from players in the illustrations, but ultimately, I drew Kizmel, and all other NPCs, the same as any player.

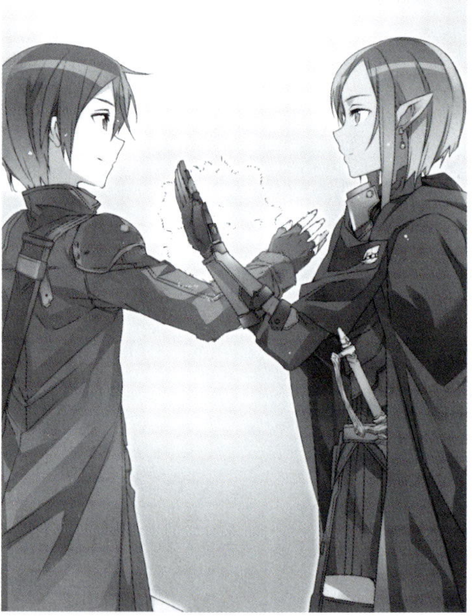

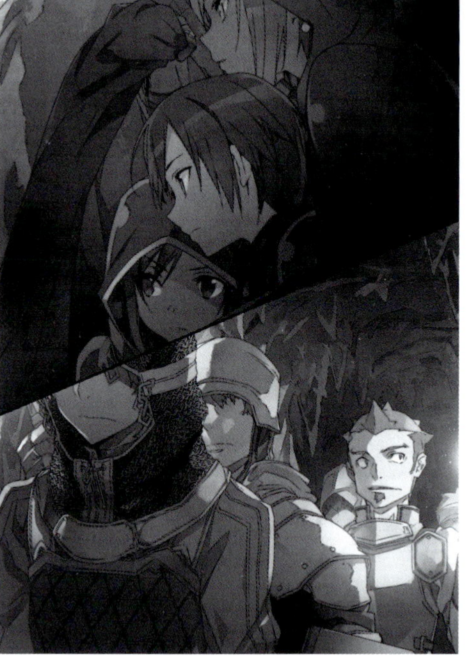

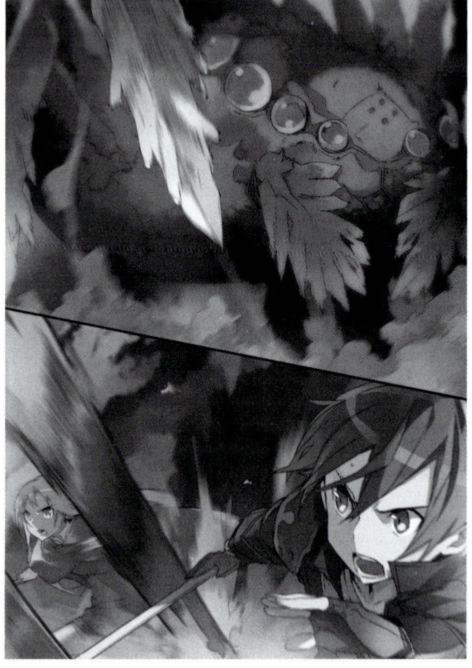

Dengeki Bunko
Sword Art Online Progressive 2
Illustration: December 2013

At some point, I came to the realization that spiders are surprisingly cute.

Dengeki Bunko
Sword Art Online Progressive 2
Illustration: December 2013

I like the huge difference between the serious scenes and the comedic scenes.

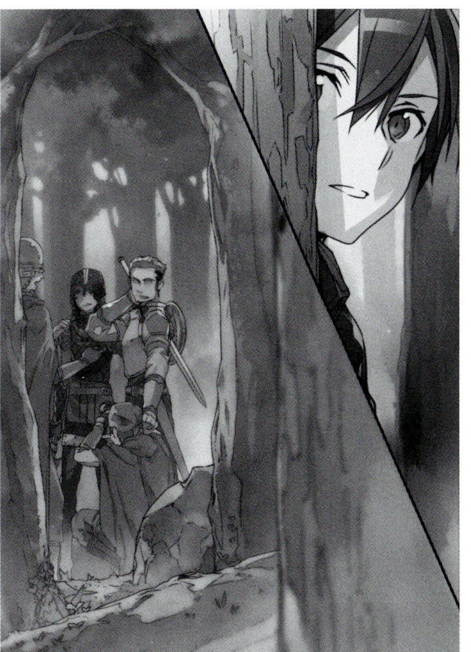

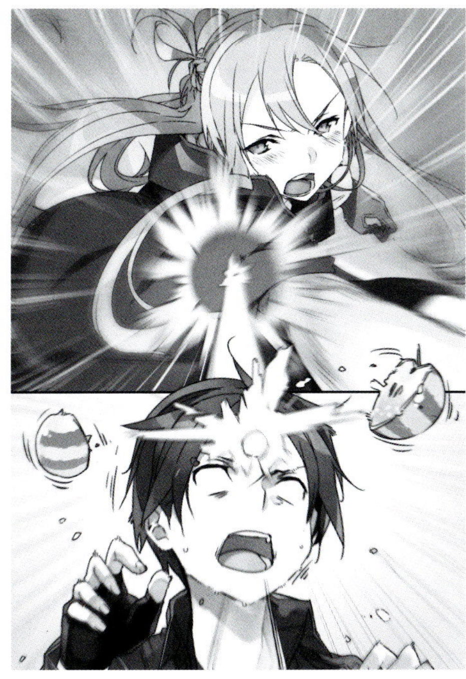

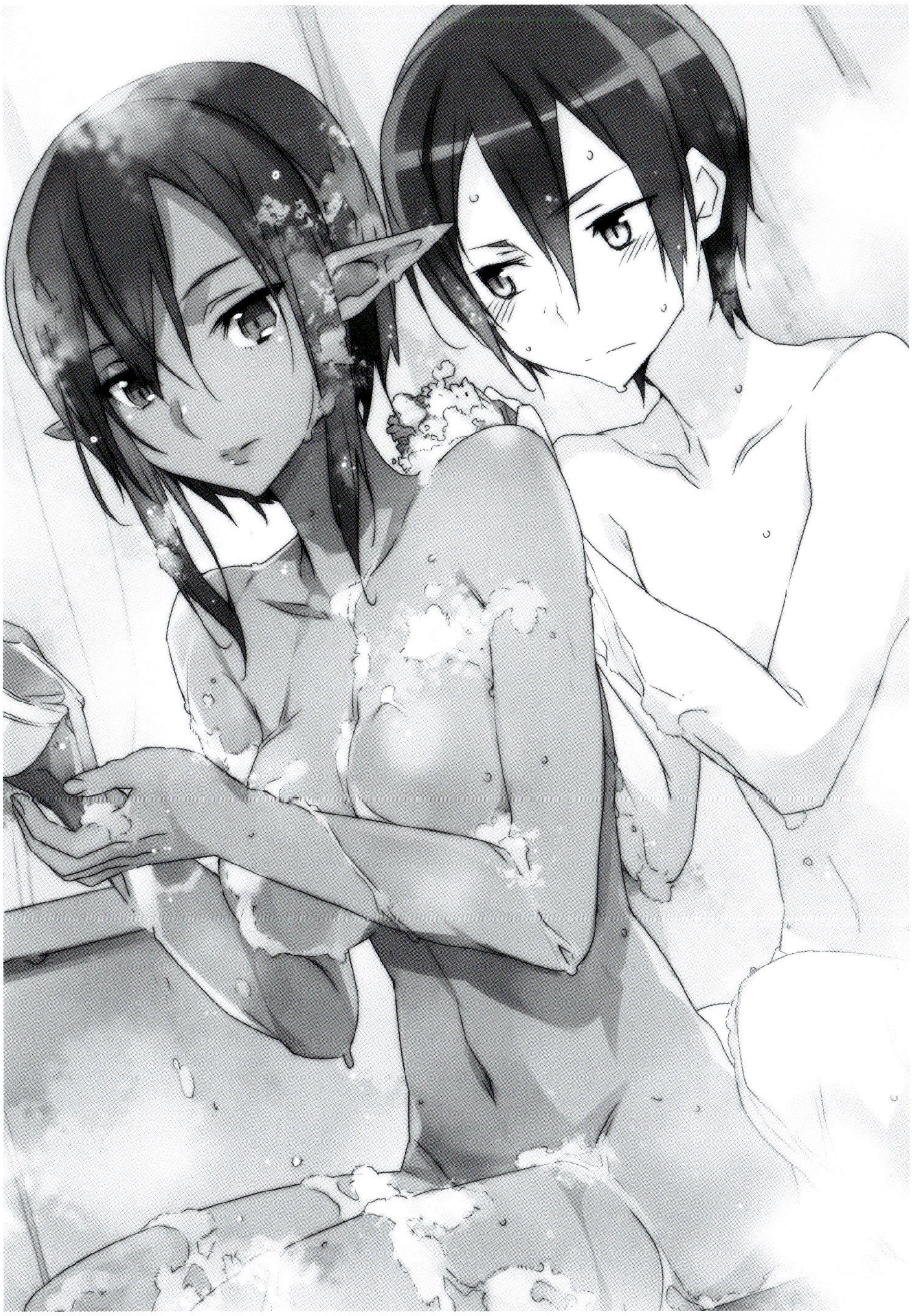

Dengeki Bunko
Sword Art Online Progressive 2
Illustration: December 2013

Normally with story illustrations, I'd use steam and stuff to haze over all the detail, but the contrast with her darker skin just makes it look even more sexy. I didn't have any other option, so that makes it okay!

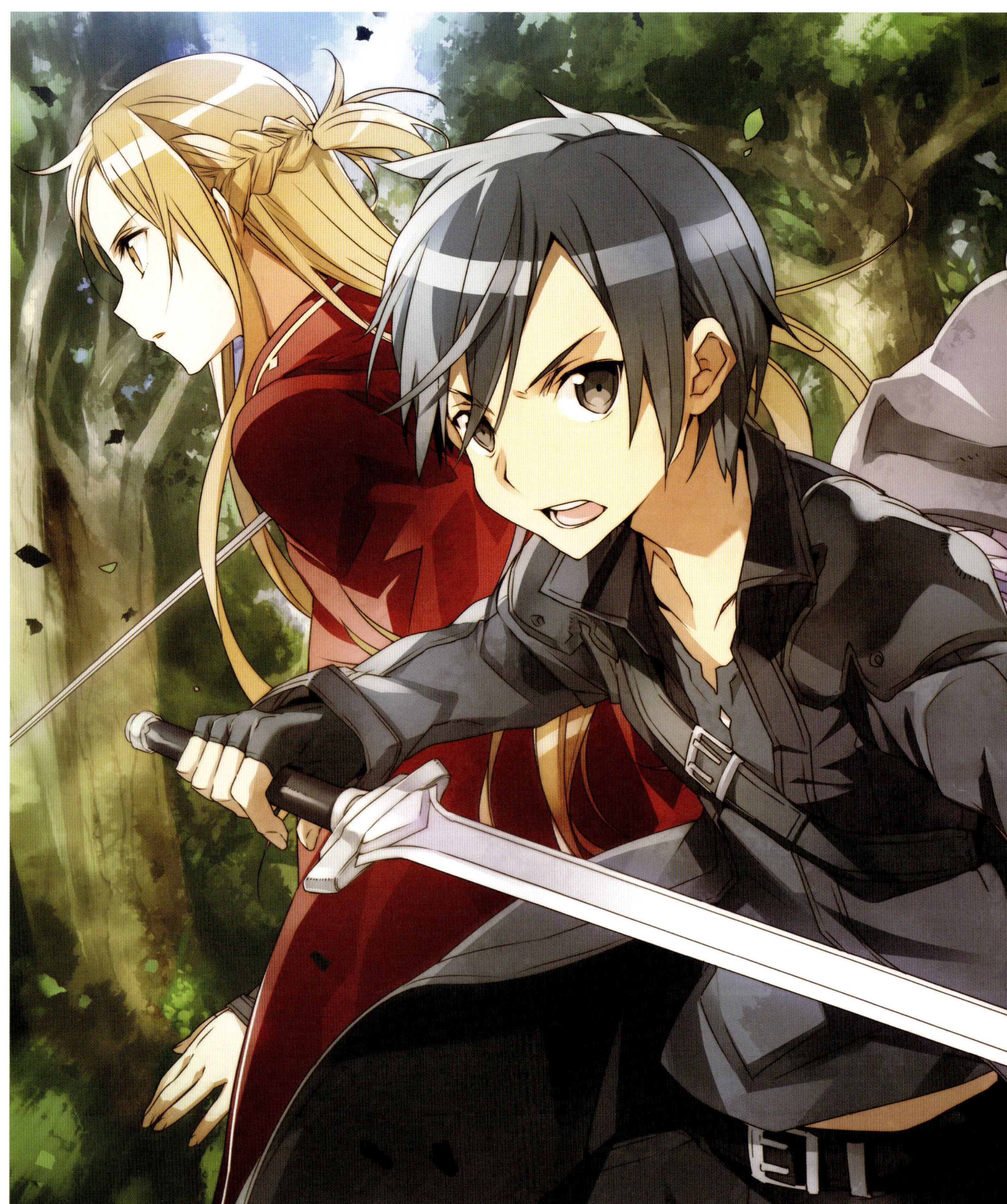

Dengeki Bunko
Sword Art Online Progressive 2
Frontispiece: December 2013

The trio fighting together. You know a powerful dark elf NPC who helps out the party is going to be popular. But it also makes me sad to think about taking the other story route that would make her the enemy.

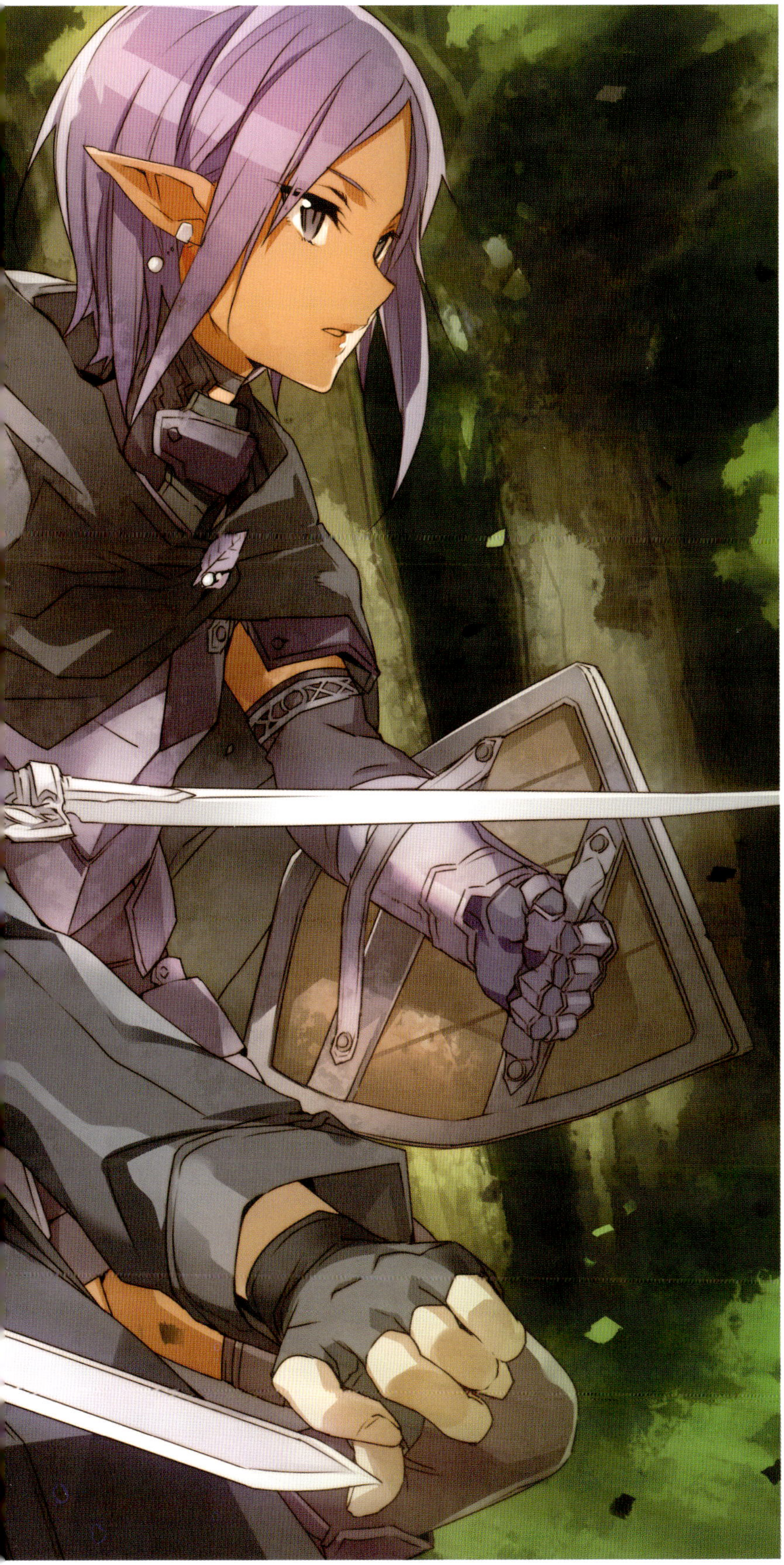

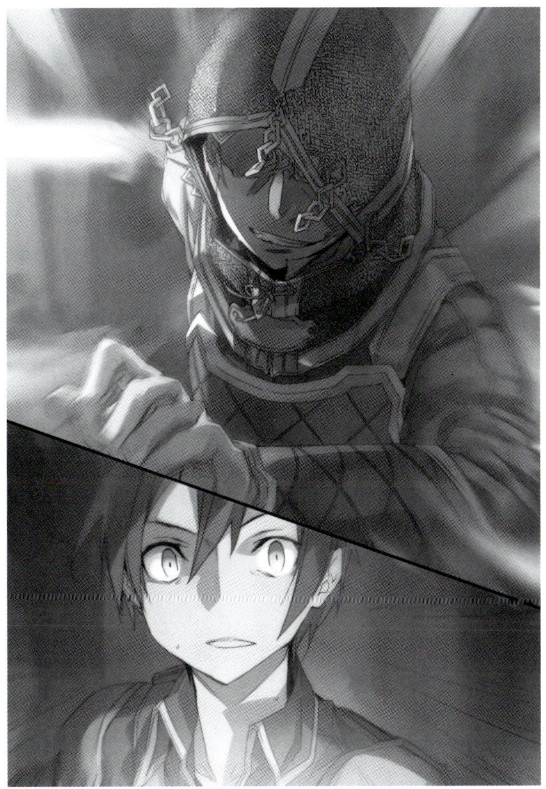

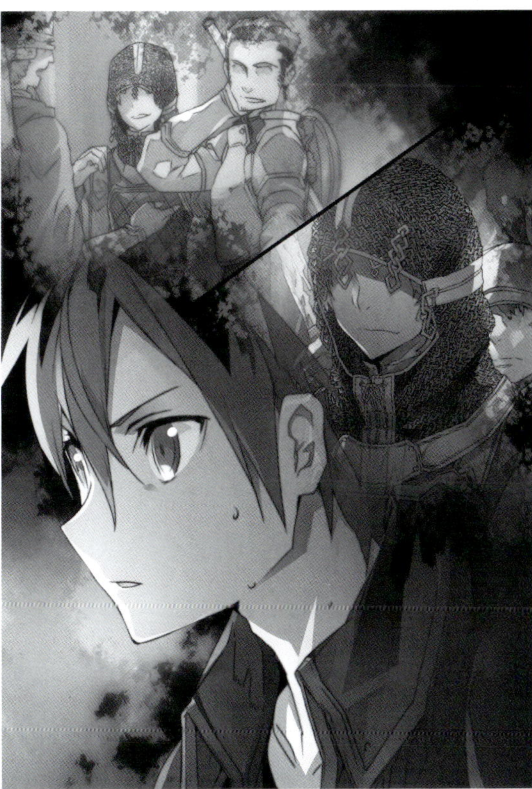

Dengeki Bunko
Sword Art Online Progressive 2
Illustration: December 2013

You'd be surprised how much of a pain that chain hood is to draw.

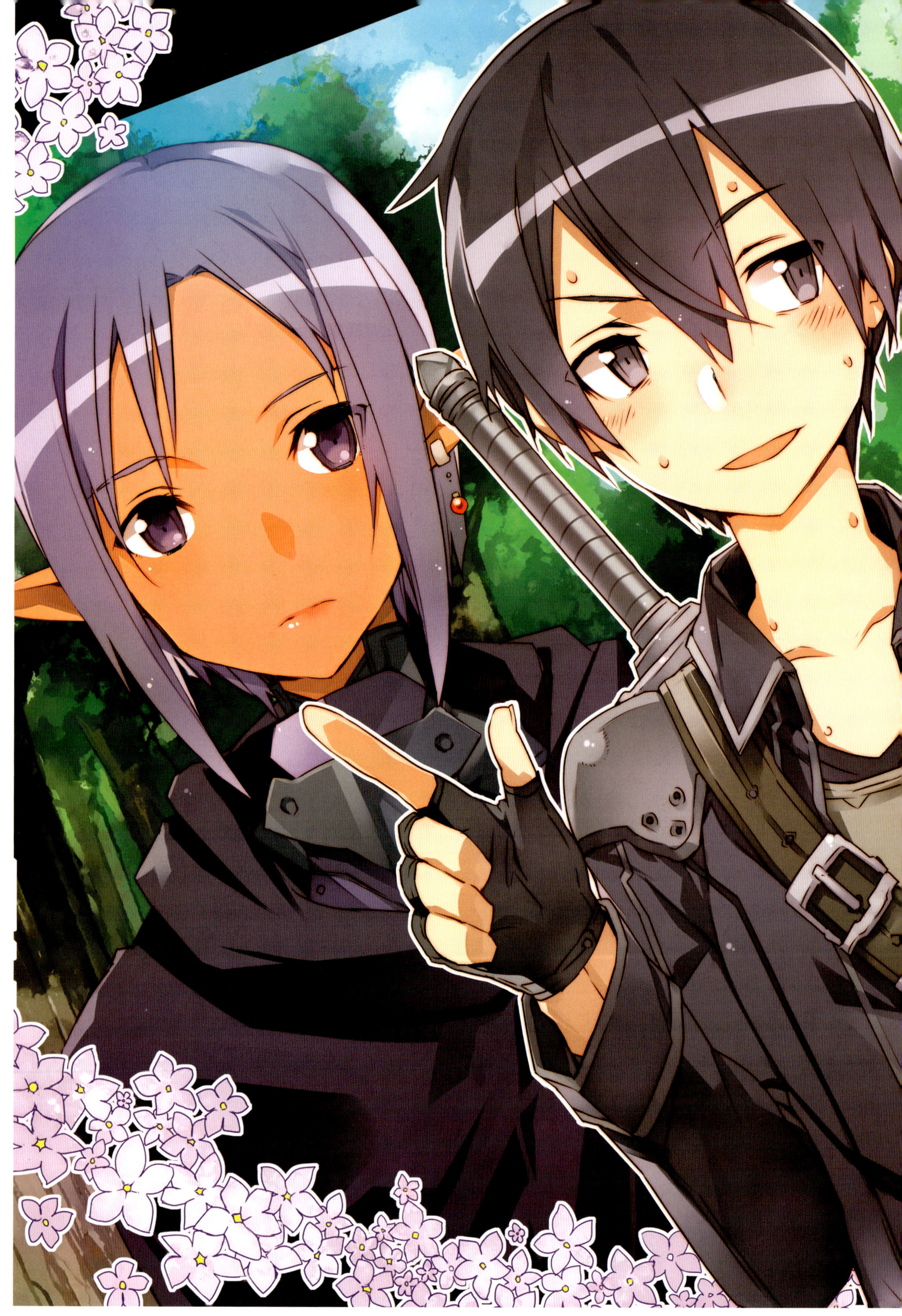

Dengeki Bunko, *Sword Art Online Progressive 2*
Frontispiece: December 2013

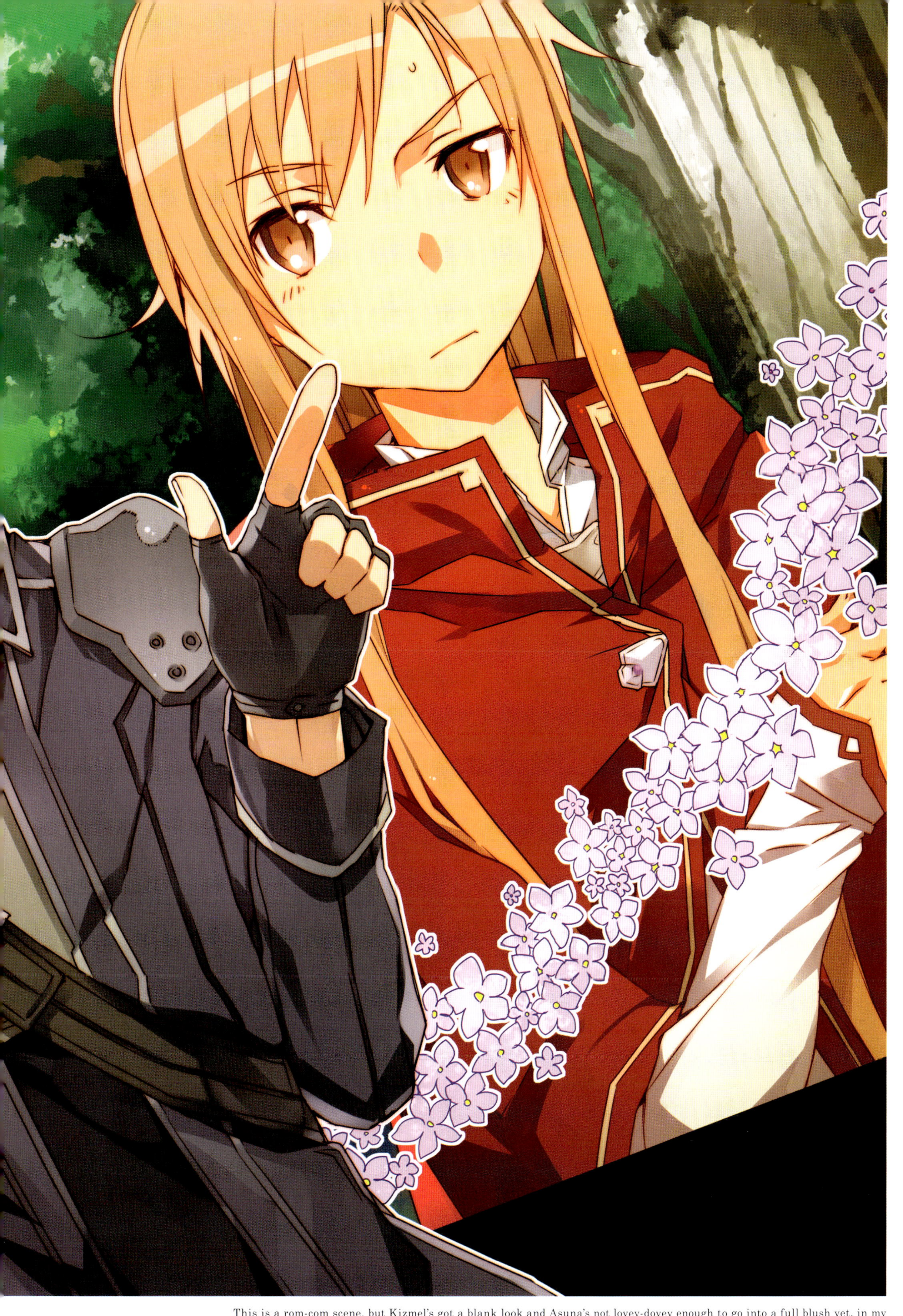

This is a rom-com scene, but Kizmel's got a blank look and Asuna's not lovey-dovey enough to go into a full blush yet, in my opinion. But the result is that it looks like Kirito's just getting hung out to dry with a bad joke! I mean, that's accurate, but...

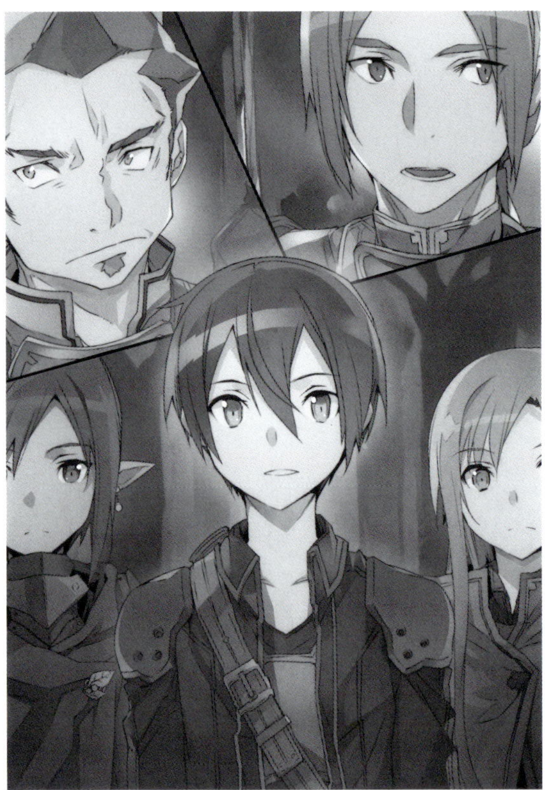

Dengeki Bunko
Sword Art Online Progressive 2
Illustration: December 2013

A conversation scene. The frontline gang is not hanging together well.

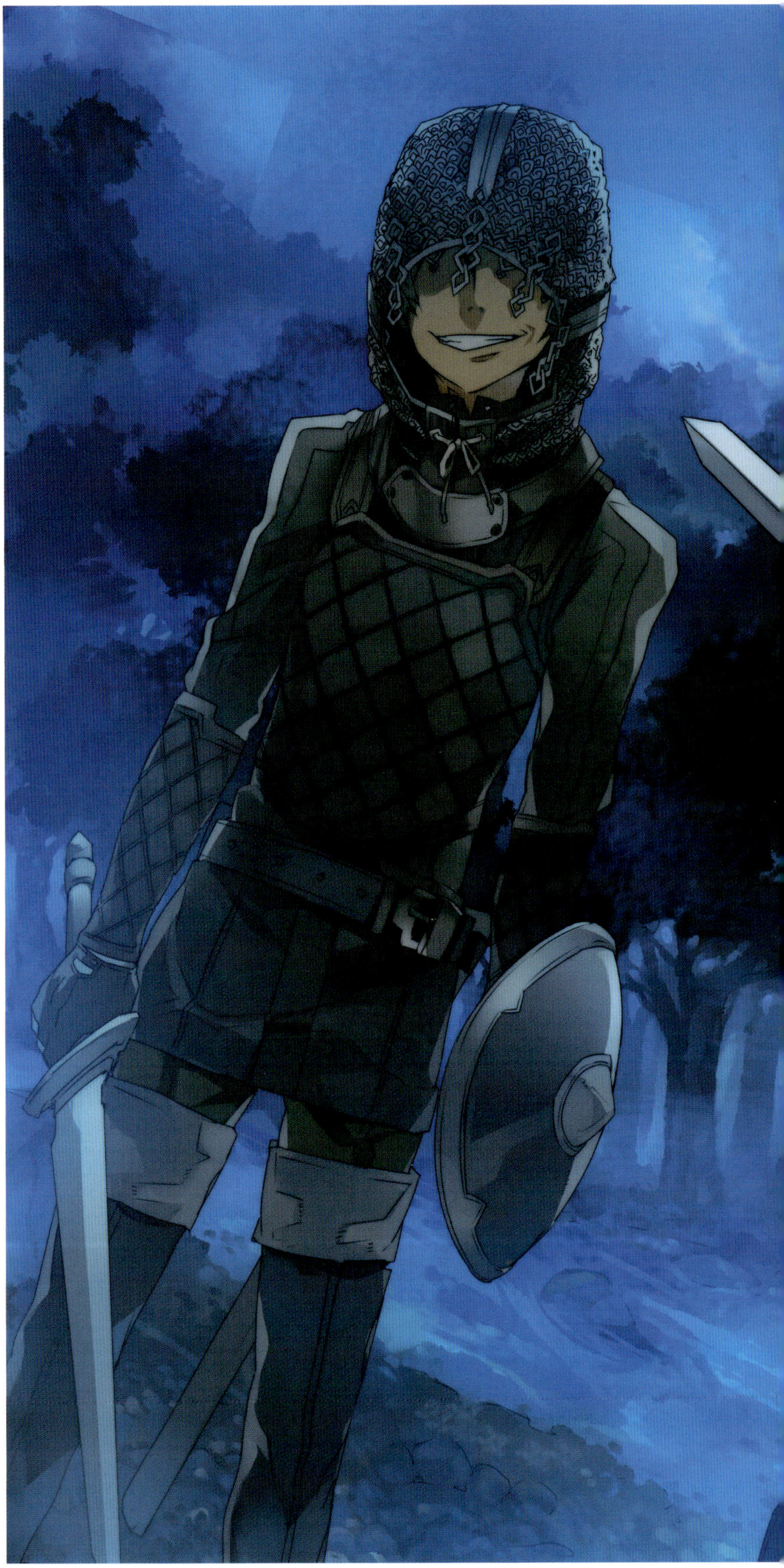

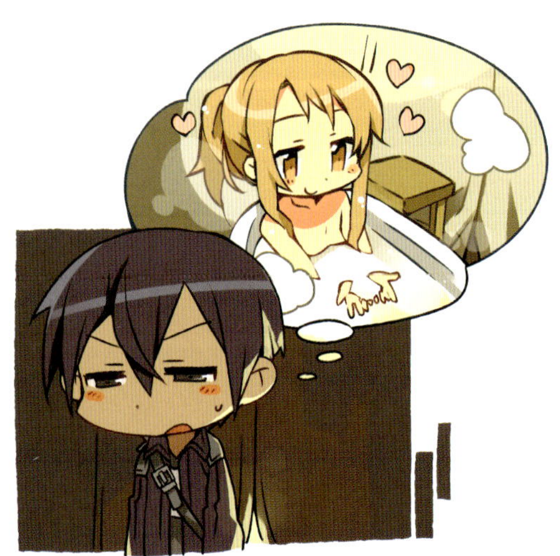

Dengeki Bunko
Sword Art Online Progressive 2
Back Cover: December 2013

Rom-com!

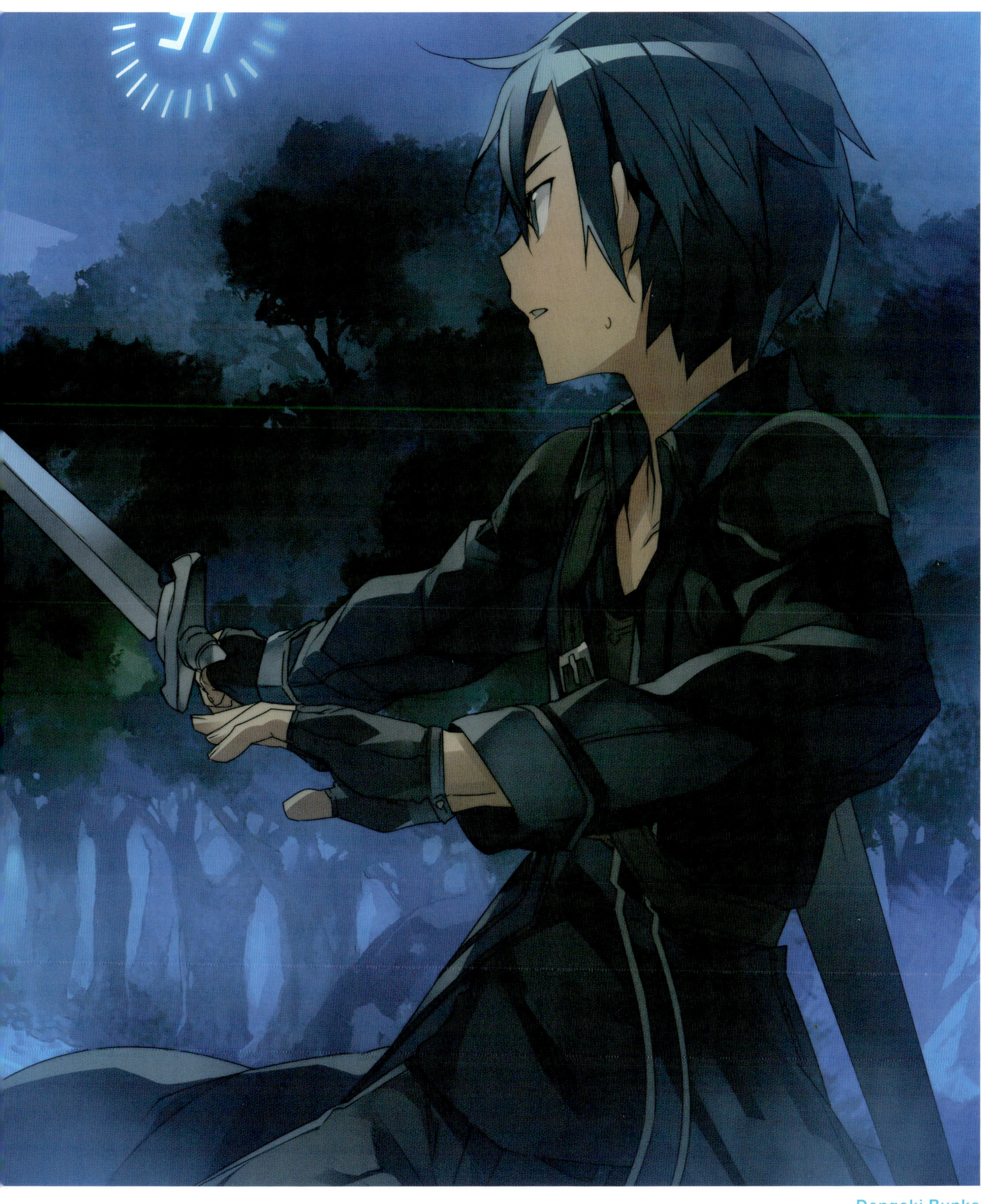

Dengeki Bunko
Sword Art Online Progressive 2
Frontispiece: December 2013

I actually like Morte's design a lot. I wanted this one to look eerie, with the background and everything.

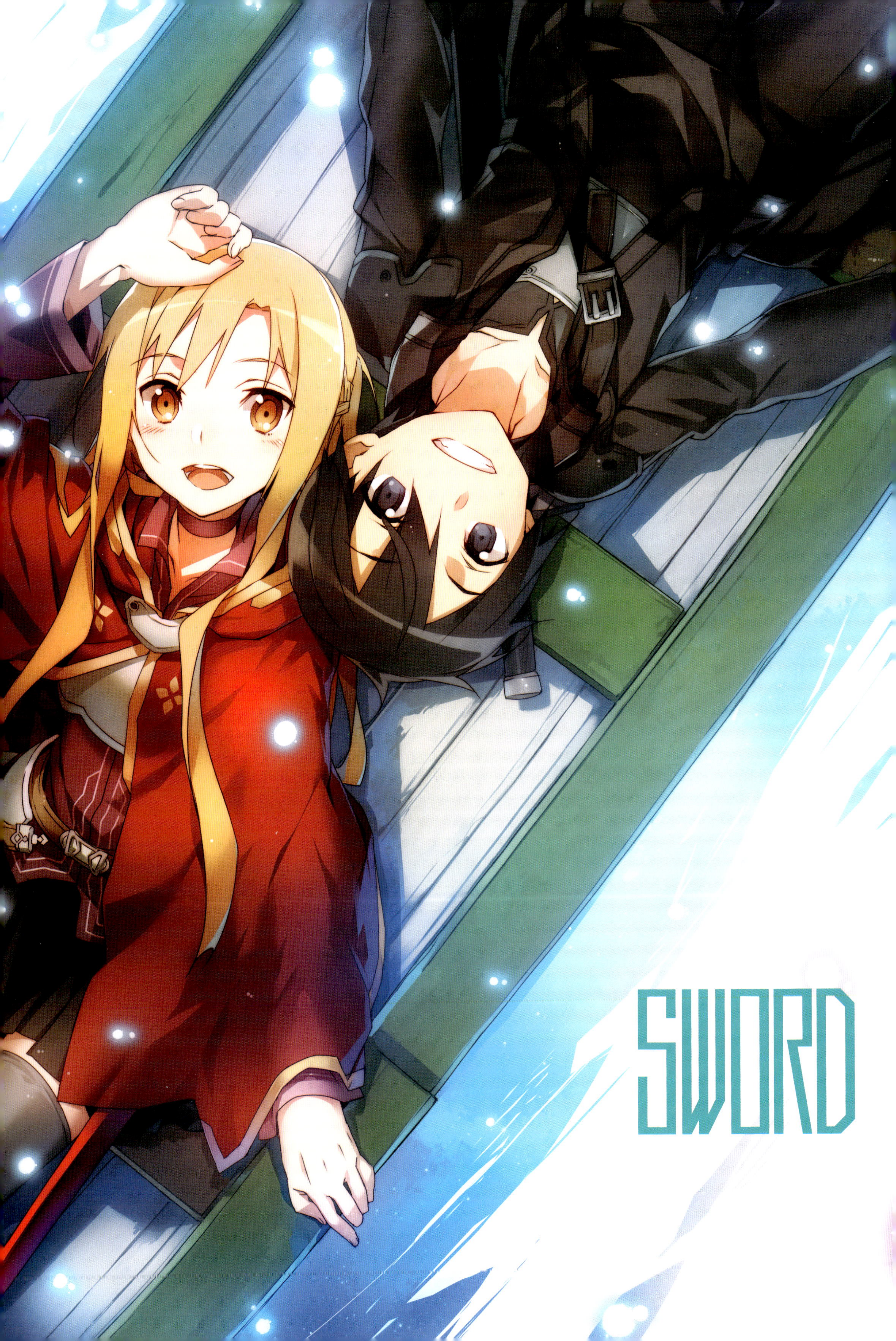
SWORD

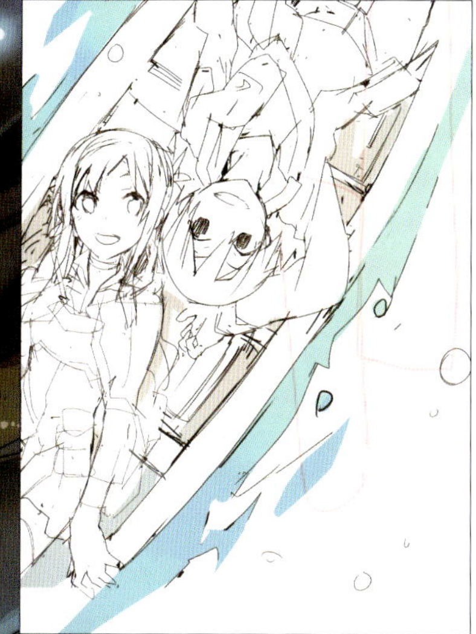

Dengeki Bunko
Sword Art Online Progressive 3
Cover: December 2014

This one is Kirito and Asuna floating in the gondola. Just a good old gondola date.

Alternate Illustration Sketches

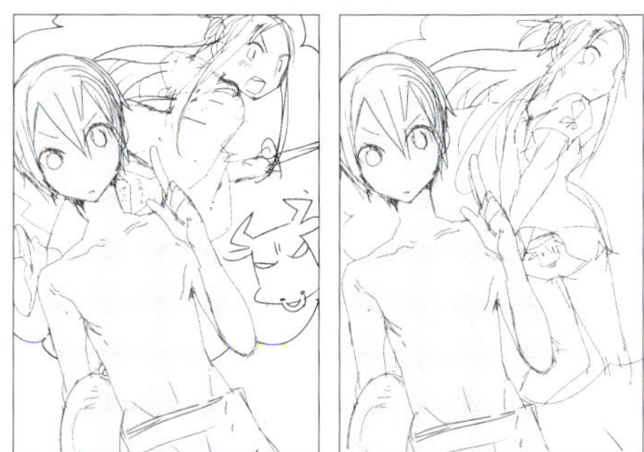

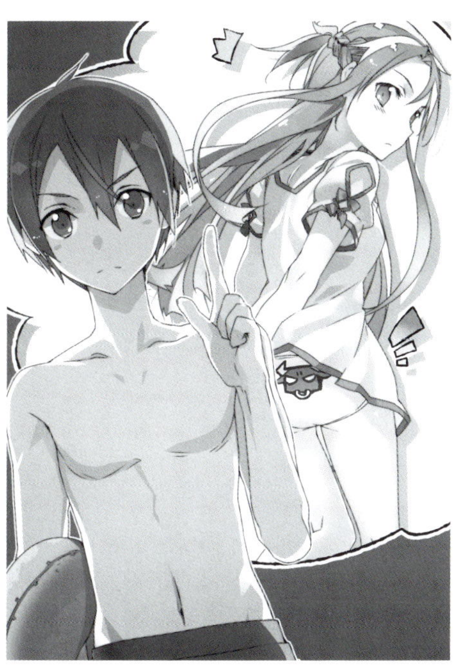

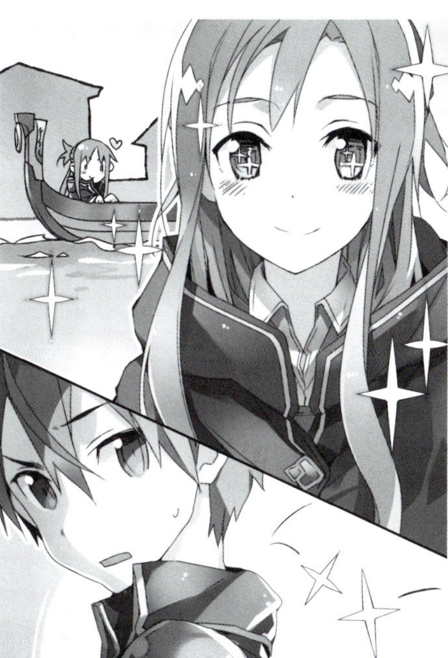

Dengeki Bunko
Sword Art Online Progressive 3
Cover: December 2014

I draw a lot of bath scenes, but for some reason, I held back and proposed a different idea here. It's a rather preposterous scenario, isn't it? Also, their rom-com level is so off the charts it makes you wonder if they're actually going to split up after this. But it gave me the chance to draw lots of lighthearted illustrations. Sparkly Asuna is adorable.

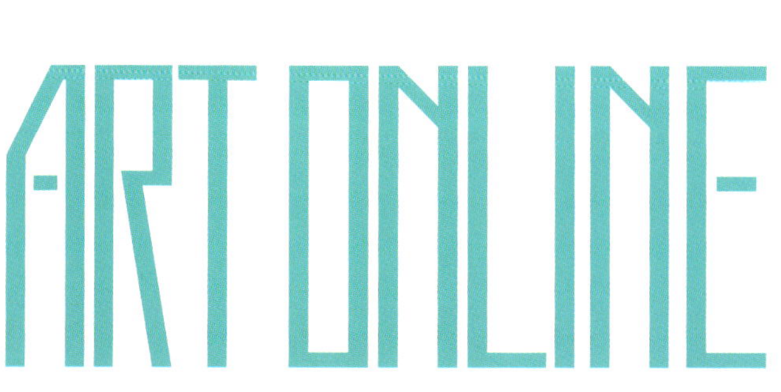

003 PROGRESSIVE

The story turns to the watery fourth floor of Aincrad. There are lots of scenes on water this volume, because they're floating around in a gondola.

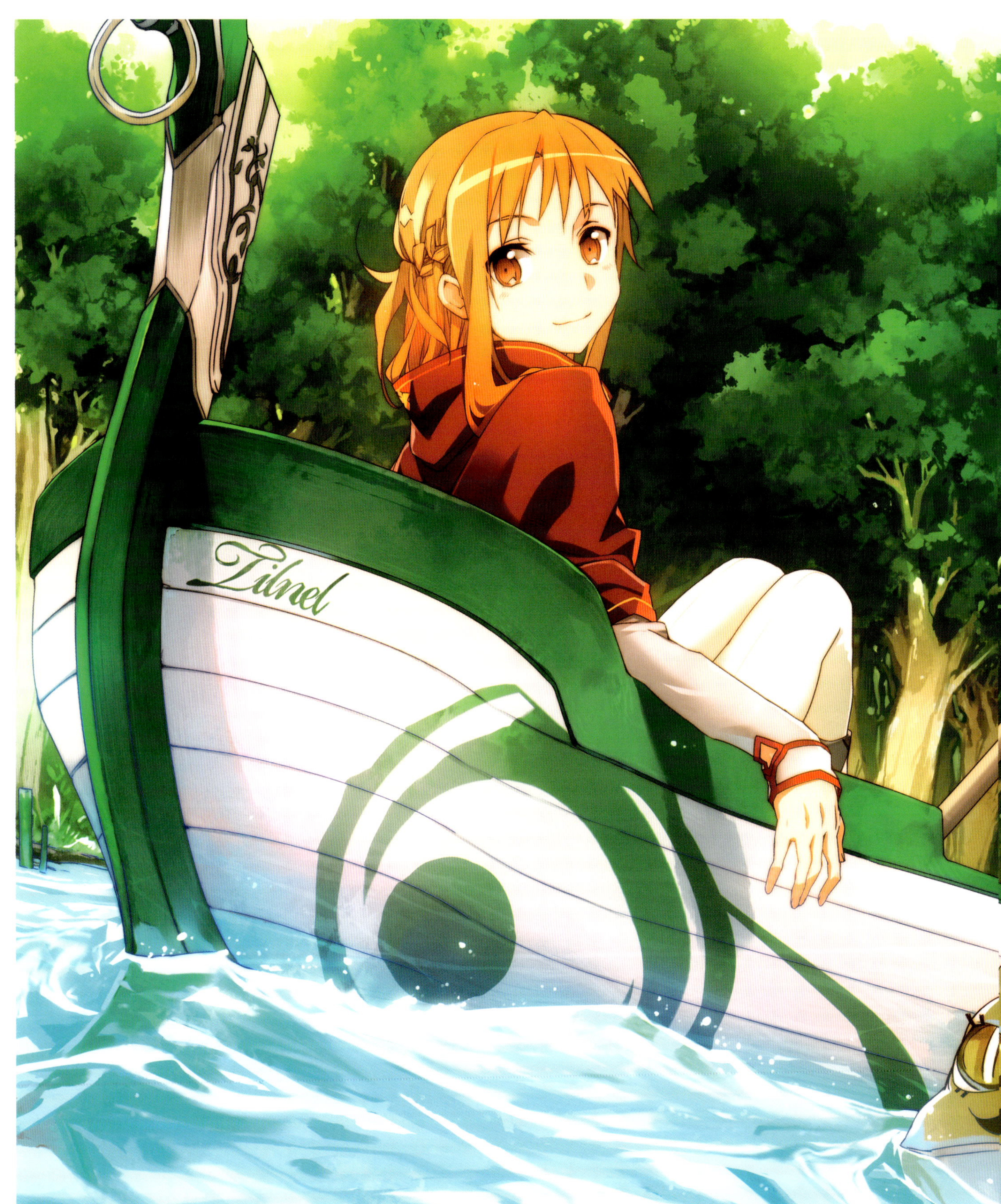

Dengeki Bunko
Sword Art Online Progressive 3
Frontispiece: December 2014

I'm serious, it's just a straight-up gondola date! Also, apparently it's sea turtles whose arms and legs make flippers. I drew a turtle in the first art book and got feedback on it, which is when I learned that fact. I think there was probably some mystical VR-world power that kept them from adapting to go on to land.

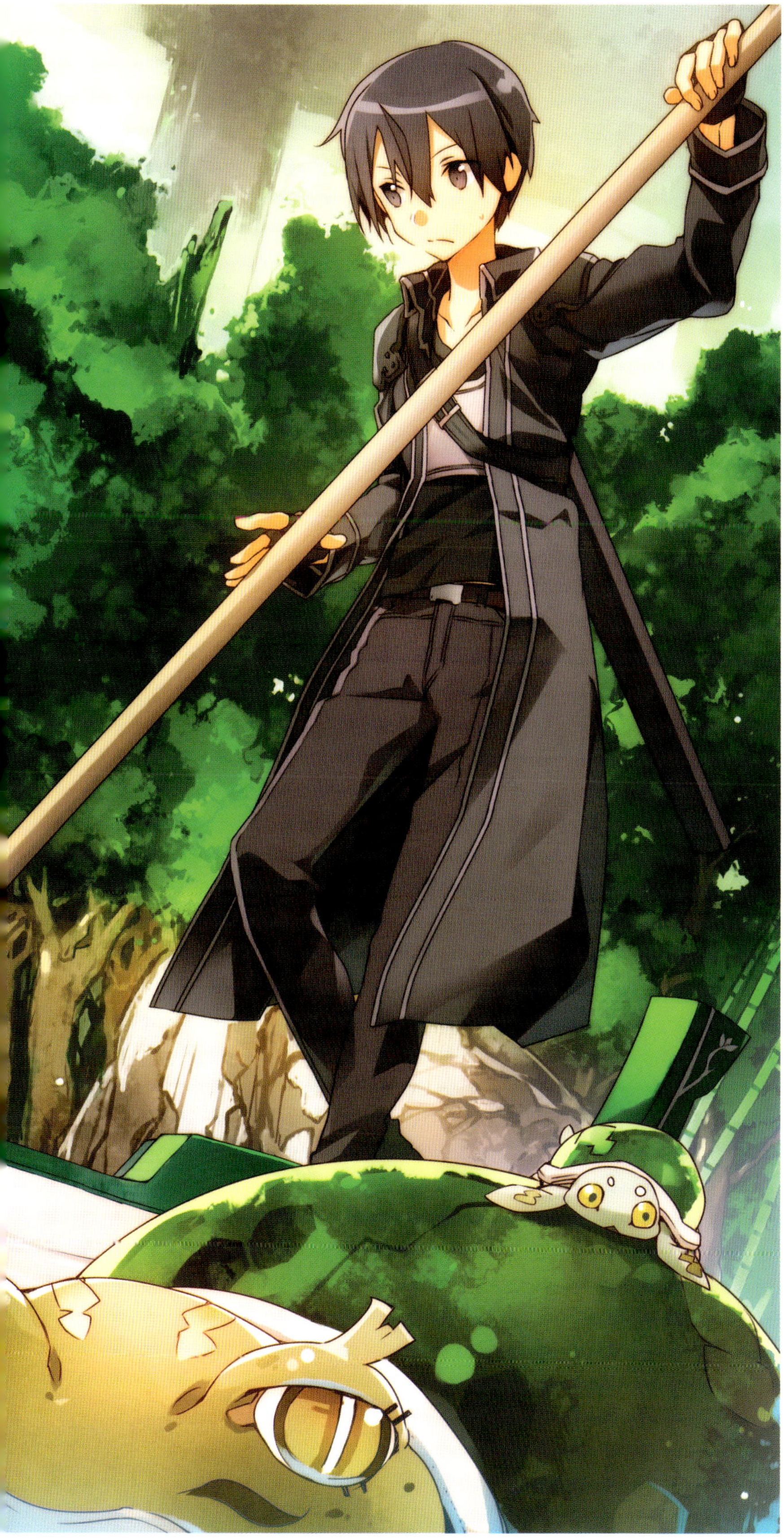

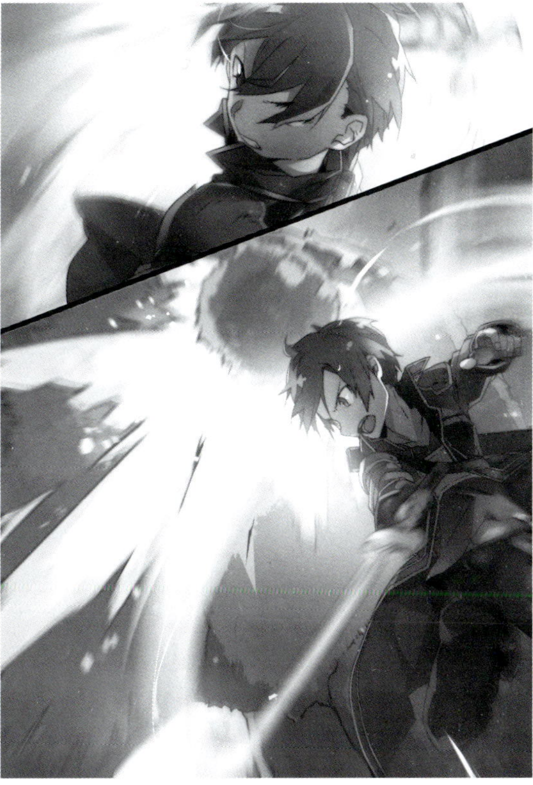

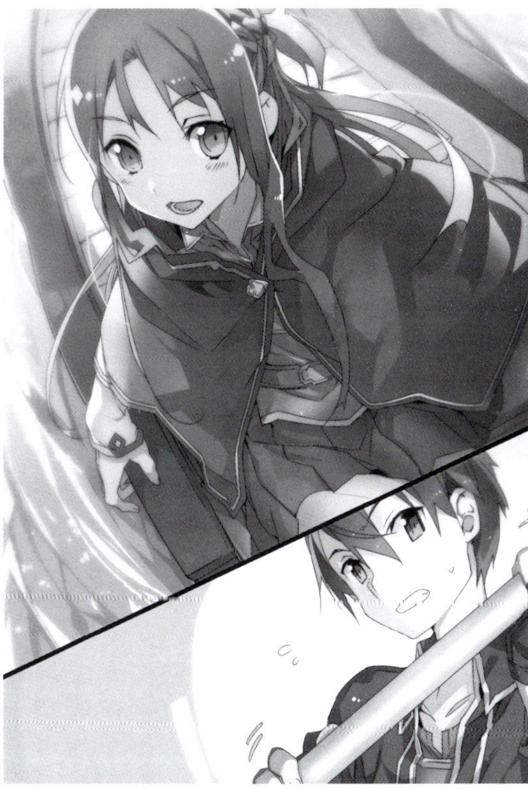

Dengeki Bunko
Sword Art Online Progressive 3
Illustration: December 2014

The upper illustration is Kirito attacking the giant bear's tail, but you can't tell that just from the picture alone. The illustrations are meant to enhance the text, and sometimes the text enhances the image. How much information the illustration itself contains is something I agonize over.

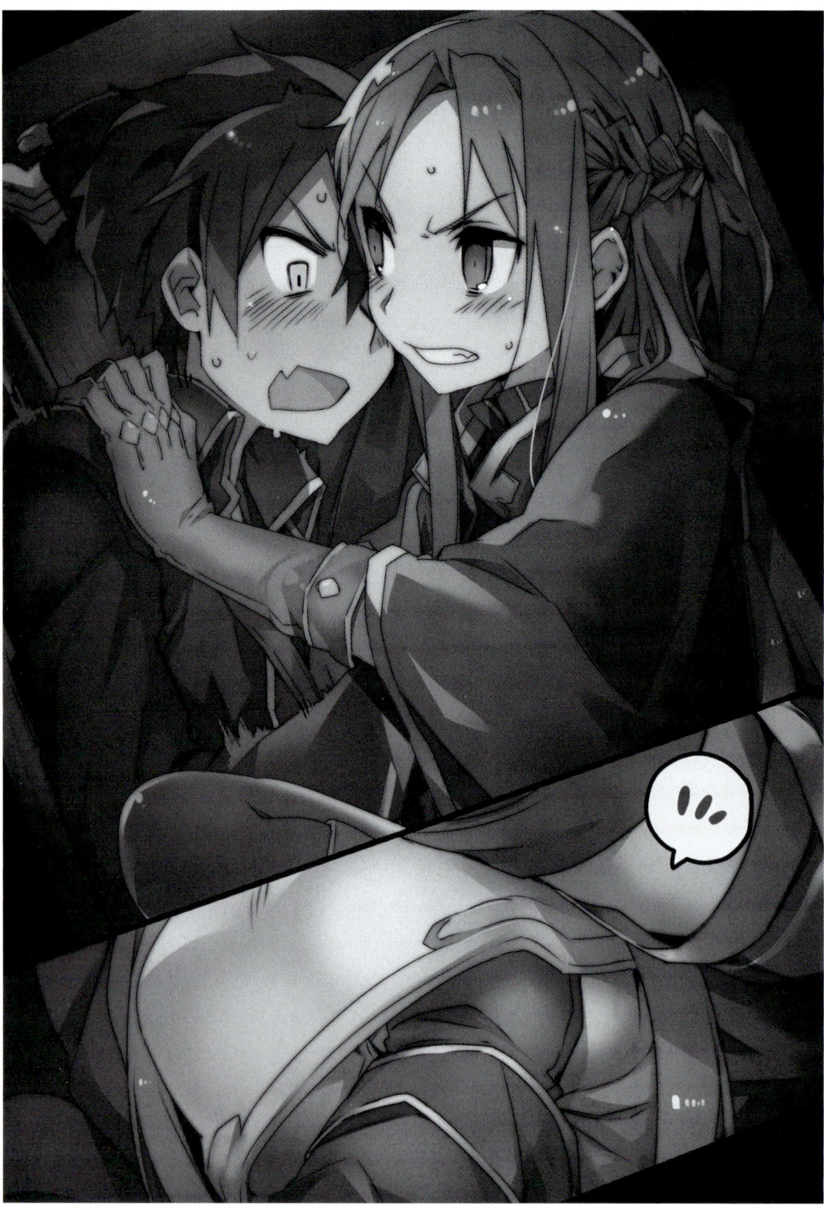

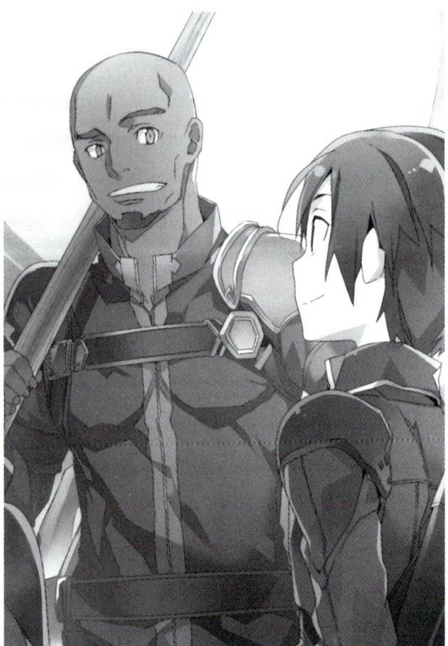

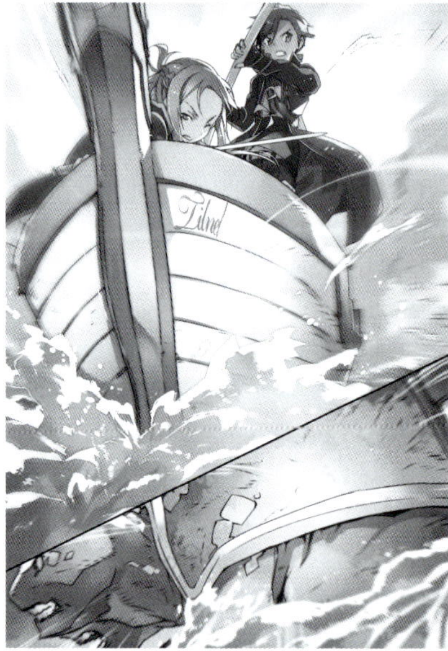

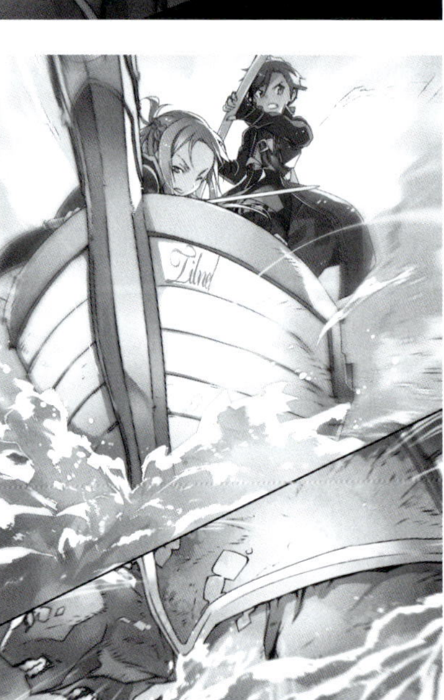

Dengeki Bunko
Sword Art Online Progressive 3
Illustration: December 2014

The one on top is a lucky pervy scene, but it's pretty difficult to put into a picture. On the bottom right, I like how much momentum I managed to get into the scene of the gondola blazing toward the giant turtle boss.

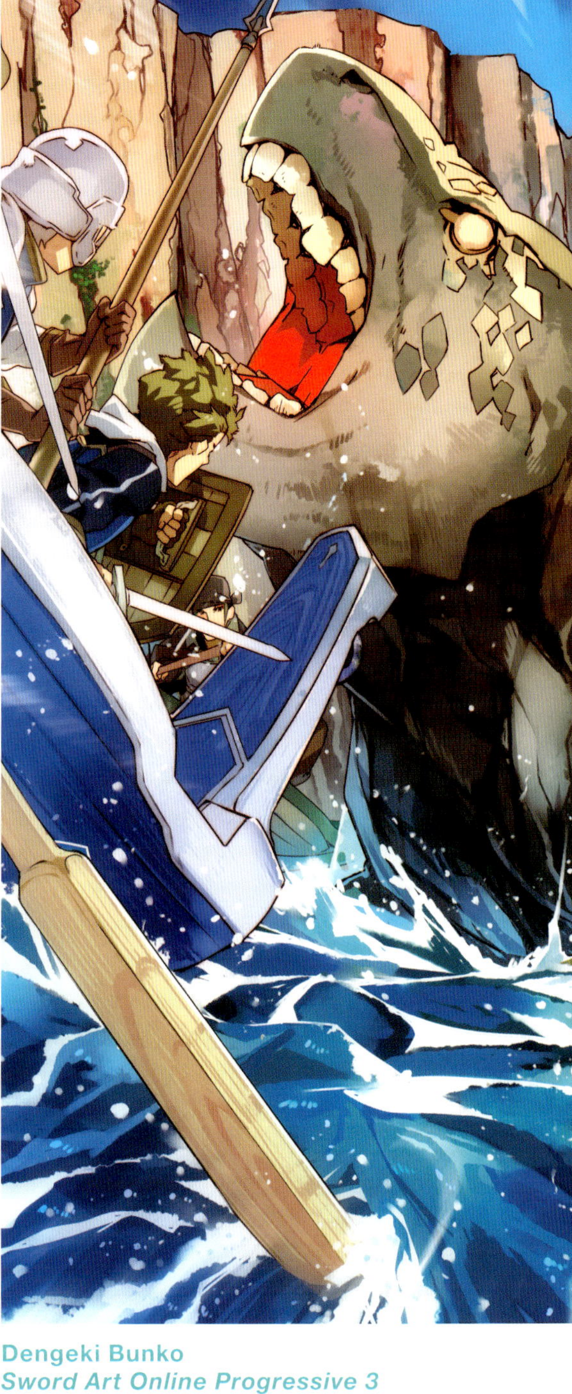

Dengeki Bunko
Sword Art Online Progressive 3
Frontispiece: December 2014

The giant turtle field boss battle scene. I like the feeling of velocity in the water. I just really love big battle scenes where you see a bunch of characters charging at a giant monster.

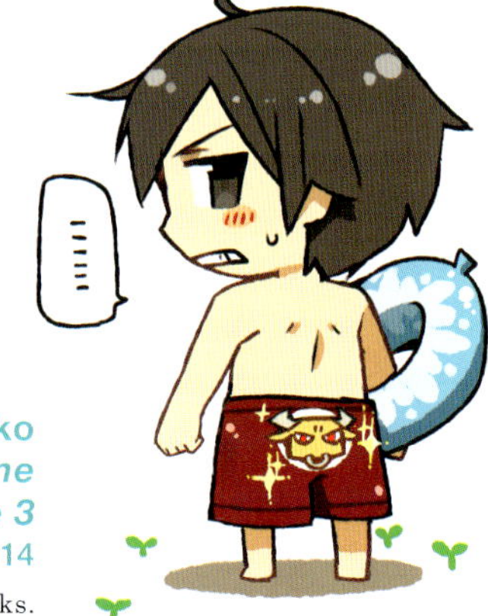

Dengeki Bunko
Sword Art Online Progressive 3
Back Cover: December 2014

Kirito with the bull-symbol trunks. This is fan service!

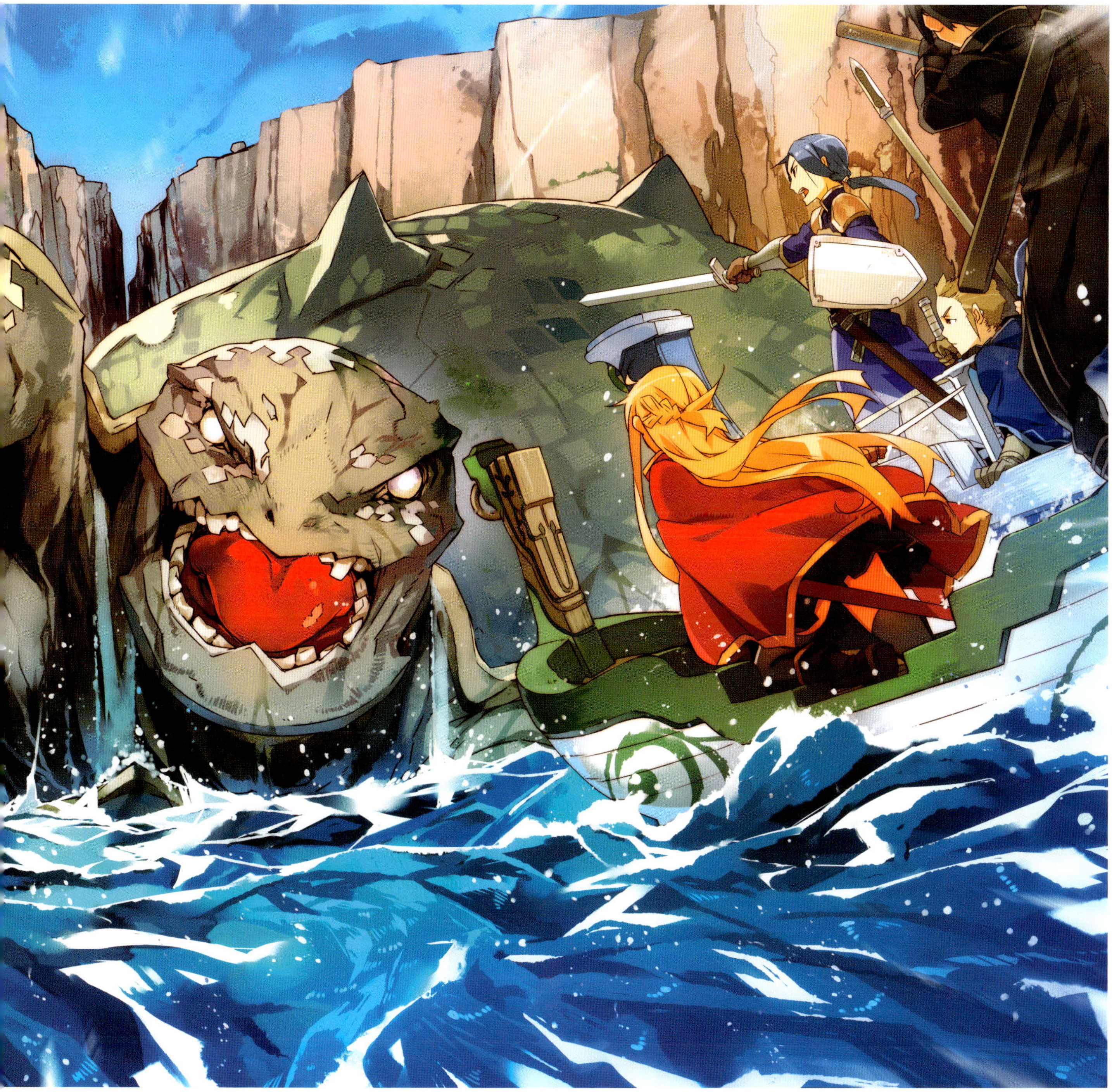

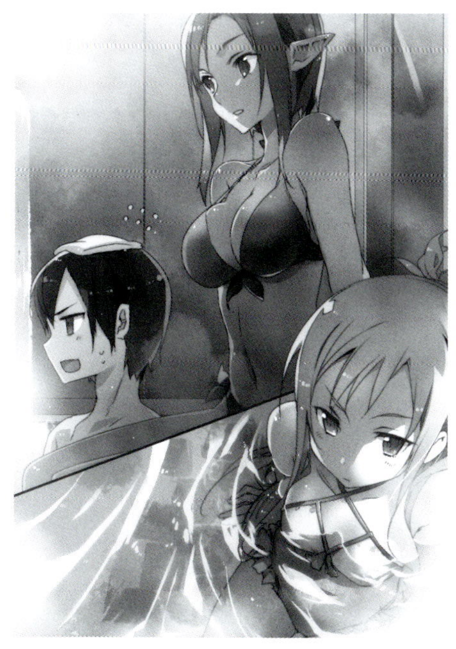

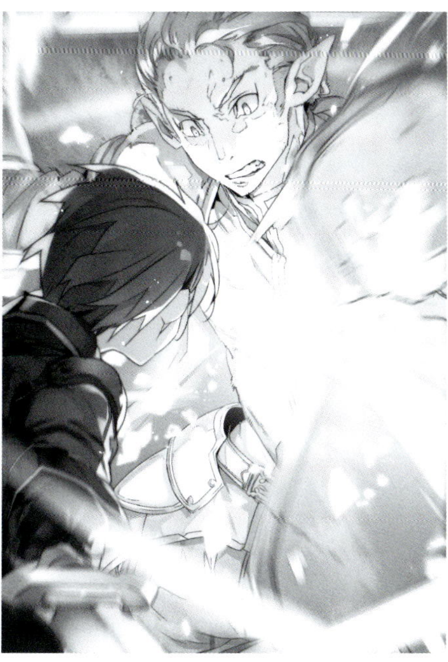

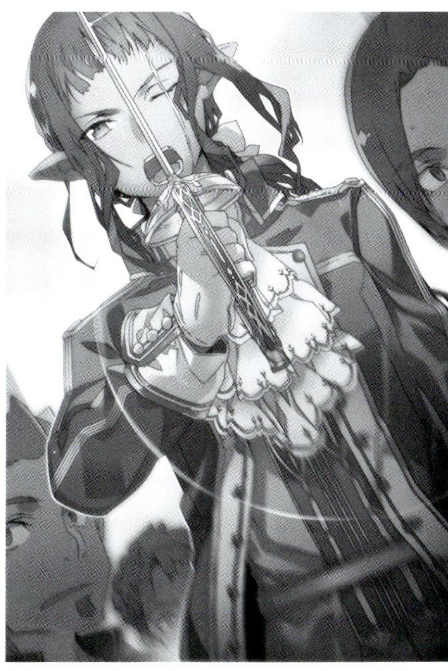

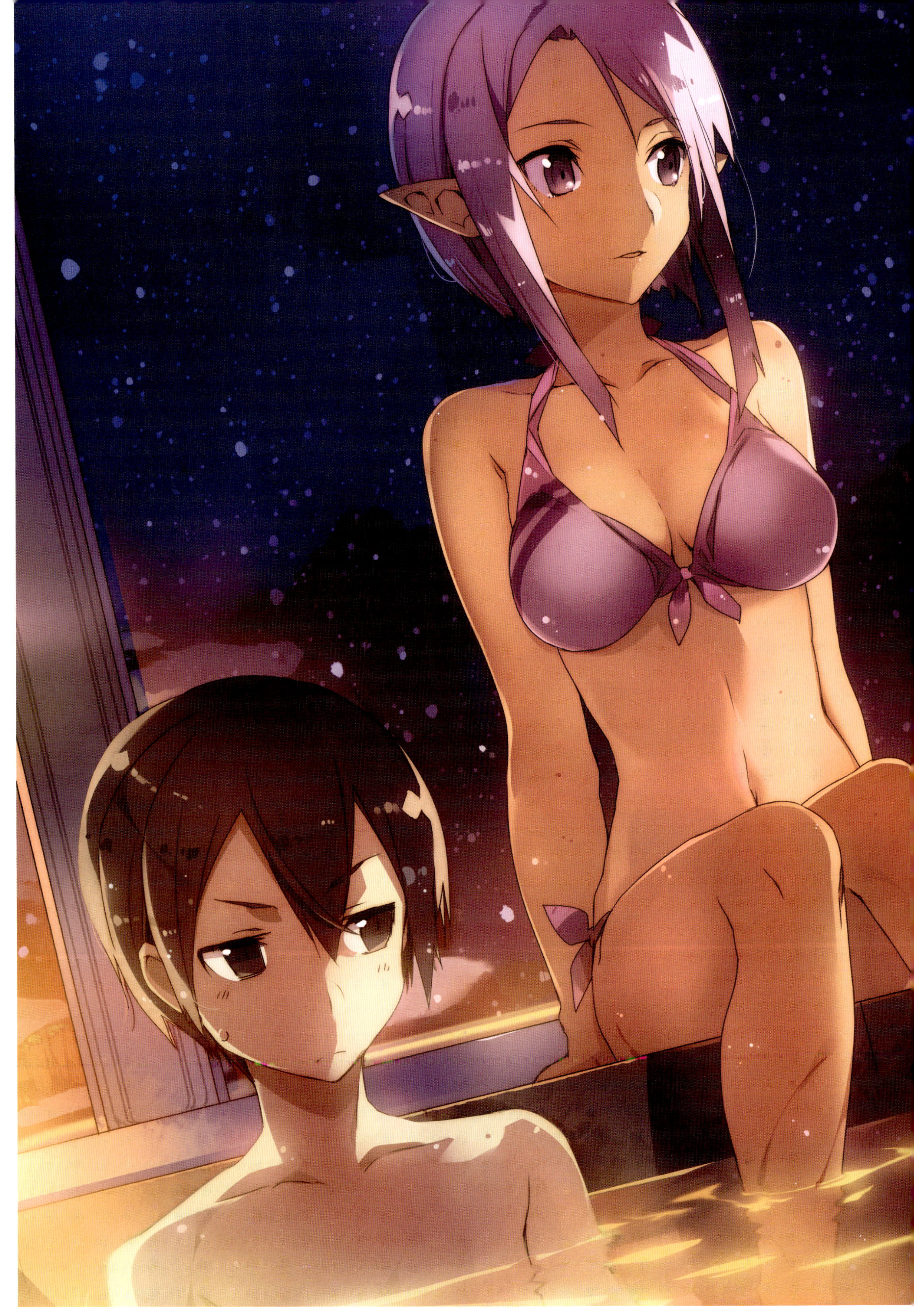

Dengeki Bunko, *Sword Art Online Progressive 3*
Frontispiece: December 2014

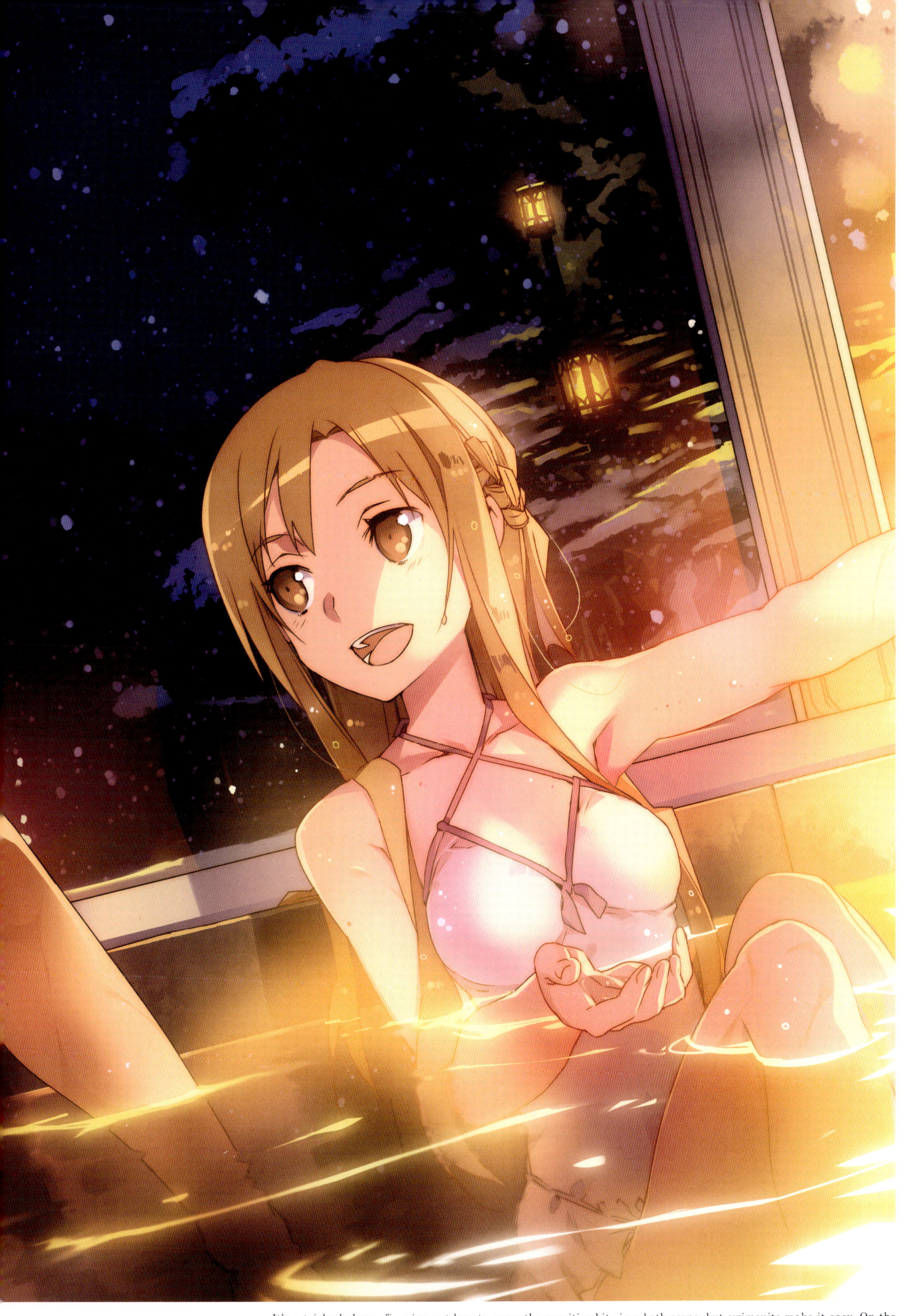

It's a tricky balance figuring out how to cover the sensitive bits in a bath scene, but swimsuits make it easy. On the other hand, a swimsuit makes the "bath" vibe weaker. I was worrying about a lot of little things like whether or not her long hair should be touching the water, but I ultimately decided it was okay, since it's a video game. Even in real-life settings, I'll often have long hair trailing in the water if I need it to cover the character's chest.

SWORD ART ONLINE media mix 4

This section is primarily comprised of illustrations for theatrical features and video games.

Yomiuri Shimbun & Asahi Shimbun, National Morning Edition
Promotional Illustration: January 2017

Of all the illustrations I drew for *Ordinal Scale*, this one expresses the aesthetic of the work the best. It's hard to tell, but that's the ground at Kirito's feet. One of my regrets is that I didn't make it clearer that he's standing on regular, real asphalt, but even still, I really like this one.

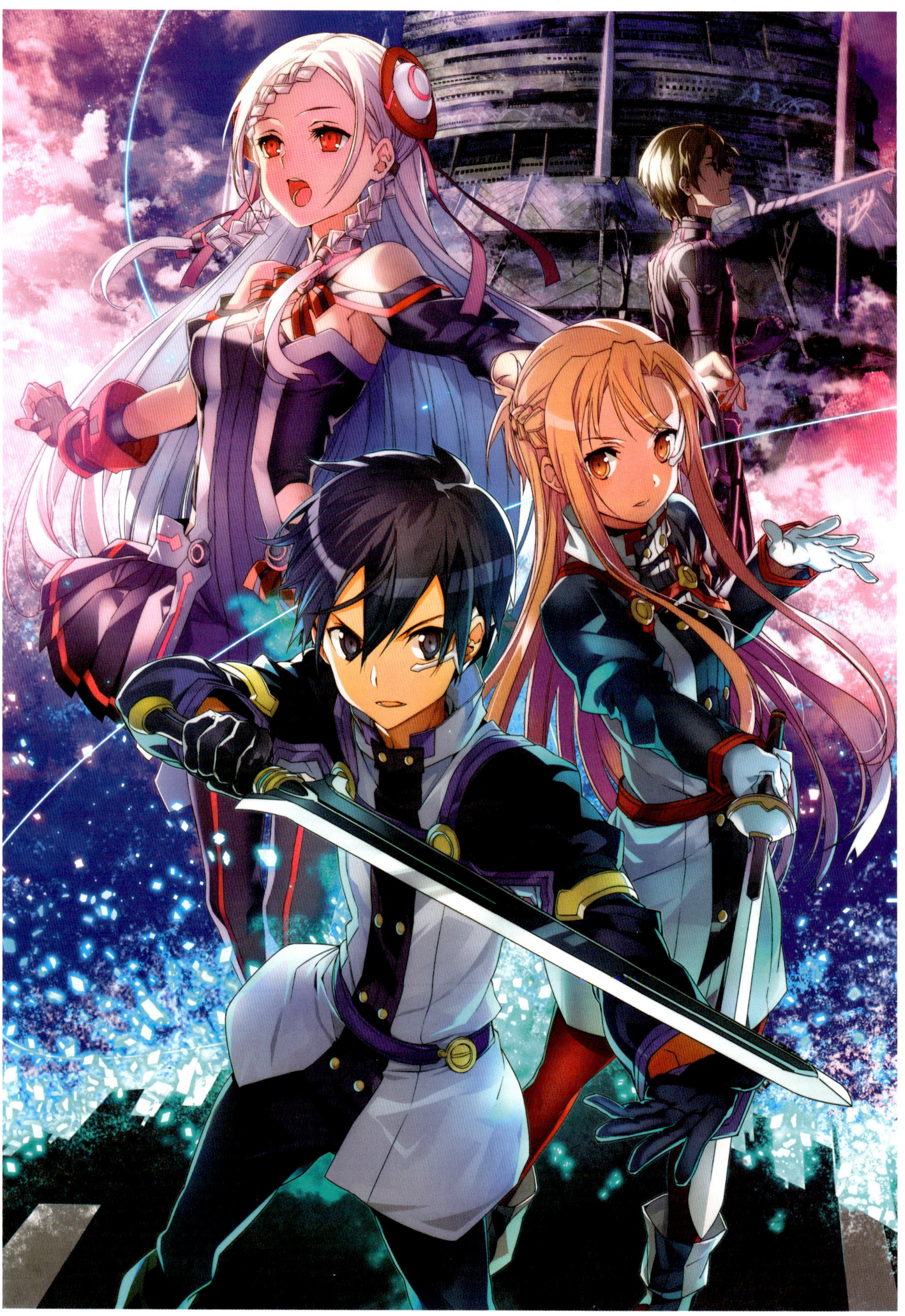

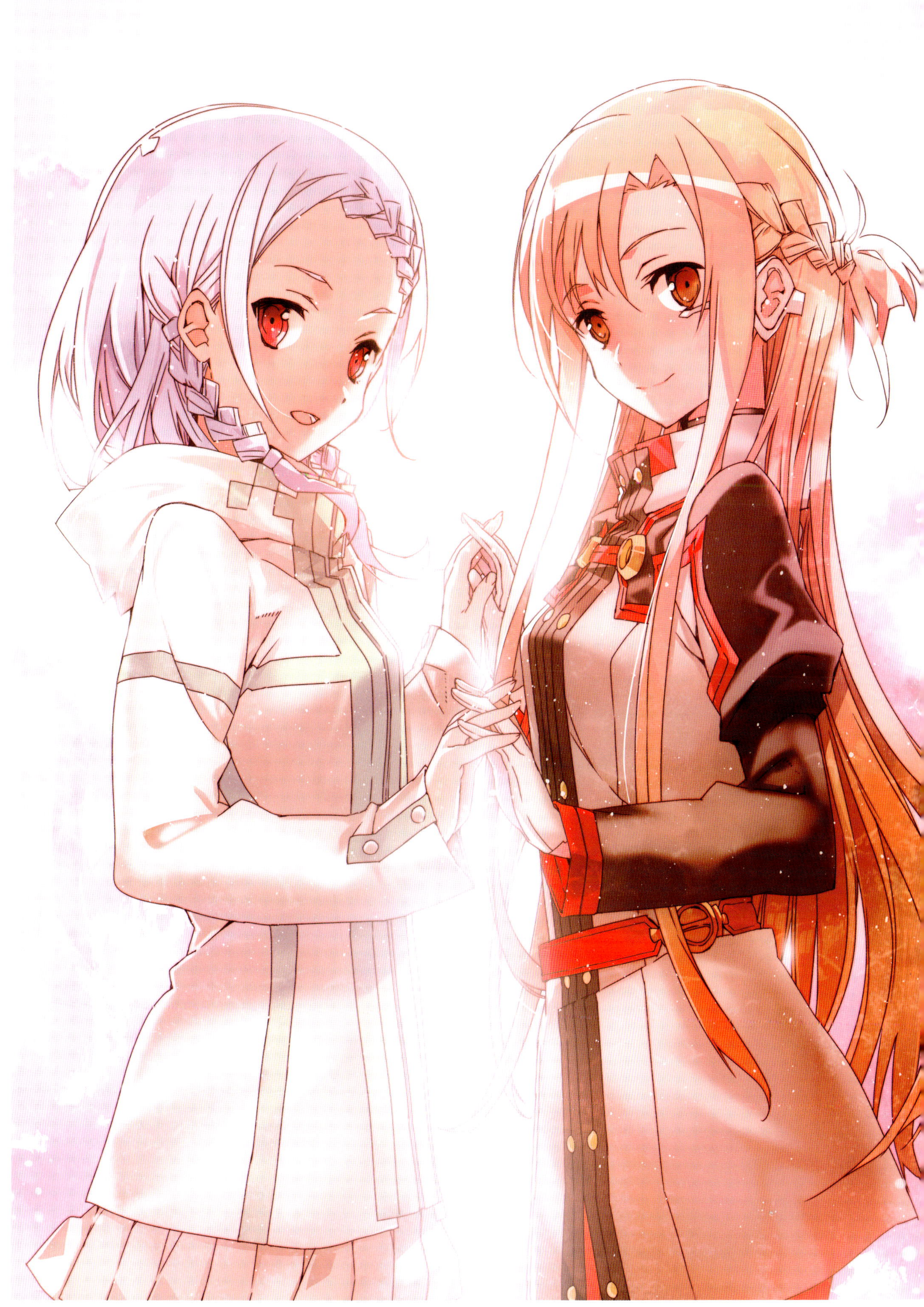

Theatrical Feature
***Sword Art Online The Movie: Ordinal Scale* BD/DVD**
Preorder Bonus Illustration Card: August 2017

Yuna and Asuna. I haven't done many illustrations with pale colors, so I went with that this time.

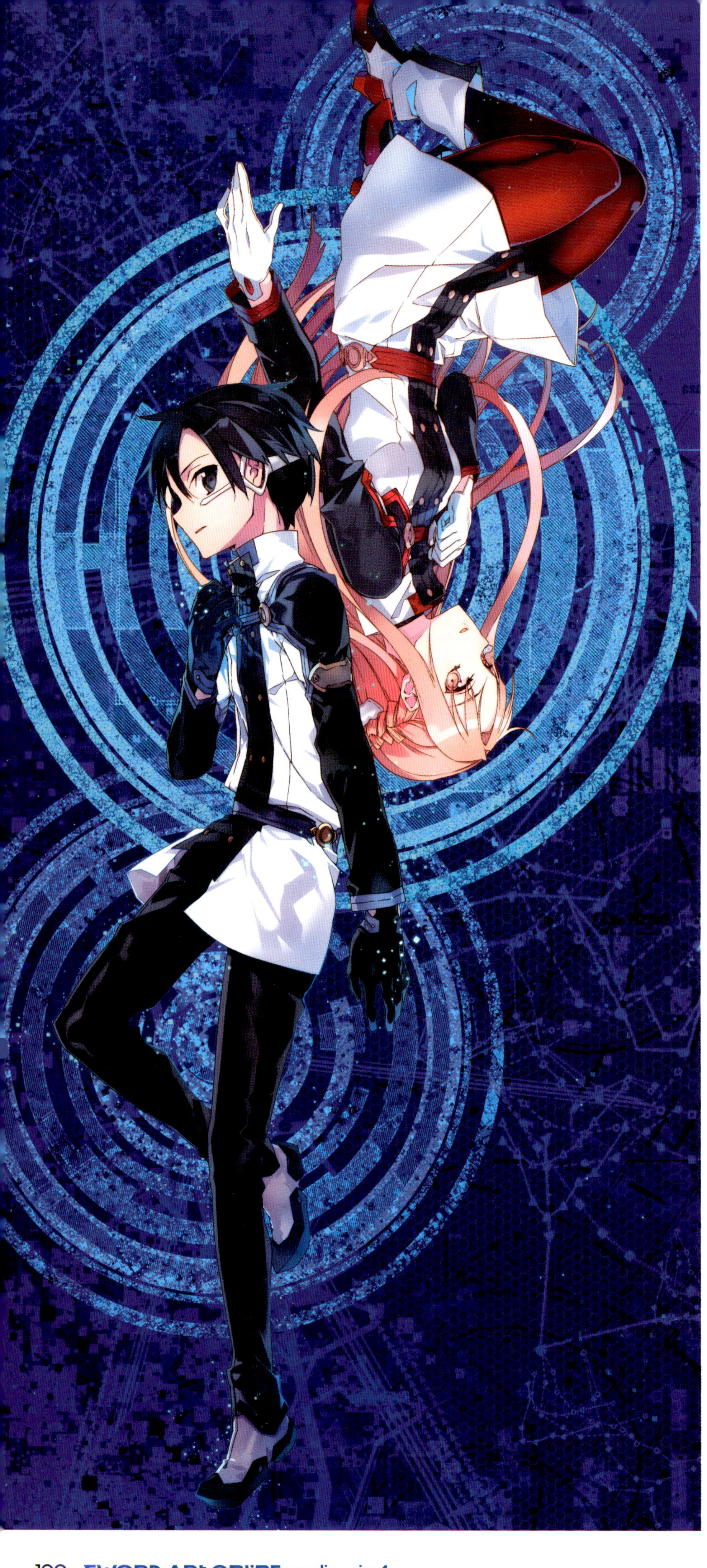

Sword Art Online The Movie: Ordinal Scale

Initial Key Visual: March 2016

This was the first image for the movie and the initial reveal of the costumes, but looking at it now, I think the overall color is too dark and blue, which makes it harder to tell how the clothes really look. Not sure about this one.

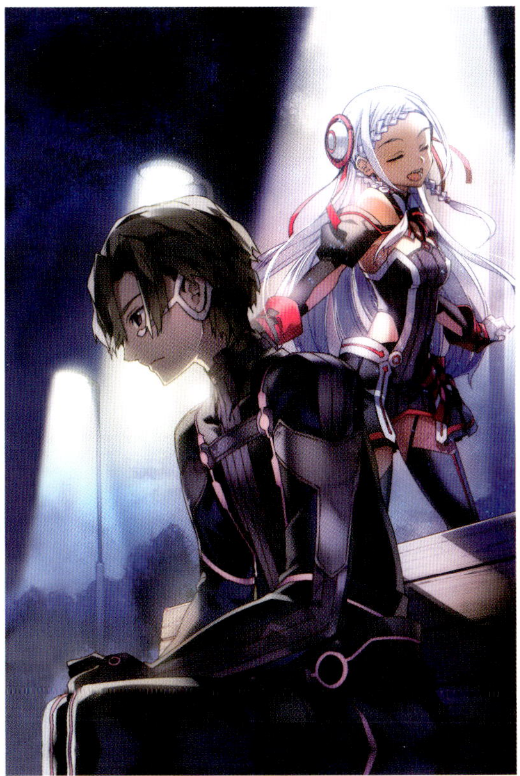

***Sword Art Online The Movie: Ordinal Scale* 3rd Week Theatrical Bonus: *Hopeful Chant* Novel**

Cover: March 2017

This was the cover for a special bonus novel, so this was based on its contents. Even when Yuna is singing happily, these two can't help but look sad together.

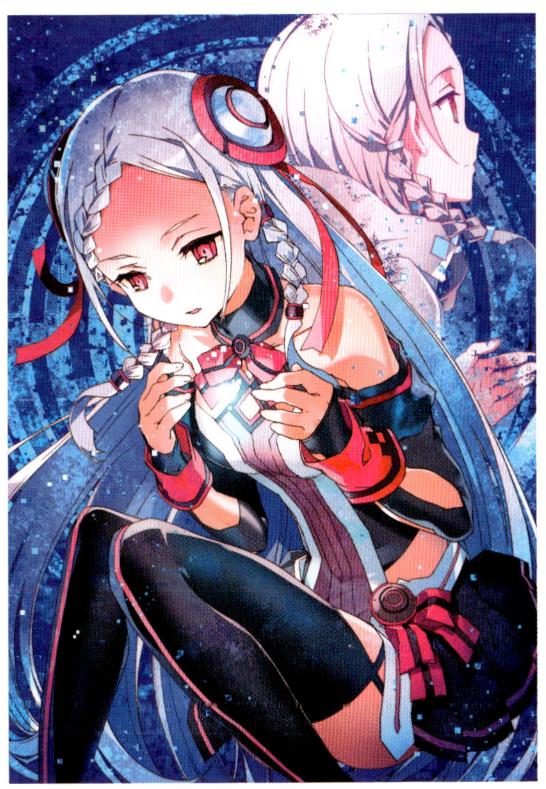

***Sword Art Online The Movie: Ordinal Scale* BD/DVD Limited Edition Bonus: *Cordial Chord* Novel**

Cover: August 2017

Two Yunas. The background and texture is reused from the first key visual.

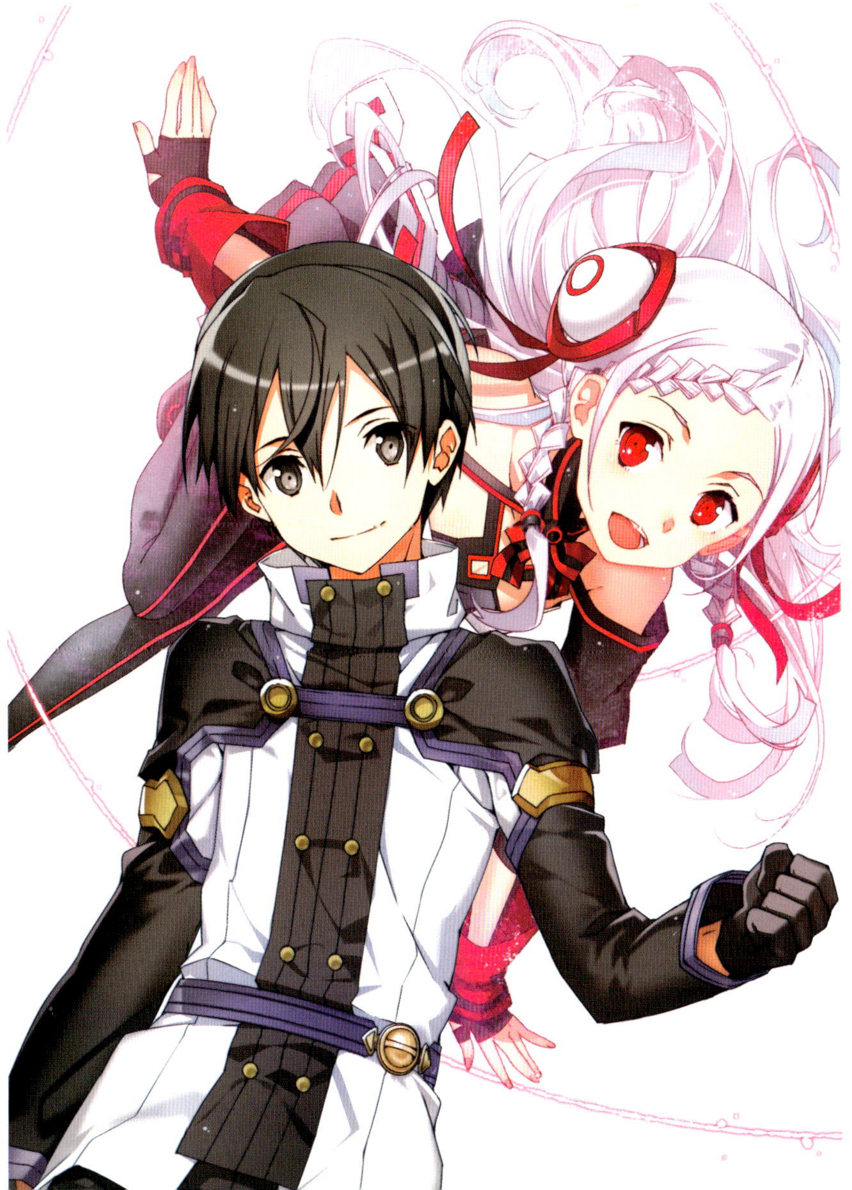

***Dengeki Bunko Magazine*, Vol. 54**

Cover: February 2017

Cover illustrations for *Dengeki Bunko Magazine* are generally on a blank white background, so I made the color combination bright to match it.

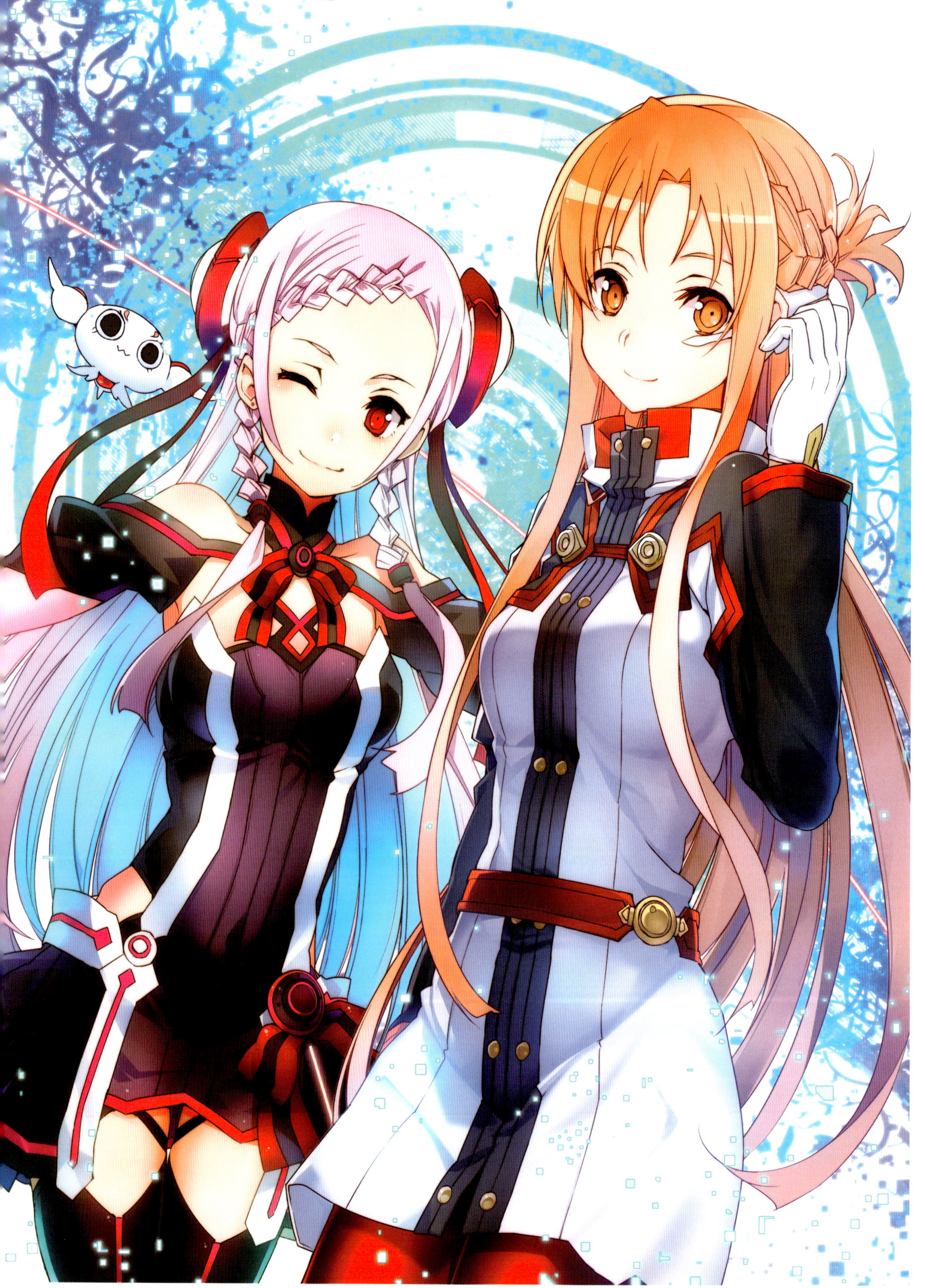

***Dengeki Bunko Magazine*, Vol. 53**
Cover: December 2016

Despite the covers of *Dengeki Bunko Magazine* not needing backgrounds, I drew one for this piece. Because of that, the color hues trended toward blue to match. I tend to like having a background in order to provide the right level of visual information.

Sword Art Online The Movie: Ordinal Scale

6–7th Week Theatrical Bonus
Mini Shikishi: March 2017

I drew these as a set of four mini shikishi. While blocking them out, I imagined the order of Yuna, Kirito, Asuna, Eiji, but I drew them in such a way that Yuna and Eiji could go side by side.

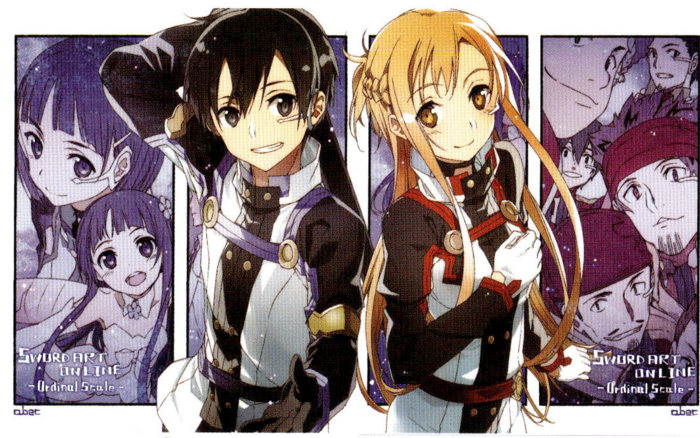

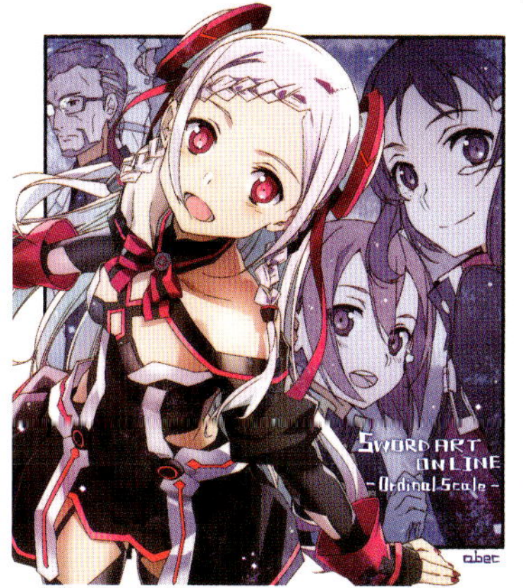

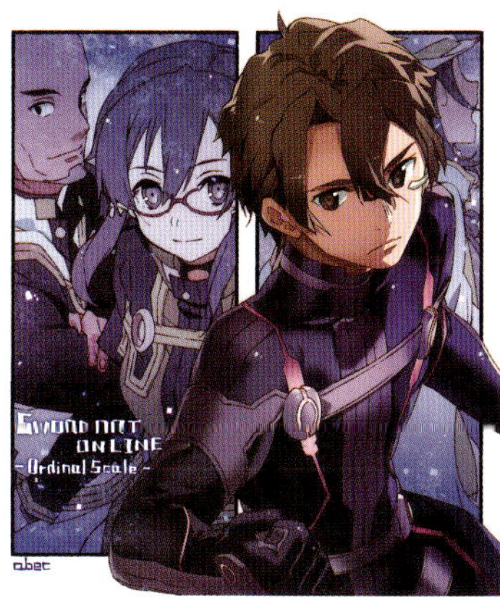

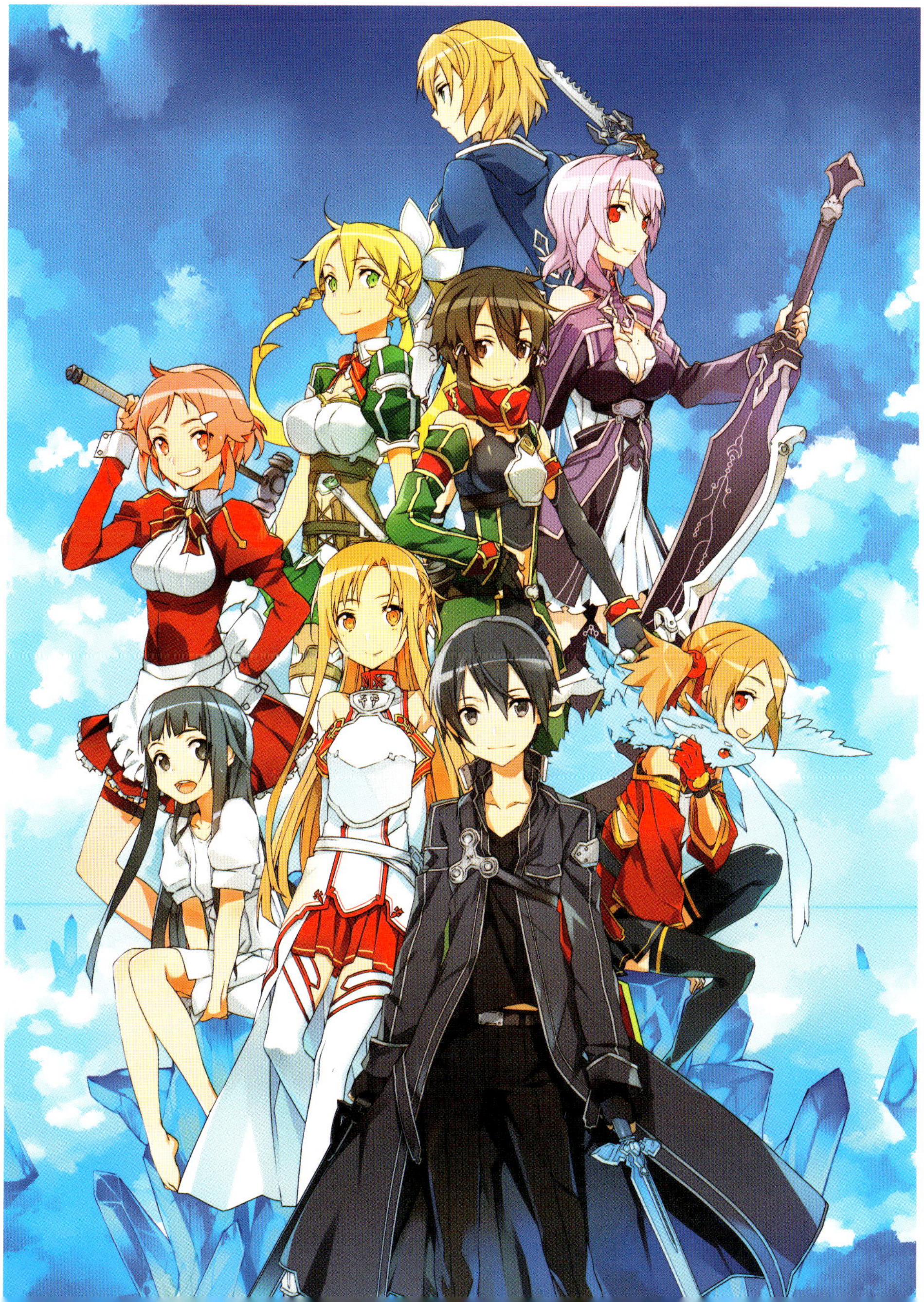

PS Vita Game *Sword Art Online: Hollow Fragment*

Limited Edition Package
Illustration: April 2014

This is a game cover. People might be split on them, but one of the great things about games is that you can depict scenarios that would never happen in the novels. So this cover features outfits for Leafa and Sinon, who were never in Aincrad.

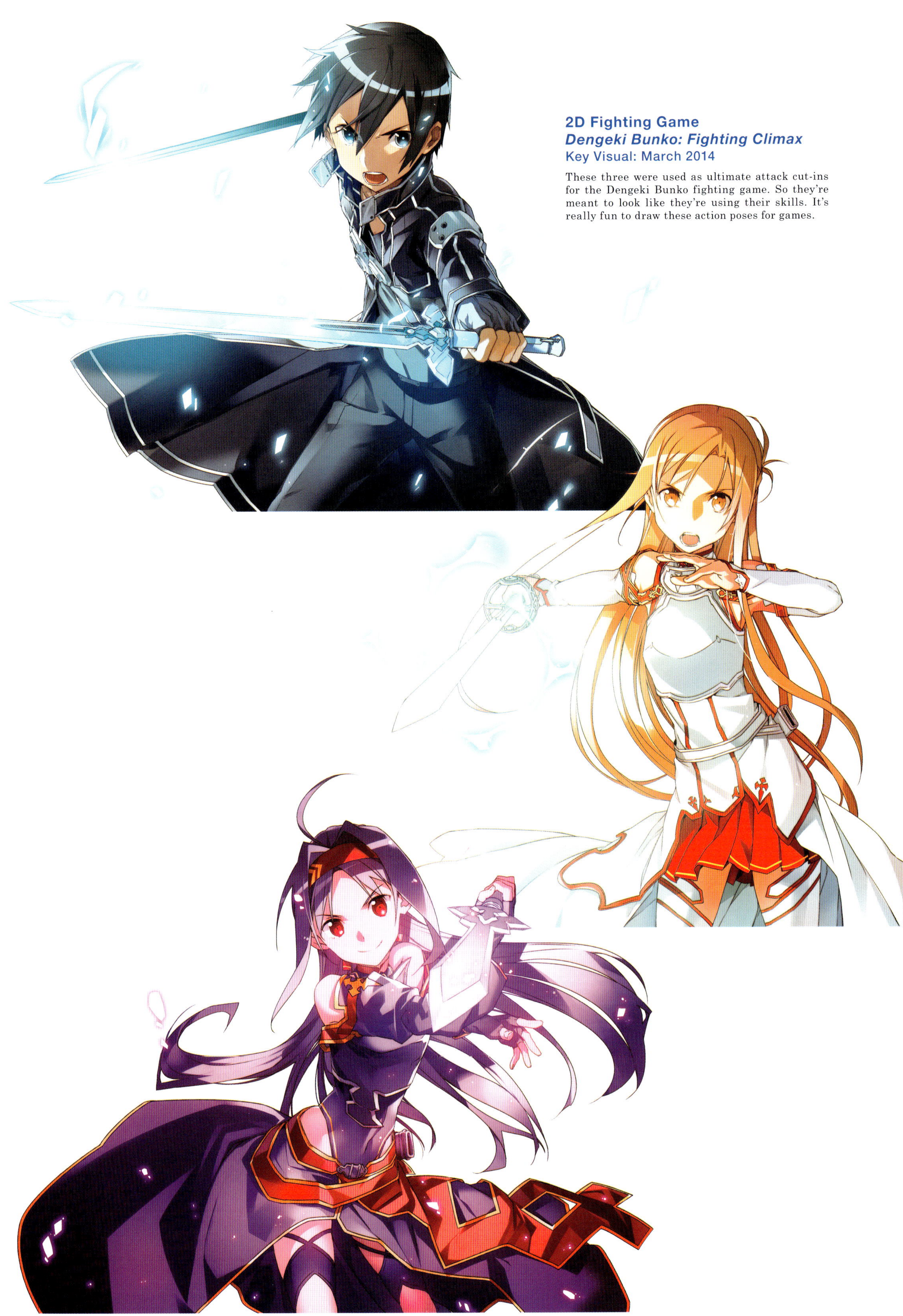

2D Fighting Game
Dengeki Bunko: Fighting Climax
Key Visual: March 2014

These three were used as ultimate attack cut-ins for the Dengeki Bunko fighting game. So they're meant to look like they're using their skills. It's really fun to draw these action poses for games.

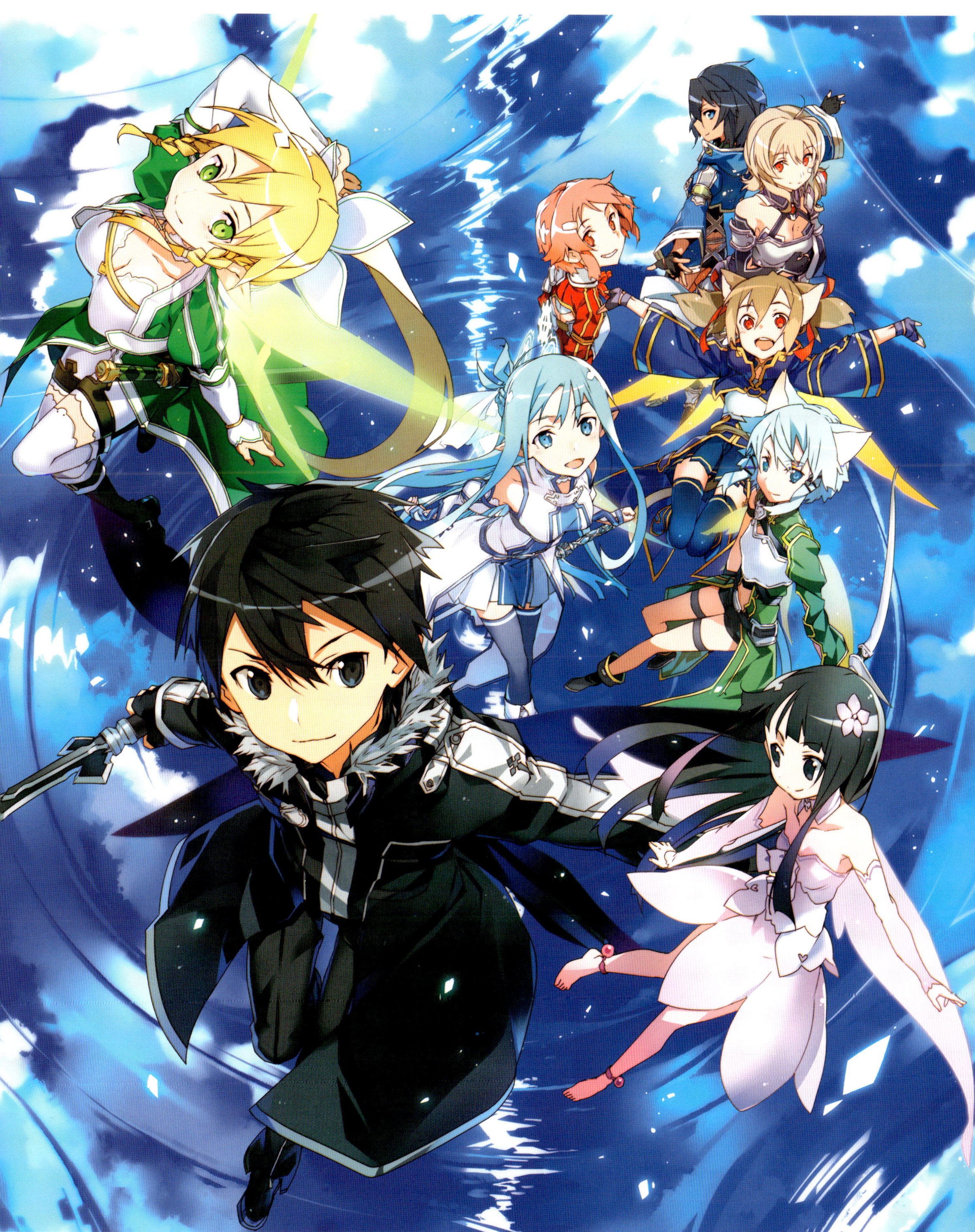

PS3/PS Vita Game
Sword Art Online: Lost Song
Limited Edition Box Illustration: March 2015

Since there's a flight mode in this game, I drew them flying. That makes it much easier to place them in the image, and frees them up for more varied action.

Strategy Guide
Sword Art Online: Hollow Realization: The Complete Guide
Cover: November 2016

This is a *Hollow Realization* book, so Kirito and Asuna are wearing their outfits from the game. They're difficult to draw, because there's a lot of detail. The designs on Premiere's robe are also surprisingly tough.

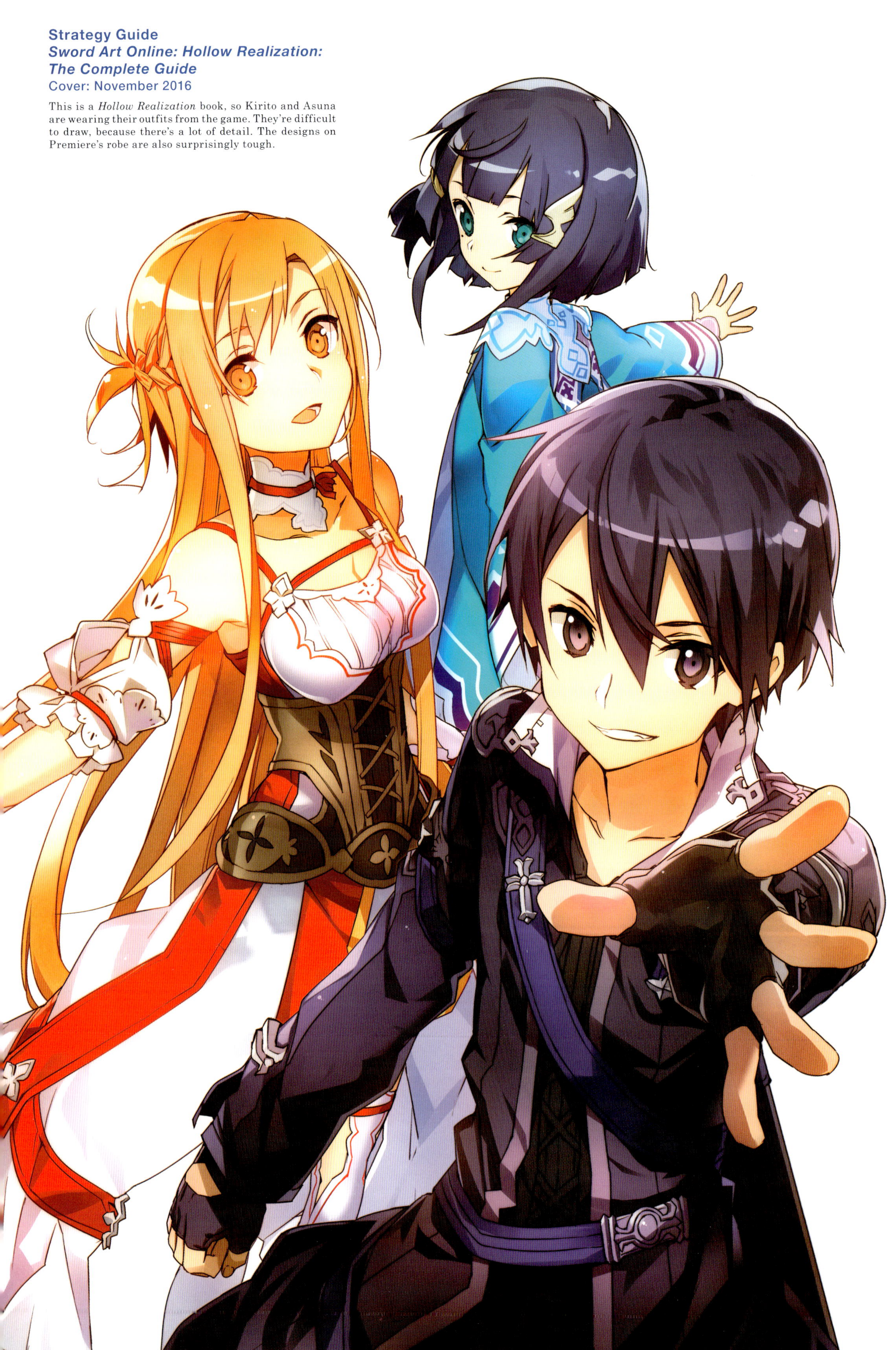

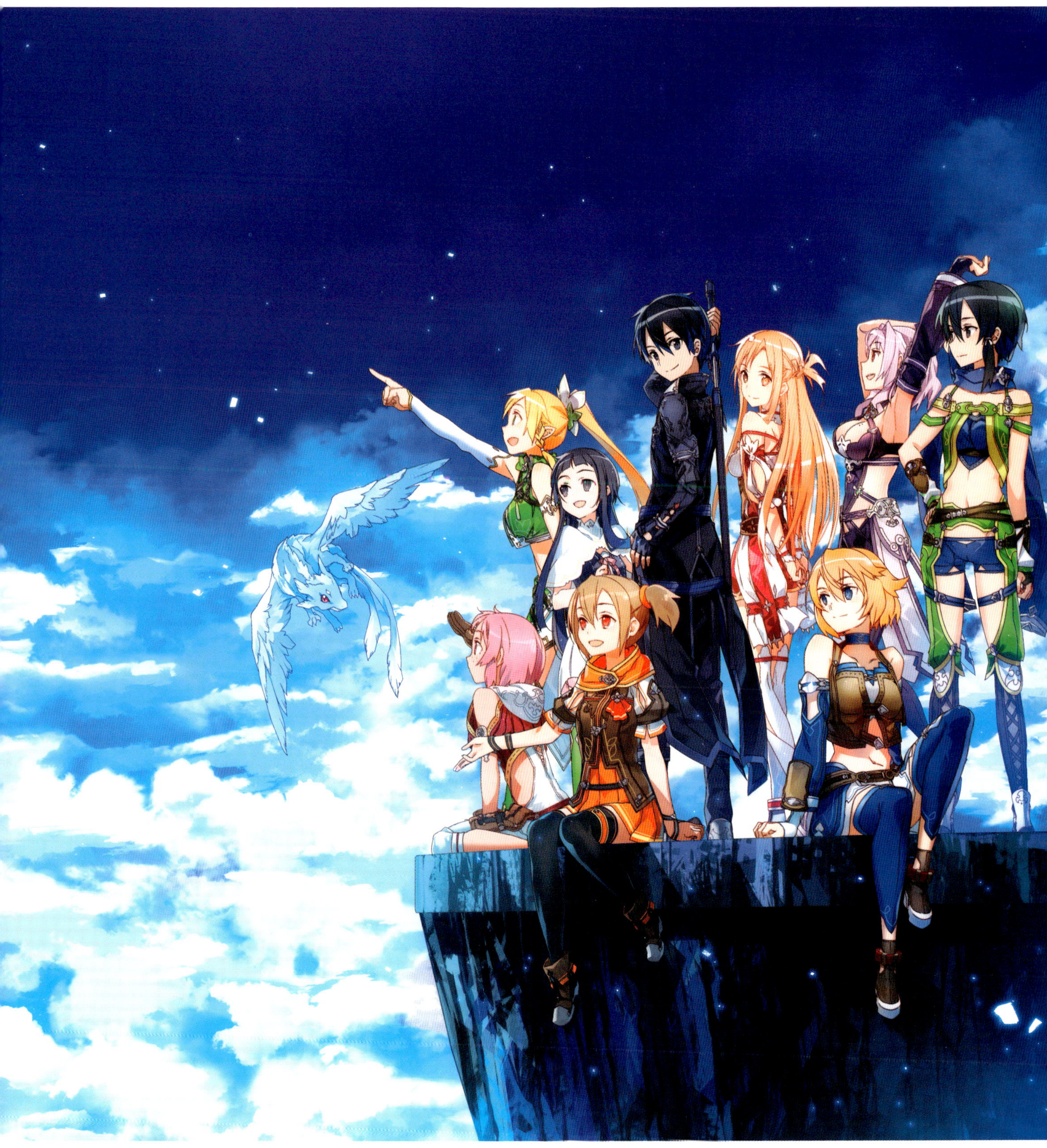

PS4/PS Vita Game
Sword Art Online: Hollow Realization
Limited Edition Box Illustration: October 2016

Pina's camouflaged into the background! I have no input on the game's design, but I've noticed there's definitely an elevated level of skin exposure here.

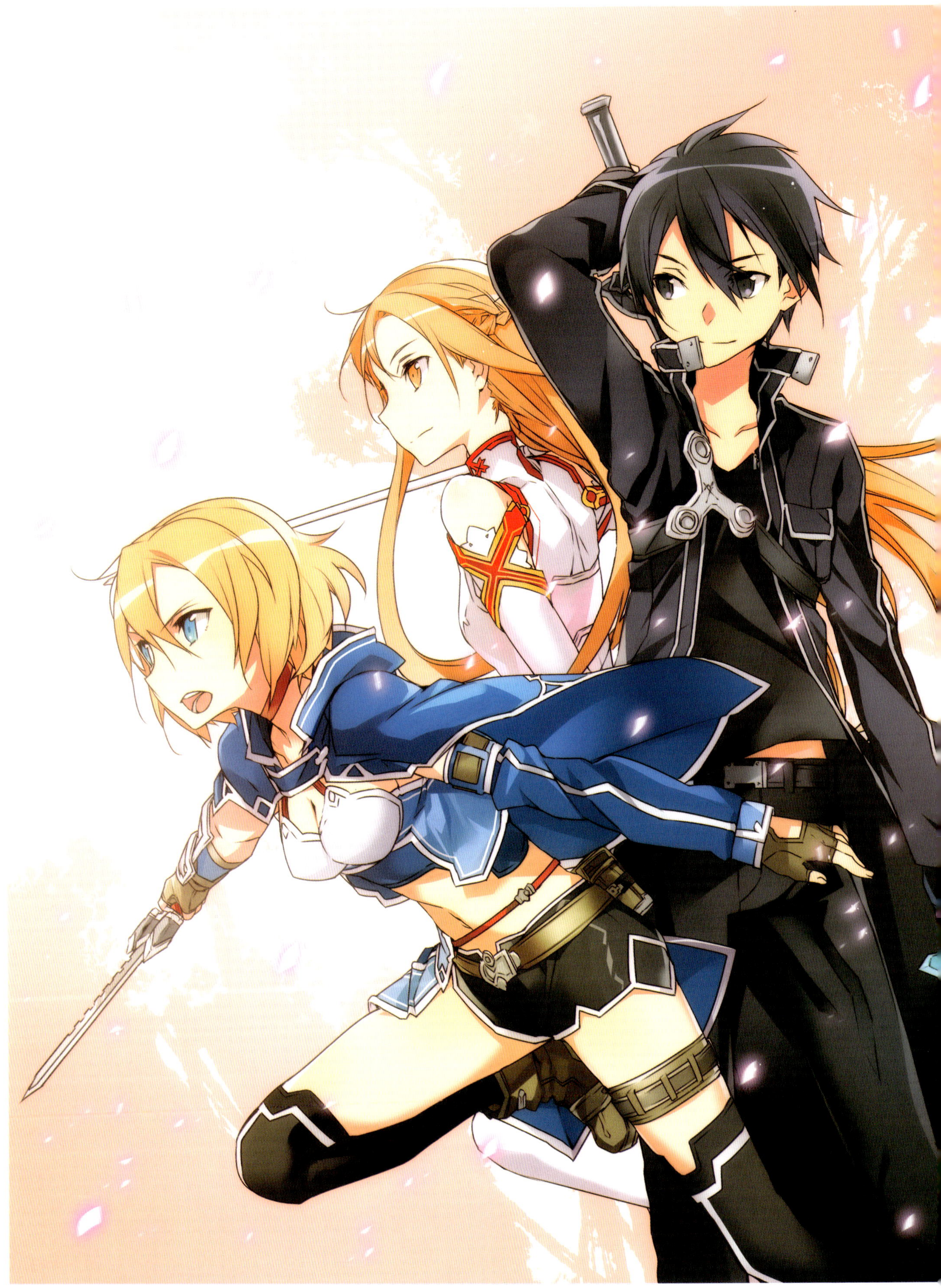

***Dengeki PlayStation*, Vol. 565**

Cover: April 2014

A magazine cover; I believe this one was a wraparound to the back. On the left edge, there were borders that blocked the top and bottom, so when you see the full image, it looks a little empty. It's also the rare magazine cover that doesn't have the characters looking at you.

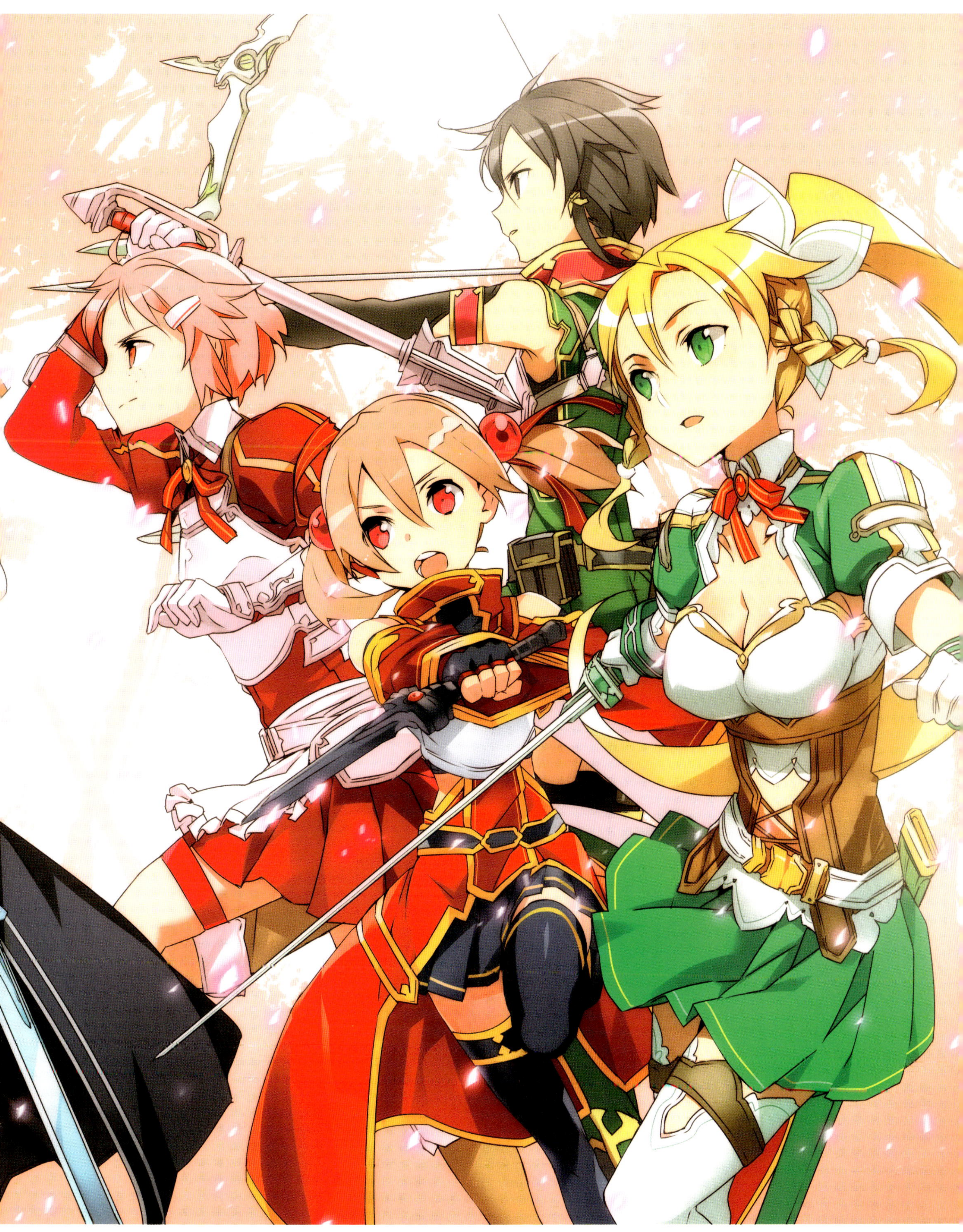

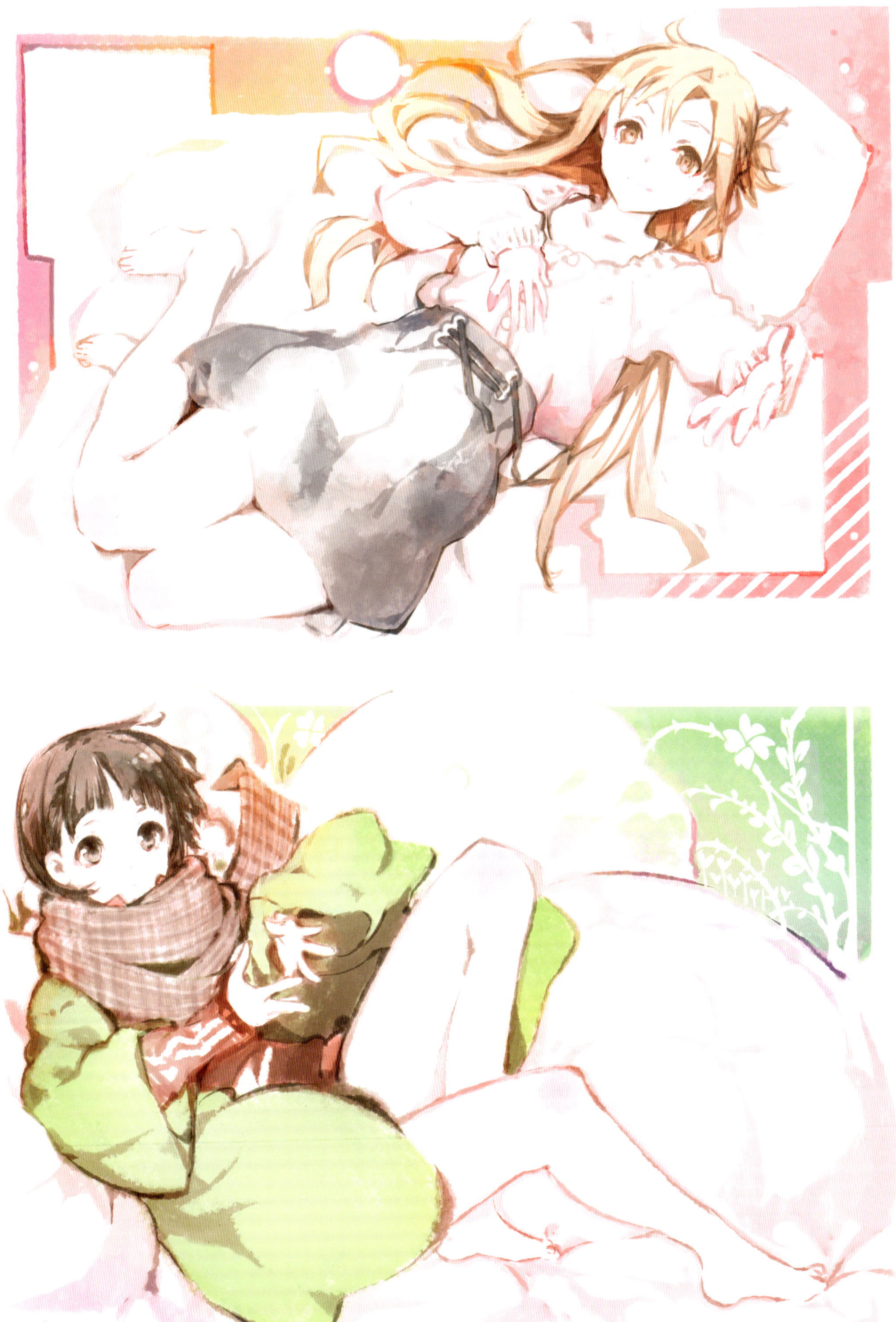

Never Commercially Published

These were drawn for the art book. The ones I did new for this book, including the cover, were drawn with different brush settings and styles than I usually use—except for Kirito. These ones in particular, I don't think I could have done unless it was for my own art book. I'd like to be able to improve in this style in the future.

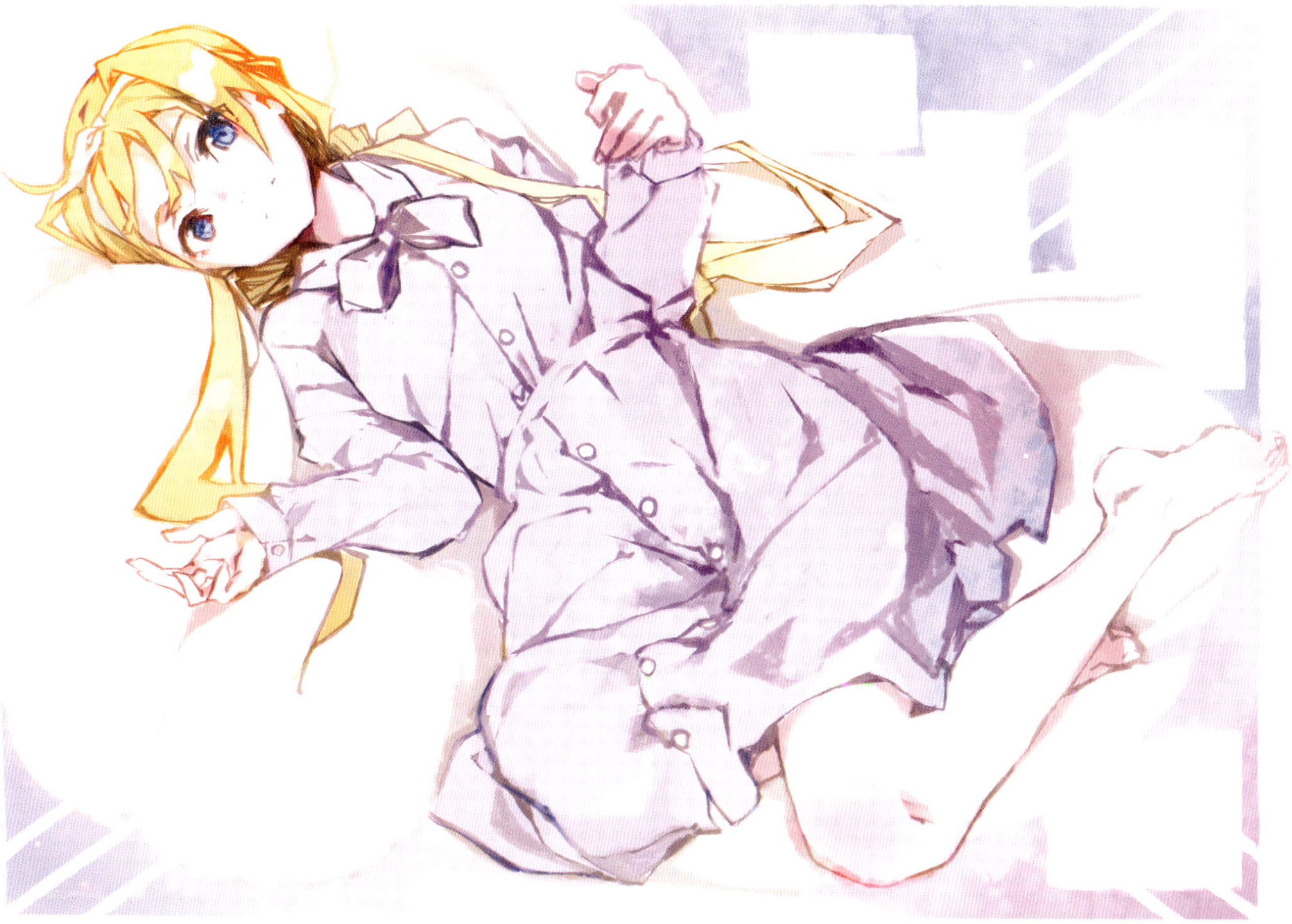

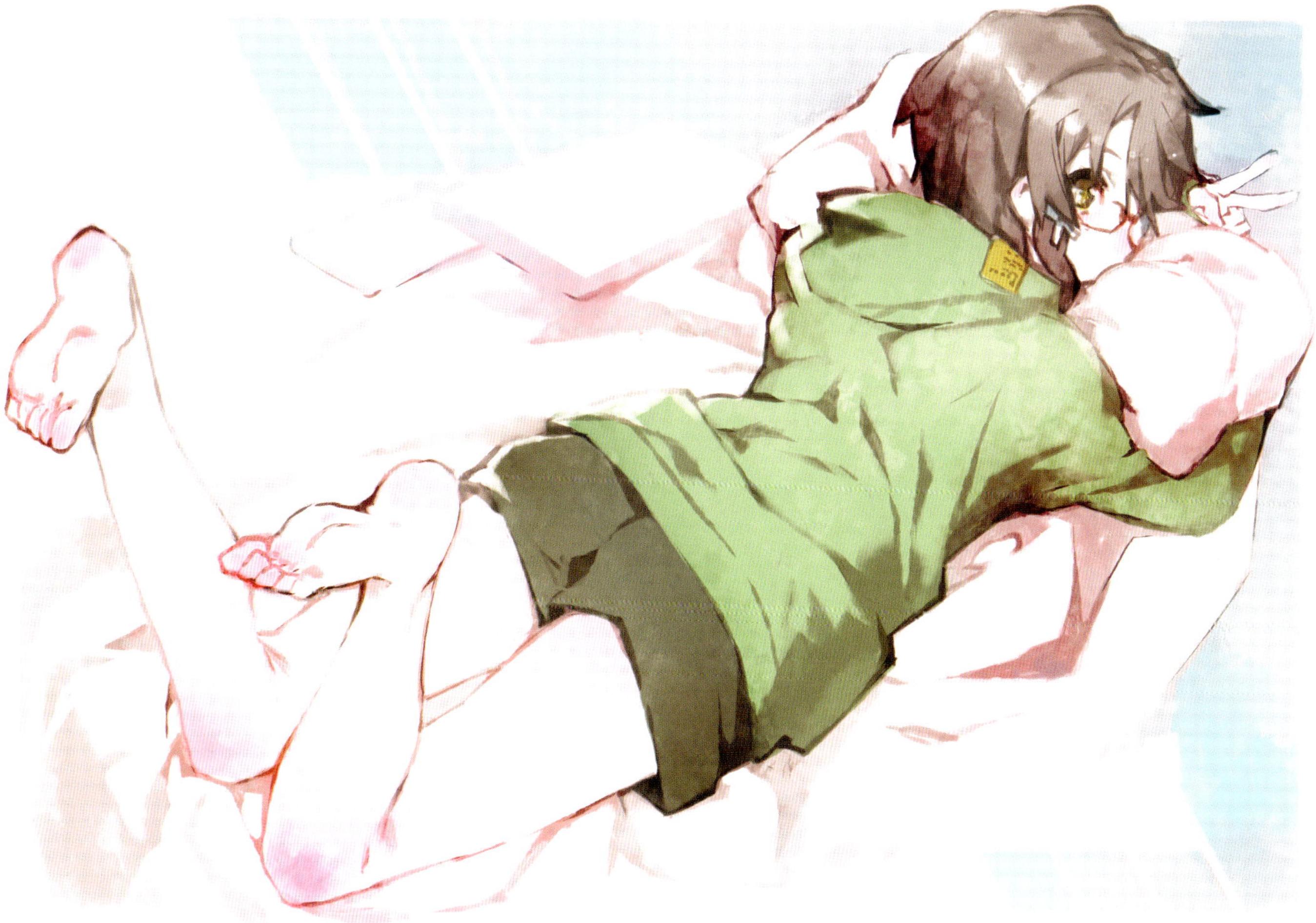

Never Commercially Published

It all started with the Suguha on the bottom left, which I drew as a bit of a breather between other work, and I liked it so much that I drew the other three soon after. My mind was completely blank as I drew her, which is why her padded kimono and tracksuit are so unfashionable, but I think the linework is the most relaxed there, which is why I like it so much.

SWORD ART ONLINE
model sheet for animation

Usually, character design for publishing is done for the author and editors to approve of, and for the artist's own reference, and is not a precursor to an animated adaptation. Naturally, when there is an anime, the animators redo it for their own purposes, but before that point, I also redid my own designs.

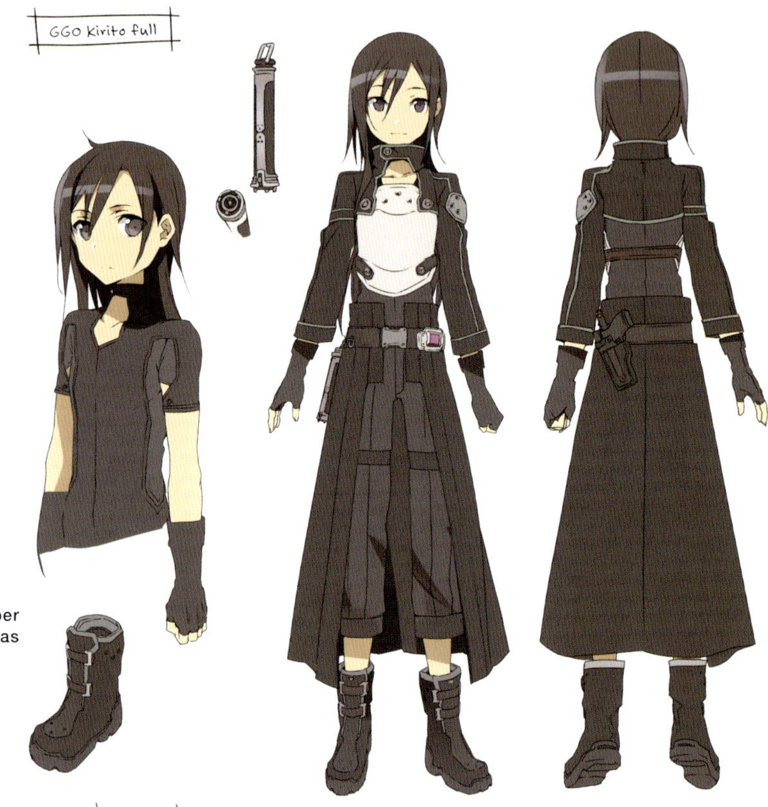

When working on the novels, I drew the upper half and cut the rest. Even from the start, I was drawing this Kirito with a feminine face.

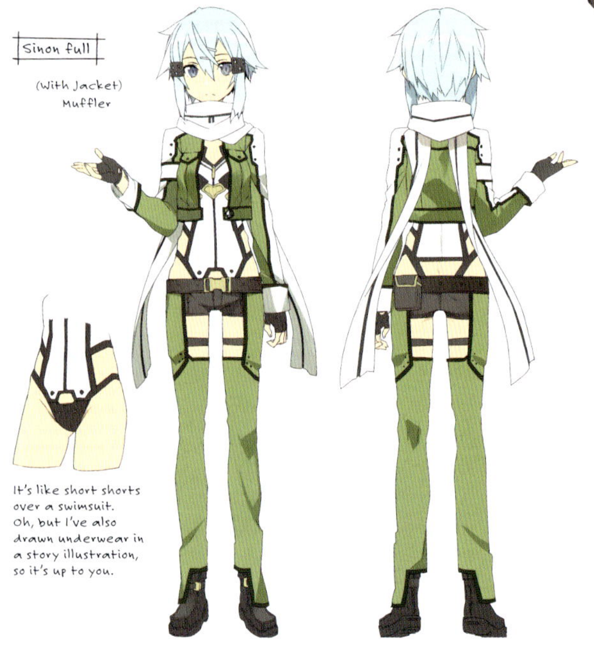

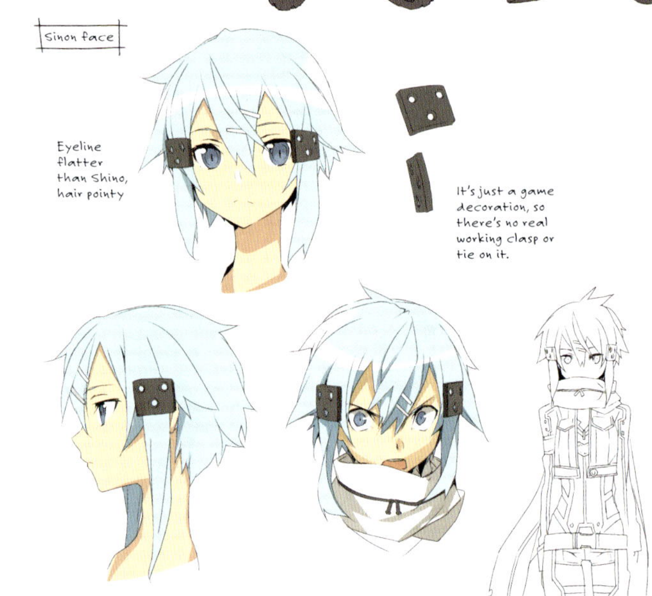

When I saw the anime, I realized her butt sticks out a lot more than I thought (laughs). I wasn't sure if revealing clothing really fit Shino as a person, but I decided that since Sinon is just her avatar in *GGO*, she probably focused on statistical benefits only and didn't worry about looks. Yeah, I bet those hot pants are for stats only!

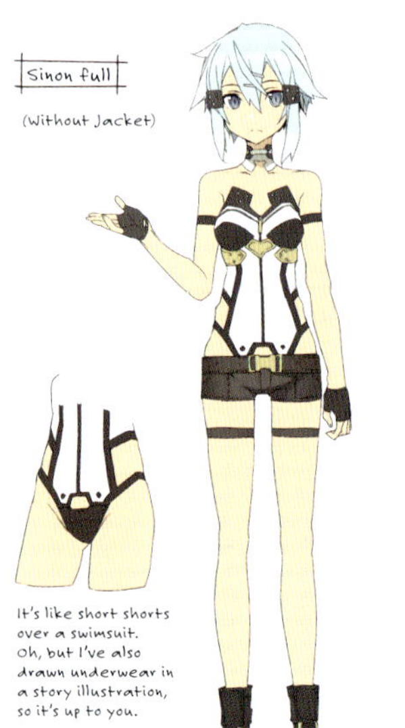

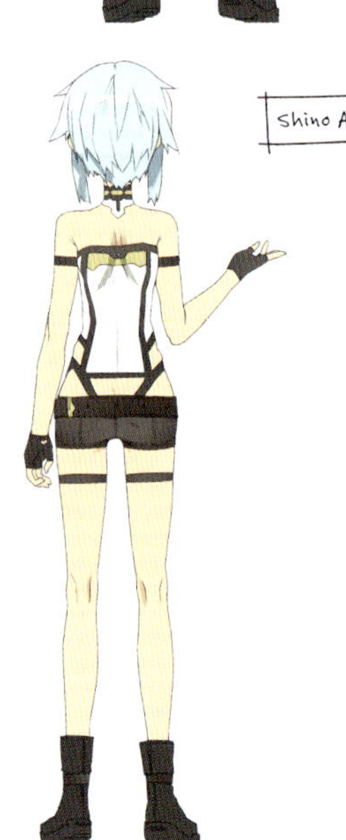

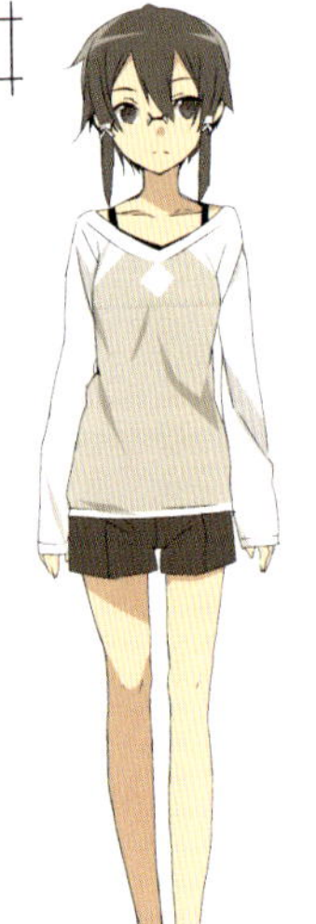

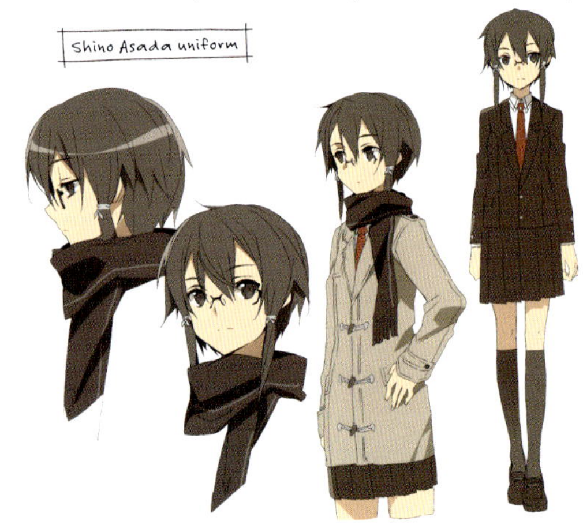

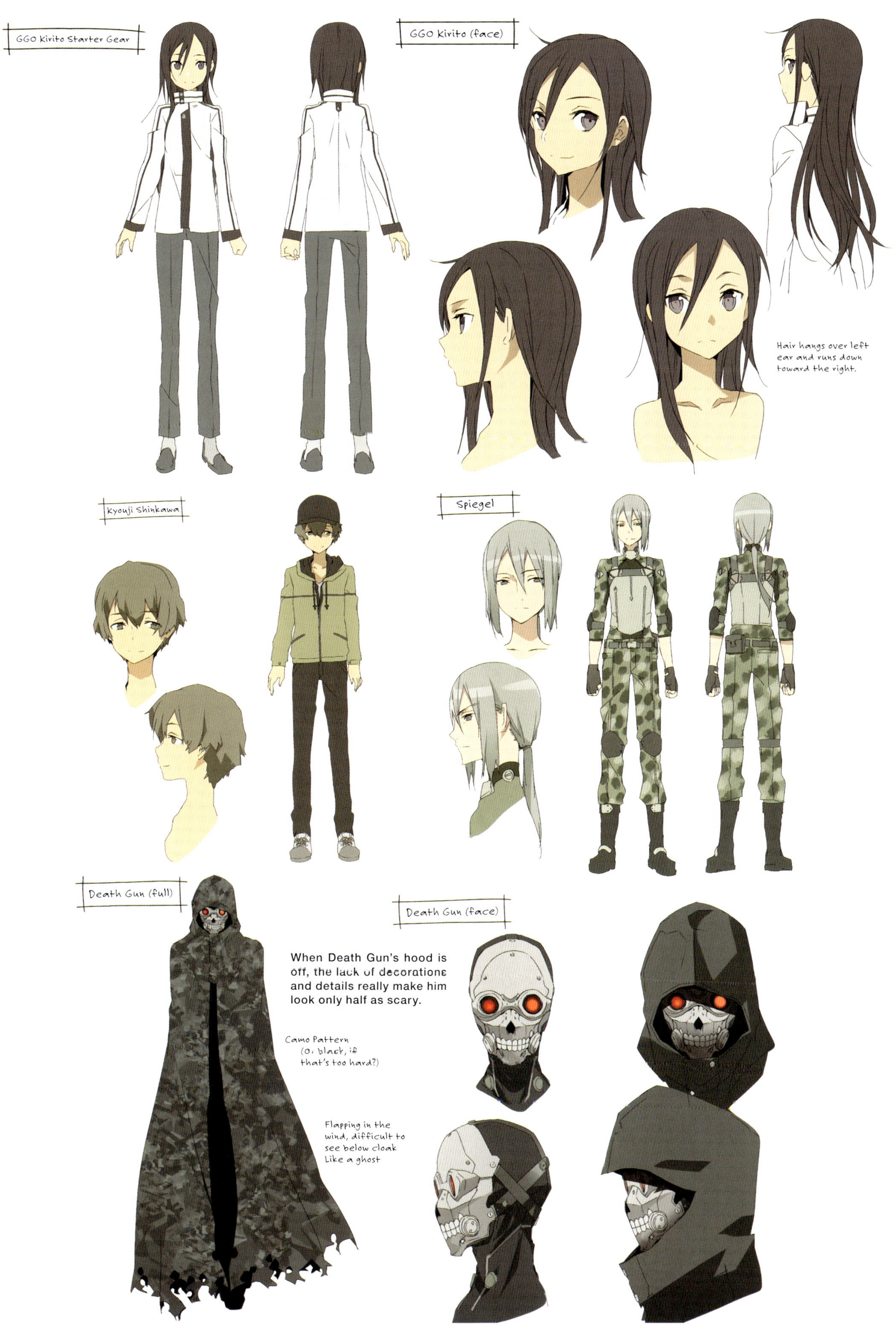
GGO Kirito Starter Gear
GGO Kirito (face)
Hair hangs over left
ear and runs down
toward the right.
Kyouji Shinkawa
Spiegel
Death Gun (full)
Death Gun (face)
When Death Gun's hood is
off, the lack of decorations
and details really make him
look only half as scary.
Camo Pattern
(or black, if
that's too hard?)
Flapping in the
wind, difficult to
see below cloak
Like a ghost

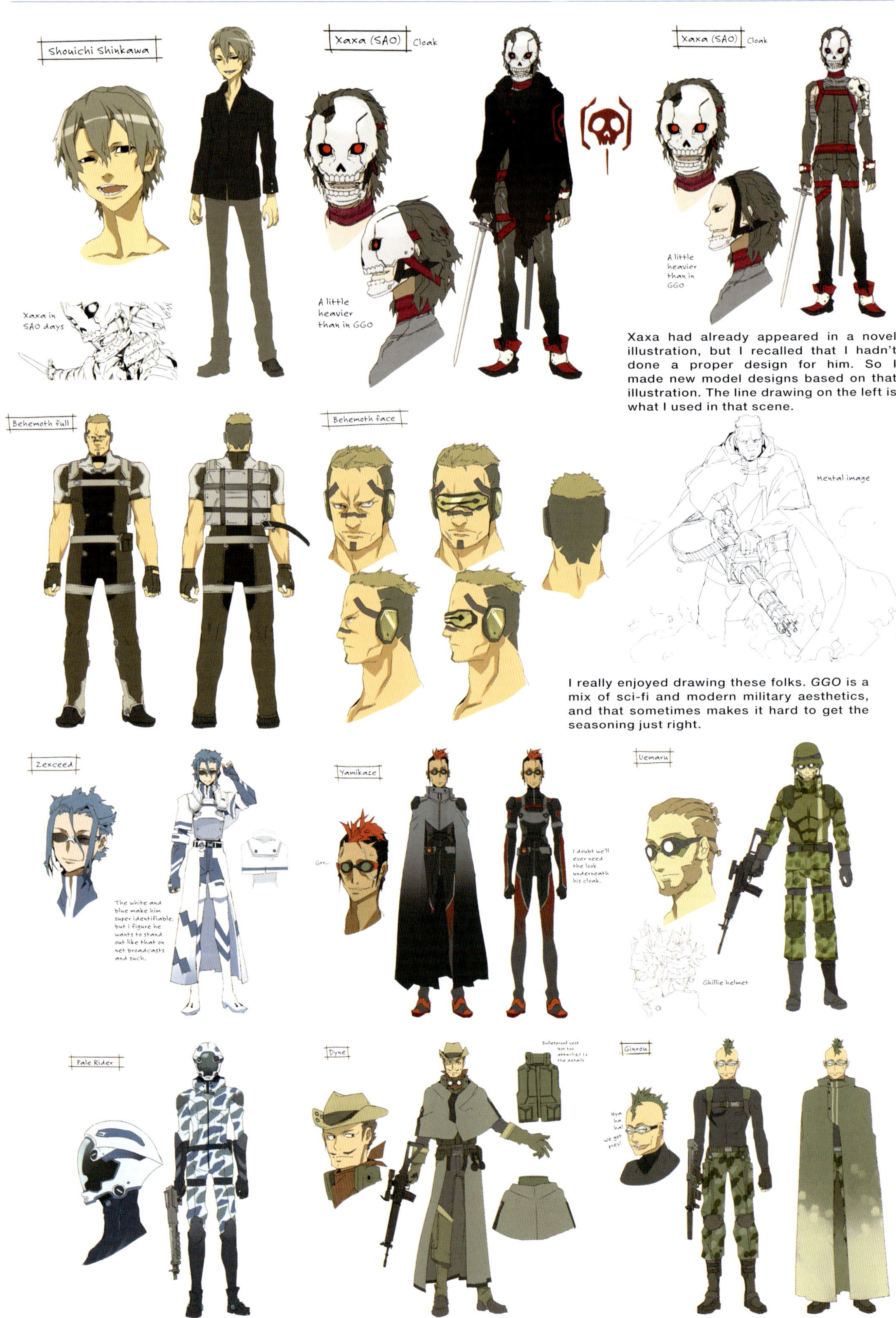

Xaxa had already appeared in a novel illustration, but I recalled that I hadn't done a proper design for him. So I made new model designs based on that illustration. The line drawing on the left is what I used in that scene.

I really enjoyed drawing these folks. *GGO* is a mix of sci-fi and modern military aesthetics, and that sometimes makes it hard to get the seasoning just right.

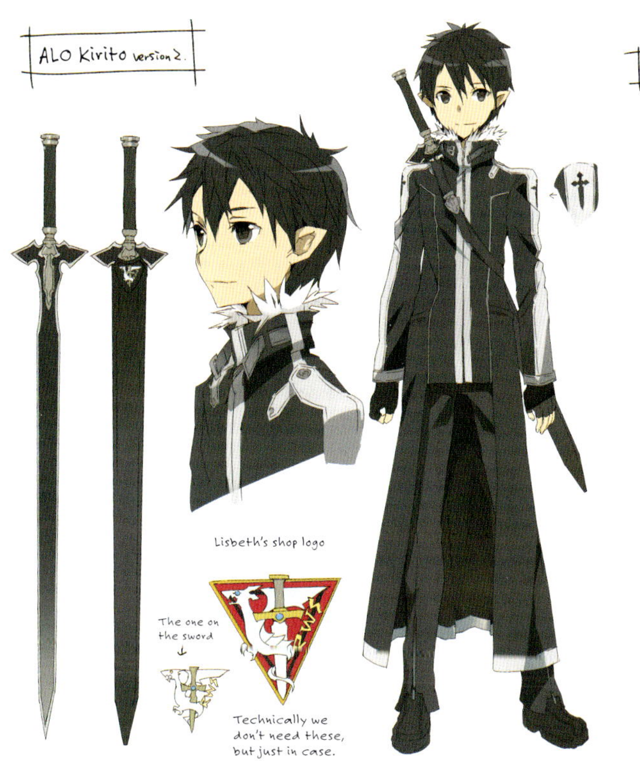

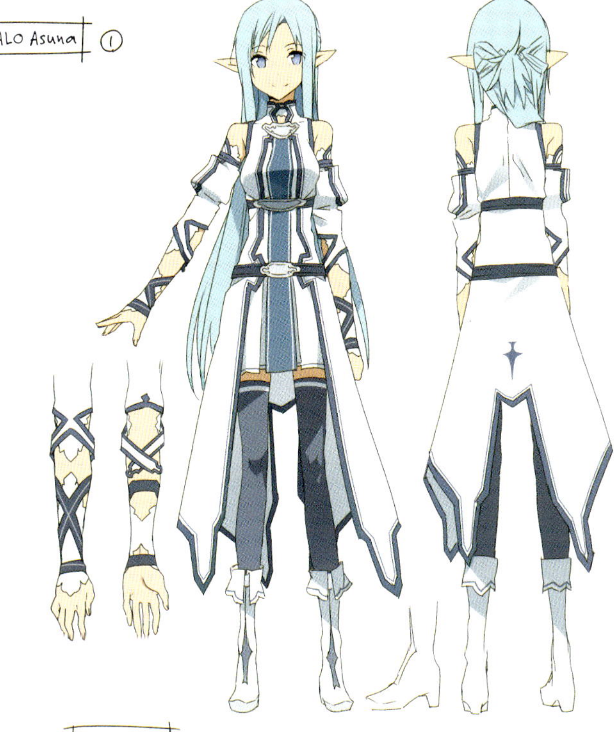

For the main characters in *ALO*, I only added the parts that were missing from my initial novel designs. Since the animators are so good, I often only drew the front and let them handle the rest (laughs).

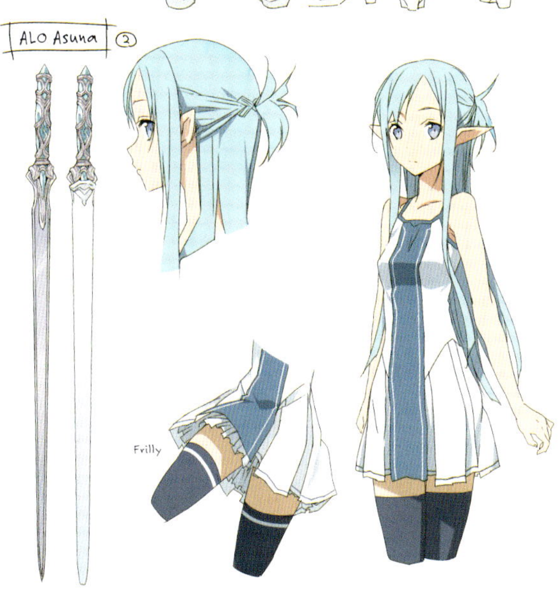

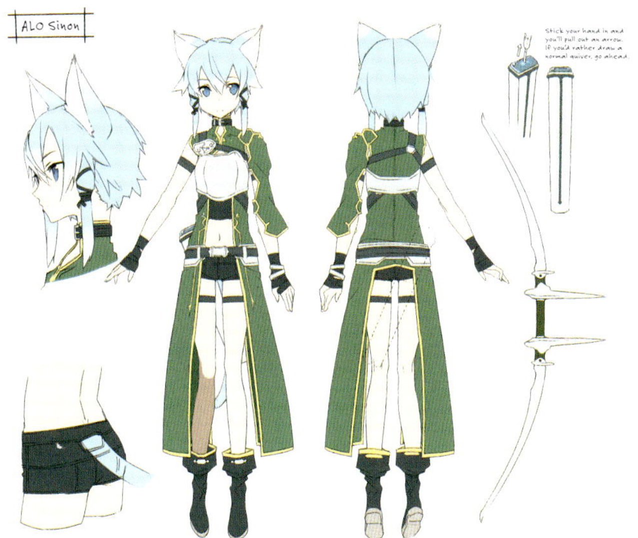

ALO Asuna and Yuuki having skirts was a compromise, because I just couldn't do better than this look. As I was designing them, I made up my own excuses, like imagining that the underside of the skirt would be in permanent darkness to protect against panty glimpses.

Since you can fly in *ALO*, I just assumed that everyone would want to wear proper bottoms. That's why Silica and Liz have pants on.

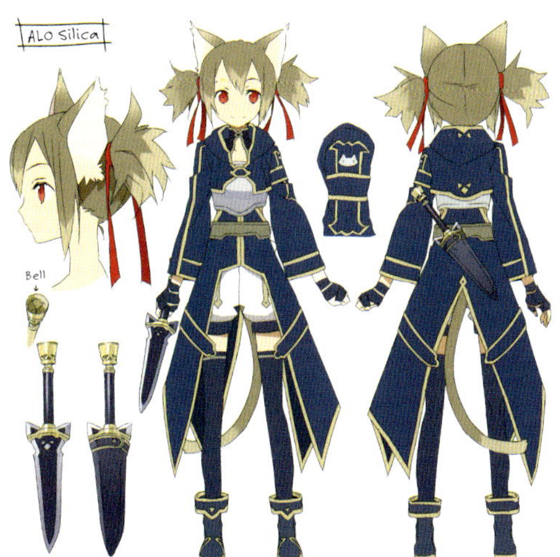

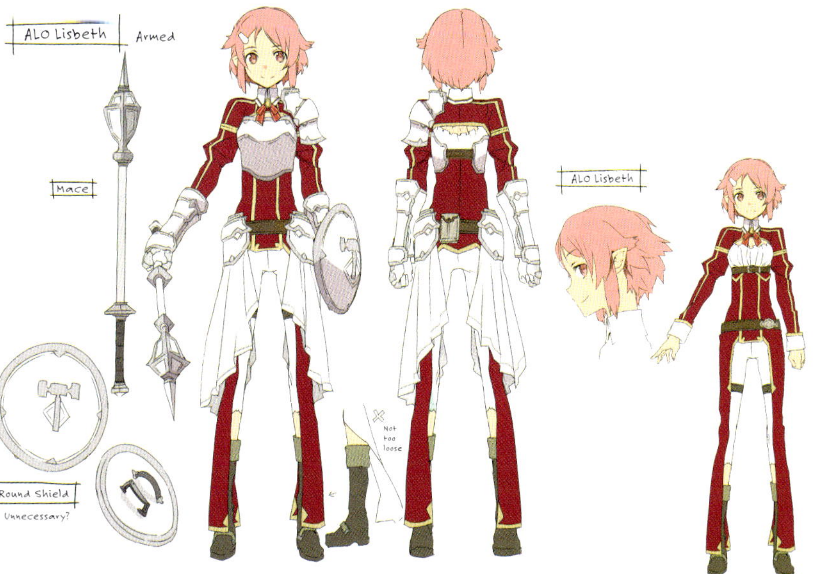

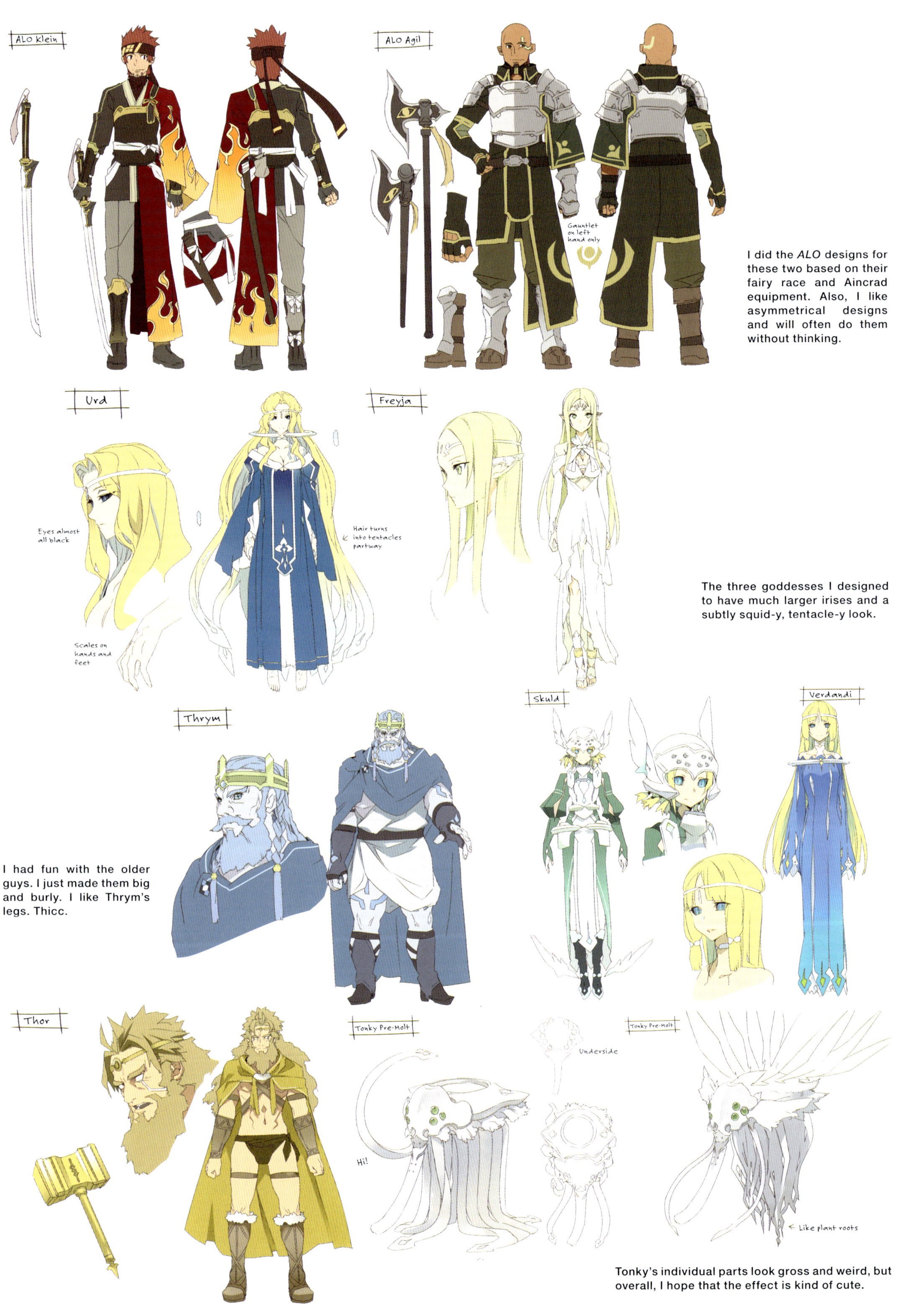

I did the *ALO* designs for these two based on their fairy race and Aincrad equipment. Also, I like asymmetrical designs and will often do them without thinking.

The three goddesses I designed to have much larger irises and a subtly squid-y, tentacle-y look.

I had fun with the older guys. I just made them big and burly. I like Thrym's legs. Thicc.

Tonky's individual parts look gross and weird, but overall, I hope that the effect is kind of cute.

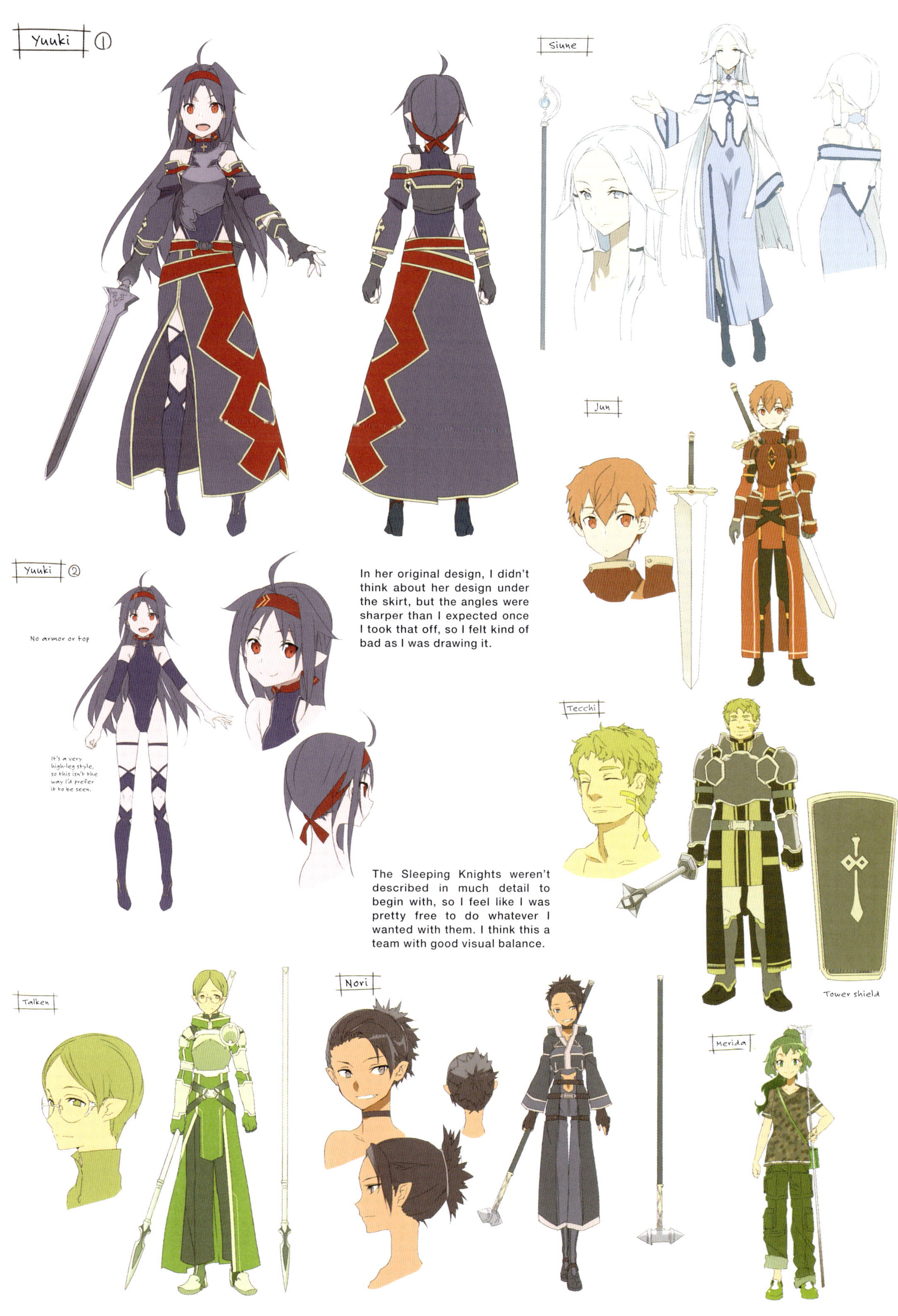

In her original design, I didn't think about her design under the skirt, but the angles were sharper than I expected once I took that off, so I felt kind of bad as I was drawing it.

The Sleeping Knights weren't described in much detail to begin with, so I feel like I was pretty free to do whatever I wanted with them. I think this a team with good visual balance.

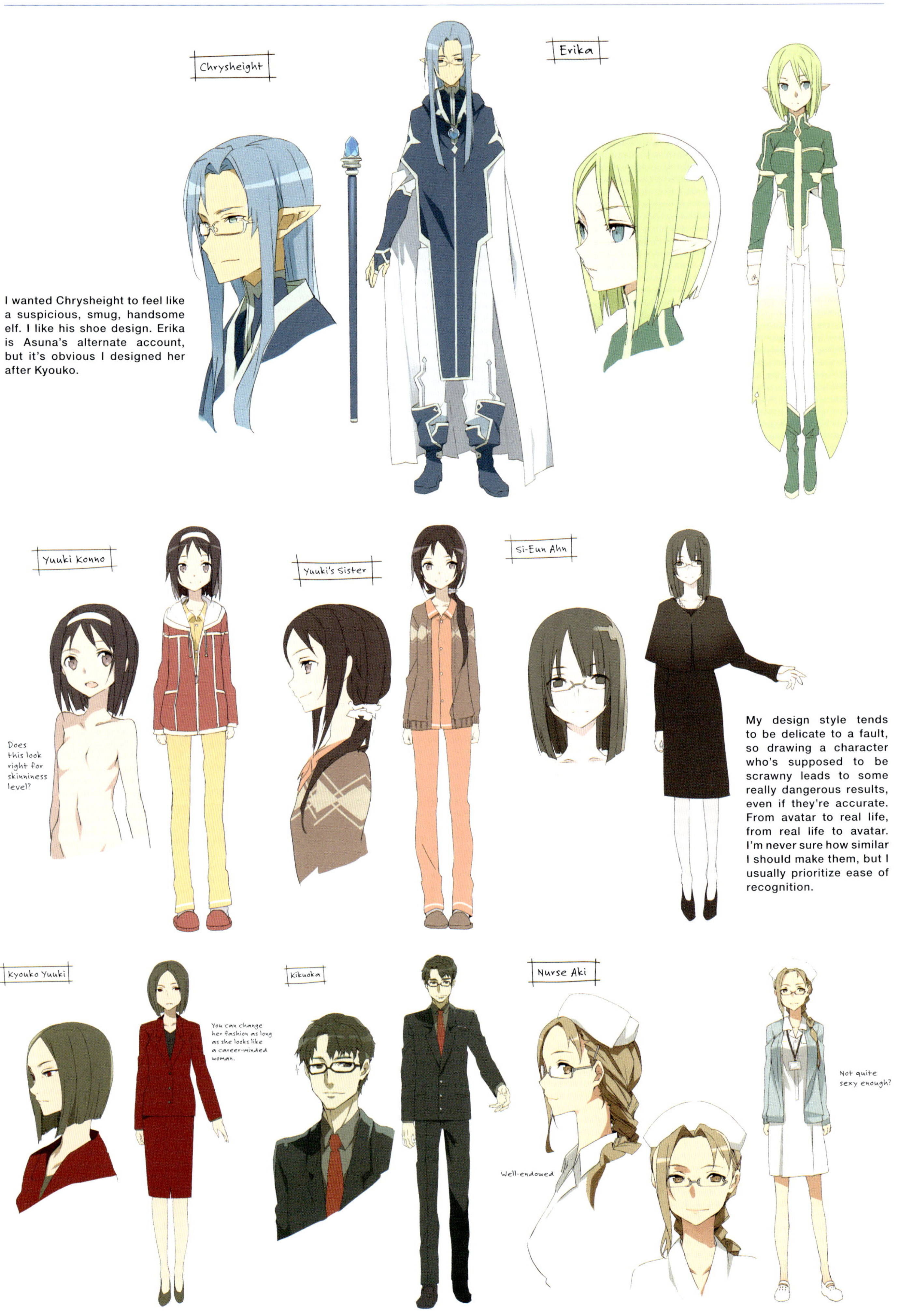

I wanted Chrysheight to feel like a suspicious, smug, handsome elf. I like his shoe design. Erika is Asuna's alternate account, but it's obvious I designed her after Kyouko.

My design style tends to be delicate to a fault, so drawing a character who's supposed to be scrawny leads to some really dangerous results, even if they're accurate. From avatar to real life, from real life to avatar. I'm never sure how similar I should make them, but I usually prioritize ease of recognition.

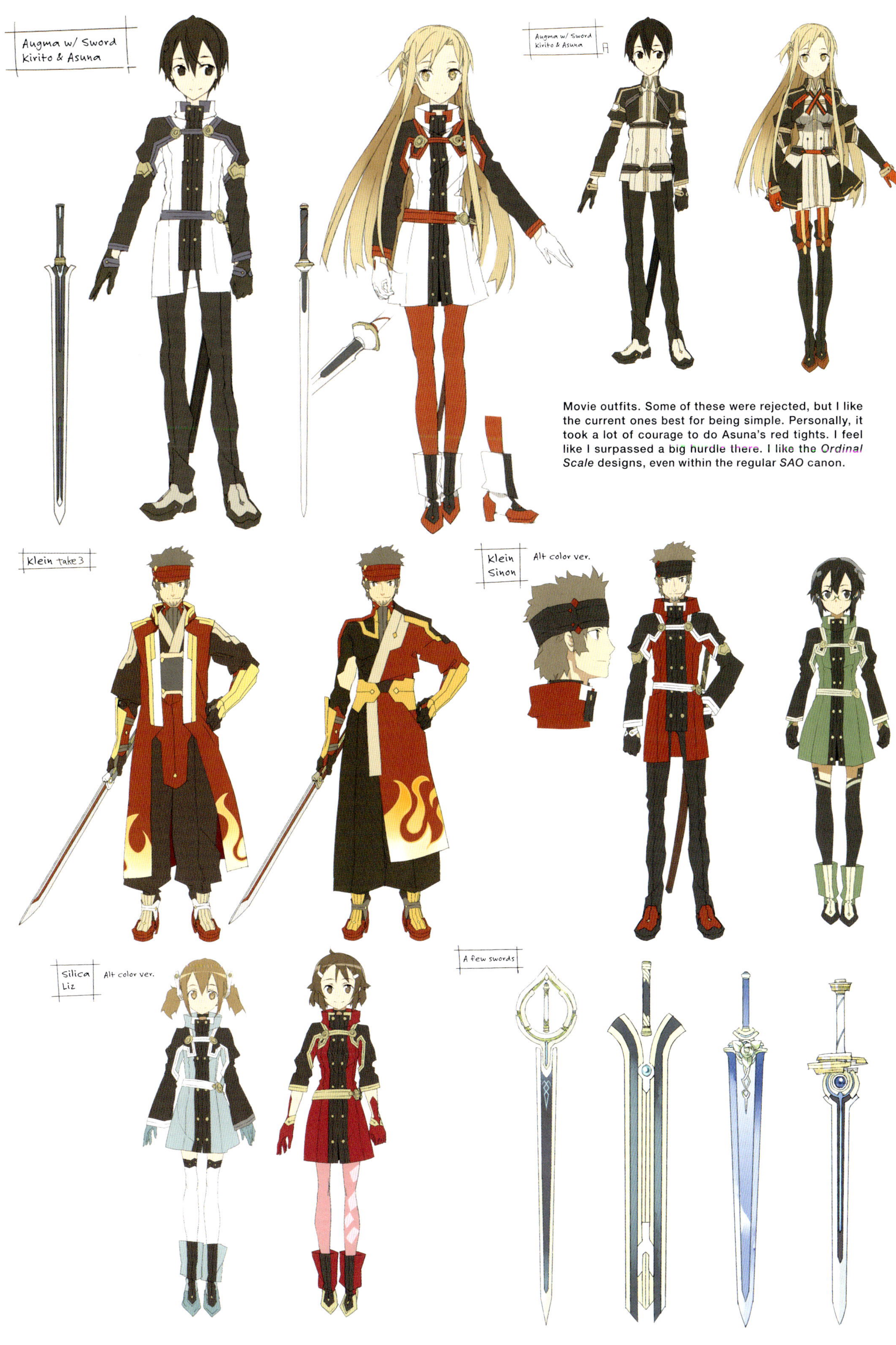

Movie outfits. Some of these were rejected, but I like the current ones best for being simple. Personally, it took a lot of courage to do Asuna's red tights. I feel like I surpassed a big hurdle there. I like the *Ordinal Scale* designs, even within the regular *SAO* canon.

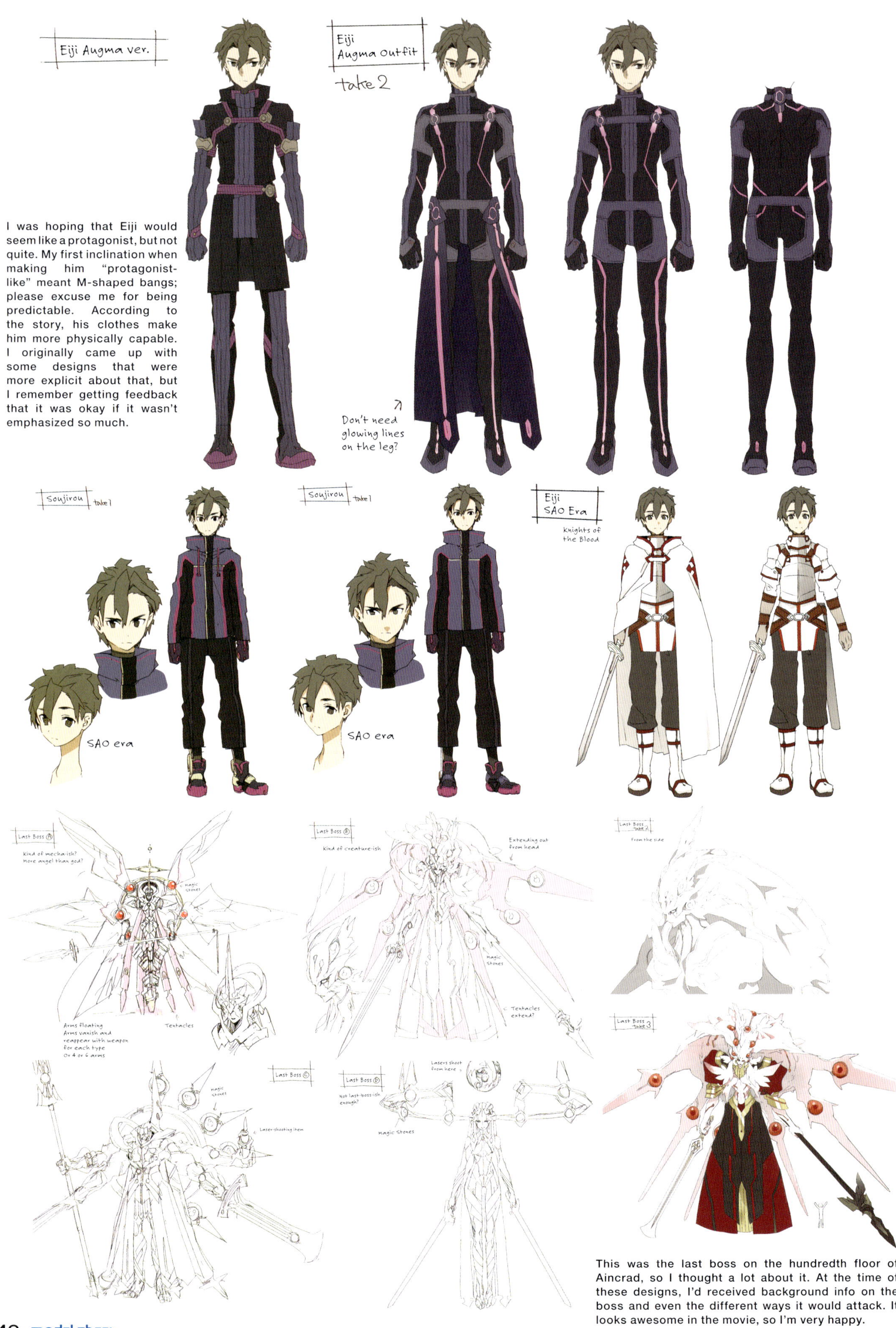

I was hoping that Eiji would seem like a protagonist, but not quite. My first inclination when making him "protagonist-like" meant M-shaped bangs; please excuse me for being predictable. According to the story, his clothes make him more physically capable. I originally came up with some designs that were more explicit about that, but I remember getting feedback that it was okay if it wasn't emphasized so much.

This was the last boss on the hundredth floor of Aincrad, so I thought a lot about it. At the time of these designs, I'd received background info on the boss and even the different ways it would attack. It looks awesome in the movie, so I'm very happy.

Yuna has braided bangs with her forehead exposed, so I was worried people might not take to her. She has three different forms, so while it's not that extreme of a feature, I wanted something that would be easily identifiable.

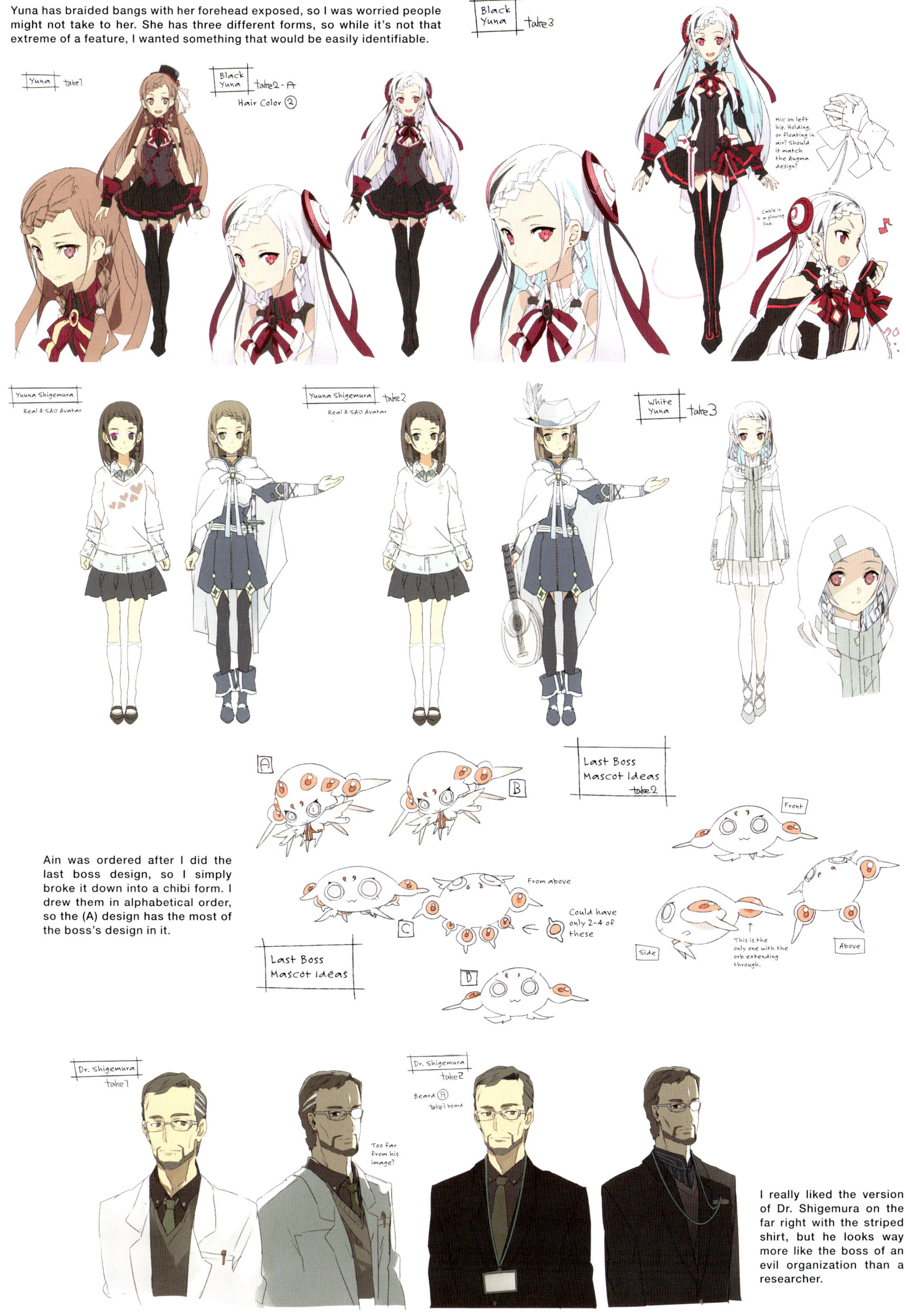

Ain was ordered after I did the last boss design, so I simply broke it down into a chibi form. I drew them in alphabetical order, so the (A) design has the most of the boss's design in it.

I really liked the version of Dr. Shigemura on the far right with the striped shirt, but he looks way more like the boss of an evil organization than a researcher.

SWORD ART ONLINE model sheet for novel

When doing character designs for the novel illustrations, I just do simple line art, then usually decide on colors when they need to go on a frontispiece or cover. When I have time, or I'm really undecided, I'll often go straight to coloring on the first pass, too.

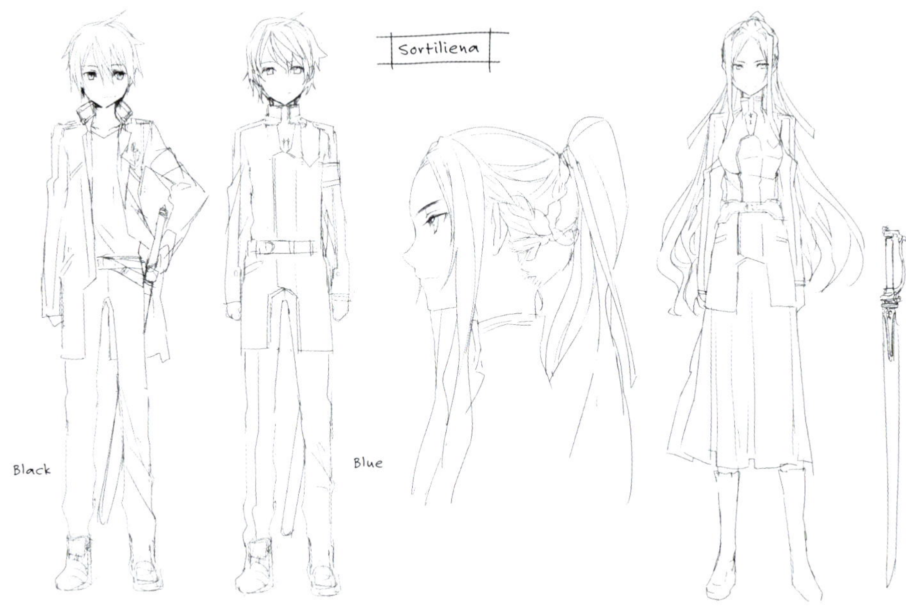

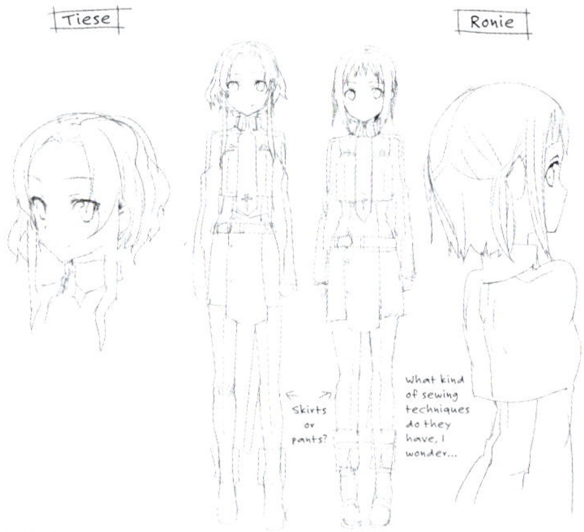

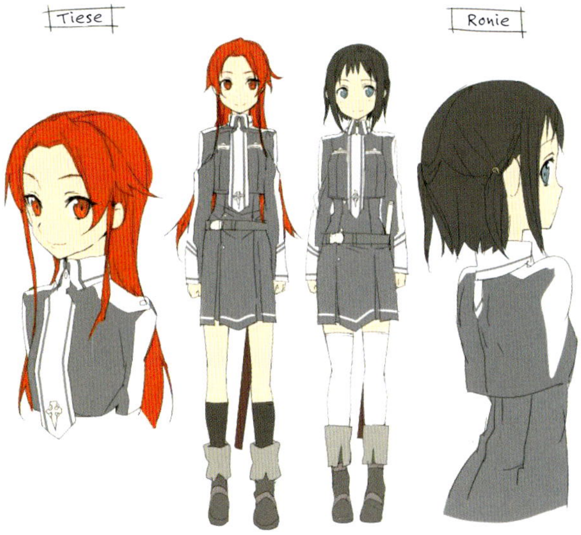

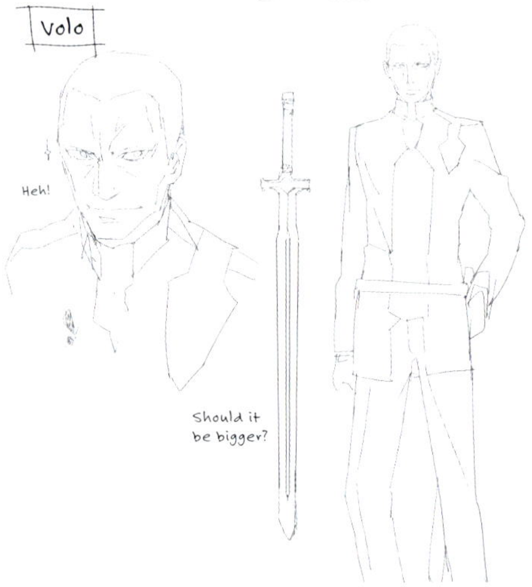

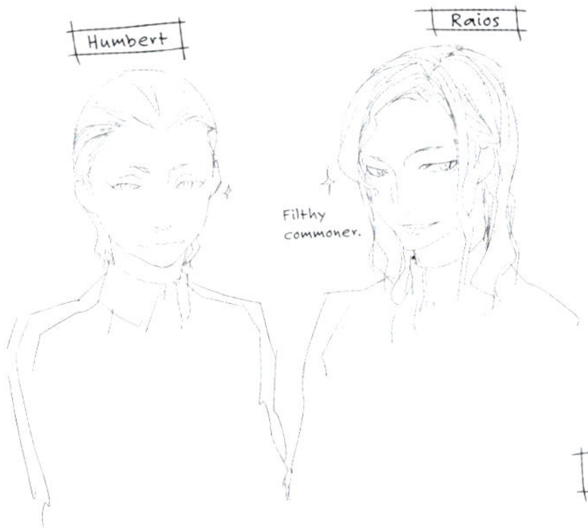

Ronie and Tiese are important characters, of course, but I also wanted to get the primary trainee uniforms for girls figured out. I think the version of Tiese with shorter, wavy hair is really cute.

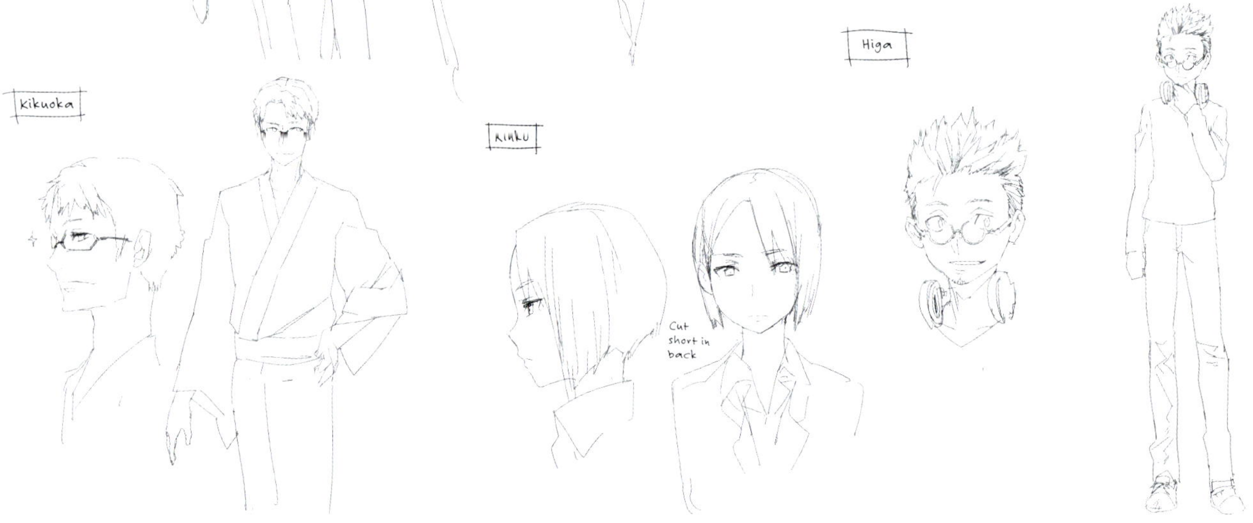

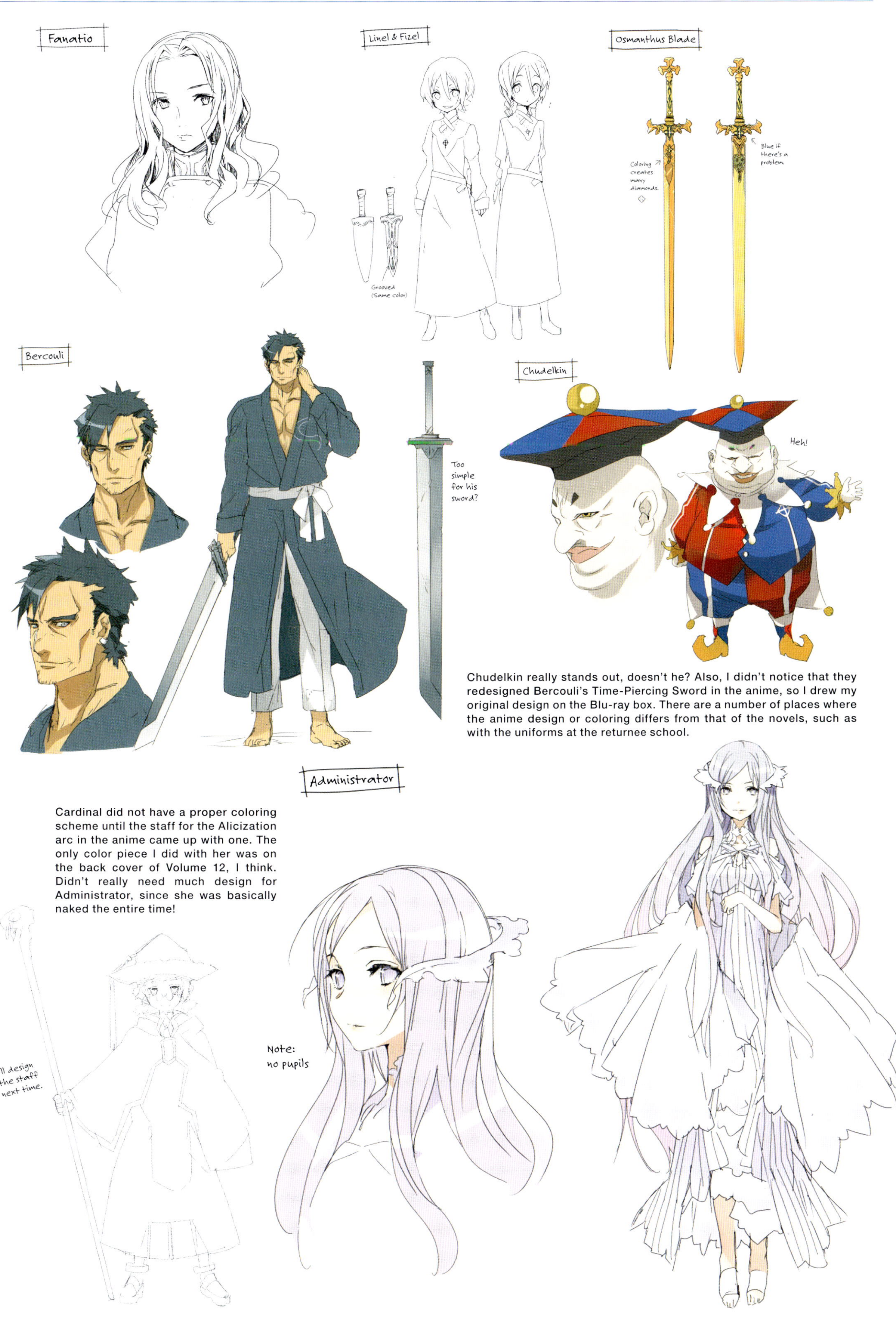

Chudelkin really stands out, doesn't he? Also, I didn't notice that they redesigned Bercouli's Time-Piercing Sword in the anime, so I drew my original design on the Blu-ray box. There are a number of places where the anime design or coloring differs from that of the novels, such as with the uniforms at the returnee school.

Cardinal did not have a proper coloring scheme until the staff for the Alicization arc in the anime came up with one. The only color piece I did with her was on the back cover of Volume 12, I think. Didn't really need much design for Administrator, since she was basically naked the entire time!

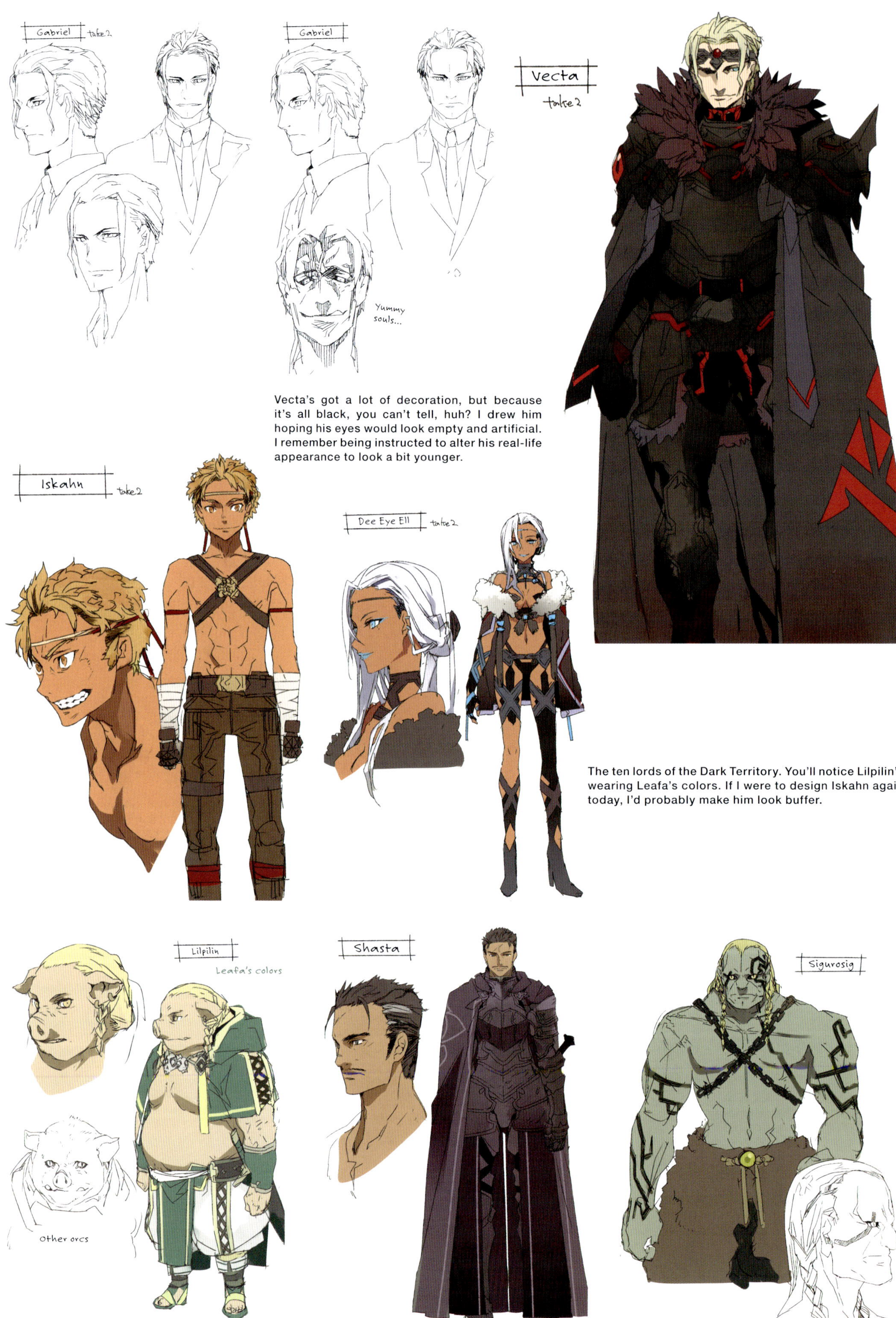

Vecta's got a lot of decoration, but because it's all black, you can't tell, huh? I drew him hoping his eyes would look empty and artificial. I remember being instructed to alter his real-life appearance to look a bit younger.

The ten lords of the Dark Territory. You'll notice Lilpilin's wearing Leafa's colors. If I were to design Iskahn again today, I'd probably make him look buffer.

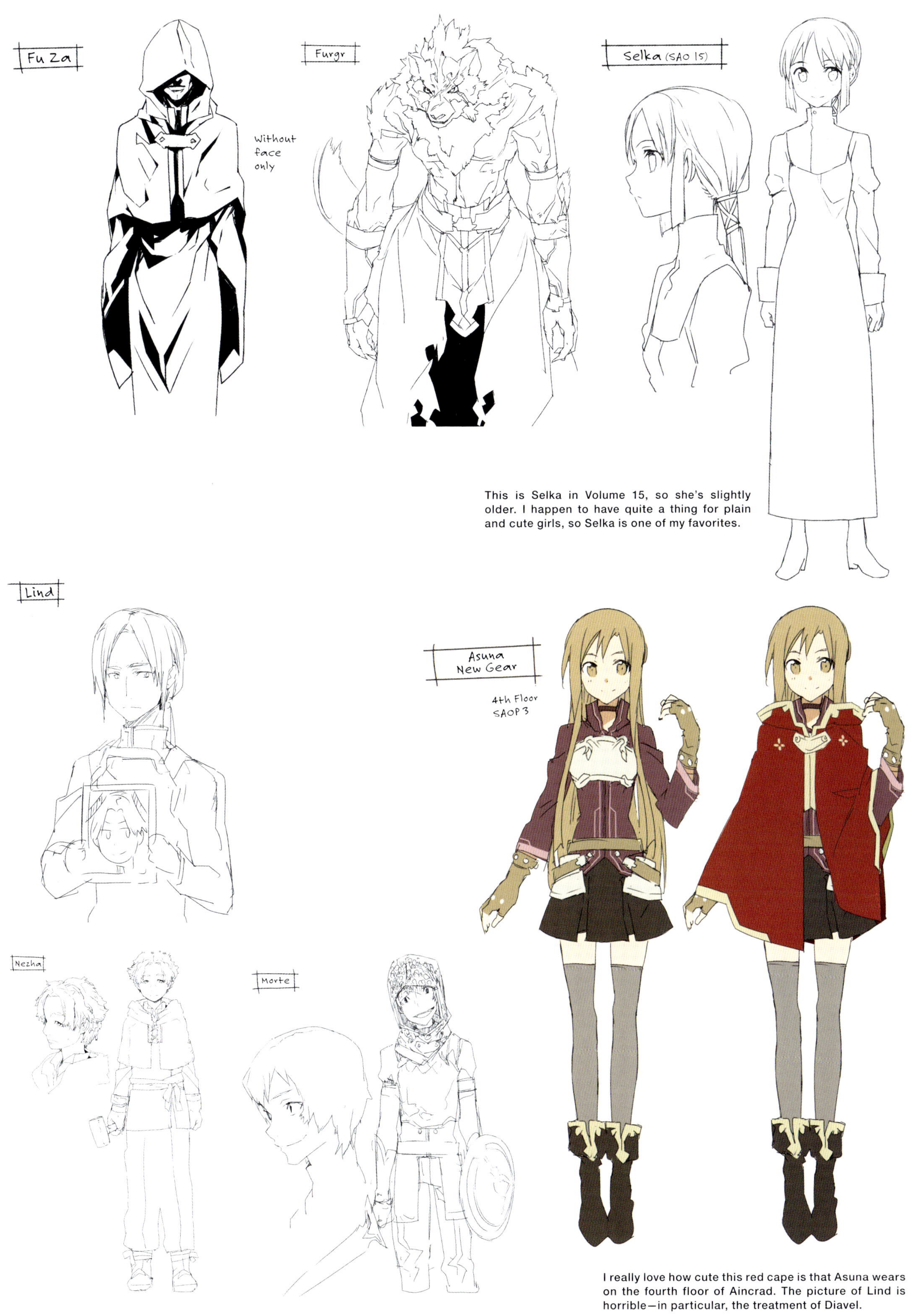

This is Selka in Volume 15, so she's slightly older. I happen to have quite a thing for plain and cute girls, so Selka is one of my favorites.

I really love how cute this red cape is that Asuna wears on the fourth floor of Aincrad. The picture of Lind is horrible—in particular, the treatment of Diavel.

SWORD ART ONLINE

Prismatic Colors

Reki Kawahara Illustration by abec

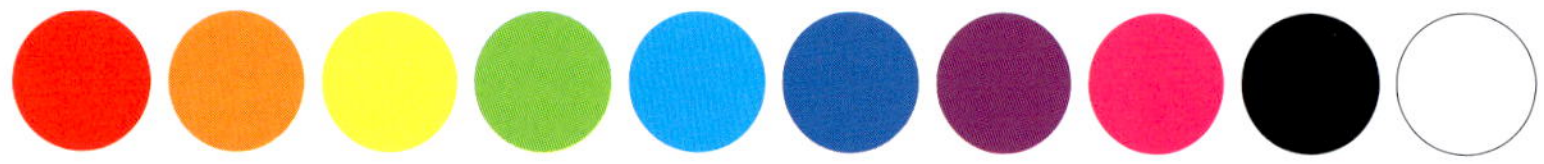

Author of *SAO*, Reki Kawahara, presents a new short story. This takes place during the Alicization arc, while Kirito and Eugeo are elite disciples at the academy. And it might include a certain character who appeared in the first artbook...?

"Um, Kirito…are you sure we shouldn't be paying a visit to Raios and Humbert?" Eugeo asked.

He was polishing the table with a wet cloth, so the comment came as a complete surprise. I grimaced and replied, "Why should we…? They're not hoping to see us, that's for sure."

I returned to cleaning the tea set, but Eugeo persevered with his concern.

"The thing is, Raios is the first seat elite disciple, and Humbert is the second. We're fifth and sixth, so if we don't at least pay them a respectful visit, they're only going to give us more grief when they come back, won't they?"

So Eugeo was less concerned for their well-being, and more for the potential trouble after they came back to school. Even that was more than they were worth, in my opinion.

Three weeks had passed already since they were bitten by poisonous crabs. The effects weren't fatal, but the numbness in their legs was apparently quite persistent, and if the hushed stories were true…

"…They might not be back for a whole year, right? By that time, both you and I will have graduated. Who cares what they say after we're gone? Doesn't affect us."

"But they might get out early; you never know. This morning, Third Seat Wegin and Fourth Seat Elcar were talking about how they paid the two a visit in the hospital. It made me wonder what might happen…"

"Hrmm…"

Wegin Sorby and Elcar Marscull, the third and fourth seats of the elite disciples, were both young men from rich families. They weren't nearly as snide and nasty as Raios and Humbert, but we weren't exactly close with them, either.

"…Well, they are from higher noble families. Maybe their families know each other, so there was a social reason they needed to go visit."

"I mean, by that logic, you and I are the only elite disciples who *aren't* of noble birth. So wouldn't that mean everyone would pay them a visit?"

"What? No way, they can't *all* be nobles," I protested, but the truth was, I still didn't even have the faces and names of the other ten disciples in our dorm memorized. "Let's see, you're the fifth, I'm the sixth, then seventh is Somelier, and eighth is Lushe..."

With Eugeo's eventual help, I managed to list off the first ten disciples' names. Just then, a voice burst into the living room, startling us.

"Oh! They're still working!"

A girl with long red hair tied in the back was emerging from the door to Eugeo's bedroom. That was Eugeo's page, the primary trainee Tiese Schtrinen.

"You guys, cleaning is for Ronie and me to do! You don't need to do any of it!"

My partner and I shared a look and grimaced. I glanced back at Tiese and said, "I know, but it just makes us so antsy…"

"We've been looking after ourselves ever since we left our hometown, so it just feels wrong to watch you do all the work," Eugeo agreed. In truth, Eugeo was almost entirely looking after *me*, but I couldn't bring myself to lounge on the sofa while the girls were tidying my messes—even if that was the tradition for elite disciples.

"At least let me polish this…It's the only thing left," I pleaded, holding up the tea pot. Somehow, though, my page, Ronie Arabel was right there next to me and snatched it out of my hands.

"No! Cleaning is part of the page's duties!"

"…You're getting pretty good at catching me unawares, Ronie," I said, holding my hands up in surrender. But on the inside, I was promising, *I'm gonna help clean tomorrow, and this time, you won't catch me*.

"So, what were we talking about?" I asked Eugeo.

"We were trying to see if you could name all the elite disciples. You've got two more to go."

"Aaah...um, the eleventh is…Oh! Phinea! And the twelfth is… Ohhh, ugh, urrrf…"

Despite my best attempts, I could not remember the final name. Well, this made it seem like I was disrespecting the twelfth seat! I had to prove I was different than Raios and Humbert, who looked down their noses at anyone in a lower position. The problem was that I couldn't even think of the first letter of the person's name. At last, with great regret, I admitted defeat and lifted my hands.

"I can't do it! Can't remember. Who's the twelfth, again?"

"Ha-ha, well, by your standards, you tried pretty hard. The twelfth seat is…"

Eugeo stopped talking abruptly, earning him a curious look from me. My partner's eyes wandered, looking at nothing in particular, until eventually, he spoke in a voice more frail and uncertain than I expected.

"Um…that's weird. The twelfth is, uh…"

"Wait a minute, Eugeo. Are you telling me *you* don't remember, either?" I asked, smirking heartily and glancing toward our pages. But Tiese and Ronie were simply standing there stock-still, holding their brooms and dusters.

"Uh…hang on, you two don't know, either?"

"Oh, no…we have the names of the elite disciples memorized, of course…I thought," said Tiese uncertainly.

Ronie looked just as baffled. "I know that I learned them all by heart on the day I received the page's title…"

"......"

That one left me stumped, too. Was it somehow possible for the memories related to the twelfth seat elite disciple to be deleted from our minds...or the minds of the entire student body of Swordcraft Academy, or from all the residents of the world?

That couldn't be possible, I decided, but that wasn't going to solve this problem. I patted my knees and stood up, shouting, "Okay! Then let's go find out, right now!"

"Huh...?"

I grabbed Eugeo by the left arm and pulled him up next. "The twelfth seat has to be in this dorm somewhere. I'm sure we'll remember when we see their face. Ronie and Tiese, keep going with the cleaning!"

And with that, I tugged my partner right out of the room.

The elite disciples' dorm at North Centoria Imperial Swordcraft Academy was a round building, almost like a playhouse, with a mess hall and training area on the first floor and students' living spaces on the second and third floors. Eugeo and I shared a room on the third floor, so we descended the stairs to the second floor and stopped in front of the door to the common room that the eleventh and twelfth seats shared.

"Are you really going to knock, Kirito?"

"You think I'm going to walk all the way here and then turn around?"

Part of me was worried about the twelfth seat being similar to Raios, but at the very least, I knew that the eleventh seat, Phinea Suvale, was a quiet and reserved girl, so we weren't likely to get kicked out. I summoned up my determination and rapped twice on the door.

At least five seconds passed before a woman's soft voice said, "Come in." Perhaps that was Phinea. Eugeo and I chimed "Pardon us" and opened the door.

The interior of the shared living room was the same as ours, but there was a faintly sweet scent in this one—as well as something strange. I wrinkled my nose, wondering what it was as we walked around the front screen.

"Whoa!" Eugeo muttered. I almost reached for my sword belt on the left side, but I wasn't actually wearing it.

The source of our surprise was an enormous dog sitting on the floor straight ahead. Its thick fur was white with just a hint of gray, and its ears were long enough to be small wings. A large bell hung from its collar, and its blue eyes seemed friendly—for now.

Then I looked up and saw, standing behind it, a thin woman wearing the elite disciple's uniform. It was not Phinea. Her ponytailed hair was the color of cofil tea with plenty of milk. She was also wearing glasses, which were rare in the Underworld. Her attractive features could belong to someone from the western empire. Or the eastern. In fact...the more I studied her, the more I wondered if I'd met her before...

"...Who are you?" she asked in a flat voice.

I hastily straightened up. "Ah...P-pardon me. I'm Elite Disciple Kirito, and this is Elite Disciple Eugeo."

We gave the knight's salute, which she quickly returned.

"I'm Ceba. This is Droolie."

...Droolie? That was a very creative name to give a dog. But more than that, it wasn't the sort of name people in the human realm gave their dogs, period. Then I realized that the name of the dog wasn't the important thing here.

Ceba. I did...*not* remember that. But how could that be true? If she was an elite disciple like us, she must have lived with us in the primary trainee dorm for a year. We would have met during the testing matches, perhaps even faced each other in combat.

Like me, Eugeo was frozen with shock. He didn't seem to remember Ceba, either. The situation was becoming alarming.

But she didn't seem to notice or care about our obvious confusion. In the same tone of voice, she asked, "So what do you want?"

"Oh, er...Well, since being named elite disciples, we'd already met and introduced ourselves to Phinea, but we hadn't done the same with you, Ceba, so..."

"Uh-huh. Well, that's very polite of you. Would you like some tea?"

"Er, no, don't bother yourself. Um, anyway, it's nice to meet you..." I said awkwardly, extending my hand. I'd decided that we had fulfilled the purpose of our visit, as unsatisfying as it was. Ceba grabbed my hand, then shook Eugeo's.

I suddenly sensed the strange smell getting stronger. I glanced at my hand and saw a small spot of blue on my index finger, so I lifted it to my nose and sniffed. It smelled like turpentine...no, paint. It smelled like oil paint.

Instantly, it felt like something in my head had split. I looked at Ceba's face, then down at Droolie on the floor, then up at Ceba again.

"...Oh...is that you again?! From Alfheim...when we fought the secret boss on the fifth floor of New Aincrad..."

As soon as the words left my mouth, I knew I had made a mistake. I shouldn't have been letting Eugeo hear any of this. I was worried about how to explain away what I'd just said—but when I looked at Eugeo, I was shocked again.

Eugeo was as still as a statue. And it wasn't just him. The steam rising from the tea cup on the table had stopped, too, and even the birds in the sky outside the window were suspended in the sunset. The only things moving in the world were Ceba and Droolie...

"Oh dear. So you remembered," she said, taking a step closer.

"Of course I wouldn't forget...says the guy who forgot you completely until just now. What does this mean?!"

"I'm passing through worlds where my art does not yet exist. When the painting I'm meant to finish is complete, I vanish from that world—and from the memory of those I met there. Though every now and then, I run into one of them again."

"You pass through worlds...? You mean VRMMO worlds? How did you dive into the Underworld?"

"That's not really important, is it? I'm like light refracted through a prism...I shine upon a single world with the full spectrum of color for a time, and when the angle on the prism changes, I'm shining upon a different world," she explained, which didn't clear anything up at all. Then she pointed at the door behind me. "Well, you should be going. Once you've passed through that door, you'll forget about me again."

"...Just tell me one thing before I go," I said to the mysterious girl. "Back in *ALO*, you painted on the biggest canvas that existed in that world—the guild flag. What are you going to paint on here?"

Ceba just gave me a faint smile and looked out the window. I followed her gaze and saw, beyond the trees, the white surface of Central Cathedral, glowing a brilliant orange with the light of the setting sun.

The End

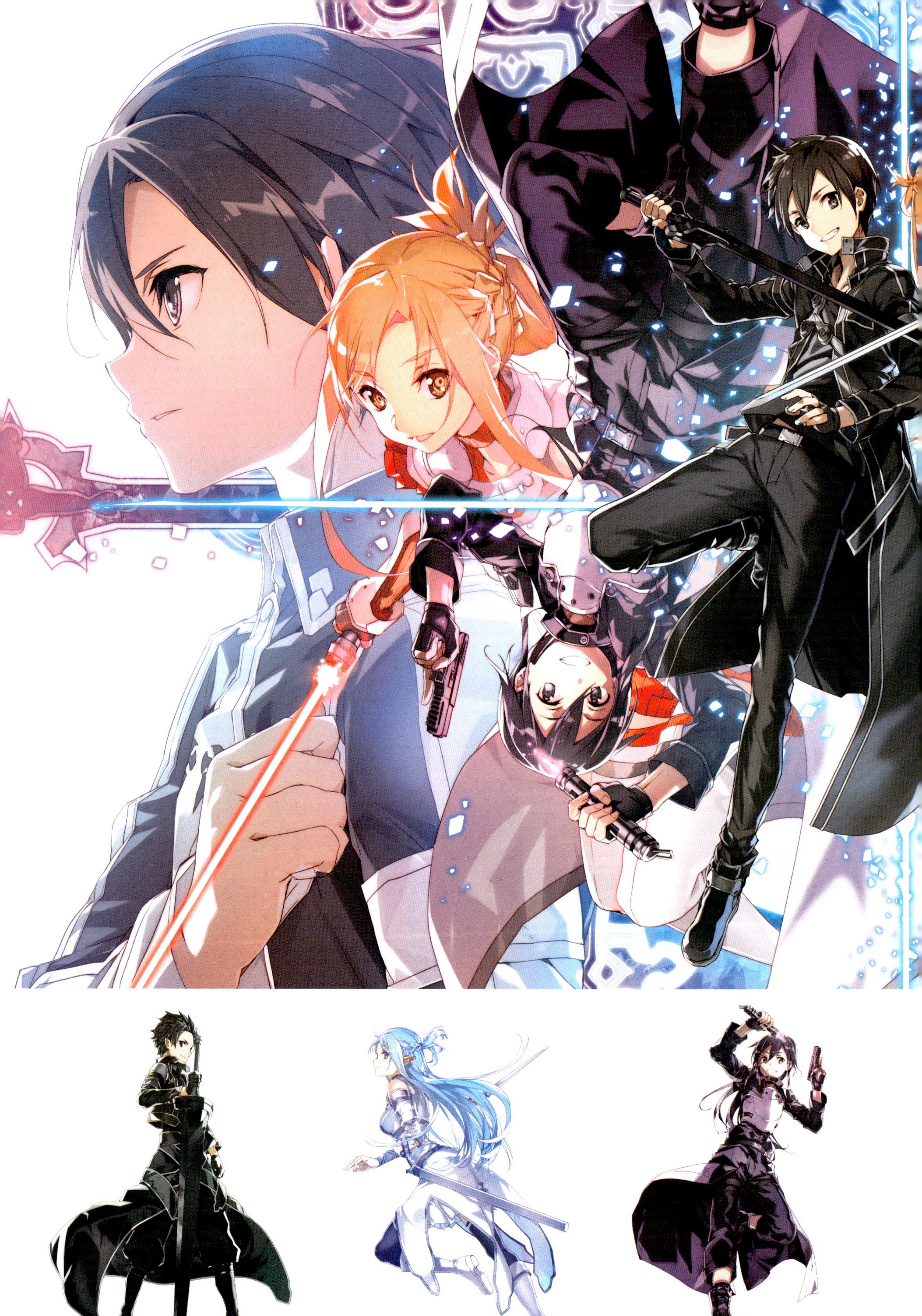

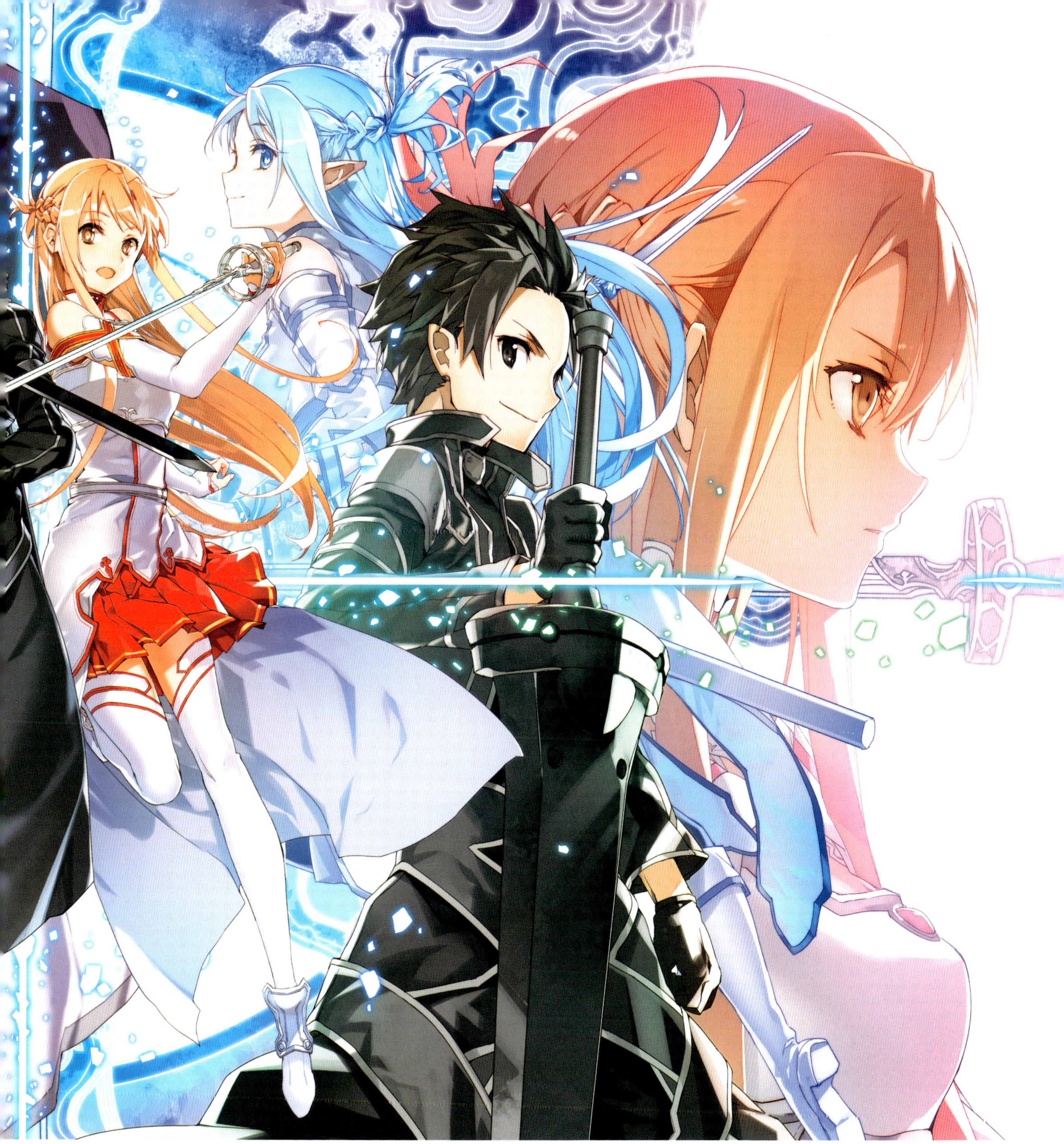

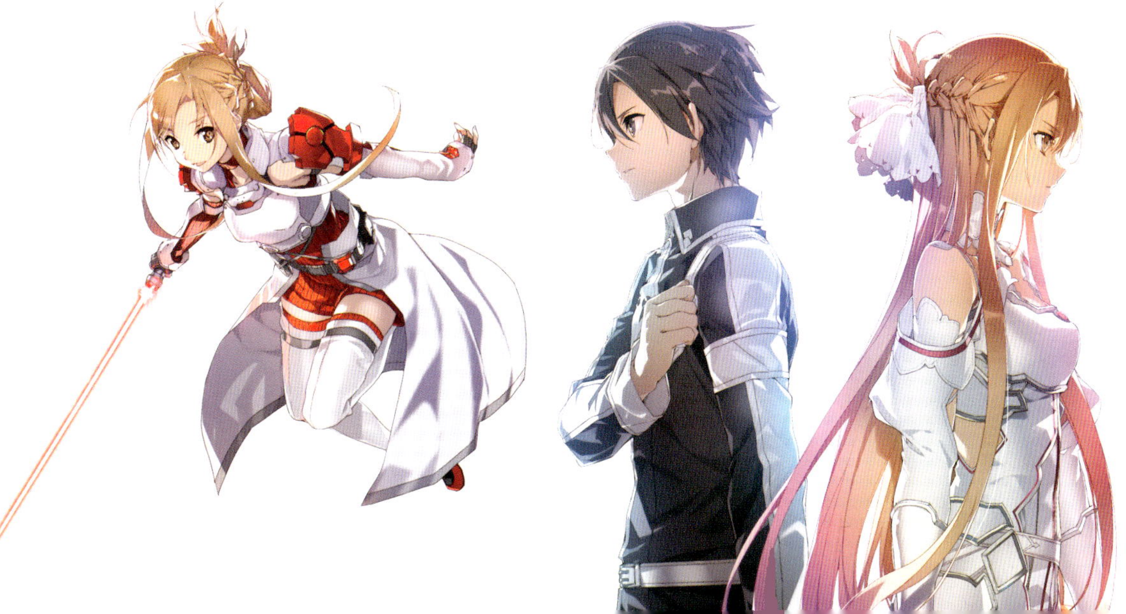

Reki Kawahara &
***Sword Art Online*, 10th Anniversary**
Cover: December 2012

Since it's been ten years, I drew four different pairings of Kirito and Asuna. *GGO* Asuna was a new design I did for the anime. Also, they were all done separately so they could be arranged for custom covers (it ended up being an obi strip instead) so it was quite difficult. The background I used came from the key visual for the first season of the anime.

SWORD ART ONLINE
abec Artworks

ILLUSTRATION BY **abec**

- Translation: Stephen Paul
- Lettering: Abigail Blackman

Yen Press
150 West 30th Street, 19th Floor
New York, NY 10001

Visit us at yenpress.com
facebook.com/yenpress
twitter.com/yenpress
yenpress.tumblr.com
instagram.com/yenpress

First Yen Press Edition: June 2022

Library of Congress Control Number: 2017946003

ISBNs: 978-1-9753-3493-2 (paperback)
978-1-9753-3494-9 (ebook)

APS

Printed in China

10 9 8 7 6 5 4 3 2 1

Special Thanks
- KANA ISHIDA
- GREEN TANUKI
- SAO Project
- SAO II Project
- SAO MOVIE Project
- SAO-A Project
- BANDAI NAMCO ENTERTAINMENT

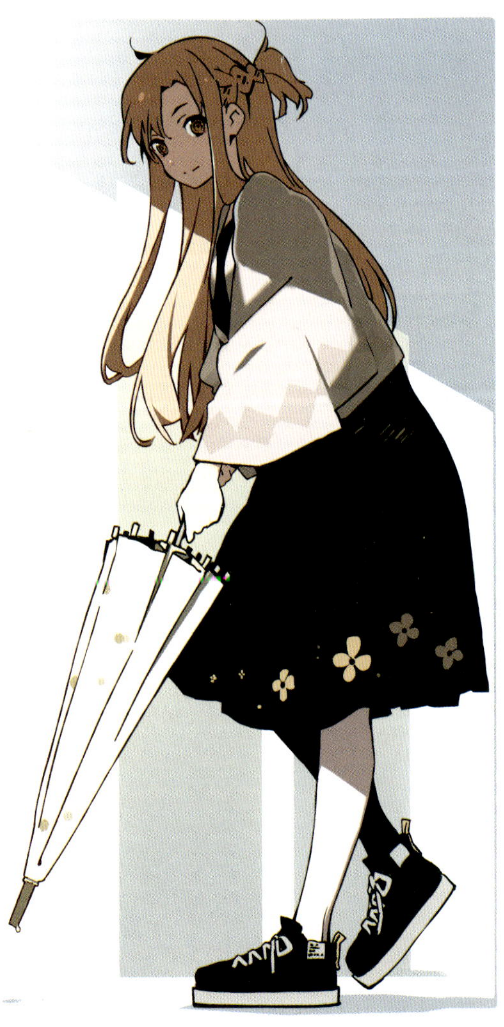